COGNITIVE PROCESSES IN CHOICE AND DECISION BEHAVIOR

COGNITIVE PROCESSES IN CHOICE AND DECISION BEHAVIOR

edited by
THOMAS S. WALLSTEN
University of North Carolina at Chapel Hill

LEA LAWRENCE ERLBAUM ASSOCIATES, PUBLISHERS
1980   Hillsdale, New Jersey

This work relates to Department of the Navy
Contract N00014-78-C-0170 issued by the Office
of Naval Research. The United States Government
has a royalty-free license throughout the world
in all copyrightable material contained herein.

Lawrence Erlbaum Associates, Inc., Publishers
365 Broadway
Hillsdale, New Jersey 07642

Library of Congress Cataloging in Publication Data

Main entry under title:

Cognitive processes in choice and decision
  behavior.

  Proceedings of a conference held June 22–24,
1978 at the University of North Carolina at
Chapel Hill.
  "Contract N00014-78-C-0170 issued by the Office
of Naval Research."
  Bibliography: p.
  Includes index.
  1. Decision-making—Congresses. 2. Choice
(Psychology))—Congresses. 3. Cognition—
Congresses. I. Wallsten, Thomas S.
BF441.C53   153.8′3   79-27553
ISBN 0-89859-054-X
Printed in the United States of America

Contents

Preface

Decision theory is a uniquely interdisciplinary field of study with contributions from economics, statistics, mathematics, philosophy, operations research, and psychology. Recent years have seen important changes in research on behavioral decision theory in terms of a shift from a reliance on economic and statistical models to an emphasis on concepts drawn from cognitive psychology. In order to explore the reasons why these changes have come about, and to discuss the future directions to which they point, a conference was held from June 22–24, 1978, at Quail Roost, an idyllic conference center run primarily for the University of North Carolina at Chapel Hill. This volume contains the proceedings of that conference, and should be of interest to cognitive psychologists, decision theorists, decision analysts, and related scientists.[1]

The schism that, until recently, has existed between behavioral decision theory and the rest of cognitive psychology has been unfortunate, although understandable. Pitz (1977) is probably correct in his analysis that this separation occurred because the the roots of decision theory lie squarely in economics and statistics, whereas those of cognitive psychology can be found in the early schools of association and rationalism. Estes (this volume) presents a similar perspective. It is useful to consider certain aspects of decision-oriented and cognitive research to see how each can benefit from the other and to understand why the two fields may be growing closer together.

Research in behavioral decision theory has been concerned primarily with developing, testing, and reformulating relatively sophisticated formal models,

---

[1]A paper by Kahneman and Tversky (1979) was also presented at the conference, but is not included here because it has been published elsewhere.

most of which are normative in character. This work has focused both on global evaluations of the models and on testing various axioms from which the models flow, on measuring subjective probability and utility, and on developing probalistic models to pit against the normative algebraic ones. (Reviews of much of this earlier literature can be found in Becker & McClintock, 1967; Edwards, 1954, 1961; and Rapoport & Wallsten, 1972.)

Although individual models have been successful in the sense that a particular model can account for a good deal of the variance in a particular situation, there is a feeling among many researchers that the overall approach has not been fruitful. For one thing, it has not been possible to apply the results from one paradigm or with respect to one model to other paradigms or other models in any satisfying way. Perhaps more important than the lack of generalizability have been the findings that various axioms are systematically violated under a variety of conditions, utility is frequently not risk invariant, and people often do not make decisions so as to optimize some well-specified objective function. This apparent lack of progress in psychological decision theory was made starkly evident in the preface to *Contemporary Developments in Mathematical Psychology* (Krantz, Atkinson, Luce, & Suppes, 1974) in which the editors wrote:

> Perhaps the most striking exclusion (in the set of topics covered) is the entire area of preferential choice. There is no lack whatever of technically excellent papers in this area, but they give no sense of any real cumulation of knowledge. What are the established laws of preferential choice behavior?... [p. *xii*].

It is decidely not the case that researchers have simply catalogued descriptive successes or failures of normative models. Rather, in the search for more complete or useful descriptive models, investigators have been led to concepts and findings in various areas of cognitive psychology (see Hogarth, 1975, or Slovic, Fischhoff, & Lichtenstein, 1977). The alternative theories being suggested derive from the acknowledgment that decision making is a complex cognitive task, frequently situation dependent, which humans perform in a manner determined by their limited memory, retention, and information-processing capabilities. In certain respects, recent developments are similar to those advocated by Simon (1957) and, as Lockhead (this volume) points out, also by Bruner, Goodnow, and Austin (1956). Discussions of how cognitive limitations affect decision processes appear repeatedly throughout this book, but can be found explicitly in the chapters by Einhorn; Pitz; Payne; Fischhoff, Slovic, and Lichtenstein; Lockhead; MacCrimmon, Stanbury, and Wehrung; Wallsten; and Estes.

It is clear that decision researchers have come to realize the importance of cognitive concepts and cognitively oriented theories in understanding choice behavior. However, it is less obvious that cognitive psychologists yet acknowledge the importance of choice behavior in understanding intellectual processes such as memory, problem solving, letter recognition, or the like. This point is developed by both Estes and Lockhead in this volume. Indeed, because the majority of tasks studied by cognitive psychologists involve people making choices of one sort or another, Lockhead goes so far as to suggest that perhaps we should study "choice and decision behavior in cognitive processing" rather than the reverse.

Both Kubovy and Healy (this volume) and Estes (this volume) remind us that signal-detection theory is a normative choice model employed in a wide range of cognitive theories. Furthermore, the distinction between amount of information and criterion for a choice implied by this theory is also implicitly accepted by many cognitive theorists. However, in general, this decision aspect of a cognitive theory is relegated to a black box insensitive to the context within which it is placed, and rarely is the area of behavioral decision theory called upon to supply helpful concepts or findings for the purpose of improving the cognitive theory. It is to be hoped that these proceedings might stimulate cognitive psychologists to attend more carefully to the decision aspects of their subjects' tasks.

Both Lockhead and Estes point out that, generally, decision theorists have been concerned with formal descriptions of the task environment and with optimal strategies for performing such tasks, and consequently, have studied behavior within a narrowly defined range of situations. Alternatively, cognitive theorists have been concerned primarily with processes that cut across tasks and consequently have studied behavior in a wider range of richer but less well understood environments. The chapters in this book represent clear attempts to merge these two approaches.

Some of the participants in this conference were invited to describe the present structure of their theoretical framework, indicating the roots from which it grew, how it ties in with other areas of psychology or decision theory, and future prospects stemming from it. It was anticipated that these papers would fall relatively neatly into certain classifications that would form a basis for partitioning this book. Other participants (Carroll, Estes, Lockhead, and Luce) were each invited to discuss and provide commentary on a specific set of papers from the perspective of his particular specialization in psychology. The papers that were assigned to the discussants, naturally enough, are those that immediately precede their chapters in the book. All the authors responded to their invitations in such a comprehensive fashion that, happily, it has become impossible to classify the papers. There are numerous interrelated messages in each paper, and furthermore, the discussion chapters for the most part extend so far beyond the specific papers assigned to them that they stand as useful and important contributions in their own right.

Broadly speaking, three themes are woven throughout all the chapters. One is that we must enlarge the range of paradigms studied. Another is that we must broaden the scope of the underlying psychological theories employed. The third is that we must utilize mathematical models in less simplistic fashions. Truthfully and trivially, charges of this sort can be leveled against all research in all areas.

The contributions of the chapters lie not in the charges, but in the directions of the solutions they propose.

If one wishes to read chapters that focus to a substantial degree on fruitful ways we can enlarge the range of paradigms, then one would turn to Ebbesen and Konečni; Corbin; Payne; Carroll; Fischhoff, Slovic, and Lichtenstein; Lockhead; Schum; and Estes. Ebbesen and Konečni discuss their recent research relating laboratory and field studies of legal decision making. They find systematic differences in behavior between college students and legal professionals in the laboratory, and also between the behavior of the professionals in the laboratory and in the real world. They go on to suggest that although one might use laboratory experiments to study specific cognitive limitations, or processes, it would be a mistake to imagine that there exist a small number of laws of decision behavior that can be uncovered in the laboratory and then applied in a straightforward way to real world decisions. Thus, laboratory and observational studies should proceed hand-in-hand.

Corbin, in her chapter, suggests that we will learn much more about decision processes by studying the determinants that inhibit or allow choices to be made than by studying the choices themselves. Thus, we should focus to a considerably larger extent than we have on prechoice environments and behaviors. By providing a conceptual organization to the range of barriers that must be overcome prior to the making of a choice, Corbin suggests a framework for future empirical and theoretical research.

Payne, too, provides ways to usefully study the decision process from the subject's first introduction to the task, through his or her understanding of it, to the final set of choices. Payne suggests that a range of measures, such as verbal protocols, order of information search, eye movements, and so on, be collected to provide a fuller understanding of the process.

Carroll suggests that our models have dictated to too large an extent the paradigms in which we have collected data. If we consider decision makers as adaptive and at the same time beset with certain cognitive limitations, we will realize that they are adapting to the task as they view it, and consequently that we must expand the range of situations studied.

Fischhoff, Slovic, and Lichtenstein are concerned primarily with the elicitation of value judgments from decision makers. They point out that often these values are poorly defined or formulated by the subject, and that, as a result, the particular judgments elicited will depend to a large degree on the method of questioning. These authors demonstrate that we may achieve greater insight into the nature of people's values by posing diverse questions and studying the nature of the apparently inconsistent responses.

Lockhead shows the close theoretical correspondence among paradigms studied in decision research, problem solving, and certain aspects of psychophysics. The specific questions asked in each of these areas are relevant to the other areas, and Lockhead demonstrates ways in which it would be beneficial to look across the paradigms.

Schum is interested in the inductive use of equivocal information when that information is nonindependent and hierarchically related to the hypotheses in question. In itself, this is an important advance over the usual paradigms involving simple probabilistic linkages between hypotheses and data. However, Schum goes on to show that formal models and behavioral theories of the process can be aided by studying the law concerning use, interpretation, and admissibility of courtroom evidence.

Estes' chapter relates contemporary behavioral decision research to certain long-term trends in psychology, and in so doing suggests a variety of ways that our paradigms might be broadened. We should, for example, devote more attention to experimental situations in which the choice alternatives are not well defined, in which memory for information can be assessed, and in which individual differences can be systematically explored.

If one wishes to read chapters emphasizing ways in which psychological aspects of decision theories can be enriched, then one would look at those by Einhorn; Pitz; Lockhead; MacCrimmon, Stanbury, and Wehrung; Wallsten; Kubovy and Healy; and Estes.

Einhorn demonstrates that theories of learning must be included in our understanding of the decision process. People learn action–outcome linkages, and frequently they see causal linkages where none exist. The question is, how do people's experiences give rise to the range of normative and heuristic rules that they bring to bear in various situations? Einhorn suggests that we must particularly study the nature of outcome feedback, reviews his research on that topic, and develops a theory concerning how subjects learn in a choice situation based on their misinterpretation of feedback.

Pitz relies heavily on Newell and Simon's (1972) "production systems" to develop a class of theories concerning how people encode and process the distributional properties of outcomes. Within this context, he demonstrates how subjects' internal representations of tasks can depend on certain cognitive limitations, and how heuristic rules can be derived.

Payne also relies heavily on the information processing theory of Newell and Simon to suggest that we develop models that include the subject's internal representation of the environment, or his or her problem space, as well as descriptions of the environment itself. Payne reviews his research showing that the subject's problem space, and therefore his or her decision strategy, depends on the task and on how it is presented.

As previously indicated, Lockhead argues that decision processes, problem solving, and psychophysics can profitably be studied jointly in a manner that will enhance the commonalities among the theories involved.

MacCrimmon, Stanbury, and Wehrung employ a very simple mathematical model of risk to analyze the data obtained from their business executive subjects, and as a consequence demonstrate the importance of context on people's choices. They interpret these data by developing a theory incorporating selective perception and simple decision making.

Wallsten's chapter presents a general theory relating selective attention and simple task-specific decision rules to a wide range of choice situations. The theory is developed in a manner intended to be consistent with the findings on bounded rationality and heuristics, but is formulated so as to allow specific predictions and the relation of behavior in one situation to that in another. The approach is illustrated by applying it to the study of probabilistic inference.

Within the framework of signal-detection theory, Kubovy and Healy present and study classes of psychological theories concerning probabilistic inference, or categorization, as they call it. They are concerned in particular with how subjects learn, form their choice rules and decision criteria, and evaluate the probabilistic nature of information. Kubovy and Healy discuss some of their research that rules out, or makes less likely, certain classes of theories, each of which encompasses various specific models.

Finally, Estes suggests ways in which decision theorists might focus less strongly on particular tasks and devote more attention to developing theories about basic processes that cut across tasks. He proposes that the distinction currently made in many areas of cognitive psychology between structural and control processes will be useful in understanding decision behavior, and in relating decision processes to other areas of psychology.

The chapters that provide explicit examples of how mathematical models can be applied to behavioral decision research in less simplistic ways include those by MacCrimmon, Stanbury, and Wehrung; Schum; Wallsten; and Kubovy and Healy.

As already mentioned, the analyses by MacCrimmon, Stanbury, and Wehrung are guided by relatively elementary mathematical models of risk. However, the relationship between model successes or failures and features of the choice alternatives is traced in such a fashion that our knowledge of the determinants of subjective risk is enhanced considerably.

Schum specifies classes of Bayesian models that tease out and formalize the logical connections between evidence and hypotheses when the evidence is indirect, nonindependent, and hierarchical. Such a situation occurs, for example, when multiple unreliable witnesses report an event. This allows Schum to develop a scheme for classifying evidence in terms of its source and the nature of its relationship to the facts at issue. Schum's approach provides a framework for systematically studying complex inferences and relating it to other cognitive processes. In his discussion of Schum's chapter, Luce uses concepts from signal-detection theory to demonstrate some of the problems involved in combining multiple reports of an event.

Wallsten's chapter makes use of algebraic composition rules in a manner that explicitly interprets the parameters in terms of psychological constructs. This provides a means for relating predictive failures of models to substantive theory and for generalizing results from one paradigm to another. The focus of research thus shifts from whether a model is right or wrong to the development of a general descriptive theory of the decision process, which, however, is modeled differentially, depending on the task.

Kubovy and Healy superimpose on signal-detection theory formal representations of learning processes and of various psychological considerations that could lead to suboptimal performance. This approach provides a taxonomy of theories for the probabilistic categorization task and a systematic means for evaluating the theories.

It is clear that research in behavioral decision theory is changing dramatically. The chapters in this book represent a good assessment of the reasons the changes are coming about and some of the merits and problems of the directions in which we are moving. In that sense, the chapters are speculative, and as such, there is more than occasional disagreement between them. I hope the result is thought provoking to the reader.

I express my sincere appreciation to the authors for their thorough, thoughtful, and timely responses to my editorial comments. Their cooperation made my job as editor far easier and more enjoyable than I was led to believe it would be. Special thanks are due Michael Kubovy for assistance in organizing the conference, Curtis Barton for handling many of the details, and Elizabeth Schopler for secretarial assistance above and beyond the call of duty. The conference was made possible by support from the Office of Naval Research through contract N00014-78-C-0170.

Thomas S. Wallsten

Chapel Hill, North Carolina

REFERENCES

Becker, G. B., & McClintock, C. G. Value: Behavioral decision theory. *Annual Review of Psychology*, 1967, *18*, 239-286.

Bruner, J. S., Goodnow, J. J., & Austin, G. A. *A study of thinking.* New York: Wiley, 1956.

Edwards, W. The theory of decision making. *Psychological Bulletin*, 1954, *51*, 370-417.

Edwards, W. Behavioral decision theory. *Annual Review of Psychology*, 1961, *12*, 473-498.

Hogarth, R. Cognitive processes and the assessment of subjective probability distributions. *Journal of the American Statistical Association*, 1975, *70*, 271-293.

Kahneman, D., & Tversky, A. Prospect theory: An analysis of decision and risk. *Econometrica*, 1979, *47*, 263-291.

Krantz, D. H., Atkinson, R. C., Luce, R. D., & Suppes, P. (Eds.), *Contemporary developments in mathematical psychology* (Vol. 1). San Francisco: Freeman, 1974.

Newell, A., & Simon, H. A. *Human problem solving.* Englewood Cliffs, N.J.: Prentice-Hall, 1972.

Pitz, G. F. Decision making and cognition. In H. Jungermann & G. De Zeeuw (Eds.), *Decision making and change in human affairs*. Dordrecht, Holland: Reidel, 1977.

Rapoport, A., & Wallsten, T. S. Individual decision behavior. *Annual Review of Psychology*, 1972, *23*, 131-176.

Simon, H. A. *Models of man: Social and national*. New York: Wiley, 1957.

Slovic, P., Fischhoff, B., & Lichtenstein, S. Behavioral decision theory. *Annual Review of Psychology*, 1977, *28*, 1-39.

COGNITIVE PROCESSES IN CHOICE AND DECISION BEHAVIOR

1 Learning from Experience and Suboptimal Rules in Decision Making

Hillel J. Einhorn
Graduate School of Business
Center for Decision Research
University of Chicago

Current work in decision-making research has clearly shifted from representing choice processes via normative models (and modifications thereof) to an emphasis on heuristic processes developed within the general framework of cognitive psychology and theories of information processing (Payne, this volume; Russo, 1977; Simon, 1978; Slovic, Fischhoff, & Lichtenstein, 1977; Tversky & Kahneman, 1974, 1980). The shift in emphasis from questions about how well people perform to how they perform is certainly important (e.g., Hogarth, 1975). However, the usefulness of studying both questions together is nowhere more evident than in the study of heuristic rules and strategies. This is because the comparison of heuristic and normative rules allows one to examine discrepancies between actual and optimal behavior which then raise questions regarding why such discrepancies exist. The approach taken here is to focus on how one learns both types of rules from experience. The concern with learning from experience raises a number of issues that have not been adequately addressed; e.g., under what conditions are heuristics learned? How are they tested and maintained in the face of experience? Under what conditions do we fail to learn about the biases and mistakes that can result from their use?

The importance of learning for understanding heuristics and choice behavior can be seen by considering the following:

1. The ability to predict when a particular rule will be employed is currently inadequate (Wallsten, this volume). However, concern for how and under what conditions a rule is learned should increase one's ability to predict when it is likely to be used. For example, if a rule is learned in situations in which there is

1

little time to make a choice, prediction of the use of such a rule is enhanced by knowing the time pressure involved in the task.

2. A concomitant of (1) is that it should be possible to influence how people judge and decide by designing situations in which tasks incorporate or mimic initial learning conditions. The implications of this for both helping *and* manipulating people are enormous (Fischhoff, Slovic & Lichtenstein, 1978; this volume).

3. Consideration of learning focuses attention on environmental variables and task structure. Therefore, variables such as amount of reinforcement, schedules of reinforcement, number of trials (= amount of experience), and so on, should be considered in understanding judgment and decision behavior (cf. Estes, 1976). Although the importance of the task for understanding behavior has been continually stressed (Brunswik, 1943; Castellan, 1977; Cronbach, 1975; Dawes, 1975; Edwards, 1971; Einhorn & Hogarth, 1978; Simon & Newell, 1971), psychologists seem as prone to what Ross (1977) calls the "fundamental attribution error" (underweighting environmental factors in attributing causes) as anyone else.

4. A major variable in understanding heuristics is outcome feedback. Because outcome feedback is the main source of information for evaluating the quality of our decision/judgment rules, knowledge of how task variables both affect outcomes and influence the way outcomes are coded and stored in memory becomes critical in explaining how heuristics are learned and used.

5. The area of learning is the focal point for considering the relative merits of psychological versus economic explanations of choice behavior. Some economists have argued that although one does not act "rationally" all the time, one will learn the optimal rule through interaction with the environment. Vague assertions about equilibrium, efficiency, and evolutionary concepts are advanced to bolster this argument. Therefore, study of how (and how well) people learn from experience is important in casting light on the relative merits of psychological and economic theories of choice.

LEARNING FROM EXPERIENCE: HOW?

It is obvious that decision making is action oriented; one has to choose what action to take in order to satisfy basic needs and wants. Therefore, it is important for any organism to learn the degree to which actions will lead to desirable or undesirable outcomes. This means that a great deal of learning from experience must involve the learning of action–outcome linkages. Furthermore, because actions and outcomes are contiguous, people are prone to interpret the links between them as representing cause-and-effect relationships (Michotte, 1963). Therefore, the strong tendency to see causal relations can be considered an outgrowth of the need to take action to satisfy basic needs. Moreover, as pointed out by Tversky and Kahneman (1980), the learning of causal relationships and the organizing of events into causal "schemata" allow people to achieve a coherent interpretation of their experience. Finally, the learning of action-outcome links is important for understanding how people learn their own tastes or utilities. For example, consider a child who chooses a particular vegetable to eat, experiences an unpleasant taste, and thereby learns to associate a negative utility with that food. Note that it is typically by choosing that consequences can be experienced and utility learned. Therefore, the learning of action–outcome links and the learning of utility are closely tied together.

Although we learn from experience by taking action, how does one initially learn which alternative to choose? Undoubtedly, much initial learning occurs by trial and error—that is, people randomly choose an option and observe the outcome (cf. Campbell, 1960). The process by which trial-and-error learning gives way to the development of strategies or rules is not well known (cf. Siegler, 1978). However, one can speculate that both reinforcement from trial-and-error learning and generalization (both stimulus and response) play an important role (Staddon & Simmelhag, 1971). In any event, the rules we develop seem directly tied to learning what outcomes will follow from particular actions. As previously described, learning from experience is basically inductive in nature; that is, one experiences specific instances or cases and heuristics are developed to provide some generality for dealing with them. The inductive nature of learning from experience has several implications regarding heuristics:

1. Specificity of Rules. If learning occurs inductively via specific cases, then heuristic rules should be extremely context dependent. Much evidence now suggests that this is indeed the case (Grether & Plott, 1979; Lichtenstein & Slovic, 1971; Simon & Hayes, 1976; Tversky & Kahneman, 1980). The way in which a problem is worded or displayed, or a particular response is asked for, all seem to make an important difference in the way information is processed and responses generated. A dramatic example of this specificity can be seen in the work of Simon and Hayes (1976) on "problem isomorphs." They have shown that different surface wordings of structurally identical problems (i.e., problems that can be solved using identical principles) greatly change how people represent the problem in memory and consequently solve it. An important implication of this result is that in order to make heuristic models more predictive, one must contend with the task as represented and not necessarily with the task structure as seen by an experimenter. A particularly timely example of the importance of this phenomenon in predicting behavior is provided by observing that behavior depends on whether a tax cut is represented as a gain or a smaller loss (Kahneman & Tversky, 1979).

2. Generality of Rules. If heuristics are rules learned through induction, it is necessary to group tasks by similarity or else there would be as many rules as situations. Because this latter possibility is unacceptable, heuristics must have some generality over tasks. However, this conclusion contradicts what was said previously about context dependence and specificity of rules. This paradox can be resolved if one considers the range of tasks to which a rule can be applied. For example, consider the rule: "Never order fish in a meat restaurant." Although such a rule is general with respect to a certain type of restaurant, it is certainly more specific than the rule: "Judge the probability with which event B comes from process A by their degree of similarity" (Tversky & Kahneman, 1974). The latter heuristic is clearly at a much higher level of generality. In fact, it may be that heuristics such as representativeness, availability, anchoring and adjusting, are "metaheuristics"—that is, they are rules on how to generate rules. Therefore, when confronted by problems that one has not encountered before (such as judging probabilities of events), or problems whose specificity makes them seem novel, metaheuristics direct the way in which specific rules can be formed to solve the problem. The idea of a metaheuristic allows one to retain the generality that any rule necessarily implies, yet at the same time allows for the important effects of context, wording, response mode, and so on. In order to illustrate, consider the study by Slovic, Fischhoff, and Lichtenstein (1976) in which people were asked to judge the relative probabilities of death from unusual causes. For example, which has a higher probability: being killed by lightning or dying from emphysema? When confronted with such a question, there are many ways to attempt an answer. One rule that could be used would be: "Think of all the people I know that have died from the two causes and pick the event that caused more deaths." In my own case, I would choose emphysema (which does have a higher probability, although most people pick being killed by lightning). However, I could have just as easily developed a rule that would lead to the opposite answer; e.g., "Think of all of the cases of being killed by lightning and of death from emphysema that I have ever *heard about* (newspapers, television, etc.)." If this were my rule, I would choose being killed by lightning as being more probable. Note that in both cases I have used an availability heuristic. Clearly, the way in which a question is phrased could induce specific rules that lead to different results, yet these specific rules could be classified under a single more general strategy, or metaheuristic.

   3. Strength of Heuristics.   If heuristics are learned inductively, then learning occurs over many trials with many reinforcements. As is discussed later, because of the way feedback occurs and the methods that we use to test rules via experience, positive reinforcement can occur even for incorrect rules (Wason, 1960). Moreover, in addition to the large number of reinforcements that we experience, the size or intensity of reinforcement can be large. For example, gaining a sizable amount of money following the use of some rule for picking stocks should have a considerable reinforcement effect. Therefore, unlike laboratory studies of human learning, in which ethical considerations prevent large positive and negative reinforcements, our own experience poses no such constraints.

LEARNING FROM EXPERIENCE: HOW WELL?

The question of how well we learn from experience focuses attention on comparing heuristic rules to optimal rules. Therefore, it must be asked how the latter are learned and what the implications are for applying them in our own experience? Optimal rules, such as Bayes' theorem, optimization, and so on are learned *deductively.* In fact, much of what can be called formal learning is of a deductive character; that is, we are taught scientific laws, logical principles, mathematical and statistical rules, and so on. Such rules are by their very nature abstract and context independent. Furthermore, when context can influence the form of a rule, one is frequently told that the rule holds, "other things being equal." Of course, in our own experience, other things are rarely equal, which makes the learning of optimal rules via induction so difficult. (The original discoverers or inventors of optimal rules overcame these difficulties; however, this distinguishes them from the rest of us.)

The abstract nature of deductive rules has important implications regarding the difficulty people have in applying optimal methods to specific situations. This difficulty centers around the ability to discern the structure of tasks that are embedded in a rich variety of detail. Therefore, when one is faced with a specific problem that is rich in detail, and in which details may be irrelevant or redundant, one's attention to specifics is likely to divert attention from the general structure of the problem. In fact, the very abstractness of deductively learned optimal rules may prevent them from being retrieved from memory (cf. Nisbett, Borgida, Crandall, & Reed, 1976). Therefore, abstract rules may not be very "available" in specific cases. However, this begs the question because it is important to know *why* these rules are not available.

Consider the way action–outcome combinations are likely to be organized and stored in memory. In particular, consider whether such information is more likely to be organized and stored by content or task structure. It would seem easier and more natural to organize action–outcome combinations by subject matter rather than by structure; for example, experiences with schools, parents, members of the opposite sex, and so on, rather than Bayesian problems, selection situations, optimization problems, and the like. That content can differ while structure remains the same is quite difficult to see (Kahneman & Tversky, 1979; Simon & Hayes, 1976). Therefore, I think it unlikely that most people organize their experiences by task structure. This is not to say that one could not be trained to do so. In fact, much of professional training is exactly this; for instance, one is taught to recognize problems as belonging to a class of problems having a given structure and (sometimes) a known solution. Therefore, optimal rules can be "available" through extensive training. Of course, there is the danger of such rules being *too* readily available; that is, problems are forced into a structure that is not appropriate because a solution within that structure exists. It is a truism that when presented with a problem, professionals view the problem within the structures they have been trained to see. Therefore, although professional training does involve a concern for structure, such training is generally within a narrowly defined content area.

Further evidence illustrating the need to group problems by content rather than structure is provided by considering the way public knowledge about the world is organized and taught. For example, departmentalized education, professional training, cataloguing of information in libraries and encyclopedias, and so on, illustrate the organizing of information by content rather than structure. Although there are great advantages in organizing knowledge in this way, there are also costs. The difficulty of applying optimal rules developed in one content area to structurally similar problems in other content areas may be one such cost. However, at the level of the individual learner, other difficulties are now considered that may be even more costly.

Although task structure is difficult to discern, outcomes are not; they are highly visible, available, and often unambiguous. Therefore, consideration of reinforcement via outcome feedback is essential in understanding how heuristics are maintained in the face of experience. Furthermore, if outcomes are a function of task structure to a considerable degree and the decision maker's knowledge of such structure is lacking, then rules that are irrelevant or even poor may still be reinforced by positive outcome feedback (for example, "superstitious" behavior in animal learning; see Staddon & Simmelhag, 1971).

Following are two examples of how normatively poor heuristics can lead to good outcomes and in which awareness of the poor quality of the rule may be lacking. Consider shopping in a supermarket and coming to cans of juice with the following prices and overall quality levels (adapted from Tversky, 1969):

Brand	Price	Quality
X	40¢	High
Y	35¢	Medium
Z	30¢	Low

Assume that I use the following rule to choose between the three brands: If the price difference is 5¢ or less, choose the brand with the higher quality; if the price difference is greater than 5¢, choose according to price. Such a simple rule (which is a lexicographic semiorder) leads to:

$$X > Y$$
$$Y > Z, \text{ but}$$
$$Z > X$$

Therefore, this rule leads to intransitive choices, which are clearly irrational. However, note that after I choose X over Y, I may then eliminate Y from the remaining set and compare X with Z. Therefore, I end up with Z, which may be quite acceptable after I taste it. I then congratulate myself on what a good shopper I am—I saved money and I got a reasonable product. The important point to note here is that by not making the *Y* vs. *Z* comparison, I remain unaware that my rule leads to an intransitive choice. All I *am* aware of is that I made a choice with minimal fuss and strain and the outcome was satisfactory. Therefore, positive outcome feedback reinforces a normatively poor rule, and awareness that something is wrong is missing.

The second example is a probabilistic one (cf. Schum, this volume). Imagine that you are a military general in a politically tense area and that you are concerned that your enemies will invade your country. Furthermore, from past experience it is known that when enemy troops mass at a border, the probability of invasion is .75. However, you do not have direct access to information about enemy troops, but must rely on a report of such activity by your intelligence sources. As it turns out, every time your intelligence sources report that troops are massing, they are really there. Consider that you now receive a report from your sources that enemy troops are at the border. What is the probability of invasion? More formally, let:

$$H = \text{hypothesis of being invaded}$$
$$D = \text{troops massing at the border}$$
$$D^* = \text{report of troops massing at the border}$$

The problem states that $p(H|D) = .75$ and $p(D|D^*) = 1.0$, and asks you for $p(H|D^*)$. If you are like most people, you probably answered .75. However, the information given is not sufficient to answer the question in the normatively correct way. In fact, it is possible that in the preceding problem, $p(H|D^*) = 0$. Because most people find this very difficult to believe, consider Fig. 1.1, which illustrates the problem by means of a Venn diagram. Note that the intersection of H with D^* is null, so that the conditional probability, $p(H|D^*)$, is zero. The reason that people find this result so surprising is that they have made a logical

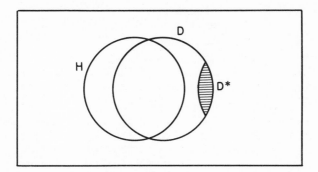

FIG. 1.1.   Venn diagram showing the relationship between the hypothesis (*H*), datum (*D*), and report of datum (*D**).

fallacy of the form: If D^* implies D, then D implies D^*. Although D occurs whenever D^* is given, the reverse is not necessarily the case. In fact, an intuitive way to see the issue is to think that the enemy is particularly cunning so that your intelligence sources see their troops only when there is no invasion planned. However, when an invasion is planned and troops are at the border, they are hidden so that your sources do not report them.

This example illustrates the difficulty of applying optimal rules (in this case, the rules of formal logic) to a specific task. Although very few people would make the logical error when it is presented in a recognizable form, the importance of the example is that it shows how the specifics of the problem hide its real structure so that optimal rules are easily violated (cf. Kahneman & Tversky, 1979). A second point can be made with respect to this example. Consider that the general makes the logical error and estimates the chance of war at .75. He then sends *his* troops to the border, thereby causing an invasion by the enemy. Therefore, the faulty reasoning of the general is reinforced by outcome feedback—"after all," he might say, "those SOB's did invade us, which is what we thought they'd do."

The two examples just discussed illustrate the basic point of this chapter, viz. without knowledge of task structure, outcome feedback can be irrelevant or even harmful for correcting poor heuristics. Moreover, positive outcome feedback without task knowledge tends to keep us unaware that our rules are poor because there is very little motivation to question how successes were achieved. The conditions under which outcome feedback does not play a correcting role vis-a-vis heuristics and strategies are denoted *outcome irrelevant learning structures* (OILS). Such structures may be much more common than we think. Before examining one such structure in detail, consider probabilistic judgments within the framework of OILS, because much of the work on heuristics is directly concerned with this type of judgment. Consider that you judge the probability of some event to be .70. Let us say that the event does not happen. What does this outcome tell you about the quality of the rules used to generate the judgment? One might argue that any *single* outcome is irrelevant in assessing the "goodness" (i.e., degree of calibration) of probabilistic judgments. Therefore, in an important sense, immediate outcome information is irrelevant for correcting poor heuristics. It is only if one keeps a "box score" of the relative frequency of outcomes when one judges events with a given probability that one can get useful feedback from outcomes. However, this is likely to be a necessary but not sufficient condition for making well-calibrated judgments. First, over what time period does one keep the box score before deciding that the judgment is or is not calibrated? Furthermore, how close is close enough in order to say that the judgment is accurate (in the sense of being well calibrated)? Note that this whole mode of evaluating outcomes involves reinforcement that is delayed for long time periods. Therefore, it is not clear that such feedback will have much of a self-correcting effect. Second, in order to learn about the goodness of rules for estimating probability, one's box score must include not only one's estimates and the resulting outcomes, but also one's rules for deriving those estimates. For example, if I kept a record of outcomes that resulted for 100 cases in which I gave estimates of .70, what would the information that 53 of those times the event happened tell me about the quality of the rules I used? Because it is likely that many different rules could have been used to estimate probabilities in the 100 different situations, the outcome information is irrelevant and outcome feedback is not useful unless one is both aware of one's rules and a record is kept of their use (cf. Nisbett & Wilson, 1977 on whether we are aware of our own cognitive processes).

The preceding example does not imply that it is impossible to learn to make well-calibrated probability judgments. If one makes *many* probability judgments in the *same situation,* such as weather forecasters and horse-racing handicappers do, and outcome feedback is quickly received, such conditions may not be outcome irrelevant, and feedback can be self correcting. However, such conditions would seem to be the exception rather than the rule for most of us.

Although probabilistic judgments typically occur in OILS, what about non-probabilistic judgments? Surely, if one makes a prediction about something, one can check to see if the prediction is correct or not. Therefore, it would seem that outcomes should be relevant for providing self-correcting feedback. The remainder of this chapter discusses this issue within the context of one general and prevalent task structure, although the specific content of such tasks may be quite different.

SELECTION TASK[1]

A very general task involving nonprobabilistic judgments is now examined because outcome information seems both available and relevant for providing self-correcting feedback. The task considered is one in which judgments are made for the purpose of choosing between alternative actions. For example, consider a situation with two possible actions, A and B. Denote by x an overall, evaluative judgment, which may itself be a function of various types and amounts of information. Furthermore, let x_c be a cutoff point such that:

if $x \geq x_c$, take action $A;$
if $x < x_c$, take action B. (1.1)

Although simplistic, Eq. (1.1) applies to many judgment/decision situations, for example: job hiring, promotion, admission to school, loan and credit granting, assignment to remedial programs, admission to social programs, journal article acceptance, grant awarding, and so on. In these cases, a judgment of the degree

---

[1]Much of this section is drawn from Einhorn & Hogarth (1978).

of "deservedness" typically determines which action is to be taken because the preferred action cannot be given to all.

In order to compare judgment to a standard, the existence of a criterion, denoted y, is assumed to serve as the basis for evaluating the accuracy of judgment. Although the practical difficulties of finding and developing adequate criteria are enormous, the focus here is theoretical: It is the concept of a criterion that is necessary for this analysis. To be consistent with the formulation of judgment, it is further assumed that the criterion has a cutoff point (y_c) such that $y \geq y_c$ and $y < y_c$ serve as the basis for evaluating the outcomes of judgment. Thus, as far as learning about judgment is concerned, representation of outcomes in memory is often of a categorical form, i.e., successes and failures (cf. Estes, 1976).

It is very important to note that the structure of the task is one in which judgments (predictions) lead to differential actions and that outcomes are then used as feedback for determining the accuracy of the predictions. The formal structure can be seen by considering the regression of y on x and the four quadrants that result from the intersection of x_c and y_c, as illustrated in Fig. 1.2.

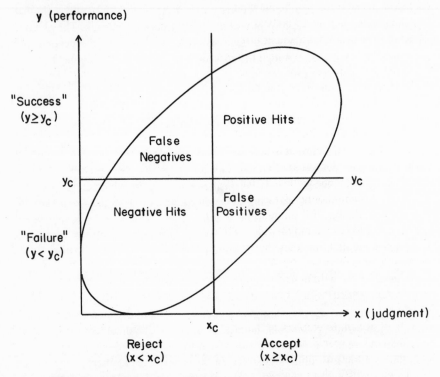

FIG. 1.2.   Action–outcome combinations that result from using judgment to make an accept/reject decision.

Denote the correct predictions as positive and negative hits, and the two types of errors as false positives ($y < y_c | x \geqslant x_c$) and false negatives ($y \geqslant y_c | x < x_c$). To estimate the relationship between x and y (i.e., the correlation between x and y, ρ_{xy}) it is necessary to have information on *each* judgment–outcome combination. Assume first that such information becomes available over time (i.e., sequentially) and consider the experimental evidence concerned with learning the relationship between x and y in such circumstances. Research on the ability to judge the contingency between x and y from information in 2 × 2 tables (Jenkins & Ward, 1965; Smedslund, 1963, 1966; Ward & Jenkins, 1965) indicates that people judge the strength of relationship by the frequency of positive hits (in the terminology of Fig. 1.2), while generally ignoring information in the three other cells. These results are extremely important because they indicate that *even when* all of the relevant outcome information is available, people do not use it. This means that in laboratory studies that have outcome-relevant learning structures, people have transformed them into outcome-irrelevant learning structures. How can this be explained?

The explanation advanced here is that our experience in real world tasks is such that we develop rules and methods that seem to work reasonably well. However, these rules may be quite poor and our awareness of their inadequacy is profound. This lack of awareness exists because positive outcome feedback can occur in spite of, rather than because of, our predictive ability. As an illustration, consider the study by Wason (1960) in which he presented subjects with a three-number sequence, for example: 2, 4, 6. Subjects were required to discover the rule to which the three numbers conformed (the rule being three ascending numbers). To discover the rule, the subjects were permitted to generate sets of three numbers that the experimenter classified as conforming or not conforming to the rule. Subjects could stop at any point when they thought they had discovered the rule. The correct solution to this task should involve a search for disconfirming evidence rather than the accumulation of confirming evidence. For example, if someone believed that the rule had something to do with even numbers, this could only be tested by trying a sequence involving an odd number (i.e., accumulating vast amounts of confirming instances of even number sequences would not lead to the rule). The fact that only 6 of 29 subjects found the correct rule the first time they thought they did illustrates the dangers of induction by simple enumeration. As Wason (1960) points out, the solution to this task must involve "a willingness to attempt to falsify hypotheses, and thus to *test those intuitive ideas which so often carry the feeling of certitude* [p. 139; author's emphasis]."

It is important to emphasize that in Wason's experiment, where actions were *not* involved, a search for disconfirming evidence is possible. However, when actions are based on judgment, learning based on disconfirming evidence becomes more difficult to achieve. For example, consider how one might erroneously learn an incorrect rule for making judgments by focusing on the hypothetical case of a manager learning about his or her predictive ability concerning the potential of job candidates. The crucial factor here is that actions (e.g., accept/do not accept) are contingent on judgment. Therefore, at a subsequent date, the manager can only examine *accepted* candidates to see how many are successful. If there are many successes (which, as is shown later, is likely), these instances all confirm the rule. Indeed, the important point here is that it would be difficult to disconfirm the rule, even though it might be erroneous. One way in which the rule could be tested would be for the manager to accept a subset of those he or she judged to have low potential and then to observe their success rate. If their rate was as high as those judged to be of high potential, the rule would be disconfirmed. However, a systematic search for disconfirming evidence is rare and could be objected to on utilitarian and/or even ethical grounds; one would have to withhold the preferred action from some of those judged most deserving and give it to some judged least deserving. Therefore, utilitarian and/or ethical considerations may prevent one from even considering the collection of possible disconfirming information. Note that the tendency not to test hypotheses by disconfirming instances is a direct consequence of the task structure in which actions are taken on the basis of judgment. Furthermore, as Wason (1960) points out: "In real life there is no authority to pronounce judgment on inferences: the inferences can only be checked against the evidence [p. 139]." Therefore, large amounts of positive feedback can lead to reinforcement of a nonvalid rule.

Although outcomes contingent on the action not taken may not be sought, it is still the case that one can examine the number of positive hits and false positives as a way to check on the accuracy of one's predictions. Therefore, although such information is incomplete for accurately assessing the relationship between predictions and outcomes, such information is what most people have available. It is therefore important to consider the factors that affect these variables.

FACTORS AFFECTING POSITIVE HITS
AND FALSE POSITIVES

In order to examine the number of positive hits and false positives that will result from making predictions in selection tasks, some notation is necessary. Let:

N = number of total decisions to be made; i.e., total number of "applicants."

$p(x \geq x_c) = \phi$ = selection ratio; i.e., the unconditional probability of receiving action A.

$p(y \geq y_c) = br$ = base rate; i.e., the unconditional probability of exceeding the criterion.

$p(y \geq y_c | x \geq x_c) = ph$ = positive hit rate.

$p(y < y_c | x \geq x_c) = fp$ = false positive rate.

ρ_{xy} = correlation between predictions and outcomes.

Let us denote the number of positive hits as N_p and the number of false negatives as N_f. These can now be defined as:

$$N_p = N \, p(y \geq y_c, \, x \geq x_c)$$
$$N_f = N \, p(y < y_c, \, x \geq x_c). \tag{1.2}$$

However, the joint probabilities can be replaced by conditional probabilities multiplied by their respective marginal probabilities; i.e.:

$$N_p = N \, p(y \geq y_c | x \geq x_c) \, p(x \geq x_c) = N \, ph \, \phi$$
$$N_f = N \, p(y < y_c | x \geq x_c) \, p(x \geq x_c) = N \, fp \, \phi. \tag{1.3}$$

Because $ph = 1 - fp$,

$$N_p = N \, ph \, \phi$$
$$N_f = N(1 - ph) \, \phi. \tag{1.4}$$

If people evaluate the total feedback effect of outcomes by the ratio N_p/N_f, then the positive hit rate determines whether feedback is positive or negative. When $ph > .5$, $N_p > N_f$. On the other hand, if people evaluate the total feedback effect by the difference $N_p - N_f$, it is easily shown that:[2]

$$N_p - N_f = N \, \phi(2 \, ph - 1), \tag{1.5}$$

in which case, if $ph > .5$, $N_p > N_f$ (see Einhorn & Hogarth, 1978, for a more complete model). Therefore, regardless of whether people evaluate $N_p - N_f$ or N_p/N_f, the issue comes down to whether $ph > .5$. This is now examined in detail.

Consider Fig. 1.2 again, in which it can be seen that three factors affect the positive hit rate:

1. Predictive ability as measured by ρ_{xy}, the correlation between x and y
2. The unconditional probability of being judged above the cutoff; the selection ratio (ϕ)
3. The base rate or unconditional probability of exceeding the criterion (br).

The effects of these three factors on the positive hit rate are well known. Taylor and Russell (1939), for example, have shown that one can increase the positive hit rate, for any given ρ_{xy} and base rate, by reducing the selection ratio (ϕ), i.e., by giving the preferred action to a smaller percentage (assuming $\rho_{xy} \neq 0$). Therefore, even if ρ_{xy} is low, it is possible to have a high positive hit rate depending on the values of ϕ and br. Taylor and Russell (1939) provide tables of positive hit rates for a wide range of values of ρ_{xy}, ϕ and br. Examination of these tables shows that low correlations between judgments and criteria are compatible with large positive hit rates.

---

[2] $N_p - N_f = N \, ph \, \phi - N(1 - ph) \, \phi = N \, ph \, \phi - N\phi + N \, ph \, \phi = 2N \, ph \, \phi - N \, \phi = N \, \phi (2 \, ph - 1)$

In addition to the three factors already mentioned, a fourth factor must be considered. This can be illustrated by imagining the following experiment. Assume that a series of judgments is made about some persons. Of those judged to be above x_c, *randomly* assign half to action A and half to action B. Similarly, do the same for those judged below x_c. At some later point in time, measure performance and calculate the proportion of persons with $y \geq y_c$ in each cell (each person is assigned a 0 or 1 to indicate whether he or she is below or above the cutoff on y—the proportion above y_c being simply the mean of that cell). This is a 2×2 factorial design with one factor being "judgment" and the other "type of action." Note that because the criterion cannot be measured immediately before the decision (indeed, if it could, there would be no need for judgment), people receiving actions A and B have also received different experimental treatments. If this experiment were done, one could test for the main effect of judgment (which measures its accuracy); the main effect for the action, i.e., whether receiving A or B in itself causes differences in performance; and the interaction between judgment and action. Observe that the advantage of the experiment is that it allows one to untangle the accuracy of judgment from the treatment effects of the action. However, such an experiment is rarely done, even conceptually, and especially not by people without extensive training in experimental design. Therefore, judgmental accuracy will almost always be confounded with possible treatment effects due to actions. Furthermore, and with reference to the earlier discussion, this experiment allows one to examine disconfirming information. Therefore, in contrast to most real judgmental tasks, it would permit one to disconfirm the hypothesis of judgmental accuracy *as well as* to estimate any treatment effects due to the action.

To illustrate how treatment effects can influence outcomes, consider the decision to award or not to award grants to researchers.[3] Assume that grant applications are judged on some basis of potential such that those judged above x_c receive awards and those judged below x_c are denied. Assume also that the granting agency wishes to determine whether its judging procedures produce satisfactory results. To this end, it develops a criterion that reflects both quantity and quality of completed research. It then examines funded projects and calculates the proportion considered successes. (If the agency were wise, it might also try to discover the proportion of successful projects it had refused to fund. The difficulty in doing this, however, illustrates the earlier point about the rarity of having complete information to evaluate judgment). If the proportion of successes for those given grants is high, the agency might feel that its judgmental procedures are quite accurate. However, note that the treatment effect of receiving a grant is completely confounded with judgmental accuracy; e.g., obtaining a grant can give a researcher time and resources to do more and better work. If there were a main effect for the action (in the direction assumed here), one might

---

[3]This example is used for illustrative purposes only.

still experience a high positive hit rate, even if the accuracy of the judgment were low (or perhaps zero). Note that the true experiment would be difficult to do because it would imply withholding grants from some "deserving" cases while awarding grants to some who do not "deserve" them. Consequently, the *assumed* validity of judgment can be continually reinforced by experience.

A MODEL FOR DETERMINING POSITIVE HIT RATES

A model is now developed in which the positive hit rate is shown to be a function of four factors: (1) ρ_{xy}, the correlation between judgments and outcomes (in the absence of treatment effects); (2) the selection ratio, ϕ; (3) the base rate, *br;* (4) treatment effects due to actions, *t*. The assumptions of the model are that in the absence of any treatment effects, both x and y are standardized and they are distributed as bivariate normal. Furthermore, attention will be limited to a possible additive treatment effect for those judged to exceed x_c. Under these assumptions, the relationship between x and y can be expressed as:

$$y = \rho_{xy} x + zt + \epsilon \qquad (1.6)$$

where z = dummy variable with the specification

$$z = \begin{cases} 1 \text{ if } x \geq x_c \\ 0 \text{ if } x < x_c \end{cases}$$

t = treatment effect in units of the standard deviation of performance (y). For example, $t = .5$ means that for those judged above x_c, the treatment increases y by $.5$.

ϵ = random disturbance term with mean of 0.

Note that the model could also incorporate a negative treatment effect (i.e., people below x_c receive an action that reduces their y scores) by changing the specification of the dummy variable when $x < x_c$ from 0 to -1. It follows from Eq. (1.6) that the conditional expectation of y is

$$E(y|x, \rho_{xy}, z, t) = \rho_{xy}x + zt. \qquad (1.7)$$

Therefore, the conditional probability of observing a success, i.e., an outcome above y_c for any $x \geq x_c$, can be found by making use of the conditional distribution of y given x; that is:

$$p(y \geq y_c|x, \rho_{xy}, z, t) = \int_{y_c}^{\infty} \{2\pi(1 - \rho_{xy}^2)\}^{-\frac{1}{2}} \exp\left[\frac{-(y - \rho_{xy} x - zt)^2}{2(1 - \rho_{xy}^2)} \right] dy.$$

$$(1.8)$$

From Eq. (1.8), it can be seen that the probability of observing a successful outcome is dependent on:

1. y_c, and thus the base rate, br
2. x_c, and thus the selection ratio, ϕ, because z is a function of x_c
3. ρ_{xy}, true judgmental ability
4. t, the size of the treatment effect.

Treatment effects are illustrated in Fig. 1.3. The dotted ellipse is that shown in Fig. 1.2 and represents the true relationship between judgments and outcomes. The shaded portion indicates those outcomes that can be observed; hence, only values for which $x \geq x_c$ are shown. The treatment effect occurs in that the outcomes (i.e., performance) of all those given action A are increased by a constant amount so that the number of positive hits is greater than would have been observed in the absence of treatment effects. From a psychological viewpoint, the key aspect of Fig. 1.3 is that the nature of feedback to the judge is contaminated; the number of positive hits is inflated, and the number of false positives is reduced.

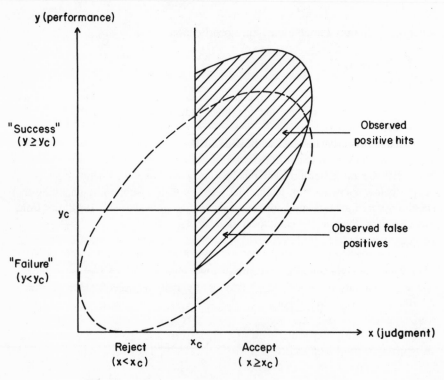

FIG. 1.3.   Effect of treatment on the observed positive hit rate.

In order to quantify the effects of the factors previously discussed on the positive hit rate, Einhorn and Hogarth (1978) performed a simulation experiment in which various levels of treatment effects, selection ratios, base rates, and predictive abilities were varied in a factorial design. The dependent variable was the positive hit rate. The results of that simulation can be summarized as follows:

1. In general, the positive hit rate is greater than .50. When treatment effects exist, the positive hit rate can be high even when $\rho_{xy} = 0$.

2. When $\phi < br$, positive hit rates are particularly high. Furthermore, the positive hit rate is sensitive to treatment effects at low values of ρ_{xy}. This means that in highly selective situations, poor predictive ability is most likely to be reinforced by positive outcome feedback.

3. When $\phi > br$, positive hit rates are lowest. However, small treatment effects have a substantial impact on raising positive hit rates in these situations.

The simulation results demonstrate that positive feedback can exist when predictive ability is poor. Moreover, awareness of this is usually very low because of the failure to adequately understand the task structure. Therefore, although one might suppose that nonprobabilistic judgments are made in an outcome-relevant learning structure, when judgments are made for the purpose of deciding between actions, outcome information may be irrelevant for providing self-correcting feedback.

CONCLUSION[4]

The basic theme of this chapter has been that outcome information, without knowledge of task structure, can be irrelevant for providing self-correcting feedback about poor heuristics. Furthermore, it has been argued that knowledge of task structure is difficult to achieve because of the inductive way in which we learn from experience (cf. Hammond, 1978, on Galilean versus Aristotelian modes of thought). These conclusions raise two issues that are now briefly discussed.

It may be the case that even with knowledge of task structure, one chooses to act in such a way that learning is precluded. For example, consider a waiter in a busy restaurant. Because the waiter does not have time to give good service to all the customers at his or her station, a prediction is made about which customers are likely to leave good or poor tips. Good or bad service is then given depending on the prediction. If the quality of service has a treatment effect on the size of the tip, the outcomes confirm the original predictions. Note that the waiter could perform an experiment to disentangle the treatment effects of quality of service

---

[4] I would like to thank J. E. R. Staddon for raising the points discussed in this section.

from the predictions if he or she was aware of the task structure; i.e., he or she could give poor service to some of those judged to leave good tips and good service to some of those judged to leave poor tips. However, note that the waiter must be willing to risk the possible loss of income if the judgment is accurate, against learning that the judgment is poor. The latter information may have long-run benefits in that it could motivate the person to try to make better predictions or, if this is not possible, to use a strategy of giving good or poor service randomly, thus saving much mental effort. In the case of organizational decisions, the long-run benefits from knowing about the accuracy of one's predictions could be substantial. For example, if selection interviews do not predict performance (independent of treatment effects), why spend money and time using them? Therefore, the costs and benefits of short-run strategies for action versus long-run strategies for learning needs to be more fully investigated.

The second issue can be raised by stating the following question: If people learn and continue to use poor rules, doesn't this contradict the evolutionary concept of survival of the fittest? I take this question to mean that those who use bad rules should be less likely to survive than those who use better rules (they are more fit). However, the use of better rules can still be quite removed from the use of optimal rules. The concept of most fit involves a relative ordering whereas optimality implies some absolute level. Therefore, the fact that suboptimal rules are maintained in the face of experience is not contradicted by Darwinian theory. Perhaps the most succinct way of putting this is to quote Erasmus: "In the land of the blind, the one-eyed man is king."[5]

ACKNOWLEDGMENTS

This research was supported by a grant from the Illinois Department of Mental Health and Developmental Disabilities, Research and Development #740-02. I would like to thank Robin Hogarth for his comments on an earlier version of this chapter.

REFERENCES

Brunswik, E. Organismic achievement and environmental probability. *Psychological Review*, 1943, *50*, 255–272.
Campbell, D. T. Blind variation and selective retention in creative thought as in other knowledge processes. *Psychological Review*, 1960, *67*, 380–400.

---

[5]The intent of this quotation is to point out that *relative* advantages vis-a-vis one's environment are important. No slur is meant or intended toward blind people. Tom Wallsten makes the following comment: "In the land of the blind, the one-eyed man could only survive by closing his eye, because the environment would be arranged to rely on other senses." Although this is a fascinating comment, I disagree because the one-eyed man would still have all of his other senses in addition to the seeing advantage.

Castellan, N. J., Jr. Decision making with multiple probabilistic cues. In N. J. Castellan, D. B. Pisoni, & G. R. Potts (Eds.), *Cognitive Theory*, (Vol. 2). Hillsdale, N.J.: Lawrence Erlbaum Associates, 1977.

Cronbach, L. J. Beyond the two disciplines of scientific psychology. *American Psychologist*, 1975, *30*, 116-127.

Dawes, R. M. The mind, the model, and the task. In F. Restle, R. M. Shiffrin, N. J. Castellan, H. R. Lindman, & D. P. Pisoni (Eds.), *Cognitive Theory, 1*. Hillsdale, N.J.: Lawrence Erlbaum Associates, 1975.

Edwards, W. Bayesian and regression models of human information processing—a mypoic perspective. *Organizational Behavior and Human Performance*, 1971, *6*, 639-648.

Einhorn, H. J., & Hogarth, R. M. Confidence in judgment: Persistence of the illusion of validity. *Psychological Review*, 1978, *85*, 395-416.

Estes, W. K. The cognitive side of probability learning. *Psychological Review*, 1976, *83*, 37-64.

Fischhoff, B., Slovic, P., & Lichtenstein, S. Fault trees: Sensitivity of estimated failure probabilities to problem representation. *Journal of Experimental Psychology: Human Perception and Performance*, 1978, *4*, 330-344.

Grether, D. M., & Plott, C. R. Economic theory of choice and preference reversal phenomenon. *American Economic Review*, 1979, *69*, 623-638.

Hammond, K. R. Toward increasing competence of thought in public policy formation. In K. R. Hammond (Ed.), *Judgment and decision in public policy formation*. Denver, Colorado: Westview Press, 1978.

Hogarth, R. M. Cognitive processes and the assessment of subjective probability distributions. *Journal of the American Statistical Association*, 1975, *70*, 271-289.

Jenkins, H. M., & Ward, W. C. Judgment of contingency between responses and outcomes. *Psychological Monographs: General and Applied*, 1965, *79*, Whole No. 594.

Kahneman, D., & Tversky, A. Prospect theory: An analysis of decisions under risk. *Econometrica*, 1979, *47*, 263-291.

Lichtenstein, S., & Slovic, P. Reversal of preferences between bids and choices in gambling decisions. *Journal of Experimental Psychology*, 1971, *89*, 46-55.

Michotte, A. *The perception of causality*. New York: Basic Books, 1963.

Nisbett, R. E., Borgida, E., Crandall, R., & Reed, H. Popular induction: Information is not necessarily informative. In J. S. Carroll & J. W. Payne (Eds.), *Cognition and social behavior*. Hillsdale, N.J.: Lawrence Erlbaum Associates, 1976.

Nisbett, R. E., & Wilson, T. D. Telling more than we can know: Verbal reports on mental processes. *Psychological Review*, 1977, *84*, 231-259.

Ross, L. The intuitive psychologist and his shortcomings: Distortions in the attribution process. In L. Berkowitz (Ed.), *Advances in experimental social psychology*, (Vol. 10). New York: Academic Press, 1977.

Russo, J. E. The value of unit price information. *Journal of Marketing Research*, 1977, *14*, 193-201.

Siegler, R. S. The origins of scientific reasoning. In R. S. Siegler (Ed.), *Children's thinking: What develops?* Hillsdale, N.J.: Lawrence Erlbaum Associates, 1978.

Simon, H. A. Information-processing theory of human problem solving. In W. K. Estes (Ed.), *Handbook of learning and cognitive processes*, (Vol. 5). Hillsdale, N.J.: Lawrence Erlbaum Associates, 1978.

Simon, H. A., & Hayes, J. R. The understanding process: Problem isomorphs. *Cognitive Psychology*, 1976, *8*, 165-190.

Simon, H. A., & Newell, A. Human problem solving: The state of the theory in 1970. *American Psychologist*, 1971, *26*, 145-159.

Slovic, P., Fischhoff, B., & Lichtenstein, S. Cognitive processes and societal risk taking. In J. S. Carroll & J. W. Payne (Eds.), *Cognition and social behavior*. Hillsdale, N.J.: Lawrence Erlbaum Associates, 1976.

Slovic, P., Fischhoff, B., & Lichtenstein, S. Behavioral decision theory. *Annual Review of Psychology*, 1977, *28*, 1–39.

Smedslund, J. The concept of correlation in adults. *Scandinavian Journal of Psychology*, 1963, *4*, 165–173.

Smedslund, J. Note on learning, contingency, and clinical experience. *Scandinavian Journal of Psychology*, 1966, *7*, 265–266.

Staddon, J. E. R., & Simmelhag, V. L. The "superstition" experiment: A reexamination of its implications for the principles of adaptive behavior. *Psychological Review*, 1971, *78*, 3–43.

Taylor, H. C., & Russell, J. T. The relationship of validity coefficients to the practical effectiveness of tests in selection: Discussion and tables. *Journal of Applied Psychology*, 1939, *23*, 565–578.

Tversky, A. Intransitivity of preferences. *Psychological Review*, 1969, *76*, 31–48.

Tversky, A., & Kahneman, D. Judgment under uncertainty: Heuristics and biases. *Science*, 1974, *185*, 1124–1131.

Tversky, A., & Kahneman, D. Causal schemas in judgments under uncertainty. In M. Fishbein (Ed.), *Progress in social psychology*. Hillsdale, N.J.: Lawrence Erlbaum Associates, 1980.

Ward, W. C., & Jenkins, H. M. The display of information and the judgment of contingency. *Canadian Journal of Psychology*, 1965, *19*, 231–241.

Wason, P. C. On the failure to eliminate hypotheses in a conceptual task. *Quarterly Journal of Experimental Psychology*, 1960, *12*, 129–140.

2

On the External Validity of Decision-Making Research: What Do We Know About Decisions in the Real World?

Ebbe B. Ebbesen
and Vladimir J. Konečni
University of California, San Diego

THE ISSUE

Many current models of decision making are based on evidence obtained from laboratory experiments in which a relatively limited set of "simulated" decision problems have been used. For example, in the area of probabilistic inference, subjects are often presented with gambles differing in the amounts of money that can be won or lost and in the probabilities associated with such outcomes (e.g., Anderson & Shanteau, 1970; Kahneman & Tversky, 1979; Lichtenstein & Slovic, 1973; Payne, 1975; Slovic & Lichtenstein, 1968). Even when the choice alternatives do not involve monetary gain or loss, the decision problems are usually decomposed in such a way that probabilistic information is presented numerically rather than experientially (e.g., Kahneman & Tversky, 1973). In fact, the majority of what are considered to be important results in the decision-making area has been obtained with procedures in which the decision task was, at least to some extent, already decomposed into the dimensions that were of primary interest to the researcher (cf. Slovic & Lichtenstein, 1971, and Slovic, Fischhoff, & Lichtenstein, 1977). For example, when the interest is in comparing the role that certain key variables play in normative models with the actual effects of these variables on decisions, relevant decision tasks are not found in the real world, but rather are constructed in such a way that these key variables are presented in a decomposed form.

Even when decision-making models are applied to specific real-world decisions, much of the decision analyst's time is spent redefining the decision task facing the client so that its format conforms to the structure of laboratory simulations (Keeney, 1973, 1977). For example, in applying decision theory to the

21

problem of the distribution of fire engines in a city, Keeney (1973) first had to "discover" the attributes of fire fighting that the decision maker thought were relevant, then "elicit" the utility functions associated with these attributes. Probabilities were also "elicited" but from experts rather than from the decision maker.[1] In short, the decision problem was decomposed such that the choice alternatives made available to the client were presented as lists of attributes, each with an associated value and probability. This was done even though the original decision problem was described in a completely different manner.

In research that has been guided by linear rather than normative models, the decision tasks are somewhat less constrained to fit a preexisting theoretical mold. Nevertheless, the data being fit by the linear model have generally been obtained from people making decisions in what are obviously simulations of the relevant decision problems. Thus, it is typical that only some of the predictors that might be relevant in similar real-world decision tasks are included in the simulated task and, more importantly, the ones that are presented are usually in decomposed form (although there are exceptions, e.g., Einhorn, 1974; Exp. 2 in Phelps & Shanteau, 1978). That is, the decision maker is usually given a *list* of the levels of the relevant factors (not some holistic representation of the predecision situation) and is told to reach a decision (e.g., Anderson, 1974; Naylor & Wherry, 1965; Exp. 1 in Phelps & Shanteau, 1978; Slovic, 1969). For example, in response to a request for greater face validity of the decision tasks used to study stockbrokers' investment decisions (Slovic, Fleissner, & Bauman, 1972), Ebert and Kruse (1978) asked professional securities analysts to consider a large number of cues that had been constructed from the actual performance data of relevant securities. Thus, although the range of levels of the cues probably matched those usually seen by the analyst, the cues were still presented, one at a time, in the standard list format. Furthermore, although a major purpose of the study was to improve the realism of past research, the subjects were clearly told that their decisions were hypothetical and therefore had no monetary consequences. Finally, the authors did not report whether the intercorrelations of the cues (Hammond, Stewart, Brehmer, & Steinmann, 1975) used in the experimental task matched those in the real world.

---

[1] A major problem with applying some normative models to real-world decision problems is that some of the constructs in the models refer to subjective variables whose values cannot be observed directly. Often, the levels of these variables are obtained from ratings made by subjects. Therefore, all of the problems associated with "reactive" measurement (Webb, Campbell, Schwartz, & Sechrest, 1966) should be relevant to such applications. Unfortunately, very little attention seems to be paid to the fact that values (and other subjective states) may be *constructed* by the decision maker for the first time when asked about them. It is generally known in social psychology, for example, that attitudes are consistent with action only under very special circumstances (Zimbardo, Ebbesen, & Maslach, 1977). If our measures are tapping basic and stable states, why do multiple measures of the "same" state correlate so poorly (cf. Fischhoff, Slovic, & Lichtenstein, this volume)?

Even in several instances in which the decision task has involved stimuli presented in a holistic format, the subjects are told that their decisions are hypothetical and are also typically fully aware that their decisions are being evaluated (e.g., Phelps & Shanteau, 1978). Thus, the consequences of the decisions are rarely the same as those naturally occurring in the real-world task being simulated.[2]

One explanation for the overrepresentation of laboratory simulations in past research on decision making is that researchers have been primarily concerned with discovering what are thought to be basic psychological rules or processes. If one begins with the assumptions (1) that such rules exist; (2) that their number is probably small; and (3) that the different rules do not interact in any important way, then the major consideration in selecting a decision task should be that it will allow the researcher to clearly demonstrate the operation of one or more of these rules or processes. Because real-world decision making is bound to be clouded by a host of irrelevant and potentially confounding factors, constructing a decision task provides the opportunity to conduct more controlled and inexpensive research. In fact, because the results from such research are likely to reflect the operation of a "pure" process or rule, unconfounded by other factors, the conclusions that are reached about decision making on the basis of laboratory simulations should have great generality.

THE EVIDENCE

What evidence do we have to support such a view of laboratory simulations? We would argue, little or none. In fact, what evidence there is suggests that this view might be incorrect.

Task Specificity

Consider first the picture that is emerging from the laboratory simulations currently being used in decision-making research. Humans are portrayed as intellectual cripples, limited in their capacity to think, and biased by cognitive processes that interfere with rational decision making (e.g., Dawes, 1976; Slovic, Fischhoff, & Lichtenstein, 1976). They are oversensitive to variables that are not

---

[2]It is also true that when holistic stimuli are used (e.g., Einhorn, 1974; Phelps & Shanteau, 1978), the subjects are often asked to evaluate the levels of the relevant cues as well as to reach a final decision. Thus, the experimenter still defines the relevant cue dimensions for the subject. In addition, it is unclear in which direction the causal arrow flows in such studies. The cue evaluations might well be constructed from an anticipatory decision rather than the decision being caused by an evaluation of the cues. Furthermore, the reactivity of having to make cue evaluations of the holistic stimuli might impose a limit on the external validity of these studies.

included in normative theories (e.g., Kahneman & Tversky, 1972) and undersensitive to variables that are (e.g., Kahneman & Tversky, 1973). They become more variable when given more information (e.g., Einhorn, 1971; Hayes, 1964) and increase their confidence in the accuracy of their judgments when they should not (e.g., Kahneman & Tversky, 1973; Slovic & Lichtenstein, 1971).

If we eliminate the derogatory tone of these conclusions, what is left is a simple descriptive statement suggesting that decision makers are sometimes responsive to task characteristics that are not specified by prior normative or theoretical conceptions (Olson, 1976) and that researchers do not know when such oversensitivities will emerge. In some tasks, certain variables have smaller effects than expected; in other tasks, the effects are larger than expected. Put differently, there are no theories to tell us when people will be Bayesian, when they will average, when they will add, when they will be subjective–expected-utility maximizers, when they will be sufficiently sensitive to characteristics of data samples, when they will show appropriate hindsight, when they will retrieve information from memory that is not typical but is actually representative, when they will know what they do not know, and so on. What features of tasks control when and which of these many different processes will have causal effects on decisions? How and when might these different processes interact?[3]

If features of simulated decision tasks that are not included in the existing models of basic processes are controlling the subjects' decisions, even to some extent, then one has at least two options. The first is to broaden current models to include these features of the task and thus manage to retain the assumption that simulated decision tasks tap basic processes. This seems to be the popular response. Invoking heuristics (cf. Pitz, this volume), biases, transformation of variables previously thought not to require them (cf. Kahneman & Tversky, 1979), and postulating several decision strategies where before there was only one (cf. Wallsten, this volume) are the frequently used strategies for explaining results that do not fit an expected outcome.

A more radical alternative is to change one's view of decision making. Rather than think of decision making as controlled by a few basic processes that can be discovered by studying a limited and arbitrarily selected set of decision tasks, one could assume that decision rules and processes are *created* to fit the specifics of each particular decision task. In this view, features of a decision task and of measurement procedures (cf. Fischhoff, Lichtenstein, & Slovic, this volume) that have little or no theoretical relevance to the researcher might be expected to

---

[3]Another way of speaking about the fact that decision-making processes seem to be highly task specific is to say that the causal relationships between specified cues and measures of decision making vary with the context. It cannot be concluded that base-rate information is ignored because sometimes it is not (Kassin, 1979; Wells & Harvey, 1977). It cannot be concluded that sample size has little or no effect on decisions because sometimes it does (Olson, 1976). In short, causal relationships may be less consistent over minor variations in the nature of decision tasks than is generally believed.

determine, at least in part, the results one observes. After adopting this view, one would not be surprised to find that features of tasks, such as the context, the order in which information is presented, the salience of different cues, the number of times a decision is made, the response scales used, the way in which the task is described, the abstractness of the information, the amount of time given to decide, and so on, might affect the decisions of subjects. Rather than "explain" these effects by assuming the existence of all sorts of cognitive limitations and biases, one might think of people as continually shifting their strategies to meet the demands placed on them by contrived decision tasks.

Comparison of Laboratory Simulations With Real-World Tasks

Several studies that have compared the results from simulated decision tasks to results obtained from unobtrusive (Webb et al., 1966) observations of the decision situations being simulated have recently emerged. These provide a different and more direct source of evidence against the utility of the view that most decision tasks tap basic decision processes.

Bail Setting. In a study of bail setting (Ebbesen & Konečni, 1975, in press a), we presented San Diego County judges, who had had first-hand experience with bail setting, with simulated cases and asked them to set bail, in dollars, *exactly* as they would if the case were a real one. The cues that the judges were to use in reaching their decisions were presented in decomposed form on a sheet of paper. Following a brief description of background information (which included the same charge for all cases), the following information was presented: (1) prior record; (2) the extent to which the accused was tied to the local area (for example, owned a home, was employed, and was married); (3) a dollar amount recommended by the district attorney; and (4) a recommendation by the defense attorney, also in dollars. Prior observation of *actual* bail hearings showed that these cues were typically presented to the judges prior to their decisions and that little other information was presented or otherwise available to the judges. Interviews with the judges and official bail-setting guidelines both suggested that local ties would be the most important factor in the decision. The levels of the various cues were organized so that they formed a complete factorial design. Analysis of variance of the bail amounts indicated that all but the defense attorney's recommendation had significant effects, and in obvious directions. There were no interactions. The local ties variable did indeed account for the most variance, by far.

Taking an untypical next step, we also trained observers to code, *unobtrusively,* the levels of the same variables, as well as to record the final amount of bail set in *actual* bail hearings presided over by the *same* judges used in the simulations. The judges were completely unaware that these observations were being made. The reliability of the coding was virtually perfect. Multiple regression analyses of these naturalistic data indicated that it was possible to account for almost all of the variance in the bail decisions (95%) with the same four factors manipulated in the simulation (plus the severity of the crime). More importantly, a quite different pattern of results emerged. The district attorney's recommendation accounted for the most variance; the defense attorney's recommendation was significant; local ties accounted for a nonsignificant portion of the variance; several interactions emerged. Two related interpretations for the differences in the results between the simulated and the actual bail decisions are: (1) that the range of values of the various cues was different in the two studies and (2) that the interval scale spacing of the levels of the cues used in the multiple regression did not match the judges' subjective spacings of the cue levels in the simulation. To test both of these possibilities, a dummy variable multiple regression that utilized only those cases in which the cues took on values very close to those used in the simulation was performed. The results indicated that the district attorney's recommendation was able to account for almost all of the predictable variance in this data set.[4]

In short, the picture of the judges' bail-setting strategies that emerged from the simulation was quite consistent with the bail-setting guidelines; local ties seemed to be the most important factor in the decision. In contrast, analysis of the decisions in the actual bail hearings suggested that judges were primarily influenced by the district attorney's recommendation and that local ties played only a minor role and even then in a direction largely opposite to that found in the simulation! It is of interest to note that the district attorney's recommendation was predicted primarily by the severity of the crime and not by local ties.[5]

Sentencing of Adult Felons.   As part of the same extensive project on legal decision making in which the previously described bail-setting results were obtained (Ebbesen & Konečni, 1976, in press b; Konečni & Ebbesen, in press a, in press b; Konečni, Mulcahy, & Ebbesen, in press), we have examined the factors that control the sentencing of adults convicted of felonies (a crime punishable by a year or more in state prison). In two simulation experiments, volunteer college

---

[4] It is possible that the results of the simulation would have been more like those in the actual hearings had severity of the crime been varied as well as the other factors. On the other hand, if the results that are obtained in simulations depend so heavily on including all of the "right" factors as variables, how does one determine what all the right factors are without collecting data in the real world?

[5]Another explanation for the differences between the simulation and the actual hearings is that the severity of the crime (or some other variable) might be correlated with the district attorney's recommendation. The first possibility was assessed by examining the *additional* variance accounted for by the district attorney's recommendation, *after* the crime was included as a predictor. The identical pattern of results emerged. The latter possibility could not be assessed directly; however, observation of the actual hearings suggests that such a factor would be difficult to discover. Even if one or more such factors could be discovered, it is important to note that the resulting picture of bail setting would *still* be very different from that obtained from the simulation.

students were used as subjects. They were asked to sentence people convicted of a felony on a scale from 0 to 25 years in prison. Cues were presented in decomposed form but embedded in a longer "case description." Four cues were manipulated in a complete factorial design: severity of the crime (forgery versus burglary versus armed robbery), prior record (none versus two previous felony convictions), social history (broken home and bad family life versus solid middle-class life), and feelings of remorse about the criminal activity (none versus a lot). All aspects of the two experiments were identical except that one employed a between-subjects design and the other a complete within-subjects design. No interactions were found in either design. All four main effects were highly significant in the within-subjects design. All but the social history factor were significant in the between-subjects design. Severity of crime and prior record accounted for the most variance in both designs, but crime accounted for slightly more in the within-subjects design, whereas prior record did so in the between-subjects design. In short, slightly different conclusions might have been reached had only one or the other simulation study been conducted.

We repeated similar simulation studies with superior court judges and probation officers as subjects. The latter write extensive reports detailing the criminal activity, prior record, social background, and previous legal history of the offender. These reports are given to the presiding judge the day before he is to sentence the offender. The reports conclude with a detailed sentence recommendation. A major purpose of these reports is to provide the judge with background information about the felon and about the crime because the sentencing hearing often provides the judge with his first encounter with the defendant. During the actual sentencing hearing, the district attorney and defense attorney briefly argue for more and less (respectively) severe sentences. The probation officer is usually present but rarely speaks.

Five factors were varied in both experiments. For the judges they were: severity of crime, prior record, method of guilt determination (plea versus trial), social history, and the probation officer's recommendation. For the probation officers, degree of remorse replaced the probation officer recommendation factor. Both experiments employed within-subjects factorial designs. Unlike the college student studies, however, a time-in-prison scale was not used as the dependent variable.[6] Instead, the judges were asked to write down the exact

---

[6]Contrary to the views of many college students, in most state sentencing systems, the judge does *not* set the number of years in prison. More often than not, the law defines a minimum and/or a maximum sentence. Furthermore, the *actual* length of time that a felon spends in prison is usually controlled by a parole board rather than the judge (Carroll & Payne, 1976; Maslach & Garber, in press; Wilkins, Gottfredson, Robinson, & Sadowsky, 1973). The judge's decision, therefore, is not time in prison but whether to send the felon to state prison or not; and if not, whether the felon should be confined for a brief time (less than a year) to the sheriff's custody (the county jail facilities), be merely released on probation, or be confined to the sheriff's custody and then be released on probation. Had we tried to formulate the decision task with these options for college students, they would not have known what we were talking about. Had we asked the judges to rate years in prison, they would have laughed us out of the chambers.

sentence, with all of the details, that they would give this offender were the description a real case. The sentencing options available to superior court judges are to send the offender to state prison (where he/she remains until released on parole), to confine the offender in county jail (sheriff's custody) for not more than one year and then to follow the jail term with a period of probation (a period of time during which the offender's behavior is restricted and supervised in lieu of confinement), or to merely impose a period of probationary supervision (not more than 5 years per conviction) with no confinement. Other options are available but are rarely used and generally only in special circumstances (Konečni, Mulcahy, & Ebbesen, in press). The probation officer has the identical array of recommendation options available. The results of an analysis of variance of the number of prison sentences given and recommended are presented in Table 2.1. As can be seen, somewhat different patterns of results emerged for the two types of sentencing experts. Although crime and prior record produced the largest F values in both cases, the order of the effect sizes was different. In addition, social history had a significant effect on the probation officer's recommendation but not on the judge's decision, whereas method of guilt determination had a significant effect on the judge's sentencing decision but not on the probation officer's recommendation. There was also a marginally significant crime by prior record interaction for the probation officers.

Comparing these results to the data for college students from the within-subjects design, we find that the students behaved in a manner similar, but not identical, to the judges. Both responded slightly more to the crime than to prior record; however, social history was a significant factor for students and not for the judges. Although the differences between students, probation officers, and judges might be due to any number of factors, sentencing decisions do not appear to be driven by identical rules with identical parameter values in the three instances. Nevertheless, it is possible that in the case of sentencing, the data for the experts are representative of their decision-making strategies in the real world.

TABLE 2.1
F-values For Analyses of Variance of the Number of Prison
Recommendations by Probation Officers and of Prison Decisions
by Judges in Simulated Decision Tasks

Factors	Probation Officers	Judges
Crime	13.70	27.68
Prior record	81.81	25.84
Social history	8.33	1.73
Plea/Trial	1.49	8.80
Remorse	8.94	
Probation recommendation		6.69
Crime × Priors	3.84	

TABLE 2.2
Relationship Between Probation Officers' Recommendations and
Judges' Sentencing Decisions[a] (Number of Cases)

Probation Officer Recommendation	Judges' Decisions		
	Prison	Probation and Sheriff's Custody	Probation Only
Prison	103	32	5
Probation and sheriff's custody	15	396	42
Probation only	1	34	142

[a] Total agreement = 87.1%.

The number of factors that can potentially be considered by a judge in actual sentencing hearings is enormous. An attempt was made to code most of these by content analyzing all of the written documents available to the judge prior to the sentencing decision and by recording the stream of verbal interchanges in the hearing (using a time-sampling system in which the identity of the person speaking and the content of the speech were recorded every 10 seconds). Nonverbal factors, such as the appearance and demeanor of the offender, were also recorded. Data for over 3000 cases have been collected. The present results are based upon the 800 or so cases that have been analyzed thus far. A complete description of the methods and coding systems are available in Ebbesen and Konečni (in press b) and Konečni and Ebbesen (in press b).

Of all of the many factors coded, only a very small number accounted for a substantial portion of the variation in the sentencing decisions of judges. By far the best predictor of the sentence was the probation officer's recommendation. Table 2.2 is a contingency table showing the number of cases in which the probation officer recommended prison, probation plus some time in the sheriff's custody, or probation with no period of confinement, and in which the judge gave one of these same three major categories of sentence. As can be seen, the recommendation and the final sentence were in the same category in over 85% of the cases. It is of some interest to note that when there was a discrepancy, judges were slightly more likely to disagree on the lenient (10%) than the severe (6%) side.

When considered separately, we also found that the likelihood of more severe sentences (those involving incarceration) increased as the severity of the crime that the offender had been convicted of increased, and as the prior record of the offender increased. Tables 2.3 and 2.4 show these relationships for broad crime categories and for the number of previous felony convictions.

Another factor that, to our surprise, was also highly associated with the sentence was the manner in which the accused spent the time between arrest and

TABLE 2.3
Percent of Sentences in Prison, Probation and Sheriff's Custody,
and Probation Only Categories as a Function of Severity of Crime[a]

Crime Category	Number of Cases	Prison	Sentence Probation and Sheriff's Custody	Probation Only
Possession of drugs	(106)	9	61	30
Forgery	(97)	18	47	35
Theft	(220)	14	65	22
Burglary	(225)	12	67	20
Sale of drugs	(57)	14	56	30
Robbery	(106)	29	62	8
Rape	(15)	27	67	7
Armed robbery	(26)	46	54	0
Homicide	(21)	62	29	10

[a] Ordering of crimes is based upon average ratings of severity by the same judges whose decisions were observed in sentencing hearings.

conviction—in legal jargon, the status of the offender. Was the defendant released on his or her own recognizance, released on bail, or not released (i.e., remained in jail)? Table 5 presents the relationship between status and the final sentence. As can be seen, being in jail is associated with a greater percentage of severe sentences than being released on one's own recognizance.

Although a few other factors accounted for a small but significant portion of the variance in sentencing, the four factors previously described here were, by far, the best predictors of the sentence. Little is lost, therefore, by ignoring these other factors in the current description.

TABLE 2.4
Percent of Sentences in Prison, Probation and Sheriff's Custody,
and Probation Only Categories as a Function of Number of Prior
Felony Convictions

Number of Prior Felony Convictions	Prison	Sentence Probation and Sheriff's Custody	Probation Only
None	12	60	28
One	10	59	29
Two	13	62	25
Three	19	62	19
Four	30	57	13
Five and up	29	62	9

TABLE 2.5
Percent of Sentences in Prison, Probation and Sheriff's Custody,
and Probation Only Categories as a Function of the Defendant's
Status Between Arrest and Final Sentencing

Status of Defendant	Sentence		
	Prison	Probation and Sheriff's Custody	Probation Only
Released on own recognizance	6	61	33
Released on bail	21	43	36
In jail	37	52	11

A number of causal explanations can, of course, be generated for the results presented thus far. All four predictors might be differentially correlated with some unmeasured factor that is the single real causal variable. Alternatively, the four factors might be correlated with several different causal factors, each to a varying degree. Although these explanations cannot be discounted, it is difficult to imagine what these other causal factors might be, given the number of variables examined in our work. Still another view, consistent with the simulation work, is that these four factors are cues in the judge's decision and are, therefore, all causally important.

A somewhat different view of the process is to assume that the variables are related to each other in a causal chain (Heise, 1975). Thus, it might be that only one or two of the four factors are direct causes of the sentence and that other factors are causes of these causes. Several temporal features of the system make certain chains less likely than others. For example, it is always the case that prior record, status, and severity of the charge at conviction are determined earlier in time than the probation officer's recommendation and the judge's sentence. Although it is not impossible to imagine a view of the system in which the final sentence caused prior record (say, via selective reporting or alteration of rap sheets on the part of probation officers), the occurrence of activities such as these was very unlikely in the studied circumstances. Accepting the temporal order, for the moment at least, as useful causal evidence, it is possible to construct several reasonable causal models relating the five variables to one another. Fig. 2.1 presents a diagramatic representation of three such models. In the top model, prior record, severity of crime, and status are assumed to be direct causes of the probation officer's recommendation. But, these variables are assumed to have no direct causal link to the sentence decision. Only the probation officer's recommendation is given this distinction.

The second model proposes that the three early factors have direct effects on the probation officer's recommendation and on the judge's decision, but the latter

THREE REASONABLE CAUSAL MODELS OF SENTENCING

PROBATION OFFICER AFFECTS JUDGE

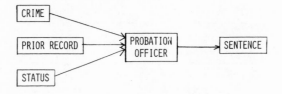

PROBATION OFFICER AND JUDGE REACH INDEPENDENT DECISIONS

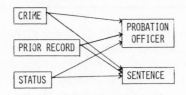

JUDGE AFFECTS PROBATION OFFICER

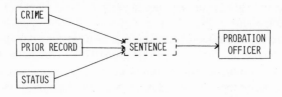

FIG. 2.1.   Three causal models for the relationships between crime, prior record,
status, probation officer recommendation, and sentence. The arrows represent the
existence and direction of causal relationships between a pair of variables.

are not causally related. In this view, the high agreement shown in Table 2.2
between the probation officer and the judge is assumed to be a spurious consequence of the fact that both variables are being caused in the same manner by the
same set of prior variables.

The third model actually reverses the temporal order of events and argues that
the probation officer's recommendation is directly caused by the judge's sentence, which is, in turn, caused by the three prior factors. One reasonable
interpretation of this temporal reversal is to assume that the judge is committed to
a specific sentence agreement made between the district and defense attorneys in
exchange for a plea of guilty (contrary to the popular opinion represented by
Perry Mason television shows, over 85% of all felony convictions are obtained as
a result of guilty pleas, rather than as a result of jury trials) and that the probation

officer writes his/her report and recommendation in correct anticipation of the judge's decision and is motivated to match and justify this sentence agreement.[7]

Each of the above causal models implies that observed cell frequencies in the five-way data table (crime by prior record by status by probation officer recommendation by actual sentence) should be due to a particular set of "main" and "interaction" effects. These effects can be represented as log odds ratios in a linear model. Specifically, each variable and interaction between variables adds to (or subtracts from) the odds (in logarithms) of an observation falling into a given cell. The causal relationships (arrows in Fig. 2.1) that are assumed by a particular causal model constrain the set of odds ratios (effects) that are to be used to predict the observed frequencies. For example, the first model in Fig. 2.1 assumes that the two-way "interaction" between the three prior variables and actual sentence are all zero (there are no arrows between these variables), whereas the second and third models do not impose this constraint. The predicted (by a given causal or log-linear model) cell frequencies can be estimated from appropriate marginals and then tested against the observed frequencies by an ordinary χ^2 test of fit. Because the details of this analysis approach have been described elsewhere (Ebbesen & Konečni, in press b; Goodman, 1973), we simply report the major results here. When each of the three models outlined in Fig. 2.1 were fitted to the observed frequencies, the first model was best able to account for the data. In addition, the fit of this model to the observed pattern of frequencies was excellent, even in absolute terms (χ^2 likelihood ratio (189) = 136.44, $p > .5$).

Further evidence in support of the first model was obtained by examining the relationship between the prior variables and the sentence when the covariation in the probation officer's recommendation was partialled out and by examining the relationship between the prior variables and the probation officer's recommendation when the covariation in the judge's sentencing decision was partialled out. In the latter analysis, prior record was still significantly associated with the recommendation. In the former analysis, however, all relationships with the sentence were nonsignificant.[8]

Because sentence agreements are not obtained in all cases, it was possible to examine the relationship between the probation officer's recommendation and

---

[7]It should be noted that given the method used to assess the utility of these three models, the third model is isomorphic with the causal model assumed by the previously described factorial simulations, namely, that severity, prior record, status, and the probation officer's recommendation are all direct causes of the judge's final decision. One need merely reverse the direction of the arrow between sentence and probation officer in the third model in Fig. 2.1 to see that this is so.

[8]This test assesses whether the variation in the three prior variables can "get through" to the last factor when the intervening variable is held constant, statistically. If the first model is correct, holding the probation officers' recommendations constant should prevent crime, prior record, and status from being related to the sentence. This is exactly what happened. The logic of the reverse test is similar and supported the present view.

the sentence for just those cases in which no agreement was made. If the high agreement between the two decision makers seen in all of the data (Table 2.2) is due to a presentence arrangement with the district attorney, then one might expect the agreement between the judge and the probation officer to be considerably less in this selected sample of cases because the probation officers would not feel constrained to match their recommendations to a preexisting agreement. Table 2.6 shows the relationship for cases in which a presentence agreement was not reached. As can be seen, an equally strong relationship between the recommendation and final sentence was found here as was found in all of the data.

Once again, the picture emerging from an unobtrusive analysis of real-world decisions is different from that obtained from experimental simulations. Although there are other causal interpretations of the naturalistic data previously presented, they are also quite different from the conclusions that would have been reached had we stopped with the simulations. It appears that in the real world the judges respond primarily to the probation officers' recommendations and that case factors have their effects on the final outcome only indirectly by affecting the probation officers' recommendations.

Selecting cases to match the levels used in the simulations supports the claim that decisions in the simulations were based on different rules than those in the real world (Konečni & Ebbesen, in press b). Specifically, (1) the simulations yielded many more sentences involving prison and jail terms than actually occurred in the real world; (2) factors significant in the simulations were not significant (even when considered singly) in the actual hearing (for example, the method of guilt determination was not significant in actual sentences whereas it was in the judge's simulated decisions and remorse was not associated with the actual recommendations of probation officers whereas it did have an effect on their simulated decisions); (3) the agreement between the probation officer's recommendations and the judge's sentencing decisions was much more in the

TABLE 2.6
Relationship Between Probation Officers' Recommendations and
Judges' Sentences When no Preplea Bargain Agreement was Made[a]

	Judges' Decisions		
Probation Officers' Recommendations	Prison	Probation and Sheriff's Custody	Probation Only
Prison	18.8	5.3	.4
Probation and sheriff's custody	1.2	45.7	5.7
Probation only	0.0	3.3	19.6

[a] N = 245. Numbers in table are percent of total cases falling in each cell. Total probation officer–judge agreement = 84.1%.

real world (over 85%) than in the simulations (approximately 40%); and (4) the relative importance (variation explained) of the several factors were different (the probation officer's recommendation was the most important factor in the actual decisions, whereas it was one of the lesser factors in the simulation). Another important difference that emerged is that the simulation results implied that the judges and the probation officers were responding to somewhat different cues (see Table 2.1). However, when the real-world results were analyzed, treating the judge and probation officer as independent decision makers, we found that their decisions seemed to be responsive to virtually identical cues and in the same order of importance, not surprisingly, given the high agreement between them. Still another difference, not yet discussed, is that several interactions between cues were detected in the real-world data (for example, crime by prior record, crime by status) that did not emerge in the judges' simulation (although, in a rather different pattern, a marginally significant crime by prior record interaction was found for probation officers in their simulated decisions). Finally, the best-fitting decision rules for the judges were different in the two studies: In the real world, judges seemed to decide simply on the basis of the probation officers' recommendations, whereas in the simulation, they seemed to linearly combine crime, prior record, method of guilt determination, and the probation officers' recommendations.

Automobile Driver Behavior.   A study of driver decision making has suggested that experimental simulations can yield different results than those obtained from unobtrusive observation in decision situations involving risk (Ebbesen, Parker, & Konečni, 1977). In this study, we found that drivers seemed to decide whether to turn in front of an oncoming car (or let it go by before turning) at a T-intersection on the basis of the *temporal* gap between the driver's car and the oncoming car. When we attempted to construct a "holistic" simulation of this situation in the laboratory, we found that experienced drivers seemed to respond, separately, to the speed and the physical distance of the oncoming car rather than to a direct perception of the temporal gap. Had we only conducted the laboratory simulation, we would have concluded that distance and speed were being independently evaluated and weighted, and then configurally combined to reach a decision. Instead, the field data suggested that the turning decision was a direct and simple function of the temporal gap between the two cars and that the drivers were merely applying a simple threshold rule to the temporal gap dimension in deciding whether to turn.

Judging Swine.   Phelps and Shanteau (1978) have reported that livestock judges took many more cues into account in their judgments of swine when the cues were presented as a fully crossed factorial design in decomposed form than when pictures of swine, rather than feature lists, were evaluated. Although a major conclusion of this work (with which we agree) was that the currently popular conception of decision makers as being limited in their capacity to take a large number of factors into account in making decisions is in error, the fact remains that differences in decision results and, therefore, in the apparent underlying process were obtained across the two tasks. One among many reasonable alternative explanations for these differences is that the factors were correlated in one task and not in the other. As we (Ebbesen, Parker, & Konečni, 1977) and others (Brunswik, 1956) have argued, whether the correlations between potential cues deviate from zero may well be yet another feature of decision tasks that alters the decision strategy people use.

Arguments For and Against the Task-Specificity Approach

A number of arguments might be raised against the evidence cited in the previous section. It is conceivable that the simulations were poor representations of the decision tasks being simulated and that had they been better, the results from the different procedures would have been more similar. Although this argument cannot be refuted until the "better" simulations are conducted, two comments about it should be noted. First, had the real-world data never been collected, no one would have known how "bad" the simulations were. When we first began our present line of research, the real-world data were included as an afterthought. We did not think of the simulations as simulations. Instead, they were designed to provide the *real* causal evidence for what we expected to observe (only as correlations) in the real-world settings. Of course, it could be argued that we, and we alone, are poor at designing simulations. On the other hand, pie diagrams, brief verbal sketches, or a single sentence describing the percentage of people who fall into a certain category do not seem far removed from the simulations that we constructed.

Second, the argument applies equally well, in reverse, to *all* simulation studies. Because data for real-world decision tasks are usually missing from reports utilizing simulation methods, the possibility exists that many of these simulations are also poor representations of the decision tasks they are simulating. Being cautious scientists, the reasonable view is to assume that the results are *not* representative until shown otherwise.

Another argument against the view that simulations generally create task-specific decision strategies is that the real-world decision data we have reported are all correlational and, therefore, solid evidence about real *causal* decision processes can never be obtained from them (Phelps & Shanteau, 1978). Thus, it is possible that the discrepancies are due to our inability to tease apart real from spurious causal relationships in the real-world data. Although this argument has merit in most contexts, we feel that in the present case it lacks strength. It can reasonably be maintained that *all* decision models, whether based on data from simulations or from observations of real-world events are, in fact, only *paramorphic representations* (Hoffman, 1960) of the *actual* decision processes of the subject. Our models merely simulate—that is, are correlated with—the input–output relationships that we observe (Payne, Braunstein, & Carroll, in press). Even when the claim that deep decision processes are being discovered is buttressed with reaction time, eye movement (e.g., Russo & Rosen, 1975), and/or verbal protocol (e.g., Carroll & Payne, 1976) data, input–output relationships are still being dealt with. One simply has more types of output to consider. After all, people can think about things they are not looking at and speak about things that they would not otherwise think about.

The attack on correlational data is weak for another reason. True experiments do not eliminate the possibility that causal relationships other than those proposed as explanations might be producing the results. The fact that randomization generally breaks the correlation between one variable and all prior variables has absolutely no implications for the correlations between that one variable and all following variables. A given manipulation might create quite a number of mediating variables and processes each of which might play a causal role in the final decision (Costner, 1971). Because these mediating processes might well be correlated with each other, we wind up in a similar position to the researcher dealing with real-world data. The best we can hope for is that our models will describe and *predict* patterns in data.

Whether or not our counter argument is accepted, a review of decision-making research suggests that the specific decision strategies used by subjects are very sensitive to a wide range of task variables. It is possible to argue from this evidence alone that decision tasks do not tap a few simple and basic processes.

It might be argued that there is actually no problem with the results from the laboratory simulations, per se. What needs to be done is to change the way that simulations are thought about. Rather than naively assume that subjects in experiments characterize the decision problems that are given to them in a manner identical to the characterization that our theories and models assume, one should, instead, attempt to discover what the subjects are *trying to do* in the task (Simon, 1969; cf. Pitz, this volume). Having done so, it might be found that the subjects are not playing by the ground rules required by current theories. Furthermore, if tasks were constructed so that subjects perceived them in a manner consistent with theoretical assumptions, simulation results might then provide a much better match to the real-world data. On the other hand, how do we discover what the subjects are *really* trying to do? If the concept of trying-to-do-something is central, then why not assume that it plays an important role in real-world decisions as well? Asking the judges what they were trying to do in sentencing yielded quite an array of responses, even from the same judge. Answers focused on such topics as rehabilitation, recidivism, protection of the public, retribution, deterrence, the extent of guilt, the likelihood of future employment, mental illness, cost to taxpayers, what was best for everyone concerned, the strength of the evidence, taking everything that is important into account, and so on. Which of these many possibilities represents what the judges are, in fact, trying to do?

Another attack on our position is that we are preaching scientific nihilism. After all, if laboratory tasks create specific, rather than tap into basic, decision processes, then why not assume that real-world tasks also create just as task-specific decision strategies? We would agree with the latter point, but disagree that nihilism is the consequence. What we are suggesting is that in the area of decision-making, the really important truths are to be found in the real world rather than in laboratory simulations, no matter how high the *face* validity of the latter might be. We would prefer to base our conjectures about how people make various types of decisions on observations of *those* people making *those* decisions. We are not arguing that laboratory simulations should be abandoned altogether. There are conditions in which they might serve as useful tools in teasing apart certain questions about the real-world process. Rather than *assume* that the simulations are good, however, one ought to collect sufficient evidence to test whether the constructed tasks have captured the necessary detail of the real world to be *real simulations*. One ought to be required to show that the simulations can mimic data from various aspects of the real world before claiming that one is tapping basic processes.

We are not arguing against the continued search for basic, highly generalized rules of decision making. We are claiming, however, (1) that such rules or models are going to be very hard to discover; (2) that findings from a few laboratory simulations do not establish the generality of a model or process of decision making; and (3), most importantly, that it will be impossible to utilize such basic rules to predict decisions in real-world tasks unless a great deal is known about the task and the decision maker prior to application of the rules, i.e., unless real-world data have already been collected.

The latter claim is a consequence of the conclusion that causal relationships between cues and measures of decision making are not universal but vary over tasks (not to mention subjects). The existence of interactions with task features means that any rule, heuristic, process model, and so on will necessarily have to include parameters whose values are set according to specific features of the decision task. Furthermore, the number of such parameters will almost certainly be very large. Unless real-world data have been collected in an attempt to tie down these unspecified parameters, *a priori* prediction of real-world decisions will necessarily be quite limited.

When one is given a real-world decision task with all of its naturally occurring complexity, the theory must be made to fit the task rather than vice versa. Theoretically irrelevant features cannot be eliminated from the processes by which people make decisions by constructing a task in which such features are held constant.

SOME GENERAL IMPLICATIONS OF TASK SPECIFICITY

Experimental and methodological procedures for assessing the external validity of causal hypotheses have been described by others (e.g., Brunswik, 1956; Campbell & Stanley, 1963; Rosenthal & Rosnow, 1969; Slovic et al., 1977; Webb et al., 1966). We are by no means the first to raise the question of external validity. Psychologists have been grappling with the issue for years. It simply seemed that the time was ripe to mention the issue once again and in the current context. In part, this is because much of decision-making research seems to have a relatively obvious applied orientation, and yet, little concern about external validity issues has been expressed in the recent literature. We also felt that an emphasis on real-world decisions might focus attention on some neglected issues.

Appropriate Uses of Laboratory Decision Tasks

If it is agreed that laboratory simulations may not, in general, simulate what they are thought to simulate, then it is reasonable to ask whether there are uses to which laboratory decision tasks might be put other than simulation. One reasonable possibility is to use laboratory tasks not to discover what people do (in general), but rather to arrange demonstrations of what people can or might do (even if only in very restricted circumstances). Thus, it might be of interest to know that a task can be constructed in which decision makers do not respond to base-rate information or in which they are overconfident in the accuracy of their predictions. Although such research seems quite reasonable, an ever present danger is that it can be mistaken for a simulation and that its results will therefore be overgeneralized. For example, several recent studies have shown that people sometimes do use base-rate information (see Kassin, 1979 for a review) and that the use to which sample information is put depends on specific task features (Olson, 1976).

Another use of laboratory decision tasks might be to study the cognitive limitations of decision makers. How many factors can a decision maker take into account? How fast can decisions be made and still be accurate? How much better can experts be than nonexperts? At first thought, such questions seem well suited to analysis with laboratory decision tasks; however, it is quite possible that people's limitations change across tasks. For example, it is generally well known that the number of words that a person can remember from a list varies with the strategy the person uses to remember those words. Similarly, the speed with which decisions can be made depends on the specific nature of the question being asked (Ebbesen & Allen, 1979). Phelps and Shanteau (1978) found that many more factors were taken into account when the factors were uncorrelated than when they were intercorrelated. In short, cognitive limitations may be as specific as decision strategies.

Another critique of the use of laboratory decision tasks to assess cognitive limitations is that a theory of the initial conditions necessary to ensure that people are performing at their limits is presently unavailable. Is 20 dollars a large enough incentive or would the threat of torture push people to greater limits? Should distracting noises be masked with white noise or blocked out entirely with the use of a soundproof chamber? Until agreed-upon answers to questions such as these are obtained, the possibility that current limits might be exceeded with minor task modifications will always be present and generalization to real-world tasks will be difficult.

From a somewhat different perspective, various cognitive limitations and biases that have been demonstrated in laboratory decision tasks often seem to be avoided in real-world settings. For example, the effect that the availability of relevant instances in memory can have on judgments (Kahneman & Tversky, 1973) can be minimized, or eliminated completely, by features of naturalistic decision situations. More specifically, in the case of sentencing, judicial predictions about the future criminal behavior of defendants are not likely to be biased by the judge's tendency to base such predictions on an available subset of the defendants' prior convictions. A ''rap sheet'' that details the full extent of the defendant's prior record is in front of the judge when he/she sentences the defendant. Thus, memory for the previous criminal behavior of the defendant is externalized. This does not mean that availability plays no role in judicial decisions, however. The availability of relevant facts will almost certainly influence judicial decisions. It is merely that the availability of these facts is determined by other members of the social network who compile those facts rather than by a cognitive heuristic. In short, some real-world tasks may reduce or eliminate the influence of potential cognitive biases. Until appropriate naturalistic data is obtained, it is difficult to know the relevance that various biases and limitations have for real-world decisions.

The Role of Norms

Another issue that the task-specificity argument raises concerns the use of normative models in decision-making research. As we suggested earlier, many cognitive processes (biases) have been invented recently to explain why people do not behave in accord with predictions from normative models. The evidence for these processes comes largely from studies constructed to be reasonable representations of decision problems to which the normative model might be usefully applied. It is then implied, although not directly, that decision makers are likely to be biased by these processes whenever and wherever they make decisions.

It should be obvious that the very notion of a biasing process only makes sense in the context of a normative model. A given decision outcome cannot be biased unless there is a better one against which to compare it. Because bias is a comparative concept, the degree and type of bias that one observes necessarily depends on *both* the choice of norm and the choice of observed outcome. If this line of argument is accepted, it suggests the possibility that the biasing processes that have been *constructed* by experimenters and then used to impugn the intellectual ability of people may be specific to the norms to which outcomes are being compared, as well as to the tasks in which the normative violations have been observed.

This dependence on choice of norm would not be a problem if everyone agreed as to what the normative rules should be. Unfortunately, in the real world, consensus is hard to come by. Consider, for example, the fact that the Christian Bible, the Koran, and the Talmud serve as normative devices for a large number of real-world decisions. Are we to convince a nun, about to take her vows of chastity and poverty, that a Bayesian model of the likelihood of life after death might be preferable to the normative view she currently accepts? Or, more realistically, consider the sentencing decision of judges. What should a normative model of their decisions look like? To apply a Bayesian model, for example, requires that we think of the sentence as a prediction of some future outcome. But what should that outcome be? As we noted earlier, interviews with judges suggest that quite a large variety of outcomes might be used: rehabilitation; recidivism; deterrence; perceptions by the offender, by the victim, or by one's colleagues of the sufficiency of punishment; protection of society; agreement with colleagues; feelings of satisfaction on the part of the judge; being appointed or elected to higher office; the response of the media, and so on. To compound the problem, judges simply do not agree on what the appropriate outcomes should be. To make matters even worse, judges typically deny the utility of normative models that do not take into account the fact (as they see it) that every case is different.

Given that all of the aforementioned outcomes are not perfectly correlated with each other, and that different features of cases are likely to predict different outcomes (for example, prior record probably predicts recidivism but not deterrence), the extent to which judges will appear to be biased by sundry cognitive processes is likely to depend on which outcomes the *experimenter* uses in the normative model.

Even in the unlikely event that an agreed upon outcome could be found, there may still be disagreement about the decision rule. Should the likelihood of that outcome be maximized, would a minimum likelihood be sufficient, should the sufficient likelihood vary with the nature of the offense or some other variable, or should the likelihood of the outcome be maximized while trying to keep the likelihood of other outcomes above (or below) specified limits? Thus, the experimenter's choice of rule (as well as outcome) can make an otherwise "rational" decision seem "biased." Cognitive biases may be as much in the mind of the experimenter as in that of the subject.

Causal Chains in Decision Making

When the real world serves as a source of data, one's view of the typical decision-making process is considerably different from the view that seems common in laboratory decision tasks. In many real-world situations, decisions are actually a part of a larger social system in which the decisions of various people are interrelated in complex ways. When such is the case, it is possible to focus attention on the entire system rather than on one class of participants. The input–output relationships of the system can then be explained by the operation of underlying processes; however, in this instance, the underlying processes are the observable actions of key decision makers in the system and not the unobservable activity of retrieval processes, encoding mechanisms, or decision strategies located somewhere under the skin of the decision maker.

Our own research on decision making in the legal system takes this broader view. Several interesting discoveries emerged because of it. For example, one of the major predictors of the final sentence was the "extra legal" factor: status of the defendant between the time of arrest and the final sentence hearing (see Table 2.4). It appeared that status had its effects by controlling the sentence recommendation of the probation officer which in turn controlled the judge's final decision. But, recall that in our study of bail setting, the amount of bail that a defendant had to pay was controlled by the district attorney's dollar amount recommendation. Because defendants are less likely to be able to afford the usual 10% bail–bondsman fee as the amount of bail increases, and because people who cannot pay bail remain in jail, it is conceivable that the district attorney's bail recommendation, made 2 or 3 days after an arrest, is having a causal effect on the final sentence: a decision being made practically a year after the bail hearing! In short, the decisions of people embedded in a complex social system may be interrelated in ways than can only be discovered by examining the real-world system, *in vivo*.

SUMMARY

There is considerable evidence to suggest that the external validity of decision-making research that relies on laboratory simulations of real-world decision problems is low. Seemingly insignificant features of the decision task and measures cause people to alter their decision strategies. The context in which the decision problem is presented, the salience of alternatives, the number of cues, the concreteness of the information, the order of presentation, the similarity of cue to alternative, the nature of the decomposition, the form of the measures, and so on, seem to affect the decisions that subjects make. In addition, comparisons of results from simulated and real-world tasks suggest that decision strategies may be task-specific rather than caused by a few basic processes. One consequence of this view is that researchers should provide external validity evidence for claims that causal models derived from laboratory data apply to decisions in real-world settings. The accumulation of such evidence can only serve to broaden our understanding of decision making.

ACKNOWLEDGMENTS

Preparation of this paper was facilitated by National Institute of Mental Health Grant MH 26069 to Ebbe B. Ebbesen and National Science Foundation Grant GS 42802 to Vladimir J. Konečni.

REFERENCES

Anderson, N. H. Information integration theory: A brief survey. In D. H. Krantz, R. C. Atkinson, R. D. Luce, P. Suppes (Eds.), *Contemporary developments in mathematical psychology* (Vol. 2). San Francisco: Freeman, 1974.

Anderson, N. H., & Shanteau, J. Information integration in risky decision making. *Journal of Experimental Psychology,* 1970, *84,* 441–451.

Brunswik, E. *Perception and the representative design of psychological experiments* (2nd Ed.). Berkeley, Calif.: University of California Press, 1956.

Campbell, D. T., & Stanley, J. C. *Experimental and quasi-experimental designs for research.* Chicago: Rand McNally, 1963.

Carroll, J. S., & Payne, J. W. The psychology of the parole decision process: A joint application of attribution theory and information processing psychology. In J. S. Carroll & J. W. Payne (Eds.), *Cognition and social behavior.* Hillsdale, N.J.: Lawrence Erlbaum Associates, 1976.

Costner, H. L. Utilizing causal models to discover flaws in experiments. *Sociometry,* 1971, *34,* 398–410.

Dawes, R. M. Shallow psychology. In J. S. Carroll and J. W. Payne (Eds.), *Cognition and social behavior.* Hillsdale, N.J.: Lawrence Erlbaum Associates, 1976.

Ebbesen, E. B., & Allen, R. B. Cognitive process in implicit personality trait inferences. *Journal of Personality and Social Psychology,* 1979, *37,* 471–488.

Ebbesen, E. B., & Konečni, V. J. Decision making and information integration in the courts: The setting of bail. *Journal of Personality and Social Psychology,* 1975, *32,* 805–821.

Ebbesen, E. B., & Konečni, V. J. *Fairness in sentencing: Severity of crime and judicial decision making.* Paper presented in a symposium entitled "Seriousness of crime and severity of punishment" held at the 84th Annual Convention of the American Psychological Association, Washington, D.C., September, 1976.

Ebbesen, E. B., & Konečni, V. J. An analysis of the bail system. In V. J. Konečni & E. B. Ebbesen (Eds.), *Social–psychological analysis of legal processes.* San Francisco: W. H. Freeman, in press. (a)

Ebbesen, E. B., & Konečni, V. J. The process of sentencing adult felons: A causal analysis of judicial decisions. To appear in B. D. Sales (Ed.), *Perspectives in law and psychology (Vol. 2): The jury, judicial, and trial processes.* New York: Plenum, in press. (b)

Ebbesen, E. B., & Konečni, V. J. Social psychology and law: Theoretical considerations. In V. J. Konečni & E. B. Ebbesen (Eds.), *Social–psychological analysis of legal processes.* San Francisco: W. H. Freeman, in press (c).

Ebbesen, E. B., Parker, S., & Konečni, V. J. Laboratory and field analyses of decisions involving risk. *Journal of Experimental Psychology: Human Perception and Performance*, 1977, *3*, 576-589.

Ebert, R. J., & Kruse, T. E. Bootstrapping the security analyst. *Journal of Applied Psychology*, 1978, *63*, 110-119.

Einhorn, H. J. The use of nonlinear, noncompensatory models as a function of task and amount of information. *Organizational Behavior and Human Performance*, 1971, *6*, 1-27.

Einhorn, H. J. Expert judgment: Some necessary conditions and an example. *Journal of Applied Psychology*, 1974, *59*, 562-571.

Goodman, L. A. Causal analysis of data from panel studies and other kinds of surveys. *American Journal of Sociology*, 1973, *78*, 1135-1191.

Hayes, J. R. Human data processing limits in decision-making. In E. Bennett (Ed.), *Information systems, science and engineering. Proceedings of the First International Congress on the information systems sciences*. New York: McGraw-Hill, 1964.

Hammond, K. R., Stewart, T. R., Brehmer, B., & Steinmann, D. Social judgment theory. In M. Kaplan & S. Schwartz (Eds.), *Human judgment and decision processes: Formal and mathematical approaches*. New York: Academic Press, 1975.

Heise, D. R. *Causal analysis*. New York: Wiley, 1975.

Hoffman, P. J. The paramorphic representation of clinical judgment. *Psychological Bulletin*, 1960, *57*, 116-131.

Kahneman, D., & Tversky, A. Subjective probability: A judgment of representativeness. *Cognitive Psychology*, 1972, *3*, 430-454.

Kahneman, D., & Tversky, A. On the psychology of prediction. *Psychological Review*, 1973, *80*, 237-251.

Kahneman, D., & Tversky, A. Prospect theory: An analysis of decision and risk. *Econometrica*, 1979, *47*, 263-291.

Kassin, S. M. Consensus information, prediction, and causal attribution: A review of the literature and issues. *Journal of Personality and Social Psychology*, 1979, *37*, 1966-1981.

Keeney, R. L. A utility function for the response times of engines and ladders to fires. *Urban Analysis*, 1973, *1*, 209-222.

Keeney, R. L. The art of assessing multiattribute utility functions. *Organizational Behavior and Human Performance*, 1977, *19*, 267-310.

Konečni, V. J., & Ebbesen, E. B. A critical analysis of method and theory in psychological approaches to legal decisions. To appear in B. D. Sales (Ed.), *Perspectives in law and psychology (Vol. 2): The jury, judicial, and trial processes*. New York: Plenum, in press. (a)

Konečni, V. J., & Ebbesen, E. B. Sentencing felons. In V. J. Konečni & E. B. Ebbesen (Eds.), *Social-psychological analysis of legal processes*. San Francisco: W. H. Freeman, in press. (b)

Konečni, V. J., Mulcahy, E. M., & Ebbesen, E. B. Prison or mental hospital: Factors affecting the processing of persons suspected of being "mentally disordered sex offenders." In P. D. Lipsitt & B. D. Sales (Eds.), *New directions in psycholegal research*. New York: Van Nostrand Reinhold, in press.

Lichtenstein, S., & Slovic, P. Response-induced reversals of preference in gambling: An extended replication in Las Vegas. *Journal of Experimental Psychology*, 1973, *101*, 16-20.

Maslach, C., & Garber, R. B. Decision making processes in parole hearings. In V. J. Konečni & E. B. Ebbesen (Eds.), *Social-psychological analysis of legal processes*. San Francisco: W. H. Freeman, in press.

Naylor, J. C., & Wherry, R. J., Sr. The use of simulated stimuli and the "JAN" technique to capture and cluster the policies of raters. *Educational and Psychological Measurement*, 1965, *25*, 969-986.

Olson, C. L. Some apparent violations of the representativeness heuristic in human judgment. *Journal of Experimental Psychology: Human Perception and Performance*, 1976, *2*, 599-608.

Payne, J. W. Relation of perceive risk to preferences among gambles. *Journal of Experimental Psychology: Human Perception and Performance*, 1975, *1*, 86-94.

Payne, J. W., Braunstein, M. L., & Carroll, J. S. Exploring pre-decisional behavior: An alternative approach to decision behavior. *Organizational Behavior and Human Performance*, in press.

Phelps, R. H., & Shanteau, J. Livestock judges: How much information can an expert use? *Organizational Behavior and Human Performance*, 1978, *21*, 209-219.

Rosenthal, R., & Rosnow, R. L. *Artifact in behavioral research*. New York: Academic Press, 1969.

Russo, J. E., & Rosen, L. E. An eye fixation analysis of multialternative choice. *Memory and Cognition*. 1975, *3*, 267-276.

Simon, H. A. *The sciences of the artificial*. Cambridge: MIT Press, 1969.

Slovic, P. Analyzing the expert judge: A descriptive study of a stockbroker's decision process. *Journal of Applied Psychology*, 1969, *53*, 225-263.

Slovic, P., Fischhoff, B., & Lichtenstein, S. Cognitive processes and societal risk taking. In J. S. Carroll and J. W. Payne (Eds.), *Cognition and social behavior*. Hillsdale, N.J.: Lawrence Erlbaum Associates, 1976.

Slovic, P., Fischhoff, B., & Lichtenstein, S. Behavioral decision theory. *Annual Review of Psychology*, 1977, *28*, 1-39.

Slovic, P., Fleissner, D., & Bauman, W. S. Analyzing the use of information in investment decision making: A methodological proposal. *Journal of Business*, 1972, *45*, 283-301.

Slovic, P., & Lichtenstein, S. The relative importance of probabilities and payoffs in risk taking. *Journal of Experimental Psychology Monograph Supplement*, 1968, *78*, No. 3, Part 2.

Slovic, P., & Lichtenstein, S. Comparison of Bayesian and regression approaches to the study of information processing in judgment. *Organizational Behavior and Human Performance*, 1971, *6*, 649-744.

Webb, E. J., Campbell, D. T., Schwartz, R. D., & Sechrest, L. *Unobtrusive measures: Nonreactive research in the social sciences*. Chicago: Rand McNally, 1966.

Wells, G. L., & Harvey, J. H. Do people use consensus information in making causal attributions? *Journal of Personality and Social Psychology*, 1977, *35*, 279-293.

Wilkins, L. T., Gottfredson, D. M., Robinson, J. O., & Sadowsky, A. *Information selection and use in parole decision making* (Supplemental Rep. 5). Davis, Calif.: National Council on Crime and Delinquency Research Center, 1973.

Zimbardo, P. G., Ebbesen, E. B., & Maslach, C. *Influencing attitudes and changing behavior*. New York: Addison-Wesley, 1977.

3 Decisions That Might Not Get Made

Ruth M. Corbin
Bell Canada and Carleton University
Ottawa, Canada

INTRODUCTION

"What is our mental image of a decision-maker?" wrote Simon in 1959:

> Is he a brooding man on horseback who suddenly rouses himself from thought and issues an order to a subordinate? Is he a happy-go-lucky fellow, a coin posed on his thumbnail, ready to risk his action on the toss? Is he an alert, gray-haired businessman, sitting at the board of director's table with his associates, caught at the moment of saying "aye" or "nay"? Is he a bespectacled gentleman, bent over a docket of papers, his pen hovering over the line marked (X)?

> All of these images have a significant point in common. In them, the decision-maker is a man at the moment of choice, ready to plant his foot on one or another of the routes that lead from the crossroads. All of them ignore the whole process of alerting, exploring and analyzing that precede that final moment [p. 272].

The current emphasis on cognitive processes in choice indicates that we have come a long way from Simon, that the psychologist is no longer content to ignore the "whole process of alerting, exploring and analyzing that precede that final moment."

But it is the timing of that "final moment" I wish to explore. In hindsight, decisions appear to occur at fixed points in time; but before they are made, their timing is not necessarily fixed or even predictable. That being the case, one is led to wonder how choice situations do come to take place and what determines when choices will get made. The decision maker, after all, has a good deal of influence over what choice situations will be entered and what will comprise the set of alternatives. Why are some decisions put off? How does one decide when to decide? Under what circumstances will decisions be avoided entirely? And finally, what relevance do these questions have for the choice that results?

Such questions lie outside the domain of most formal models and experimental tests of decision making. They urge a scrutiny of the decision maker when he or she is not busy actually choosing. Imagine yourself, for example, as a potential vacationer studying travel literature from Auckland, Chapel Hill, and Paris. You might maximize your expected value, minimize the Euclidean distance to an ideal, or proceed with elimination-by-aspects. Alternatively, however, you might write to your travel agent for literature on Athens as well; you may collect opinions and information from friends; you may get your spouse to decide; or, you may put off your vacation until next year. In short, you have the prerogative of not now choosing. Examples presented elsewhere (Corbin & Marley, 1974; Hansen, 1972) illustrate that this prerogative may be instrumental in determining what finally gets chosen. Consequently, a theory of choice cannot be based on choice alone.

The significance of "no-choice behavior" has won brief recognition in a variety of published sources. In *The Functions of the Executive,* Chester Barnard (1938) writes: "The fine art of executive decisions consists in not deciding questions that are not now pertinent, in not deciding prematurely, in not making decisions that cannot be made effective, and in not making decisions that others should make [p. 194]." Barnard appears to be pressing for a well-defined *normative* treatment of not choosing.

In a more theoretic vein, Tukey (1970) proposes a consideration ". . . which deserves a place of its own. This is the treatment of doing nothing. In most accounts of decision theory, the decision to do nothing is either ignored (which is probably the worst thing to do in practice) or treated on a par with all the other decisions [p. 210]." Tukey's solution is to develop a theory of conclusions (as opposed to decisions) that can discriminate, for example, the scientist's state of being "not yet certain" from other attitudes about a question.

The topic is also touched on briefly by Hansen (1972) in reviewing work on consumer choice. He argues that decisions that never get made nonetheless direct *future* decision processes by arousing motivations or by lending significance to particular informational stimuli in the environment. Thus, he argues, we should also be looking at "sequences that are never completed [p. 162]," decisions that are avoided, matters that are dropped. Hansen himself, however, appears to drop the matter, implying that uncompleted decisions are too complex and diverse a collection of behaviors from which to generalize.

The present chapter illustrates that organization *can* be lent to available ideas. It goes further to argue that "aspects of not choosing" constitute a useful umbrella structure for encompassing and fusing much diverse research, both theoretical and experimental.

This chapter takes, as its organizational basis, a standard procedural model of decision making. Such a model typically postulates stages of: (1) problem clarification; (2) information collection; (3) deliberation; (4) moment of choice; and (5) postchoice behavior. The exact names of the stages may vary according to the nuances that an author intends—but the five-stage structure is quite widely found. Examples appear in Engel, Kollat, and Blackwell (1968), Howard and Sheth (1969), and Hansen (1972).

But, although the existence of such stages in a decision procedure is well accepted, we have seldom focused on the obstructions at any one stage that may halt the procedure. What if the problem is not clarified in stage 1? How much information collection is required in stage 2 before the decision maker agrees to proceed? What determines the length of deliberation in stage 3? And, what if there is no choice at the stage 4 moment of choice? These questions collectively seek a characterization of stage *boundaries,* boundaries that must be crossed before the crossing of the decision finish line.

The remainder of the chapter is developed parallel to the foregoing problem description. The next section characterizes the stages of decision making according to their "obstructions." It identifies three classes of behavior under the titles Refusal, Delay, and Inattention. Behavioral research from different areas is organized into these classes, illustrating that we already have a good deal of raw material for building a connected set of ideas about not-choosing behavior. The section following the next discusses the motivations that account for refusal, delay, and inattention, and argues that these motivations must be satisfied prior to an observable choice. Hypothetical boundaries are proposed, the "crossing" of the boundaries corresponding to a satisfaction of motivations intrinsic to the process.

A BEHAVIORAL CLASSIFICATION OF NONDECISIONS

What kinds of "nondecisions" are there? Three categories of observable behavior are proposed: refusal, delay, and inattention. A discussion of each, together with the research it encompasses, follows.

Refusal

At the moment of choice, the decision maker may decide to refuse all of the offered alternatives, an option not usually considered in standard models of choice. It could be argued that this refusal option is nothing more than the "choice" of the status quo, and that, therefore, it does not undermine the validity of any standard model.

Yet, in many experiments, surveys, and discussions (e.g., S. L. Payne, 1951; Tversky, 1976), the evaluation of the status quo appears to be quite distinct in character. Some authors view it as a referent point against which other alternatives are evaluated (Tversky, 1976). In many real-life instances, the uncertainty associated with the status quo is less than for other alternatives. In many cases, too, there is less responsibility associated with the effects of "doing nothing" than with some conscious choice.

Mack (1971) supports this view of the status quo having a special significance in the choice set. Linking it with other evidence of conservatism in situations of uncertainty, she comments: "A conservative bias, we find, characterizes choice among pre-delineated acts and tends to place the do-nothing act in higher favor than it deserves [p. 12]."

At the very least, it seems desirable to keep track of the refusal option in a given model of choice, by allowing for its special properties in the formal notation, or by specifying the circumstances under which the model predicts no choice.

Two theoretical structures that include a refusal option have been proposed. One involved an extension of Tversky's (1972a, 1972b) elimination-by-aspects model. Tversky's theory is built on a covert elimination process. In this theory, each alternative is viewed as a set of aspects. At each stage in the hypothetical process, an aspect is selected, and all the alternatives that do not include the selected aspect are eliminated. The process continues until only one alternative remains.

Generalizing Tversky's mathematical model, Corbin and Marley (1974) showed that allowance could be made for a refusal option. In the original model, this option would correspond to the subject's selecting an aspect (for elimination purposes) that none of the current alternatives possessed.

A model introduced by Pruitt (1962) characterized gambles in terms of their pattern and level of risk (expected value of negative outcomes). The utility function (over risk) that the model generated was an inverted U function, beginning at $(0, 0)$ and eventually crossing the x-axis at a point $(r, 0)$. Pruitt (1962) labeled r the "maximum acceptable level of risk," adding that "the model predicts what we know from experience . . . that there is a limit to the amount of money a man will risk on a pattern which has at least one negative outcome, no matter how favorable the pattern may appear [p. 193]." In an experiment supporting the model, trials consisted of the presentation of a single gamble, which the subject could either accept or refuse.

The general notion of a criterion for refusal is easy enough to accept intuitively. As is shown in a later section, it is also a straightforward matter to account for a general refusal criterion in formal notation. But, other aspects of nondecision behavior pose more complex problems, and it is these we turn to next.

Delay

The refusal option is an aspect of no choice that may come into play at the final stage of the choice process. But, when does that final stage come? The decision maker controls a variety of *delay* options that include: (1) inspecting further alternatives; (2) tapping external sources of information; (3) deliberation; (4)

waiting for a goal object to become available. These four delay options help to classify the rich content of cognitive processes in decision making and help to organize the following discussion of the research that has been done.

Inspecting Further Alternatives.   The first delay option mentioned entails the expansion of the current context. Presented with an array of alternatives, a chooser often has the prerogative of bringing more alternatives into consideration. Consider again the vacation-seeking example. Having examined literature from three vacation spots, one is at liberty to inquire about a fourth before deciding. This kind of liberty is seldom extended to subjects in psychological choice experiments; the obviating difficulties are sometimes identified as the inability to simulate ill-defined sets that occur in real life.

The theories that structure choice experiments are equally weak, argued Simon (1959):

> The classical theory is a theory of a man choosing among fixed and known alternatives . . . But when perception and cognition intervene between the decision-maker and his objective environment, this model no longer proves adequate. We need a description of the choice process that recognizes that alternatives are not given but must be sought [p. 272].

Working in the closely related area of problem solving, Maier (1960) expressed a similar concern. He claimed that decision-making theories were inadequate to model problem-solving behavior because they failed to describe the complex process by which alternatives are created or the initial uncertainties of what the possible alternatives are. More than a decade later, Lee (1971) reiterated the problem, arguing that it leads one to question the very meaning of ''rationality'' on which most current theories are based. He cited the example of a committee of businessmen, who make a seemingly rational choice among a number of suggested sites for a new plant. But, Lee (1971) wrote: ''It is conceivable that there is a *better* plant site somewhere. Would it be rational to ignore such a possibility? . . . Deciding to search for more possible choices is very important in real life, but is usually awkward for decision theory [pp. 7–8].''

In addition to descriptive leverage, Mack (1971) attaches a prescriptive note to the widening of contexts. Optional decision strategies, she advises, should avoid focusing strictly on the alternatives currently considered: ''rather the greatest opportunity for improvement may lie in bringing still other alternatives within the compass of review [p. 2].''

Despite these brief acknowledgments of the problem, there have been few attempts in psychology to tackle it. Those that seem to come closest are experimental tests of the so-called ''secretary problem'' (e.g., Chow, Moriguti, Robbins, & Samuels, 1964; Gilbert & Mosteller, 1966). The secretary problem is the nickname given to a class of dynamic programming models that specify optimal search strategies when choice alternatives (monetary offers, say) are presented sequentially. At any stage in the search process, the decision maker may stop and select one of the currently available offers, or take another observation at some cost. Although the model has a long way to go before it can be considered a suitable theory of behavior, it provides a nice structure for designing experiments.

Experiments based on this model have uncovered various factors that determine the number of observations that decision makers are likely to take (Corbin, 1976). For example, they are likely to take greater numbers of observations when given no cues at all about a suitable strategy for setting a goal. The inference that the mere observation of alternatives aids in the *clarification of goals* is supported by Uhl and Hoffman (1958), who show that aspects of the alternatives suggest criteria for evaluation. As an empirical example, consider a manager interviewing potential secretaries, uncertain of what criteria to use in deciding among them. One candidate smokes so much during the interview that it occurs to the manager how unpleasant smoke might make the office. Thus, how much a candidate smokes may become a criterion for the eventual decision that is now incorporated into the chooser's goals. In this way, the generation of alternatives aids in what is usually called the "problem clarification" stage of a decision.

Experiments with the secretary problem have also indicated that subjects seek to extract *information* from the alternatives as they are sequentially observed, and to formulate hypotheses about the underlying distribution that governs them (see also Brickman, 1972). Examples given in Corbin, Olson, and Abbondanza (1975) and data given in Kahan, Rapoport, and Jones (1967) provide further support for the fact that alternatives themselves may convey information. Thus, the inspection of alternatives is a behavior that may also characterize the stage of decision making usually referred to as "information collection."

Finally, experiments with the secretary problem have demonstrated that, even when all relevant information is available to subjects, they may continue to inspect alternatives in pursuit of a specific goal (see also Rapoport & Tversky, 1970.) So here, the inspection of alternatives would be most appropriately classified as part of the final choice stage, the length of the stage being extended by the search for an alternative that has been "selected" but not obtained.

The potential of the secretary problem and its variants, as a paradigm for experimentation, is far from exhausted.

Tapping External Sources of Information.   A second delay strategy that the decision maker is at liberty to undertake is the acquisition of data. The *Consumer Reports* magazine, newspaper racing columns, mothers, and the Better Business Bureau are examples of information sources that a person might tap before exercising a choice.

Information acquisition of this sort has been the subject of an impressive scope of research. Experiments have documented search strategies over a wide range of cost, information and risk conditions (e.g., Irwin & Smith, 1957; Lanzetta & Kanareff, 1962; Siegel & Goldstein, 1959). Many studies focus on economic models, against which the optimality of subjects' search strategies can be measured (e.g., W. Edwards, 1965; Lanzetta & Kanareff, 1962). The Bayesian model, reviewed at length by Slovic and Lichtenstein (1971), has formed the basis of a great number of studies of information seeking in judgmental tasks. Klahr (1967) and J. W. Payne (1974) extended research to include information seeking in forced-choice experiments—that is, where the sought-for information concerned the alternatives themselves. Klahr attempted to establish directional relationships between the amount of search and various attributes of the alternatives. Search was greater, he found, when the alternatives appeared initially to be very similar. Search was also greater when partial information attested to the low quality of the alternatives. Klahr argued that amount of prior information should influence the search delay too, but he did not obtain supportive data.

Information collection appears to have a self-reinforcing property, because it is not always clear that the information will lead to better decisions. An individual in the stock market, for example, may collect information at length, even though its relevance and appropriate application are almost impossible to judge. Evidence, in fact (Stael von Holstein, 1972), as well as an intuitive cost–benefit analysis, suggest that choosing a stock at random would be the better strategy for the individual to pursue. Yet, randomness is apparently discomforting (Hogarth, 1975; Simon and Sumner, 1968). One feels one must collect the information. There is a strong desire to understand and explain events surrounding one (Shaver, 1977). Lanzetta and Driscoll (1966) demonstrate that an individual will seek out information about an uncertain outcome, even though the outcome is unavoidable and the information useless.

The implication of most of this behavioral research is that information collection is geared to the reduction of a concept called "subjective uncertainty" (e.g., Kogan & Wallach, 1964; Savage, 1954), and that decisions are postponed until uncertainty falls below some acceptable maximum. Studies that take this orientation directly, by relating amount of information to some measure of uncertainty, include Irwin and Smith (1957), Morlock (1967), and Lanzetta (1963).

Deliberation. Another stage of predecision cognitive processes entails the evaluation of all the discovered aspects of alternatives, a task that takes time. This delay is yet another source of psychological content. In examining this psychological content, two questions may be posed: Why do some choices take longer than others? What is the subject doing in these times of not choosing?

Abundant studies in reaction time have addressed themselves to the first question. Most of them concern research on perception, discrimination, and attention, rather than on preference. However, the transfer of ideas may not be long in coming if, as Irwin (1958) argues, making a discrimination and exhibiting a preference are inextricably related.

The potential of reaction times in preferences tasks has recently been investigated by Petrusic and Jamieson, (1976) and Jamieson and Petrusic (1977). One of their principal arguments concerns the efficiency of the technique in testing probabilistic models of preference. Demonstrating that reaction time is inversely related to probability of choice, they point out that reaction time data could substitute for the hundreds of trials necessary to get good probability data for models of choice.

A study using "real time," conducted by Lanzetta and Kanareff in 1962, pointed to a common motivational basis for information collection and deliberation time. They kept records of the amount of time spent and the amount of information requested. They found that subjects who collected less information did not complete decision problems any faster; they "made up the time" by rereading the problem or by thinking. Moreover, there was no evidence that these subjects had any less confidence in their eventual decisions than did subjects who had requested more information. Thus, it seemed that additional processing time was an alternate means for *decreasing uncertainty* and for inducing the readiness to decide. The complementary nature of the relationship between deliberation and information acquisition is upheld by Zajonc and Burnstein (1961) and Hansen, (1972), the latter arguing that "not only quantitative aspects of information may be applied in attempts to reduce uncertainty [p. 87]."

A different approach to deliberation activity is taken in the current research field of "cognitively simplifying heuristics." Researchers in the area would no doubt argue that reaction time is just a by-product of whatever heuristics the subject employs. Tackling more directly the question of what the subject is doing during the predecision deliberation, investigators have uncovered not only individual heuristics, but *sequences* of heuristics, during which subjects are apparently reducing a complex problem to a form compatible with the limitations of human processing abilities (e.g., Svenson, 1974). So, according to this type of research, *cognitive simplification* (rather than uncertainty reduction as argued earlier) is the goal that processing delays serve. But the important and intuitive connection is made explicit by Hogarth (1975) in his argument that reduction of uncertainty *is* a means of cognitive simplification. Such research invites a more precise elucidation of the uncertainty concept as a motivator of delay. Providing a commonality between two of the usually depicted stages of decision making (information collection and deliberation), it suggests the possibility of reworking the usual procedural model of decision making by emphasizing motivations rather than behaviors. We are led, moreover, to ask how *much* reduction of uncertainty is necessary to ensure that a choice will take place, and how we can explicitly account for the maximum acceptable uncertainty in a formal model. I return to this question in the section on motivations later in this chapter.

Waiting (A Goal-Directed Delay).   A final occasion for delay may arise if the subject's goal object, which has already been selected, is not currently available. The subject has the option of waiting. Research on "delay of gratification'' touches some aspects of the topic (Mischel 1958, 1961), with amount of waiting time a typical variable of interest.

Correspondingly, for preference tasks, we might wish to know what affects the length of time that a decision maker will wait for an ideal alternative before either choosing among what *is* available, or abandoning pursuit of the goal. The fact that a decision maker may indeed ''choose'' an unavailable alternative was argued by Walster and Festinger (1964) in their discussion of how typical choice experiments fall short of real-life situations. They investigated experimentally the effects of an unavailable ideal alternative on a forced choice among what they called the ''imperfect alternatives.''

No research known to me investigates the waiting option directly—that is, with ''time'' as the dependent variable. Research with the secretary problem paradigm previously mentioned is relevant, if one uses ''number of observations'' as a crude measure of time. The only difficulty there is the confounding of motivations. As pointed out earlier, the subject may be waiting for a specific offer to come along, but he or she may also be drawing observations for informational purposes, for gaining familiarity with the problem, or maybe just for fun. Thus, other types of tasks may prove better suited for investigating goal-oriented delays.

In summary, the delay options identified afford an organization of much of the research on cognitive processes in decision making—an organization according to different specific behaviors. These behaviors are presented as forces counteracting the ''forward drive to a decision'' that procedural models seem to assume. The basis of this assumption is no doubt the ''reward potential'' of a decision. But, research in this section collectively suggests that there are other motivations besides the expectation of reward that need to be satisfied. A natural inference is that until these motives are satisfied, a choice will *not* be made.

Inattention

A discussion of predecision delay options, such as the one previously pursued, takes for granted the individual's awareness that an occasion for choice exists. It assumes a motivation to direct one's behavior towards the resolution of a perceived conflict. But, in the absence of such conditions, many potential decision situations obviously never take place. The situational stimuli may not be structured by the individual in a way that will induce a decision. The question of why the situation fails to take on a cognitive structure appropriate for decision making is analogous to the question in the area of perception regarding why some stimuli are attended to and perceived while others go unnoticed. In terms of our procedural model, we may say that the procedure never moves beyond the problem recognition stage.

The literature that bears on this category of nondecisions is characterized by two quite different lines of thought: Some authors focus on decision situations that are consciously avoided; others discuss situations that are too fuzzy for the individual to recognize as problems for choice. Published ideas on both lines of thought are reviewed in the following section.

Avoidance.   Objective evidence of *decision avoidance* has been reported in many forms. Roman history describes how oracles were consulted for the best course of action, rituals were undertaken to determine the guilt or innocence of an accused. John Wesley, the founder of Methodism, is reported to have cast lots (by drawing one of many written messages out of a hat) to determine whether to marry, accepting the result as the will of God (Lee, 1971). Traditions encourage one to seek advice by pulling petals from a daisy, star gazing, reading tea leaves.

Our present democratic society upholds rationality and decries superstition: no oracles or daisies for us. Instead, we hire outside consultants to recruit personnel, seek stock brokers to take our risks, press waiters to tell us what to order. Of course, there is merit to expert opinions, but such opinions are typically accepted without question as personal preferences of the would-be decision maker. In this respect, experts in different areas are 20th century oracles, sought out by an individual wishing to avoid the taxing evaluation of complex alternatives.

Kaufmann (1973) reviews evidence for decision avoidance with far more serious concern. Drawing from such philosophers as Nietszche and Heidegger, from writings of Dostoevsky, and from religious and social history, Kaufmann describes "the dodges most of us use to avoid life-changing decisions [p. 79]." He implies that psychologists have given too little attention, in their enthusiastic theories of decision making, to the question of whether people can manage the effort and stress that many decisions demand. Consequently, cases of decision avoidance may hold valuable clues to the psychological components that are necessary for a decision to take place.

We might begin by asking what motivation can be proposed to explain decision avoidance. Perhaps (as Kaufmann's clinical view suggests) it is responsibility that is being avoided. A specific act on the part of a decision maker imposes a contingency between that act and the consequences of the decision, a contingency we intuitively label "responsibility." But, responsibility for consequences is not always pleasant. Recall the vacation-seeking example, where you might contemplate letting your spouse make the decision: If *you* choose, and the vacation is a disaster, you risk blame and reproach for poor judgment.

I know of no research that directly supports the hypothesis that "reluctance to accept responsibility for consequences" can explain decision avoidance. But there is much research that illustrates that avoidance of responsibility is a pervasive motive. Studies on the "risky shift" phenomenon (e.g., Kogan & Wallach, 1967), group-enhanced violence (Zimbardo, 1970), bystander apathy (Darley & Latané, 1968), and obedience (Milgram, 1963, 1965) provide distinctly different support for the same idea: One's choice of action in specific situations is affected by perceived responsibility for the outcome. Whether this diagnosis can be generalized to decision avoidance is a topic for more direct research. A conclusion we can certainly draw, however, is that *motivation to choose* is a necessary condition for a choice to take place. It is an *implied assumption* in arguments supporting the validity of any decision model. And, if we are to believe Kaufmann, the assumption is far from trivial.

Failure to Perceive an Occasion for Choice.   Further assumptions that models implicitly make include the existence of at least two alternatives (one may be the status quo), and the existence of a goal variable such as utility, financial gain, etc. These assumptions are illustrated in models ranging from the simplest mathematical formulations, Luce's (1959) choice model for example, to comprehensive descriptive models, such as that of Hansen (1972). Hansen implies that *conflict* is aroused by the recognition of alternatives to the status quo, and of a goal that the status quo does not meet. It is almost tautological that without these conditions, without the perception of an unresolved conflict, there is no impetus to act. The decision maker may therefore fail to attend to a decision situation that others perceive to exist.

Similar arguments concerning failure to act have been advanced in studies of bystander apathy. Yakimovich and Salz (1971), in an experiment on helping behavior, suggested that alternatives to the status quo may not be apparent to the subject until he or she receives sufficient cues. Baron, Byrne, and Griffitt (1974) add the possibility that appropriate goals for the situation may not be clear enough to incite a rational choice for action. They identify such a situation (in which alternatives are not perceived or goals are unformulated) as *ambiguous,* and they stress the importance of ambiguity reduction in order to prompt a conscious acknowledgment that a decision situation exists.

Although there are numerous papers on the characteristics of problem recognition, there is little direct research on what makes some problems recognized and others avoided or ignored (Liefeld, 1977). Because inattention (as well as delay and refusal) may preclude any observable choice, we need to account for the elements in a choice process that allow for completion of the process. That is, we should attempt to identify the necessary go-ahead indicators that permit the procedure to move from stage to stage. Such an attempt is the subject of the next section.

MOTIVATIONS INVOLVED IN NOT (YET) DECIDING: THEORETICAL CONCEPTS AND MEASURES

The previous section highlighted deterrents to decision making, choices we refuse to make, decisions we put off, opportunities we miss or avoid. There is empirical evidence, too, that good options for change are often refused in favor of the status quo. The conclusion that seems unavoidable is that decisions are *aversive* to varying degrees (Festinger, 1964; Janis, 1959), that there are barriers at different stages of the choice-making process that must be overcome. Obtaining a formal representation of those barriers is the subject of discussion in this section. I restrict the discussion to characteristics of an *individual alternative* that make it unchoosable at a given instant. By implication, if all alternatives entail such characteristics, then a no-choice option will be in effect. Early "valence models" of the response strength associated with alternatives (Lewin, 1935; Miller, 1944) support our attempts to identify aversion-inducing properties of choice objects, though attempts at measuring these properties have not always found success (Bilkey, 1957). Approaching the problem in this reductionist fashion will admittedly result in the omission of global properties of the decision process that stand in the way of the process's completion.

In line with inferences drawn from the review of no-choice behaviors, the hypothesized barriers are identified as "unacceptability," "uncertainty," and "ambiguity." These three descriptors, it is argued here, can be linked back to the no-choice options described in the last section, and can be represented by simplistic theoretical cutoffs in a procedural model of decision making. Again, the argument is erected by collecting and linking diverse research.

Unacceptability Cutoffs in the Later Stages

Unacceptability is straightforward enough to deal with, and was given its first formal treatment in Simon's "satisficing" model (Simon, 1955, 1956). Originally applied to choice alternatives viewed sequentially, satisficing implies that the decision maker will choose the first alternative whose "utility" exceeds some minimum criterion of acceptability. Discussions of satisficing models and related aspiration-level theories are found in March and Simon (1958), Cyert and March (1963), and Starbuck (1963).

A quantitative revival of satisficing is represented in Rapoport and Tversky's (1970) "cutoff strategy," applied to optional stopping decisions. According to this strategy, a subject decides on the minimum numerical offer that he or she is willing to accept, and stops as soon as there appears an offer at or above that level. Thus, according to Tversky and Rapoport, verification that a cutoff strategy is being used requires at least that a subject stop on a current maximum. Yet, that test appears too strict: It ignores the possibility that a subject uses a cutoff as a *part* of his or her overall strategy, but follows a cutoff rule with the use of other rules that depend, say, on the costs and risks of searching further. An experiment I ran to follow up on this idea (Corbin, 1976) demonstrated, for one thing, that subjects *would* set cutoffs, but search a bit further than the first acceptable offer *as long as that acceptable offer could be guaranteed available*. With an acceptable offer in hand, they often undertook the pursuit of even better offers. Thus, the cutoff determined what alternatives would certainly be *refused*, but was not sufficient to predict which single alternative would get chosen.

Despite this limitation as a predictor, the cutoff rule is clearly a useful mechanism for structuring a goal-directed dealy.

Backing up one step to the deliberation stage, we find application of a cutoff rule there too. In tracing "think-aloud" reports of subjects in decision-making situations, researchers often find the use of unacceptability criteria (in the context of what they call "conjunctive rules") in early stages of the evaluation process. Such rules, they claim, help the subject to "reduce the strain" of complicated decisions (Slovic, Fischhoff, & Lichtenstein, 1977) by eliminating clearly unacceptable alternatives as soon as possible.

This pervasive evidence of a satisficing-type rule predicting nonchoice is in contrast to the rather ambiguous evidence for its efficacy in predicting choice (Brim, Glass, Lavin, & Goodman, 1962; Dickins, Fanelli, & Ferguson, 1954; Kerby, 1969; Olander, 1975). Identified here as an "unacceptability cutoff," it represents a necessary condition for a choice to take place. If no alternatives in the population are formally "acceptable," then *refusal* of all options is the outcome we would expect.

Uncertainty Cutoffs in the Middle Stages

Subjective uncertainty contributes yet another aversive element to the decision-making process (Hogarth, 1975): "The notion that events are uncertain is both uncomfortable and complicating. Indeed, even in the supposedly 'rational' world of business, there is evidence that businessmen are averse to admitting uncertainty [p. 273]." (See also Johnson & Huber, 1977.) I would go further to argue that the evidence for people's (Slovic et al., 1977) "inordinately high opinions of their own predictive abilities [p. 6]" is indicative not of arrogance but of adaptiveness. (See also Fischhoff, 1975; Fischhoff & Beyth, 1975; Stäel von Holstein, 1972).

Information collection and deliberation, the review of available research implies, are geared in part to reducing the subjective uncertainty that characterizes any decision. But, when is the decision maker satisfied with the amount of data on hand? What criterion is used to help one get on with the business of choosing?

From arguments in the literature, it is tempting to turn again to the cutoff idea. Cox and Rich (1964) talk of reducing uncertainty "to the point where it would be comfortable," whereas Taylor's (1974) model of consumer behavior shows the consumer putting off his or her buying decision until the risk (which Taylor also refers to as uncertainty) is reduced to an acceptable level. Hansen (1972) also speaks of a level of "tolerable conflict" that the whole decision process is geared to meet. Implicit in these studies is that some level of certainty must be achieved before a decision is effected. This statement could be formalized in the postulation of an "uncertainty cutoff." Like the acceptability cutoff previously discussed, it would not necessarily allow us to predict when the subject will stop and choose. Indeed, according to Festinger (1964), information collection persists even after a choice is made. The cutoff idea shifts the focus to why the subject does not yet choose, and to (at least) how long he or she will delay.

Experimental support for uncertainty cutoffs comes from at least three sources. Irwin and Smith (1957) asked subjects to guess whether a deck of numbered cards had a mean above or below zero. Subjects could buy observations from the deck at a certain price, and received a prize for a correct guess. Uncertainty was varied by making the mean close to or far from 0 (e.g., .5 or 1.5) and by using card decks with differences in variance (2.0 and 7.5). After each choice, subjects gave confidence ratings about their guesses. The ratings did not differ across experimental conditions, the interpretation given in Hansen (1972) being that "presumably, subjects continued their information buying until they had reached a certain level of certainty . . . and then made their choices [p. 86]." This interpretation is supported by findings in Morlock (1967).

A different version of the same result is reported by Lanzetta (1963). He studied information acquisition in relation to the initial level of uncertainty, and to the rate at which uncertainty could be reduced. Information acquisition was pursued in three different conditions until uncertainty was reduced to approximately the same level. That is, although subjects did not search until complete knowledge was gained, they waited for a *particular level of uncertainty* to be reached, a level independent of initial uncertainty or speed with which uncertainty could be reduced.

Related research on "risk tolerance" takes us one step further, to suggest that uncertainty cutoffs exist as functions of personality variables (Brim & Hoff, 1957; Cox, 1967) and situational variables (Lamm, 1967).

Similar to the arguments concerning an acceptability cutoff, we find complementary ideas in the mathematical modeling literature. Suppose we represent an alternative in an empirical choice situation as a "gamble" that changes over time; as more information is collected about an alternative, the predictability of its outcome increases and its "variance" tightens up. Then, the existence of uncertainty cutoffs is supported by studies in variance preference (Coombs & Pruitt, 1960; W. Edwards, 1954; Slovic & Lichtenstein, 1968; Van der Meer, 1963) that suggest the presence of stable tolerances for uncertainty within individuals.

Definitions and measures of uncertainty are varied (Atkinson & Feather, 1966; Cox, 1967; Driscoll, Tognolli, & Lanzetta, 1966; Lanzetta, 1963). But there seems to be widespread belief in its aversive nature, and a consistent implication that some cutoff of tolerability exists. When uncertainty is defined as a property of individual alternatives, we can infer that no choice (outside the status quo) will be made until at least one alternative exceeds the uncertainty cutoff. Three of the delay strategies identified earlier were shown to be potential uncertainty reducers, and in this way constitute behavioral indicators of the underlying motivations suggested here.

Ambiguity Cutoffs at the Outset

To this point, it has been argued that a decision maker delays at least until one alternative is perceived as acceptable, and that prior to that, he or she collects information at least until it can be identified with some degree of certainty which alternatives are acceptable and which are not. These statements assume that alternatives can be evaluated. Indeed, this assumption is the basis of published prescriptive techniques for managers (e.g., Schlaifer, 1961) that urge prospective decision makers to first "formalize their priors"—that is, to assign win–loss probabilites to each alternative with respect to its likelihood of satisfying the individuals' goals. But, if one is unsure of what the alternatives are, or indeed of what one's goals are (a situation that, as discussed earlier, is defined by Baron, Byrne, and Griffitt (1974) as "ambiguous"), then one would be unable to generate a set of priors for the members of the choice set. It is almost tautological to say that no decision-making process can begin until ambiguity is dispelled; if the ambiguity cannot be dispelled, the opportunity for decision will not be taken up—a situation earlier categorized as "inattention."

Lee (1971) seizes on the "absence of priors" feature to construct a more formal definition of ambiguity, one that characterizes individual alternatives. Depicting an alternative as a gamble, he defines its ambiguity as a second-order variance—the variance of the distribution of its possible representations. The greater the ambiguity, the more difficult it is for the subject to evaluate an alternative's potential worth. And, indeed, Ellsberg (1961) had already shown that ambiguous alternatives *are* avoided.

Defined in terms of a second-order variance, ambiguity is a ready candidate for a cutoff model, whereby until at least one alternative exceeds a "tolerable level of ambiguity" (Winkler & Cummings, 1972), no further action would occur. Empirically, this would correspond to an argument that cognitive processes directed towards a decision will not start until at least one or more alternatives are perceived to be unambiguous—that is, until there is at least one alternative for which a prior "exists." An ambiguity cutoff provides for a formal boundary of the problem clarification stage, implying that an inability to dispel ambiguity will result in inattention to the decision.

SUMMARY AND DISCUSSION

That decision makers pass through stages in the choice process has been noted by many authors. The bounds of those stages have not previously been elucidated. The two preceding sections have organized some of the available literature according to (1) behaviors that characterize the hypothetical stages; and (2) theoretical concepts that might be used to explain those behaviors. A sketch of the organizational framework may be given as follows: Decisions cannot be made in ambiguous circumstances. Unless some *ambiguity* cutoff is exceeded, the potential decision is *not attended to,* and the cognitive processes we talk about in decision making will not proceed. Assuming that the cutoff is exceeded, the decision will be *delayed* at least until uncertainty is reduced to an acceptable level—that is, until some suitably defined *uncertainty* cutoff is exceeded. Assuming that it is exceeded, the decision will be delayed at least until one acceptable alternative becomes available—that is, until some suitably defined *unacceptability* cutoff is exceeded. If it is not exceeded, all alternatives will be *refused.* These ideas can be formally expressed in terms of mathematical models that offer very simplified representations of the boundaries between stages of the process.

Among the advantages to the present approach are these: It highlights the rich content of predecisional internal states, and reveals the rather significant assumptions implicitly taken for granted in any predictive model of choice. These assumptions provide a basis for *agreement* among models despite the possible conflicts among different models' predictions. Thus, we may be able to establish a framework that encompasses and connects a broader collection of research and ideas than has been previously possible. At the very least, the approach encourages us to seek out more comprehensive theories of choice, theories that will identify the *several* motivations inherent to decision making.

Another attractive feature of the approach is the compatibility of ideas with existing formal models. The relation to formal models extends to include some optimal models: "acceptability cutoffs," for example, are optimizing criteria in many variations of the secretary problem. The appeal of this observation is that it may help us to explain how decision makers can sometimes cope so astonishingly well in so complex an environment.

One final potential advantage must be mentioned, in respect to the topic itself: the possibilities for applications to areas where nondecisions *are* the subject of interest. Kaufmann (1973), for example, reflects on the pathology of extreme decision avoidance, and urges the clinician to recognize "decidophobia" as a significant maladaptive force in many people's lives. A second area of applications concerns social-survey taking, where nonresponse is becoming a marked problem. Surveys are special kinds of decision circumstances. They are interventions in the cognitive processes of the respondents. They may *interrupt* the process by which a respondent comes to a decision on the issue in question. Thus, a survey is likely to catch a respondent with his or her mind not yet made up. Of course (as Fischhoff, Lichtenstein, & Slovic point out elsewhere in this volume), respondents often rapidly adapt to the situational demands by coming to decisions on the spot. Often, though, they cannot. They have not yet heard of the issue, or they have not enough information about it, or they care too little to tax their overworked cognitive processing systems. So, they give a "nonsubstantive" response, one that will be efficiently coded with the whole class of nonsubstantive responses, including "do not know," "no response," "would not answer," "other." To a survey researcher, these are usually considered as nuisance responses. To a psychologist, these responses may be indicators of an unfinished decision process, affording us a rare chance to ask: "What is it about these circumstances that explains why a choice has not been made?" To my knowledge, psychologists have not yet begun to make the most of this source of data. Its value is enhanced by the practical advantages of the time taken to collect the data. That is, if indeed nonsubstantive responses represent samples of "cognitions in progress," then questionnaires might substitute in some circumstances for more lengthy decision-making experiments involving information search and deliberation.

Some progress in the analysis of nonsubstantive responses has been made by Coombs and Coombs (1976). They undertook to distinguish "item ambiguity" from "response uncertainty" in the construction of a data-dependent attitude scale. Their subsequent analyses, based on Guttman scalograms, constitute the only successful theoretical advance in the area that I have seen. The practical significance of their work is that it permits the detection and elimination of ambiguous items, thereby improving a scale's reliability and interpretability.

Empirical inroads on aspects of no choice in surveys have been made by Cannell, Oksenberg, and Converse (1977). Concerned with the marked invalidity of many survey data, they suggest that *delay time* in responding is a valuable cue for the kind of probe an interviewer should use to "follow up." On sensitive issues, such as health problems, the authors argue that there is meaning in the fact that some people take longer to report that they have nothing to report. But, there exists neither theoretical guidance nor refined techniques to capitalize on such clues to a respondent's cognitions.

Having dwelt on potential for further research, I should admit some of the limitations of the approach taken here. As a basis for the development of a *theory*, it is incomplete. It does not deal with all the possible cognitive activities that a decision process may entail. For example, "complexity reduction," which plays a major role in current psychological research, was not explicitly accounted for. Hogarth's argument (1975), alluded to earlier, that uncertainty and complexity are very much the same, immediately suggests a problem for research. Are the two simply different names for the same cognitive conflict state, and therefore amenable to a single theoretical construct? Or are they *separable* motivational states whose interaction in the choice process must be explicitly accounted for by theory?

Another limitation of the approach taken here is that it does not specify how the aversive elements of decision making enter into tradeoffs with the positive elements to account for the fact that decisions do get made. And, it has little direct research to support some of its principal ideas. This, I hope, the future will take care of.

ACKNOWLEDGMENTS

I am grateful to Dr. Thomas Wallsten for his detailed editorial comments.

REFERENCES

Atkinson, J. W., & Feather, N. T. *A theory of achievement motivation.* New York: Wiley, 1966.

Barnard, C. I. *The functions of the executive.* Cambridge: Havard University Press, 1938.

Baron, R. A., Byrne, D., & Griffitt, W. *Social psychology, understanding human interaction.* Boston: Allyn & Bacon, 1974.

Bilkey, W. J. Consistency test of psychic tension rating involved in consumer purchase behavior. *Journal of Social Psychology,* 1957, *45,* 81–91.

Brickman, P. Optional stopping on ascending and descending series. *Organizational Behavior and Human Performance,* 1972, *7,* 53–62.

Brim, O. G., Glass, D. G., Lavin, D. E., & Goodman, N. *Personality and decision processes.* Stanford: Stanford University Press, 1962.

Brim, O. G., & Hoff, D. B. Individual and situational differences in desire for certainty. *Journal of Abnormal and Social Psychology,* 1957, *54,* 225–229.

Cannell, C. F., Oksenberg, L., & Converse, J. M. Striving for response accuracy: Experiments in new interviewing techniques. *Journal of Marketing Research,* 1977, *14,* 306–315.

Chow, Y. S., Moriguti, S., Robbins, H., & Samuels, S. M. Optimum selection based on relative rank (the "secretary problem"). *Israel Journal of Mathematics,* 1964, *2,* 81–90.

Coombs, C. H., & Coombs, L. C. Don't know: Item ambiguity or response uncertainty? *Public Opinion Quarterly,* 1976, *40,* 497–514.

Coombs, C. H., & Pruitt, D. G. Components of risk in decision-making: Probability and variance preferences. *Journal of Experimental Psychology,* 1960, *60,* 265–277.

Corbin, R. M. *A no-choice option in decision-making.* Doctoral dissertation, McGill University, 1976.

Corbin, R., & Marley, A. A. J. Random utility models with equality: An apparent, but not actual generalization of random utility models. *Journal of Mathematical Psychology,* 1974, *11,* 274–293.

Corbin, R. M., Olson, C. L., & Abbondanza, M. Context effects in optional stopping decisions. *Organizational Behavior and Human Performance,* 1975, *14,* 207–216.

Cox, D. F. (Ed.) *Risk-taking and information handling in consumer behavior.* Boston: Graduate School of Business Administration, Havard University, 1967.

Cox, D. F., & Rich. S. Perceived risk and consumer decision-making. *Journal of Marketing Research,* 1964, *1,* 32–39.

Cyert, R. M., & March, J. G. *A behavorial theory of the firm.* Englewood Cliffs, N.J.: Prentice-Hall, 1963.

Darley, J. M. and Latané, B. Bystander intervention in emergencies: Diffusion of responsibility. *Journal of Personality and Social Psychology,* 1968, *8,* 377–383.

Dickins, D., Fanelli, A., & Ferguson, V. Attractive menu items. *Journal of the American Dietetic Association,* 1954, *30,* 881–885.

Driscoll, J. M., Tognolli, J. J., & Lanzetta, J. T. Choice conflict and subjective uncertainty in decision-making. *Psychological Reports,* 1966, *18,* 427–432.

Edwards, W. Variance preference in gambling. *American Journal of Psychology,* 1954, *67,* 68–95.

Edwards, W. Optimal strategies for seeking information: Models for statistics, choice reaction times, and human information processing. *Journal of Mathematical Psychology,* 1965, *2,* 312–329.

Ellsberg, D. Risk, ambiguity, and the savage axioms. *Quarterly Journal of Economics,* 1961, *75,* 643–669.

Engel, J. F., Kollat, D. T., & Blackwell, R. D. *Consumer behavior.* New York: Holt, Rinehart & Winston, 1968.

Festinger, L. *Conflict, decision and dissonance.* Stanford: Stanford University Press, 1964.

Fischhoff, B. Hindsight-foresight: The effect of outcome knowledge on judgement under uncertainty. *Journal of Experimental Psychology: Human Perception and Performance,* 1975, *1,* 288–299.

Fischhoff, B., & Beyth, R. "I knew it would happen"—Remembered probabilities of once-future things. *Organizational Behavior and Human Performance,* 1975, *13,* 1–16.

Gilbert, J. P., & Mosteller, F. Recognizing the maximum of a sequence. *Journal of the American Statistical Association,* 1966, *61,* 35–73.

Hansen, F. *Consumer choice behaviour: A cognitive theory.* London: Collier-Macmillan, 1972.

Hogarth, R. M. Cognitive processes and the assessment of subject probability distributions. *Journal of the American Statistical Association,* 1975, *70,* 271–294.

Howard, J. A., & Sheth, J. *A theory of buyer behavior.* New York: Wiley, 1969.

Irwin, F. W., An analysis of the concept of discrimination. *American Journal of Psychology,* 1958, *71,* 152–163.

Irwin, F. W., & Smith W. A. S. Value, cost and information as determiners of decision. *Journal of Experimental Psychology,* 1957, *54,* 229–232.

Jamieson, D. G., & Petrusic, W. M. Preference and the time to choose. *Organizational Behavior and Human Performance,* 1977, *19,* 56–67.

Janis, I. L. Motivation factors in the resolution of decisional conflict. In R. Jones (Ed.), *Nebraska symposium on motivation.* Lincoln: Nebraska University Press, 1959.

Johnson, E. M., & Huber, G. P. The technology of utility assessment. *IEEE Transactions of Systems, Man and Cybernetics,* 1977, *SMC-7,* 311–325.

Kahan, J. P., Rapoport, A., & Jones, L. V. Decision-making in a sequential search task. *Perception and Psychophysics,* 1967, *2,* 374–376.

Kaufmann, W. Do you crave a life without choice? *Psychology Today,* 1973, *6,* 78–83.

Kerby, J. K. Borrowing from the behavioral sciences. *Journal of Business,* 1969, *42,* 152–161.

Klahr, D. *Decision-making in a complex environment.* Doctoral thesis, Carnegie Institute of Technology, 1967.

Kogan, N. & Wallach, M. A. *Risk taking: A study in cognition and personality.* New York: Holt, Rinehart & Winston, 1964.

Kogan, N., & Wallach, M. A. Risk taking as a function of the situation, the person and the group. In T. M. Newcomb (Ed.), *New directions in psychology* (Vol. 3). New York: Holt, Rinehart & Winston, 1967.

Lamm, H. Will an observer advise higher risk-taking after hearing a discussion of the decision-problem? *Journal of Personality and Social Psychology,* 1967, *6,* 467–471.

Lanzetta, J. T. Information acquisition in decision-making. In A. J. Harvey (Ed.), *Motivation and social interaction.* New York: Ronald Press, 1963.

Lanzetta, J. T., & Driscoll, J. N. Preference for information about an uncertain but unavoidable outcome. *Journal of Personality and Social Psychology,* 1966, *3,* 96–102.

Lanzetta, J. T., & Kanareff, V. T. Information cost, amount of payoff and level of aspiration as determinants of information-seeking in decision-making. *Behavioral Science,* 1962, *7,* 459–473.

Lee, W. *Decision theory and human behavior.* New York: Wiley, 1971.

Lewin, K. A. *A dynamic theory of personality.* New York: McGraw-Hill, 1935.

Liefeld, J. *The problem recognition stage of the consumer decision process.* Technical report of the Department of Consumer and Corporate Affairs, Ottawa, 1977.

Luce, R. D., *Individual choice behavior.* New York: Wiley, 1959.

Mack, R. P. *Planning on uncertainty.* New York: Wiley, 1971.

Maier, N. R. F. Screening solutions to upgrade quality: A new approach to problem solving under conditions of uncertainty. *Journal of Psychology,* 1960, *49,* 217–231.

March, J. G., & Simon, H. A. *Organizations.* New York: Wiley, 1958.

Milgram, S. Behavioral study of obedience. *Journal of Abnormal and Social Psychology,* 1963, *67,* 371–378.

Milgram, S. Some conditions of obedience and disobedience to authority. *Human Relations,* 1965, *18,* 57–76.

Miller, N. E. Experimental studies of conflict. In J. M. Hunt (Ed.), *Personality and the behavior disorders.* New York: Ronald Press, 1944.

Mischel, W. Preference for delayed reinforcement; an experimental study of a cultural observation. *Journal of Abnormal and Social Psychology,* 1958, *56,* 57–61.

Mischel, W. Delay of gratification, need for achievement and acquiescence in another culture. *Journal of Abnormal and Social Psychology,* 1961, *62,* 543–552.

Morlock, H. The effect of outcome desirability on information required for decision. *Behavioral Science,* 1967, *12,* 296–300.

Olander, F. Search behavior in non-simultaneous choice situations: Satisficing or maximizing. In D. Wendt & C. A. J. Vlek (Eds.), *Utility, probability and human decision-making.* Dordrecht: Reidel, 1975.

Payne, J. W. *An information search and protocol analysis of decision-making as a function of task complexity.* Unpublished manuscript, Carnegie-Mellon University, Pittsburgh, 1974.

Payne, S. L. *The art of asking questions.* Princeton: Princeton University Press, 1951.

Petrusic, W., & Jamieson, D. G. Studying preferential choice with stable probability estimates: Temporal transitivity analyses. *Acta Psychologia,* 1976, *40,* 375–383.

Pruitt, D. G. Pattern and level of risk in gambling decisions. *Psychological Review,* 1962, *69,* 187–201.

Rapoport, A. & Tversky, A. Choice behavior in an optimal stopping task. *Organizational Behavior and Human Performance,* 1970, *5,* 105–120.

Savage, L. J. *The foundations of statistics.* New York: John Wiley & Sons, Inc., 1954.

Schlaifer, R. *Introduction to statistics for business decisions.* New York: McGraw-Hill, 1961.

Shaver, K. G. *Principles of social psychology.* Cambridge: Winthrop, 1977.

Siegel, S., & Goldstein, P. A. Decision-making behavior in a two-choice uncertain outcome situation. *Journal of Experimental Psychology,* 1959, *57,* 37–42.

Simon, H. A. A behavioral model of rational choice. *Quarterly Journal of Economics,* 1955, *69,* 99–118.

Simon, H. A. Rational choice and the structure of the environment. *Psychological Review,* 1956, *63,* 129–138.

Simon, H. A. Theories of decision-making in economics and behavioral science. *American Economic Review,* 1959, *49,* 253–283.

Simon, H. A., & Sumner, R. K. Patterns in music. In B. Kleinmuntz (Ed.), *Formal representations of human judgement.* New York: Wiley, 1968.

Slovic, P., & Lichtenstein, S. Importance of variance preferences in gambling decisions. *Journal of Experimental Psychology,* 1968, *78,* 646–654.

Slovic, P., & Lichtenstein, S. Comparison of Bayesian and regression approaches to the study of information processing judgement. *Organizational Behavior and Human Performance,* 1971, *6,* 649–744.

Slovic, P., Fischhoff, B., & Lichtenstein, L. Behavioral decision theory. *Annual Review of Psychology,* 1977, *28,* 1–39.

Stäel von Holstein, C. A. S. Probabilistic forecasting: An experiment related to the stock market. *Organizational Behavior and Human Performance,* 1972, *8,* 139–158.

Starbuck, W. H. Level of aspiration. *Psychological Review,* 1963, *70,* 51–60.

Svenson, O. *Coded think-aloud protocols obtained when making a choice to purchase one of seven hypothetically offered houses: Some examples*. Progress report on project of cognitive processes and decision-making. University of Stockholm, 1974.

Taylor, J. W. The role of risk in consumer behavior. *Journal of Marketing*, 1974, *38*, 54-60.

Tukey, J. W. Conclusions vs. decisions. In P. Badia, A. Haber, & R. Runyon (Eds.), *Research problems in psychology*. Reading, Mass.: Addison-Wesley, 1970.

Tversky, A. Elimination by aspects: A theory of choice. *Psychological Review*, 1972, *79*, 281-299. (a)

Tversky, A. Choice by elimination. *Journal of Mathematical Psychology*, 1972, *9*, 341-367. (b)

Tversky, A. *On the psychology of choice behavior*. Paper read at the Mathematical Social Science Board Workshop on the Theory and Measurement of Economic Choice Behavior, Berkeley, June, 1976.

Uhl, C. N., & Hoffman, P. J. *Contagion effects and the stability of judgement*. Paper read at the Western Psychological Association, Monterey, California, 1958.

Van der Meer, H. C. Decision-making: The influence of probability preference, variance preference and expected value on strategy in gambling. *Acta Psychologia*, 1963, *21*, 321-359.

Walster, E., & Festinger, L. In L. Festinger (Ed.), *Conflict, decision and dissonance*. Stanford: Stanford University Press, 1964.

Winkler, R. L., & Cummings, L. L. On the choice of a concensus distribution in Bayesian analysis. *Organizational Behavior and Human Performance*, 1972, *7*, 63-76.

Yakimovich, D., & Salz, E. Helping behavior: The cry for help. *Psychonomic Science*, 1971, *23*, 427-428.

Zajonc, R. B., & Burnstein, E. The resolution of cognitive conflict under uncertainty. *Human Relations*, 1961, *14*, 113-119.

Zimbardo, P. The human choice: Individuation, reason and order versus deindividuation, impulse and chaos. In W. J. Arnold & D. Levine (Eds.), *Nebraska symposium on motivation, 1969*. Lincoln: University of Nebraska Press, 1970.

4 Analyzing Decision Behavior: The Magician's Audience

John S. Carroll
Loyola University of Chicago

You sit in the audience as the magician makes pigeons appear and disappear. You know it is a trick, that the pigeons are stowed quietly in the magician's clothes. You watch with intense concentration to see the pigeon transferred from hand to coat or coat to hand. You are sure that it happens, but you never see it. The magician is the master of illusion, and we are enthralled by illusion.

Why can't we catch the magician? One reason is misdirection: The magician gets us to look at his or her face or hand gestures, the behaviors to which we conventionally attend. A second reason is misrepresentation: We believe we know how the trick is done and attend carefully to our "theory" of the trick, but we are wrong and the magician works the trick through unmonitored paths. Related to this, we perceive the trick as composed of those elements we can see. We underestimate the back-stage preparation—the props, the teamwork, the hours of practice. A third reason is that we have misplaced faith in our eyes: We believe that we can see any hand movement the magician makes, but we are wrong. In front of our bright and wary eyes, the magician's hands are simply faster than our perception.

In some ways, recent research reveals the decision maker and the decision analyst in the roles of magician and audience. The decision analyst is misdirected by the importance of the moment when the decision maker identifies a selection. We are seduced by language and common sense into believing that the choice *is* the decision. Yet, as Corbin points out (this volume), the choice is the end product of the decision, the moment when we see the pigeon in the magician's hand. The decision is a process of arriving at a choice, the process by which the pigeon got into the magician's hand.

The decision analyst is also caught in his or her own representation of the decision task. We believe that we understand the task well enough to abstract the critical features and embed them in a laboratory analog of the task. Yet, as demonstrated by Ebbesen and Konečni (this volume), our laboratory simulations can be markedly different than real-world decisions. Kahneman and Tversky (1979) also illustrate how decision behavior is responsive to task features that are irrelevant to some theoretical analyses, but that affect the way the decision problem is encoded. Einhorn (this volume) and others have pointed out that use of decision rules or heuristics is specific to the surface appearance of the task rather than to its formal structure.

Finally, like the audience who believes in the fundamental ability of their eyes to capture the magic trick, decision analysts believe that their methods are capable of capturing the decision process. Corbin (this volume) and Payne (this volume) present arguments for new methods of observing decision behavior, analogous to observing a magician with high-speed photography, or sneaking backstage to watch the magician practice and prepare the props. But, another potential danger in our methods is less obvious. The process of verifying our ideas about decision behavior, like the process of verifying decisions, is more confirmation biased than we realize. Our capability for creating tasks that match our theory, the adaptability of subjects, and the robustness of our models (Dawes & Corrigan, 1974) makes disconfirmation difficult. Our successes at predicting decision behavior serve to confirm our faith in the model of decision making, but our failures are not taken seriously enough to produce fundamental questions about our theory. Einhorn documents these failures to profit from experience in lay decision makers, but the principle applies as well to decision analysts. The magician's audience keeps watching the magician's hands over and over again, no matter how many times the trick is performed. This problem cannot be solved by new methods, it can only be appreciated.

What, then, can we do to better understand decision behavior? What aspects of the magician's behavior should we focus on to reveal the trick? I would suggest that we conceptualize the magician–decision maker as knowledgeable about tasks and adaptive to the task structure as he or she represents it. To assess this knowledge, observe this adaptation, and portray this representation, we need methods that remain true to the performance of interest with minimal intrusion of the decision analyst's preconceptions. Further, we have been too narrow in our study of decision behavior, often studying only choice processes. We must study decision makers from the point at which they recognize a decision could be made, through the encoding of the problem, and even including postdecisional regret and learning (cf. Corbin, this volume; Einhorn, this volume). In the remainder of this chapter, I discuss these topics in somewhat more detail.

THE KNOWLEDGEABLE DECISION MAKER

For the past several years, I have been investigating the decision process of expert parole decision makers in collaboration with John Payne. We began with a rather simple idea of how the parole decision was made. Briefly, parole was hypothesized to have two components or goals: punishment of past crimes and incapacitation for expected future crimes. Facts in the case history and the knowledge possessed by the decision maker would be used to produce a causal attribution regarding past criminal acts. The more these crimes were attributed to characteristics of the offender (particularly intentional acts), the more punishment would be assigned. The more these crimes were attributed to temporally enduring factors, the more incapacitation would be considered because future crime would appear more likely.

In testing these ideas, it became apparent that college students may think about parole in this manner, but it is an inadequate description of the experts. Expert judgment appears to be based upon specific knowledge about types of crime and types of criminals. Features of the case evoke a coherent body of knowledge that includes attribution about the causes of the crime, expectations for future behavior, as well as recommendations for treatment (Carroll, 1978). This description of decision behavior is very similar to the schema concept that recently has been developed in cognitive psychology (Abelson, 1976; Rumelhart & Ortony, 1976). Rather than considering the decision maker as exhaustively weighing the implications of case facts in accord with normative models such as Bayes' Theorem, utility maximization, or the Covariation Principle (Kelley, 1971), we portray the decision maker as possessing a rich store of knowledge organized around schemas such as the "heavy drug user," the "alcohol abuser," the "aimless follower," and so forth. Once the schema is evoked, it guides the acquisition and use of further case information. Different case information becomes relevant to evaluate and treat different types of cases. There may be strong confirmatory biases operating that prevent the schema from being easily disconfirmed by case facts (cf. Einhorn, this volume). Our task as decision analysts becomes to portray this knowledge and to determine how specific schemas are evoked by specific case information.

But what about nonexpert decision makers? Do they use schemas also or do they do something different, perhaps simpler to analyze? The preceding analysis would suggest that nonexperts would have fewer and less detailed schemas. Like novice and expert chessplayers (Chase & Simon, 1973) or an audience and a magician, the lay person has only a general idea and makes few distinctions among instances. It is also more likely that the lay person and the decision analyst will share these schemas. I believe that is what happened to my own research and it may explain why students responded to our simulated parole task the way we thought they (and we) would.

THE ADAPTIVE DECISION MAKER

If you ask a subject to decide, he or she will decide. If you make it clear that the subject need not state an opinion, he or she may not (cf. Corbin, this volume). If you give a lot of information or a little, increase the time pressure, change the reward structure, move from real life to written descriptions or mathematical scale values, the decision maker will oblige by doing something reasonable. People are adaptive to task structure; they change as the task changes. In fact, we are so good at adapting that it is automatic. People change their attitudes without realizing that they have changed (Wixon & Laird, 1976), they congratulate themselves on predicting events without realizing that they have changed their predictions to conform to the event (Fischhoff & Beyth, 1975). Perhaps such changes are the most reliable decision process.

But adaptation is not perfect. Our perceptions and memory and other information-processing capacities are limited by biology and conflicting demands (Newell & Simon, 1972). We adapt to the task as we see it, and our representations of the task have a conservative nature—we tend to see a task in terms of others with which we are familiar. Einhorn points out (this volume) that experience or professional training (even in decision analysis) consists of being able to recognize problem types, but these problem types are typically defined by content rather than structure (e.g., save-a-life versus lose-a-life problems). This poses a tremendous problem for decision analysts: Our laboratory tasks and decision analogs may produce behavior that is substantially different than the naturalistic task (cf. Ebbesen & Konečni, this volume), and subjects may not be aware of how their own behavior has changed from one task to its theoretical analog (e.g., Nisbett & Wilson, 1977). Only if we can separately get at the decision maker's representation of the task can we unconfound task content and decision processes.

THE REPRESENTATION OF THE TASK

As shown by Kahneman and Tversky (1979), it makes a great deal of difference whether the subject treats a problem as "saving 300 lives for sure or a 50% chance of saving 600 lives or zero lives" or treats it as "300 people die for sure or a 50% chance that 600 people die or zero die." Similarly, behavior varies depending on whether a tax cut is thought of as a gain or as a smaller loss. Social psychologists are also cognizant of this issue; they develop elaborate cover stories whose purpose is to influence subjects to treat a laboratory situation as a certain kind of reality and not to analyze certain features of the situation that are actually of high importance.

There are two research programs that have studied problem representation that contain illustrative methods and ideas from which decision makers could borrow. Hayes and his associates (Simon & Hayes, 1976) gave different subjects problem isomorphs—the same problem structure in different verbal contexts. For example, the Tower of Hanoi problem consists of moving disks on pegs, but the same formal problem can also be expressed as stationary disks and moving pegs, as extraterrestrial monsters of different sizes transferring different-sized objects, as a "tea ceremony" involving persons performing various tasks comprising the ceremony, and so forth. A variety of problem types have been examined. This research shows that different contents evoke different problem representations and different subsequent behaviors. Their method of determining problem representation is to collect verbal protocols from the point at which the task is *first given* to subjects, and thus observe the construction of the representation.

Siegler (1978) has studied children's performance on a Piagetian task in which a balance scale has some weights at certain distances on either side of the fulcrum. The arms are locked and subjects are asked to predict which side will go down when the arms are released. Siegler has identified four strategies for solving this problem, and these strategies represent a developmental sequence that begins after a pure guess or no rule stage:

1. Choose the side with more weight; if they are tied, guess or say "balance."
2. Choose the side with more weight; if they are tied, choose the side with weights farther from the fulcrum.
3. Examine weight and distance for implications; if the implications conflict, "muddle through" (idiosyncratic guesses).
4. Examine weight and distance for implications; if the implications conflict, compute cross products.

Notice that scientific reasoning in this case consists of the acquisition of certain lexicographic, dominance, and compensatory decision strategies. Except for the fact that this task has a normative model based on the physical sciences, it is a typical decision task. Another interesting feature is that more advanced strategies can err on problems that earlier strategies got right. For example, when three weights three units left and two weights four units right form the problem, Rules 1 and 2 get it right, but Rule 3 often misses.

Siegler studied 3- and 4-year-olds who had *no* rule for the task. He gave them 16 trials with feedback (watch the balance scale after it is released). None of ten 3-year-olds but six of ten 4-year-olds learned Rule 1 after this experience. What was behind the greater ability of the older children to learn from experience? Siegler asked a group of 3- and 4-year-olds to look at the balance scale and then reconstruct it from memory. Three-year-olds could reconstruct neither weight nor distance; in contrast, 4-year-olds could properly reproduce the weights on each side, but not the distances. After training 3-year-olds to encode weight, they were able to learn from experience. In summary, knowledge about a task depended on the ability to learn from experience, which was possible only if the task representation included the relevant task features.

It should be obvious that the questions raised by Einhorn of how decision makers can learn from experience are addressed in this research. Further, the success of Siegler's research is completely determined by the accuracy with which he identified the structure of the task and possible alternate task representations. Such a strategy might shed new light on the problem faced by Ebbe-sen and Konečni in studying how judges set bail and sentence. For example, what do judges remember about a case immediately after bail or sentence is set? Are they encoding different things in the lab than in the courtroom? It seems clear that in order to understand the determinants of decisions, it is more important to ask questions about which cues are used, and how they are related to the subject's task representation, than about the precise combinatorial rule the subject uses for evaluating cues (Dawes & Corrigan, 1974).

WHAT IS DECISION BEHAVIOR?

The Corbin, Einhorn, and Ebbesen and Konečni chapters in this volume con-verge in recommending that we broaden our realm of inquiry. Corbin suggests that we must consider prechoice behavior such as recognizing that a choice exists, determining when and how to decide, determining when to seek more information or more alternatives, and determining when *not* to decide. Einhorn demonstrates that postdecisional behaviors are crucial: What is it we learn from decisions and their outcomes that affect or fail to affect our future decision making? Ebbesen and Konečni attack decision analysts for focusing on decision processes based upon cues selected and processed by the experimenter. The very presentation of cues in this manner may circumvent the most crucial parts of the decision process. Decision research suggests that the selection, salience, or rep-resentation of aspects of the decision task are at least as important as the com-binatorial rules that are later applied. By presenting the decision maker with a few palatable, predigested cues, we may strongly and mistakenly determine the outcome. Ebbesen and Konečni also point out that a judge's decision behavior may not only occur in court, but also during impromptu chats with the district attorney.

METHODS FOR STUDYING DECISION BEHAVIOR

If I were interested in studying a magician's tricks, I would not hire people to sit in the audience and code behavior. Better strategies would be high-speed photog-raphy, interruption of the trick perhaps accompanied by physical search, careful observation of backstage events before and during the tricks, and paying the magician a large sum of money to tell me the tricks. Obviously, most people are not as aware of their decision behavior as a magician is of his or her act. However, the fact remains that decision behavior is a broad domain, and a variety of methods will yield more than a single method.

I think the decision theorist should always attempt to get as close as possible to the actual behaviors of interest. For example, we cannot study judicial sentenc-ing without first observing actual judges making actual decisions. Only then can we begin devising useful and appropriate methods. Because decision behaviors are dense over time, methods that track this rich and complex behavior are useful. Process tracing techniques (see Payne, this volume) are one set of useful techniques. However, process tracing techniques are no panacea; there are just as many devastating problems with their use as with any method yet devised. One interesting feature of these techniques bears comment. A prime function of process tracing techniques has little do with "mental" processes. Rather, these techniques can help the decision analyst represent the *task* as well as the subject's thoughts. The focus on temporal properties of behavior leads to a detailed description of what a decision maker *does,* both mentally (we hope) and physically. What information is examined, what sources are tapped, who is consulted? Often the decision maker has no access to, and therefore no knowledge of, some variable that is hypothetically important. We may not need fancy equipment and information-processing techniques to find this out, just a little common sense, an openness to gathering information about decision behavior, and an overall desire to have a detailed representation of what a decision maker does in a decision task.

CONCLUSIONS

Decision behavior often seems like magic, at least when we are not focusing on the shortcomings of the decision maker. Progress will be made, I think, by creative redefinitions of the nature of decision behavior and decision research. The creation of new ideas in a science truly verges on the magical. The Ebbesen and Konečni, Einhorn, and Corbin chapters in this volume are the material from which fundamental contributions emerge. They challenge old ideas and provide new ways of looking at decision behavior. As a result, the study of decision making grows and changes, giving the researcher more possibilities to check out, more ways of approaching the field. This is the excitement of watching a magician work, for, suddenly, the impossible is possible, the normal is unusual, and our mind is energized and intrigued by the wonders of the mundane.

ACKNOWLEDGMENTS

Support for the writing of this chapter was provided by the National Institute of Mental Health Grant 7RO1MH32855-01. I would like to thank John Payne for his helpful comments and moral support.

REFERENCES

Abelson, R. P. Script processing in attitude formation and decision making. In J. S. Carroll & J. W. Payne (Eds.), *Cognition and social behavior.* Hillsdale, N.J.: Lawrence Erlbaum Associates, 1976.

Carroll, J. S. Causal attributions in expert parole decisions. *Journal of Personality and Social Psychology,* 1978, *36,* 1501–1511.

Chase, W. G., & Simon. H. A. The mind's eye in chess. In W. G. Chase (Ed.), *Visual information processing.* New York: Academic Press, 1973.

Dawes, R. M., & Corrigan, B. Linear models in decision making. *Psychological Bulletin,* 1974, *81,* 95–106.

Fischhoff, B., & Beyth, R. "I knew it would happen"—Remembered probabilities of once-future things. *Organizational Behavior and Human Performance,* 1975, *13,* 1–16.

Kahneman, D., & Tversky, A. Prospect theory: An analysis of decision under risk. *Econometrica,* 1979, *47,* 263–291.

Kelley, H. H. *Attribution in social interaction.* Morristown, N.J.: General Learning Press, 1971.

Newell, A., & Simon, H. A. *Human problem solving.* Englewood Cliffs, N.J.: Prentice-Hall, 1972.

Nisbett, R. E., & Wilson, T. D. Telling more than we can know: Verbal reports on mental processes. *Psychological Review,* 1977, *84,* 231–259.

Rumelhart, D. E., & Ortony, A. The representation of knowledge in memory. In R. C. Anderson, R. J. Spiro, & W. E. Montague (Eds.), *Schooling and the acquisition of knowledge.* Hillsdale, N.J.: Lawrence Erlbaum Associates, 1976.

Siegler, R. S. The origins of scientific reasoning. In R. S. Seigler (Ed.), *Children's thinking: What develops?* Hillsdale, N.J.: Lawrence Erlbaum Associates, 1978.

Simon, H. A., & Hayes, J. R. The understanding process: Problem isomorphs. *Cognitive Psychology,* 1976, *8,* 165–190.

Wixon, D. R., & Laird, J. D. Awareness and attitude change in the forced-compliance paradigm: The importance of when. *Journal of Personality and Social Psychology,* 1976, *34,* 376–384.

5

The Very Guide of Life: The Use of Probabilistic Information for Making Decisions

Gordon F. Pitz
Southern Illinois University at Carbondale

It is interesting, but perhaps not surprising, that of all of applied mathematics, no topic generates more discussion among philosophers and scientists than does probability theory. The idea of a precise formal treatment of uncertainty is itself a paradox. How can we speak precisely of that which is known without precision? Apparently, we can only do so by employing the calculus of probabilities.

The perceived relevance of probability for helping us to deal with uncertainty is not new. Among the skeptics of ancient Greece, Clitomacus is said to have proposed that choosing the outcome with higher probability is a useful rule to follow (Bevan, 1913). This same principle seems to have cropped up on several occasions in the history of western thought. "To us probability is the very guide of life," stated Bishop Butler in an early 18th century theological treatise.[1] The same idea was expressed later, in greater detail, by John Maynard Keynes, a critic of the frequentist approach to probability theory that had become dominant by the end of the 19th century (Keynes, 1921). Unfortunately, until well into the 20th century, all of the proponents of a wider use of probability theory appear not to have solved the most important problem: How can we assess the probabilities of alternative outcomes in a rational way. Valid procedures for obtaining numerical assessments of uncertainty are very recent. For example, although Keynes' ideas were important in the development of nonfrequentist probability theory, he stated explicitly that for many events a numerical assessment of probability is impossible. Only the Bayesian version of probability theory developed during the last 40 years or so has promised an adequate solution to this problem.

---

[1]Bishop Joseph Butler, *The analogy of religion, natural and revealed, to the constitution and cause of nature*, 1736. Quoted by Keynes (1921).

It is now well known that, when left to their own resources, people are not always capable of following consistently the prescription of Clitomacus, Bishop Butler, and Bayes' theorem. A series of studies (e.g., Tversky & Kahneman, 1974) has shown how errors and biases make it difficult for a person to select accurately the most probable event. It is inevitable, then, that psychologists should seek to understand and, if possible, correct these flaws of human judgment. This cannot be done, of course, without understanding the decision process itself.

Failures to respond consistently might be traced to one of two sources. First, there may exist limitations on the kind of information processing of which the person is capable. We know that the limits of short-term memory make certain kinds of mental operations impossible. There are limits to perceptual sensitivity, to the ability to process information simultaneously from several sources, and to the ability to store in long-term memory rapidly occurring information. A second source of errors may be the problem solving strategies that a person brings to a task. Such errors are not due to fundamental limitations on information processing capacity, but rather to the strategies that people use in approaching the task.

As suggested by Simon (1969), a useful first cut at a descriptive theory of performance can be obtained by discovering what the person is trying to do. It is often the case that a person's strategy is one that is best suited to solving the problem as he or she perceives it. It is likely, then, that many of the observed inconsistencies in behavior are the result of inappropriate perceptions of the task. Other errors and inaccuracies may arise because a person's strategy is adapted to the constraints that are imposed by limitations on information processing abilities. These limitations may make certain kinds of cognitive operations difficult or impossible, while others are more readily available. In developing a theory of how people cope with uncertainty, it is necessary to show what cognitive operations are available to a person, and how these operations are combined to form a processing strategy. A complete understanding of decision making must depend on an adequate theory of basic processes and their use in complex strategies.

A THEORY OF PROBABILISTIC INFORMATION PROCESSING

It seems clear that, inconsistencies and errors notwithstanding, people frequently do manage to deal adequately with their uncertain environment. For example, anyone who does much grocery shopping must soon learn the random distribution of quantities such as the price of eggs. A successful shopper should be able to recognize that a particular price is unusually low or unreasonably high. What is not clear is just how this knowledge is acquired, and what form it takes. To discover how probabilistic information is learned and used, one might begin by asking what abilities the shopper must possess in order to respond appropriately in an uncertain environment.

The ability to learn the distributional properties of probabilistic information is critical to successful performance. This information must make up part of a person's general knowledge. Hence, any theory dealing with the processing of probabilistic information must first describe the information that constitutes the decision maker's knowledge. The theory must also deal with the processes that use this knowledge; it is necessary to describe how external information is translated into an internal representation, and how the decision maker uses that knowledge in making decisions. Ideally, the structure and the processes postulated by a theory of decision making should be consistent with everything else that is known about human knowledge. In practice, current theories in other areas of cognitive psychology may suggest where to look for suitable theories of decision making.

My own approach to probabilistic information processing has been to ask what information a person must have available, and what basic processes must be operating, for the person to exhibit the behavior observed in an experiment. I begin by making a number of assumptions, based on findings in other areas of cognitive psychology. First, I assume that the internal representation of the information in a decision task cannot be different in structure from the representation of other information. Hence, the structure postulated by a theory of probabilistic information processing must be quite general in its applicability. Second, I assume that, however probabilistic information is stored, it is not stored as a direct copy of the stimulus information. In representing the information internally, the decision maker exhibits both selectivity, which results in some information being ignored, and elaboration, which results in the creation of new information not contained in the stimulus itself. The process whereby a person translates the stimulus information into some internal structure I have referred to as encoding.

My third assumption is that the information processing employs certain basic cognitive operations that are quite simple, and largely universal. These operations are used both in the encoding process and in subsequent decision making that employs the internal representation of the information. A complete theory of decision making must be built up from these elementary operations. Fourth, I have assumed that both the elementary operations and the representation of the information are subject to limitations on the capacity of the human information processing system. For example, the selectivity found in processing information presumably reflects the limitations of short-term memory and limitations on the rate at which information can be stored in long-term memory. Cognitive limitations also restrict the number of items of information that can be considered simultaneously by a decision maker when a decision is being made.

Finally, and perhaps most importantly, I have assumed that any general statements that can be made about decision-making abilities and processes are limited to statements describing the structure of knowledge and the elementary cognitive operations. The way in which these operations are combined and applied to the knowledge structure is assumed to be under strategic control. Hence, one is likely to find large differences in performance from one person to the next, and in the same person as the nature of the task, or the context in which the task is presented, is changed.

As one moves from general assumptions to the development of a specific theory, the way in which the details of the theory are presented seems to some degree to be unimportant. It appears that, in general, there can be no empirical distinction between theoretical systems that are expressed broadly enough. Although a particular strong version of a theory may be falsified, any data that are adequately explained by one theoretical approach can be explained equally well in terms of some other theory. Demonstrations of this principle have been provided for serial and parallel models of information processing (J. R. Anderson, 1976; Townsend, 1972), and for issues concerning the representation of information in imagery form (J. R. Anderson, 1978). Within the area of decision making, a theoretical representation of information in one form (normative theory, information integration theory, computer simulation model) can probably be translated into any other. In constructing models to represent theories of performance in decision tasks, I have employed a particular kind of symbolic list structure that seems to be plausible, and that makes theory construction relatively easy. However, I make no claim for the unique validity of such a representation.

Before describing this structure, it may be helpful to define more explicitly the nature of the decision task that I have used in most experiments. First, I have made a distinction between the concepts of "population" and "sample." These terms are used theoretically in a sense that is related to, but broader than, the equivalent terms in common statistical usage. By a sample, I refer to the information that a decision maker has observed for any given problem; by population, I mean the presumed source of the information, which may be either known or unknown. The terms "data generator" or "data-generating process" might also describe what I have called the population. I have also made a distinction between "statistics" and "parameters," terms that refer to properties of the sample and population respectively. Again, these terms are defined in a way similar to, but broader than, their statistical usage.

It is also useful to distinguish between two categories of decision problems, which I refer to as "prediction" and "inference." In the prediction task, there is a single population, the characteristics of which are either explained to the decision maker or else are to be inferred from an observed sample. The problem is to predict which of two or more possible samples is the more likely to be observed at some future time. For the inference problem, there exist two or more populations, again with characteristics that may be given directly or inferred from prior sample information. A single sample of unknown origin is presented, and the decision maker's task is to indicate from which population the sample is thought to have been taken. Other decision tasks can be defined, but these two have been used most frequently in the study of probabilistic information processing.

To describe the structure that people might use to encode probabilistic information, I have employed symbolic list structures made up of hierarchical property lists. These property lists are derived from the encoding of information presented to the decision maker, together with information that he or she generates as part of the elaboration and decision-making process. Each property on the list consists of two elements: a name for the property followed by a description or value for the property. The description may itself be a property list, which gives rise to the hierarchical nature of the structure. An example of a simple structure for a task using quantitative information is shown in Table 5.1; further details are given in Pitz (1977a). The form of the structure was chosen for convenience in defining computer routines, not to embody any strong psychological assumptions.

What is important psychologically is the distinction within the structure between populations and samples. I have assumed that in both prediction and inference problems, the distinction between parameters of a population and statistics of a sample is the foundation of subsequent problem-solving and decision-making activity. Of course, these particular words are not necessarily those that a person would use in describing his or her own knowledge. However, insofar as it is difficult to distinguish between the sample and the population, the decision problem will be difficult to solve.

TABLE 5.1
Example of Property List Constructed for
Decision Task

POPULATION NAME [LABEL 1][a]
        PARAMETERS MEAN VALUE EXPECTED [X][a]
SAMPLE NAME [LABEL 2][a]
    SIZE 4
    SELECTION FROM [LABEL 1]
        METHOD RANDOM
    MEMBERS FIRST VALUE OBSERVED [X1][a]
        SECOND VALUE OBSERVED [X2][a]
        THIRD VALUE OBSERVED [X3][a]
        FOURTH VALUE OBSERVED [X4][a]
    STATISTICS MEAN VALUE ESTIMATED [X]

---

[a] [LABEL 1] and [LABEL 2] are names by which the population and sample can be identified. [X1], [X2], [X3], and [X4] are observed sample values; [X] is the estimated value of the sample mean, which has been used as the expected value for the population mean.

In some decision tasks, information about population and sample is presented separately, so constructing a representation that keeps population and sample properties distinct presents no problem. In other cases, however, information about the population may not be given directly. In daily experience, it is very rare that we are told explicitly what the characteristics of a data generator might be. In these cases, it is necessary for a person to infer properties of the population from information that is contained in the sample. Such tasks require a person to engage in abstraction, i.e., incorporating into the representational structure information that has not been presented directly.

The process of abstraction is one that has interested psychologists concerned with a number of different phenomena. A theoretical concept that has been employed to describe the end product of abstraction is a "prototype." The term is convenient, although its definition has been variable, and often imprecise. In studies of recognition memory, Bransford and Franks (1971) and Franks and Bransford (1971) assumed that a prototype is an abstract schema that is inferred from the specific information presented in the experiment. The concept was also used by Posner and Keele (1968) and by Reed (1972), for whom a prototype was an average stimulus, defined in a multidimensional space, and again inferred from specific stimulus items.

Not all theorists have agreed that an abstraction process must be postulated in order to explain categorization and recognition memory performance. However, whether or not it is necessary for a theory to postulate abstraction processes that involve the creation of new information is probably another of those issues that is empirically undecidable. It is not even clear that a parsimony criterion argues against an abstraction theory. In constructing theories to account for some of the data in decision tasks, it is easier to account for decision strategies by assuming the existence of an abstraction process than by assuming that the subject stores only a direct copy of the stimulus information.

I have used the term "prototype" to refer to any structure that describes that representation of information about a population that is inferred from sample information. It is still largely an open question what properties of the population might be abstracted. However, several experiments have suggested that the process of inferring an average value for uncertain quantities is a very general one, and that the estimated population average is a very important part of the prototype. These studies are reviewed in a later section of this chapter.

Most of my recent research has concerned decisions that are based on quantitative information. In such cases, it has appeared that certain unique features of the information also play an important role in a decision maker's strategies. As is noted later, there is evidence that extreme values for an uncertain quantity—that is, the smallest and largest values—are especially salient. The extremes are related to decisions based on the sample information. These findings are consistent with data from several other studies, which have suggested the importance of extreme values in learning to use probabilistic and other quantitative information. For example, Brehmer (1976) and Brehmer and Lindberg (1970) have studied how people learn the relationship between two quantitative variables. Some of their results suggest that extreme values for the two quantities are particularly important in determining the learning that takes place. Potts (1972) studied the encoding of ordinal information. He found that, when subjects answered questions based on this information, the extremes were particularly important in determining how quickly a question was answered; questions involving items from either extreme of the ordering were answered faster. Hence, it appears that the extremes serve as anchor points around which the other quantitative information is encoded.

One other set of findings is important in understanding how probabilistic information might be represented when it is quantitative in form. A number of authors (e.g., Moyer & Landauer, 1967; Potts, 1974) have argued that ordinal and numerical information may be stored in an analog fashion, so that operations using this information are similar to perceptual operations that take place with directly given stimulus quantities. I have found it convenient to assume that quantitative information is encoded in analog form. The theory can then be expressed in terms of processes that deal directly with the quantities, rather than working with the symbolic information contained in numbers. Hence, in determining which of two numbers, for example 363, 394, is closer to a third number, 371, it may not be necessary to perform any subtractions to obtain the answer.

Decision strategies can be constructed from elementary operations that work with these psychophysical comparisons. A theory of decision making needs to specify the elementary cognitive operations, from which are constructed the various strategies that a person might employ. In constructing computer programs to simulate decision-making activity, I have tried to describe basic operations that seem to be necessary, yet are psychologically plausible. Some of them have been suggested by the work of others who have dealt with more elementary tasks involving quantitative information (e.g., Buckley & Gillman, 1974). However, there is clearly a need for more systematic study of the elementary processes involving quantitative information.

Table 5.2 lists the quantitative operations that have been used in constructing models of decision strategies. Each operation requires certain quantities or other information to be active in short-term memory. These operations have so far sufficed to provide explanations of observed behavior; I make no claim, however, that they are exhaustive. The operations were defined so that they fit into a simulation language written in LISP (Pitz, 1972). It may be seen that some operations generate new quantities out of old information, whereas some operations return the value True or False after comparing two quantities. It should be noted that these functions work with internally represented quantities, not symbols. Hence, for example, EQUALP tests to see if two quantities appear to be of

TABLE 5.2
Elementary Operations Using Quantitative Information

Operation	Active Quantities[a]	Description
ENCODE	None	Generate quantity corresponding to current stimulus value
VALUE	None	Activate quantity named by current label
NAME	X	Assign label to quantity X
DIFFERENCE	X Y	Generate quantity equivalent to difference between currently active quantities
NLARGER	X Y	Activate label of larger of two quantities
NSMALLER	X Y	Activate label of smaller of two quantities
WEIGHT	X Y	Generate a quantity that expresses X and Y as a relative weight
WAVERAGE	X Y W	Generate a quantity that is a weighted average of X and Y, using weight W
EQUALP	X Y	True if X is (approximately) equal to Y
LARGERP	X Y	True if X is larger than Y
SMALLERP	X Y	True if X is smaller than Y

[a] Each quantity is part of a structure that uses the quantity as the value for some property on a property list. The label referred to in the table is the name of the property.

the same order of magnitude. These predicate functions require a level of precision for their operation, the setting of which can be an important part of a decision maker's strategy.

Especially important in dealing with quantitative information is the operation WAVERAGE (form the weighted average of two quantities). This operation is necessary to account for the importance of the averaging process in many decision tasks (Pitz, 1977a). Whether it is an "elementary" operation, in the sense that is not composed of other, more basic operations, is not clear. However, I have not been able to construct models for any information integration task without it. The importance of the averaging process in probabilistic information processing has been emphasized by several authors (e.g., Lichtenstein, Earle, & Slovic, 1975; Shanteau, 1975). Algebraic models of averaging behavior have been widely studied (see N. H. Anderson, 1974). Typically, these studies have either sought context effects in subjective averages, or have compared averaging with additive models of information integration. However, there seems to have been no attempt to examine averaging mechanisms from the point of view of cognitive theory. Given the prevalence of the averaging process, this is unfortunate.

The operations that use the quantitative information must be incorporated into a control structure. The control mechanisms that I have employed use production systems for defining decision strategies. These production systems work with information that is held in short-term memory, assuming a structure for the information like that in Table 5.1. I have described operation of the production systems in more detail elsewhere (Pitz, 1972, 1977a). Examples of the use of production systems for representing theoretical ideas are given by Pitz (1977a and 1977b). These examples are not complete; a great deal remains to be done in showing how various kinds of information processing can be modeled in this way.

METHODS USED TO STUDY DECISION MAKING UNDER UNCERTAINTY

By definition, the study of decision making presupposes that the principal response of interest is a person's choice. In the simplest case, there are only two alternatives, say *R1* and *R2*. The subjects must predict which of two samples is more likely to be generated from a single population, or must infer which of two populations has generated a single sample. The function of a theory of decision making is to explain how the response was generated, in terms of the information that preceded the choice, and other variables that might be relevant. The success of a theory that attempts to predict which response will be generated may be limited, because a minimum of information is conveyed by a single response, particularly if the response is binary. Nevertheless, a great deal of theoretical headway has been made by using a dependent variable no more complex than the proportion of responses for particular properties of the information.

Somewhat more information can be learned by assessing the degree of belief or uncertainty that accompanies a person's response. Suppose that two different decisions have been made. It is then possible to determine which of the two choices was made with greater certainty. One way of doing this is to have a person give numerical ratings, such as probability estimates. However, a difficulty with the rating procedure is the unreliability and instability of subjects' numerical judgments. There is some evidence (Martin & Gettys, 1969) that ordinal properties inferred from numerical responses are less reliable than ordinal judgments given directly. To overcome this problem, it is possible to ask subjects to assess directly which of two decisions was made with greater certainty. In one study of prediction decisions (Pitz, 1977b), I used a computer-controlled procedure in order to infer a rank ordering of decisions in terms of difficulty. Subjects were given pairs of decisions and were asked which they found to be easier. The pairing of the decisions was chosen in order to generate a complete ordering of the decisions in terms of difficulty.

When the sample information is quantitative in nature—that is, when the information consists of value for some continuously variable uncertain quantity—other methods are available for extracting more information from the decision maker. The methods involve eliciting a cutoff value for the uncertain quantity, a value that divides the range of possible values into two functionally different sets. As a simple example, consider a prediction problem for which a single population has been defined, and in which a single value (x) for an uncertain quantity (X) is presented. The subject is asked to indicate whether a future sample value is likely to be less than x or greater than x. One might seek a value x^* such that the subject believes $X < x^*$ is just as likely as $X > x^*$. This value then defines a subjective median for the population. The concept of a subjective median can be generalized to include any number of regions for which subjective probabilities are equivalent.

It is not necessary to ask the subject to estimate these indifference values directly. In a number of studies, I have used an iterative procedure for inferring indifference values from a sequence of decisions (see Pitz, 1974, 1975; Pitz, Leung, Hamilos, & Terpening, 1976). In these studies, I made use of the concept of subjective tertiles, which are two points that divide a continuum into three equally likely regions. One may define a prediction task by presenting any two values, say x_1 and x_2, and asking in which of the three regions defined by x_1 and x_2 the next value of X will fall. The values of x_1 and x_2 can be modified sequentially in such a way that they converge on the tertiles. The advantage of this procedure is that the response task is kept as simple as possible while valuable quantitative information is made available for the theoretical analysis.

In an inference task, the equivalent of an indifference point is the decision threshold. This is the value for some quantity at which a person's decision would change from favoring one population to favoring another. It may be assumed that the decision rule consists of dividing the range of values for X into a small number of regions, so that within each region the decision would be the same. In the simplest case, there would be only two regions, which could be uniquely defined by a single cutoff. There are a number of methods for estimating the cutoff value. One approach is to estimate the value statistically from a number of binary decisions for varying values of X. A second approach is to ask the decision maker to generate numerical values for the cutoff directly. It has been reported recently by Kubovy and Healy (1977) that there are no systematic differences in the decision rules employed under these two conditions. The equivalence of statistical estimates and direct estimates was also observed in a dissertation by Barrett (1970).

A third technique for assessing cutoff values uses an iterative procedure similar to that employed in assessing indifference regions in a prediction task. The value of X for a given decision can be modified so that it converges on the cutoff value. This procedure has been employed with success in a recent study (Pitz & Englert, 1979), in which we used normal distributions for X that varied in both mean and variance. When both means and variances are different, there can be two cutoff values; extreme values of X in either direction may suggest the population with the larger variance. In our study, an iterative procedure was used, first, to determine whether the subject was using one or two cutoffs, and second, to infer the location of the cutoffs.

All of the procedures discussed so far are concerned directly with a person's choice, and perhaps with the level of uncertainty that accompanies the choice. Other indications of how a person processes information can be found by examining that person's memory for the information. When a theory makes predictions about the kind of information that will be used for decision making, it is not difficult to extend the theory to make predictions about the ability to recognize information after the decision has been made. In one experiment (Pitz, 1976), I used both recognition and recall tasks to determine what information had been used in an inference task. In another study, Hamilos and Pitz (1977) used a recognition task to assess hypotheses about the abstraction process when people encode information for use in a prediction task. In general, hypotheses about the information processing involved in any decision task can often be validated by examining the information that subjects observe and subsequently remember.

A BRIEF REVIEW OF SOME EXPERIMENTAL RESULTS

Procedures discussed in the previous section can be used to determine what information is extracted from a sample and stored as part of the decision maker's knowledge. However, because knowledge becomes evident only through behavior, such a determination is often made difficult when a person does not use all of the information that has been stored. In our experiments, we have assumed that, when a relationship is found between the sample information and characteristics of the decision maker's responses, then that information must have been stored in some fashion. However, if no relationship is found, we cannot necessarily conclude that the information has not been encoded and stored. There have been a number of occasions on which information is apparently used for solving one problem but not for solving others.

The purpose of recent experiments has been to determine whether behavior exhibited in decision tasks can be accounted for by the processes listed in Table 5.2. First, to discover just how accurately people can use probabilistic information, Pitz, Leung, Hamilos, and Terpening (1976) employed sophisticated subjects in a prediction task, presenting sequences of sample information drawn from one population at a time. Knowledge of the population was inferred from the predictions, using the procedure described in the previous section for assessing subjective tertiles. The inferred tertiles were found to be systematically related to characteristics of the sample information, particularly to measures of central tendency. There was an appropriate, but less accurate, use of variability; in addition, skewness and bimodality of a distribution were recognized and used by the subjects in making their predictions.

These results were encouraging with respect to people's ability to use probabilistic information, but did not indicate how information about central tendency, variability, and other distributional properties might be stored. One possibility is that knowledge consists only of memory traces for individual items of sample information. Alternatively, properties of the population may be inferred from the sample information, a process I have referred to as the abstraction of prototypes. One experiment designed to distinguish between these possibilities was conducted by Hamilos and Pitz (1977), using a recognition task in addition to the prediction task. After subjects had seen the sample information, further values were presented, and subjects were asked whether or not these values had been included in the sample. Two important results were observed: First, confidence that an item of information had been seen earlier increased for values close to the middle of the sample distribution. Second, there was an increased ability to discriminate old information from new information at the extremes of the sample distribution; the smallest and largest values contained in the samples were recognized with greater accuracy than more central values. We also found that the recognition confidence judgments were related both to the variability and the skewness of the distribution. We concluded that information about the central tendency is abstracted as a prototype. However, it also appears that certain critical features of the sample information are stored directly; these distinctive features are the extreme values, the smallest and largest that are observed.

These results confirm the theoretical ideas presented earlier. The abstraction of average values is a simple process that is readily employed whenever subjects believe that it might be relevant. Further confirmation came from an extended study of the prediction task (Pitz, 1977b), for which a model was constructed from the operations described in Table 5.2. The results supported the model. An alternative assumption, that for each value of a quantity there exists a subjective probability that is related to the frequency of occurrence of the value, was not confirmed.

Based on these data, I am reasonably confident that the process of inferring central tendencies is important in the processing of probabilistic information. It is a process that can be carried out easily and comfortably with the analog operations of Table 5.2. However, the issue of how a person represents knowledge about variability (and other distributional properties such as skewness) is less clear. It is possible that measures of variability are inferred and stored as part of the prototype, along with information about the central tendency. The elementary operations described previously can be used to generate information about variability by finding the difference between each value and the current average value, and taking the average of these differences. However, such a procedure would place a fairly heavy load on short-term memory, and hence is unlikely to occur as a spontaneous strategy. It is also possible that information about variability could be stored as separate memory traces for individual items of information. However, if this were the only information available to a decision maker, it is difficult to see how he or she could develop a strategy for relating the information to predictions. A third possibility is that people use information about the central tendency together with their knowledge of the extreme values. The difference between the two extremes provides information about variability; the location of the central tendency relative to the extremes provides information about skewness. Strategies relating this information to decisions would be fairly easy to develop.

A recently completed experiment (Pitz & Englert, 1979) was designed to discover whether subjects abstract and store information about variability that goes beyond their knowledge of the smallest and largest values for a quantity. We used an inference task in which an iterative procedure was used to infer the cutoffs that a decision maker might use. The relationship between the cutoffs and various properties of the sample information was explored. We found that some, but not all, subjects did use information about variability that was independent of information about the extreme values. The results are consistent with the view that these subjects did abstract measures of variability. Other subjects showed no evidence of using any information about variability other than the extremes. The process of inferring sample variability using the operations listed in Table 5.2 would require a relatively large amount of cognitive effort, especially because, in the inference task, subjects must store information about two populations. It is likely that the subjects were selective in their encoding. Different subjects exhibited different kinds of selectivity, leading to individual differences in the encoding of information. On the other hand, we observed very few differences in encoding by a single subject as a function of how the information was presented. (Values were either shown simultaneously for each sample, or in random order, one item at a time, or in rank order, from smallest to largest value.) It appears that once a person has developed a strategy for encoding the information, that strategy does not change with variations in the information display.

The process of inferring and using central tendencies, and perhaps other distributional properties of information, seems to be very general. The idea is relevant to an understanding of what Kahneman and Tversky (1972, 1973) have called the representativeness heuristic. I have described elsewhere (Pitz, 1977a) a theory of representativeness and other behavior of the kind observed by Kahneman and Tversky. In general, they have found that people judge evidence by its typicality—that is, by the degree to which it is considered to be representative of some hypothesis. This process can be described by assuming an encoding of descriptive information about populations and samples in the form shown in Table 5.1. I assumed that judgments are made by comparing observed or inferred sample statistics with stated or inferred population parameters. Table 5.3 shows two problems that generate errors of representativeness in many people. These problems use quantitative information, for which central tendencies and variances seem to be the important characteristics. For both of the problems, the majority of subjects choose Sample B to be the more likely, whereas Sample A actually has the greater likelihood. In part (a), the presumed reason for the errors is that people abstract measures of central tendency from the sample information

TABLE 5.3
Problems Illustrating the
Representativeness Heuristic[a]

(a)	Sample A	Sample B
	142	141
	146	148
	148	153
	149	157
(b)	Sample A	Sample B
	148	138
	149	145
	150	154
	152	162

[a] Population Mean is 150; Standard deviation is 30. In each case, the task is to choose the more likely sample.

and compare these inferred statistics with the relevant parameters describing the population. Although Sample *A* has a greater likelihood, the mean for Sample *B* is more like the population mean. The second question contains samples that are equivalent in mean but differ in variability. This problem also induces incorrect responses, although less often than does part (*a*). A sample that has too small a variance is seen as less likely than one for which the variance is more appropriate.

A more appropriate strategy for each problem is to compare the deviation of each value from the population mean, and to aggregate these deviations.[2] However, when such a strategy is modeled from the operations of Table 5.2, it requires more use of short-term memory than does an averaging of all sample values; this may explain why representativeness occurs. It would also explain why there are fewer errors in part (*b*), because assessing variability requires more use of short-term memory than does assessing central tendency.

One important property of the information encoding process is that it is not fixed. For example, in one experiment (Pitz, 1976), I compared performance in decision making, frequency estimation, and memory tasks, using the same information for each task. When subjects were required to remember the information, specific items were recalled better than they were in the decision and frequency-estimation tasks. However, performance on the latter tasks exceeded that that was possible on the basis of specific information remembered in the memory tasks. These results suggest that subjects were encoding other information of direct relevance to the decision or frequency-estimation task. For the decision task, it seems that the subjects' strategy was to maintain in short-term

---

[2]The correct method for assessing the likelihood of each observation is more complex, and depends on whether the values given in the problem have been rounded or are strictly continuous. However, taking the deviation of a value from the population mean gives an approximation that is close enough for most cases.

memory their currently favored hypothesis, using specific information to revise this hypothesis, and otherwise forgetting the details of the information. Other task differences in encoding were observed by Hamilos and Pitz (1977). One group of subjects was given only a recognition task, using the same information as that used in other conditions. Although all subjects showed evidence of abstracting information about central tendencies, the group using recognition tasks did not show superior recognition for the extreme values. Apparently, the encoding of such critical features occurred only in the decision task when this information was presumably perceived as being relevant.

Because encoding strategies vary as a function of task differences, the encoding should be modifiable by changes in the task setting that might alter the choice of strategy. Suitable changes in the wording of a problem, or in the context in which the problem is presented, or in the sequence of problems presented, can all affect the decision maker's strategy. This conclusion is already well established in studies of problem solving. One recent demonstration that is relevant to the present discussion is a study by Mayer (1978), who examined the encoding of quantitative information in tasks similar to those used by Potts (1972, 1974). He found that the strategies reported by Potts were dependent on the way in which the problem information was presented. Because, in the case of decision making, some strategies may be normatively more appropriate than others, we may be able to improve decision making by extending these results to decision-making tasks.

I have been particularly interested in the degree to which the biases demonstrated by Kahneman and Tversky (1972, 1973) in their studies of heuristic processes can be modified through changes in the encoding of the problem. In a number of cases, I found (Pitz, 1977a) that suitable changes in the wording of a problem, or in the order in which problems are presented, can reduce the biases that occur. For example, the problems illustrated in Table 5.3 induce incorrect responses because the subjects tend to encode information in terms of sample means and standard deviations. However, it is possible to induce more appropriate encodings, in which the deviations of individual values from the population mean become more salient, by giving subjects a list of questions using single values, such as those shown in Table 5.4. Most of the subjects who made errors in Part (a) of Table 5.3, and who were then given the questions in Table 5.4, eventually answered correctly a final test question. A series of other experiments showed that the encoding of a problem can be changed by making more salient those features of the problem that are relevant to a correct response. A similar finding has been reported recently by Evans and DuSoir (1977). Ken Haxby and I have recently conducted an experiment in which we have shown that these changes can be documented by recording the kind of information reviewed by subjects as they study the problem.

These changes in a person's representation of the problem confirm the hypothesis that decision strategies are quite labile, and subject to changes with alterations in a person's perception of the task. The basic operations described

TABLE 5.4
Problems Designed to Eliminate the
Representativeness Heuristic[a]

(a)	Sample A	Sample B
	142	141
(b)	Sample A	Sample B
	149	148
(c)	Sample A	Sample B
	146	157
(d)	Sample A	Sample B
	148	153

[a] Population Mean is 150; Standard Deviation is 30. In each case, the task is to choose the more likely sample value.

earlier can be combined to produce a possibly infinite number of different strategies for processing probabilistic information. These strategies will differ, of course, in terms of the load they place on short-term memory, and in the time they take for production of a response. Hence, strategies that are simplest in these terms are likely to be most readily available. However, if other strategies are more appropriate from a normative point of view, it should be possible to encourage or train people to use them.

There are many ways in which human judgment and decision making are inconsistent and inappropriate. However, once we know how a person interprets a problem, what he or she is trying to do, and what mechanisms are available for achieving that purpose, we may be in a better position to improve the rationality of human behavior. We might do this by changing a person's perception of the task. We might also teach strategies that are more appropriate to the task, but that are within the limits of a person's cognitive capabilities. One of the most interesting, as well as useful, future developments in the study of decision making might be in the area of teaching strategies to decision makers. If the strategies are designed to be consistent with known cognitive operations, there is a greater chance that they can successfully be learned and applied.

ACKNOWLEDGMENTS

Research described in this chapter was supported by grants GB 40313 and BNS 73–00956 A01 from the National Science Foundation, and by a grant from the graduate school of Southern Illinois University at Carbondale. I am grateful to Judy Englert and Thomas Wallsten for their comments on an earlier version of this chapter.

REFERENCES

Anderson, J. R. *Language, memory, and thought*. Hillsdale, N.J.: Lawrence Erlbaum Associates, 1976.

Anderson, J. R. The status of arguments concerning representations for mental images. *Psychological Review*, 1978, *85*, 249–277.

Anderson, N. H. Information integration theory: A brief survey. In D. H. Krantz, R. C. Atkinson, R. D. Luce, & P. Suppes (Eds.), *Contemporary developments in mathematical psychology* (Vol. 2). San Francisco: Freeman, 1974.

Barrett, H. R. *The effect of payoffs and prior probabilities on decision making about normal distributions*. Unpublished doctoral dissertation, Southern Illinois University at Carbondale, 1970.

Bevan, E. R. *Stoics and sceptics*. Oxford: Clarendon Press, 1913.

Bransford, J. D., & Franks, J. J. The abstraction of linguistic ideas. *Cognitive Psychology*, 1971, *2*, 331–350.

Brehmer, B. Subjects' ability to find the parameters of functional rules in probabilistic inference tasks. *Organizational Behavior and Human Performance*, 1976, *17*, 388–397.

Brehmer, B., & Lindberg, L. The relation between cue validity and cue dependency in single cue probability learning tasks with scaled cue and criterion variables. *Organizational Behavior and Human Performance*, 1970, *5*, 542–551.

Buckley, P. B., & Gillman, C. B. Comparisons of digits and dot patterns. *Journal of Experimental Psychology*, 1974, *103*, 1131–1136.

Evans, J., St. B. T., & Dusoir, A. E. Proportionality and sample size as factors in intuitive statistical judgment. *Acta Psychologica*, 1977, *41*, 129–138.

Franks, J. J., & Bransford, J. D. Abstraction of visual patterns. *Journal of Experimental Psychology*, 1971, *90*, 65–74.

Hamilos, C. A., & Pitz, G. F. Encoding and recognition of probabilistic information in a decision task. *Organizational Behavior and Human Performance*, 1977, *20*, 184–202.

Kahneman, D., & Tversky, A. Subjective probability: A judgment of representativeness. *Cognitive Psychology*, 1972, *3*, 430–454.

Kahneman, D., & Tversky, A. On the psychology of prediction. *Psychological Review*, 1973, *80*, 237–251.

Keynes, J. M. *A treatise on probability*. London: Macmillan, 1921.

Kubovy, M., & Healy, A. F. The decision rule in probabilistic categorization: What it is and how it is learned. *Journal of Experimental Psychology: General*, 1977, *106*, 427–446.

Lichtenstein, S., Earle, T. C., & Slovic, P. Cue utilization in a numerical prediction task. *Journal of Experimental Psychology: Human Perception and Performance*, 1975, *104*, 77–85.

Martin, D. W., & Gettys, C. F. Feedback and responses made in performing a Bayesian decision task. *Journal of Applied Psychology*, 1969, *53*, 413–418.

Mayer, R. E. Qualitatively different storage and processing strategies used for linear reasoning tasks due to meaningfulness of premise. *Journal of Experimental Psychology: Human Memory and Learning*, 1978, *4*, 5–18.

Moyer, R. S., & Landauer, T. K. Time required for judgments of numerical inequality. *Nature*, 1967, *215*, 1519–1520.

Pitz, G. F. Production system interpreter PSPL: User's manual. Southern Illinois University at Carbondale, 1972.

Pitz, G. F. Subjective probability distributions for imperfectly known quantities. In L. W. Gregg (Ed.), *Knowledge and cognition*. Hillsdale, N.J.: Lawrence Erlbaum Associates, 1974.

Pitz, G. F. Bayes' theorem: Can a theory of judgment and inference do without it? In F. Restle, R. M. Schiffrin, N. J. Castellan, Jr., H. R. Lindman, & D. B. Pisoni (Eds.), *Cognitive theory* (Vol. 1), Hillsdale, N.J.: Lawrence Erlbaum Associates, 1975.

Pitz, G. F. Memory and frequency estimation processes in decision making. *Memory and Cognition*, 1976, *4*, 132–138.

Pitz, G. F. *Heuristic processes in decision making and judgment*. Unpublished paper, Southern Illinois University at Carbondale, 1977. (a)

Pitz, G. F. A model for judgments based on uncertain knowledge. *Proceedings of the International Conference on Cybernetics and Society*, 1977, 176–180. (b)

Pitz, G. F., & Englert, J. A. *Abstracting information about variability for decision making*. Unpublished paper, Southern Illinois University at Carbondale, 1979.

Pitz, G. F., Leung, L. S., Hamilos, C., & Terpening, W. The use of probabilistic information in making predictions. *Organizational Behavior and Human Performance*, 1976, *17*, 1-18.

Posner, M. I., & Keele, S. W. On the genesis of abstract ideas. *Journal of Experimental Psychology*, 1968, *77*, 353-363.

Potts, G. R. Information processing strategies used in the encoding of linear orderings. *Journal of Verbal Learning and Verbal Behavior*, 1972, *11*, 727-740.

Potts, G. R. Storing and retrieving information about ordered relationships. *Journal of Experimental Psychology*, 1974, *103*, 431-439.

Reed, S. K. Pattern recognition and categorization. *Cognitive Psychology*, 1972, *3*, 382-407.

Shanteau, J. C. Averaging versus multiplying combination rules of inference judgment. *Acta Psychologica*, 1975, *39*, 83-89.

Simon, H. A. *The sciences of the artificial*. Cambridge: M. I. T. Press, 1969.

Townsend, J. T. Some results on identifiability of the parallel and serial processes. *British Journal of Mathematical and Statistical Psychology*, 1972, *25*, 168-199.

Tversky, A., & Kahneman, D. Judgment under uncertainty: Heuristics and biases. *Science*, 1974, *185*, 1124-1131.

6 Information Processing Theory: Some Concepts and Methods Applied to Decision Research

John W. Payne
Graduate School of Business Administration
Duke University

One approach to cognition that has attracted wide interest in psychology is information processing theory (c.f. Newell & Simon, 1972). A specific focus of the information processing approach has been the study of human problem solving. Information processing models of problem solving describe behavior in terms of the interaction between the individual's cognitive system, the task environment as defined by the researcher, and a third component, the problem space. This last component of information processing models refers to the internal representation of the task environment used by a particular subject. Although the problem space will be related to the task environment as defined by the researcher, Simon (1978) stresses that a subject's particular problem space "must be distinguished from the task environment [p. 275]." Once a problem representation has been constructed, it will profoundly affect the subsequent performance of the problem solver.

Research in cognitive psychology has led to a number of generalizations about behavior. Perhaps the most important generalization is that the active processing of information is a serial process that occurs in a memory of limited capacity, duration, and ability to place information in more permanent storage. Consequently, people appear to keep the information processing demands of complex problem-solving tasks within the bounds of their limited cognitive capacity by utilizing heuristics that are highly adaptive to the damands of the task.

A number of researchers, including myself, feel that the information processing theory approach to cognition just outlined has the greatest potential for helping us to achieve a better understanding of the psychology of decisions. This chapter explores a few of the conceptual issues and methodological considerations that I believe represent important points of contact between information processing theory and the study of decision making. The first parts of the chapter focus on the general concept of problem space formulation and representation. The understanding of problem spaces has been stressed in problem-solving research and may be critical in decision research. For example, Kahneman and Tversky (1979) suggest that many anomalies in risky choice may be due to how choice problems are initially coded, edited, and represented by the decision maker. The following sections of this chapter make contact with the methods of cognitive psychology as well as with some other concepts. Simon (1976) has stressed that it is not enough just to adopt a set of suggestive metaphors from information processing theory; a researcher must also adopt research tools adequate to develop and test information processing models of behavior. The last part of the chapter contains a suggestion for research that combines a concern with the conceptual issue of problem space formulation with the process tracing method of verbal protocols.

PROBLEM REPRESENTATION

My initial efforts to examine decision behavior involved risky choice (Payne & Braunstein, 1971). Because the study of how people choose among gambles has also been one of the most active areas of decision research (Slovic, Fischhoff, & Lichtenstein, 1977), I use that task environment to begin our discussion of information processing theory and decision research.

The traditional way of describing gambles has been as probability distributions over outcomes, usually money. Choice among gambles could then be viewed as choice among probability distributions (Arrow, 1951). Such a description represented the task environment as defined by most researchers. That's fine as far as it goes. However, little or no attention was paid to the cognitive representation actually used by the individual decision maker. The result has been a variety of models that have concentrated on the moments of the underlying distributions as the determinants of choice among gambles. The predictive success of the moment models has been mixed. Models based on the means and variances of the distributions have been reasonably accurate in predicting overall statistics of decision making. On the other hand, a number of recent studies have demonstrated behavior that seem inconsistent with such models (Lichtenstein & Slovic, 1973; Tversky, 1969).

Slovic and Lichtenstein (1968b) suggested an alternative way in which gambles might be conceptualized by decision makers. In the simplest case, they proposed that a gamble could "be described by its location on four basic risk dimensions—probability of winning (PW), amount to win ($W), probability of losing (PL), and amount to lose ($L) [p. 1]." Slovic and Lichtenstein went on to suggest that the way in which decision makers combined these risk dimensions into a judgment would be affected by information processing considerations.

The concept that subjects respond to gambles in terms of a set of basic risk dimensions was examined in two related studies (Payne & Braunstein, 1971; Slovic & Lichtenstein, 1968a). These studies utilized duplex gambles, each of which consists of independent win and lose gambles. Slovic and Lichtenstein (1968a) employed parallel gambles such that for each standard two-outcome gamble there was a duplex gamble that displayed the same stated probabilities and payoffs, and was, therefore, equivalent in expected value but different in variance. Similar responses to standard and duplex gambles were found with both bidding and choice-response modes. Payne and Braunstein (1971) utilized pairs of duplex gambles that were equivalent in both expected value and variance and, therefore, that differed from each other in terms of the displayed probability and outcome values. Subjects had significant preferences between such pairs of gambles. Alternatively, when preferences among pairs of duplex gambles that differed both in the risk dimensions and in the first and second moments were considered, expected values and variances still could not account for the choices. Together, these two studies support the concept of risk dimension and preference judgments.

The concept of explicit risk dimensions has also been applied to the study of the perception of risk by Slovic (1967) and Payne (1975). Using a correlational technique, Slovic (1967) found that "perceived risk was determined primarily by the probability of losing [p. 223]." Payne (1975) expanded upon that result using an alternative experimental procedure based on pairs of specially constructed three-outcome gambles. The risk dimensions, probabilities of winning and losing, and amount to be won or lost were different for each gamble in a pair, but the expected values and variances were approximately equal. The probability of losing was again found to be most important in determining perceived risk.

Slovic (1972) used the results of Payne and Braunstein (1971) and Slovic and Lichtenstein (1968a) to propose a principle called "concreteness." Slovic's (1972) idea was that a "decision maker tends to use only the information that is explicitly displayed in the stimulus object and will use it only in the form in which it is displayed [p. 14]." A similar concept has been advanced by Aschenbrenner (1978). Kozielecki (1975) explicitly tied the work just described to a hypothetical construct concerned with the internal representations or problems spaces generated by subjects of risky task. Kozielecki stressed that performance in the choice task, perhaps as compared to a normative model, would depend on the problem representation used by the decision maker.[1] Several factors that might affect the problem-space formulation, such as the way in which probability information was made available, were suggested.

The question of the nature of the problem-space representations of gambles might be related to work in cognitive psychology concerning the effect on per-

---

[1]For a recent example of how problem representations can affect probability estimates, and a discussion of public policy implications, see Fischhoff, Slovic, and Lichtenstein (1978).

ceptual processes of interactions between stimulus dimensions (Garner, 1976). Garner distinguishes between integral and configural stimulus dimensions on the one hand, and separable stimulus dimensions on the other. Selective attention to the dimensions of a stimulus is not possible when the dimensions are integral or configural, but is possible when the dimensions are separable. Choice models that result from the traditional description of gambles as probability distributions appear to treat the dimensions of probability and amount as integral or configural. It may be more appropriate, however, to treat these dimensions as separable. Evidence supporting the idea that the probability of winning and amount to win may be coded and treated as separable dimensions is provided by Tversky (1969). He found that the way in which subjects responded to simple gambles of the form (a, p), where a represented the amount to be won and p represented the probability of winning, was affected by the discriminability along each of the dimensions. (See also Tversky, 1972.) It should be noted, however, that the question of whether or not the dimensions used in risky decision tasks are in fact separable or integral is still open.

The importance of this possible connection between risky decision making and the effects of stimulus dimensions on perceptual and cognitive processes lies in the understanding that might be gained concerning the coding and editing processes in choices. For example, discriminability of dimensions across stimuli is a recognized determinant of performance in perceptual tasks involving separable dimensions. A variety of other determinants of perceptual judgments, such as stimulus range, are also well known (e.g., Garner, 1976; Gravetter & Lockhead, 1973) and may help us to build a theory of the coding and editing processes in complex decision behavior.

To illustrate, the importance of factors such as stimulus range in perceptual judgments suggests that aspects of the overall choice set, and not just the dimensions of each separate alternative, may affect choice behavior. Support for this idea in risky choice was obtained by Payne and Braunstein (1971). They found that preferences between the gambles in a pair were related to the probability relationship within the gamble in a choice set. This led Payne and Braunstein to suggest a two-stage model of risky choice. The first stage involved problem evaluation. The evaluation was based on the probability relationship within gambles, and was thought to reflect a judgment by the decision maker on whether he or she was faced with an attractive $(PW > PL)$ or unattractive $(PW < PL)$ set of options. The second stage was a direct comparison and choice stage using a lexicographic choice process. The ordering of dimensions was assumed to be contingent upon the outcome of the evaluation process. When $PW > PL$, an attempt was made to maximize the amount to win. If the amounts were equal within a pair, the probability to win was used as a secondary criterion, and the gamble with the greater probability to win chosen. When the opposite relationship held $(PW < PL)$, the gamble with the lesser probability to lose was chosen.

The context effect involving the probability relationships within the gambles of a choice set has also been found in studies by Payne (1975) and Ranyard

(1976). The latter study, for example, also involved pairs of duplex gambles. Ranyard reports that when the probability to win was "favourable," subjects were inclined to select the gamble with the greater amount to win, but when probability to win was "unfavourable," subjects were more inclined to select the gamble with the lesser probability to lose in every case.

In spite of this empirical support, it is clear that the Payne and Braunstein (1971) model is not a general model or risky choice. However, the model does serve to illustrate a theory of decision behavior based on many of the notions contained in information processing types of models. The evaluation stage can be thought of as part of a process of problem-space formulation. The choice rule is of a heuristic nature. The decision is seen as situation dependent. Finally, there is an explicit sequence of operations.

This last idea that the response of an individual to a choice or judgment problem will involve several stages of processing is becoming increasingly popular (Kahneman & Tversky, 1979; Montgomery & Svenson, 1976; Park, 1978; Wright & Barbour, 1977). It is also an idea that can easily be traced back to Simon (1957). It does, however, represent a departure from most decision research, which has described a subject's processing activities in terms of a single-phase model (Wright & Barbour, 1977).

The trend towards a more dynamic view of human cognition is clear (Posner, 1973). Such a perspective, however, would appear to call for methods designed to provide data on the sequential (time-ordered) behavior of subjects. The next sections of this chapter discuss how two methods derived from information processing theory, the analysis of information acquisition behavior and verbal protocol analysis, might provide such data for decision researchers.

PROCESS TRACING

The information processing approach has also lead to the development of new methodologies for psychological research. Examples include new methods for observing behavior, called "process tracing" and computer simulation.

Monitoring Information Acquisition

Essentially, the process-tracing technique involves setting up the decision task so that the subject must view or select information in a way that can be easily monitored. Data can be obtained on what information the subject seeks, in what order, how much information is acquired, and for what duration information is examined. Several methods for monitoring information acquisition behavior have been used to study decision making. For example, the recording of eye movements has been undertaken by Russo and his associates (Rosen & Rosenkoetter, 1976; Russo & Dosher, 1975; Russo & Rosen, 1975), and by Van Raaij (1976). This research has identified how processing strategies may vary as a function of the interdependence of stimulus attributes (Rosen & Rosenkoetter, 1976). Support has also been obtained for the hypothesis that subjects use binary processing as a strategy in multialternative choice situations (Russo & Rosen, 1975). Finally, evidence of the use of heuristics, such as the counting of the number of dimensions favoring each alternative, in binary choice decisions has been obtained (Russo & Dosher, 1975).

Collecting eye-movement data is conceptually a straightforward method of obtaining process information. Unfortunately, there have been several technical problems associated with eye-movement recordings. First, the apparatus has been expensive and often cumbersome and uncomfortable for the subject. In order to obtain great enough accuracy of resolution in recording the eye fixations, the head of the subject is often immobilized through the use of a bite bar or some other restrictive device. When a cathode ray terminal has been used, the amount of information that was displayed was limited both by the size of the display screen and by the need to keep the information spaced far enough apart to preclude peripheral processing. Many of these technical problems, however, are in the process of being overcome.

Information acquisition has also been monitored by presenting subjects with a decision task in which they must explicitly search for information about the available alternatives. The information is usually presented to the subject in the form of an array with the alternatives listed across the top and the attribute names listed down the side, or vice versa. Each cell in the array, or matrix of information, contains the value for the appropriate alternative and attribute. The value is hidden until the subject explicitly seeks the information. Subjects are permitted to acquire as much or as little of the information as they wish prior to reaching a decision.

The technology used in explicit information-search experiments has varied considerably. The earliest, and simplest, procedures have involved the use of information boards (e.g., Jacoby, Chestnut, Weigl, & Fisher, 1976). Recently, computer controlled information retrieval systems have been employed (e.g., Payne & Braunstein, 1978). This study by Payne and Braunstein illustrates how the monitoring of information-acquisition behavior can be used to test hypotheses about how individuals process information into a decision.

Information Search and Risky Choice.   The predominant information utilization rules in decision making have assumed a compensatory or trade-off process. An example of such a rule in the area of risky decision making is the information integration model of Anderson and Shanteau (1970), which is expressed by the following equation:

$$R = W_w S_w + W_L S_L,$$

where R is the theoretical response and S_w and S_L are the basic pieces of information in a risky decision. Anderson and Shanteau argue that this information corresponds to subjective values of the risk dimensions W and L. W_w and W_L represent measures of the importance of the sources of information to the response. The weights are assumed to be subjective functions of the probabilities, PW and PL. This model is derived from a general theory of information integration in judgment (cf. Anderson, 1974).

As Anderson and Shanteau point out, their model is similar in form to the subjectively expected utility model that has often served as a normative standard against which behavior could be compared (Slovic et al., 1977). However, the weights in the integration model are more general than subjective probabilities and so do not have to sum to 1.0. In addition, Anderson and Shanteau have stressed that the fundamental purpose of the model is to describe the human thought processes involved in risky decision making, not prescribe them.

The information integration and similar models are not explicit about how decision processes would relate to information-acquisition behavior. Three very plausible implications, however, can be identified. First, the decision maker would use an interdimensional search strategy. That is, search and evaluation would be within a gamble and across dimensions. Such a strategy is in contrast to the intradimension strategy that has been observed in several studies of decision making (e.g., Bettman & Jacoby, 1976; Payne, 1976; Russo & Dosher, 1975). Second, the decision maker would process the information in a certain order. Specifically, information integration would imply that the acquisition of an item of information about a probability dimension would be followed by the acquisition of an item of information about an amount dimension, or vice versa. In contrast, a decision maker might process both probability dimensions and then both amount dimensions. The Payne and Braunstein (1971) model of risky choice assumes that a subject would evaluate both probability dimensions within a gamble before evaluating additional information. Third, a decision maker would search a constant amount of information when using a compensatory decision process. On the other hand, a variable amount of search for information across alternatives has been shown to be consistent with certain heuristic non-compensatory decision strategies (Payne, 1976). For example, the elimination-by-aspects model (Tversky, 1972) implies both a variable and intradimensional pattern of search.

These processing implications of the information-integration model, and those of other decision rules, were examined by presenting 25 subjects with a series of risky choice problems that involved an explicit search procedure. The stimuli were 12 sets of three-outcome gambles. Within the 12 sets of gambles, four sets contained two gambles, four contained four gambles, and four contained eight gambles. The number of alternatives available had been previously shown to affect the likelihood that subjects would use compensatory as opposed to non-compensatory decision processes (Payne, 1976). The information-search procedure involved a computer terminal connected on-line to a PDP-11 computer. The gambles were displayed in a matrix format on the screen of the terminal. Subjects could acquire one piece of information about one gamble at a time, for example, probability to win for gamble A. Selecting a new item of information resulted in the previous items being erased, but subjects could go back and recheck an item if they wished. This procedure provides data resembling that acquired by an eye-movement procedure, but allows for more complex decision displays. The order and amount of information examined by each subject was recorded. Also recorded were the amount of time between information requests (search time), the time between the last information request and the subject's indication of a choice (decision time), and the gamble finally selected. Five of the subjects also provided verbal protocols.

Results showed that the amount of variation in information searched per gamble increased as the number of gambles increased; some gambles were eliminated after only a limited amount of search. An increase in the number of gambles also led to a decrease in the proportion of total available information searched, and a change in the pattern of search. There was more intradimensional search as the number of gambles increased. Together, the results indicate that as the number of gambles in a choice set increases, subjects become less likely to employ a decision strategy consistent with the class of information-integration models.

The results in terms of the patterns of information acquisition across the four basic risk dimensions—PW, $\$W$, PL, and $\$L$—also suggested that a number of subjects may have employed processing rules other than those implied by the class of information-integration models. Out of the 300 search patterns exhibited by the subjects (25 subjects × 12 decision problems), 124 search patterns involved the processing of information about both probability components of the gambles and then the amount components, or the reverse. In contrast, the information-integration model implies that information is processed either within the win component of a gamble (PW & $\$W$) and then within the loss component of a gamble (PL & $\$L$), or the reverse.[2]

Information processing theory stresses the need to pay attention to the behavior of individual subjects (Simon, 1976). Table 6.1 provides a classification of subjects on the basis of search patterns. The eight subjects classified as having primarily win/loss, interdimensional, and constant patterns of search appear to be individuals whose behavior is consistent with an information-integration, or perhaps expectation, type of model. Additional support for the view that these eight subjects used those types of processes was obtained by calculating the average length of an interdimensional sequence of processing. A strict expected value process, for example, should show a sequence of three interdimensional single-step transitions, i.e., probability to win of gamble A followed by amount to win of gamble A followed by probability to lose of gamble A followed by amount to lose of gamble A. Furthermore, the average length of the sequence

---

[2]For more details on the different measures of search behavior, see Payne and Braunstein (1978).

TABLE 6.1
Classification of Subjects on the Basis of Search Patterns

Content of Search Across Risk Dimensions	Sequence of Search			
	Interdimensional Depth of Search		Intradimensional Depth of Search	
	Constant	Variable	Constant	Variable
Probabilities/Amounts		Five subjects $(1.82, 1.63, 1.40)^a$	One subject $(1.10, 2.86, 4.44)$	Two subjects $(.94, 2.41, 4.24)$
Win/Loss	Eight subjects $(2.77, 2.81, 2.84)$	Two subjects $(1.71, 1.77, 1.60)$	One subject $(.5, 3.5, 7.25)$	Four subjects $(.99, 2.44, 4.40)$
Neither	One subject $(2.73, 2.14, 2.44)$			One subject $(1.06, 2.34, 4.07)$

[a] The numbers in parentheses are the average length of the search sequences for the subjects in each of the 12 categories for the two-, four-, and eight-alternative choice situations, respectively.

should not vary as a function of the number of alternatives available. The average length of sequence for these eight subjects for the two-, four-, and eight-alternative choice situations was 2.77, 2.81, and 2.84. Only one subject showed inconsistent sequence lengths of 1.83, 1.18, and 1.83 for the two-, four-, and eight alternative situations.

Although the focus of the Payne and Braunstein (1978) experiment was not on the final choice response, it is also interesting to compare the final choices made by the eight subjects with information-integration or expectation types of search patterns with the choices of the other 17 subjects. Each subject in this study faced four situations that contained sets of gambles with unequal expected values. For the eight subjects with information-integration or expectation types of search patterns, the mean numbers of choices consistent with the maximization of expected value was 3.13. The mean number of choices consistent with the maximization expected value for the other 17 subjects in the study was 1.30. A test of the difference between the two means, $t = 4.36(23)$, was significant ($p < .01$). This apparent agreement between a standard measure of the end product of the decision process and the measures of predecisional behavior serves to validate the methodology and classification of subjects employed in this study.

Next, consider the six subjects who exhibited primarily intradimensional and variable patterns of search involving either probabilities/amounts or win/loss. Payne (1976) suggested that individuals whose information search is characterized as sequentially intradimensional and of variable depth may be using an additive difference process to select among multiple alternatives, and an elimination by aspects process to select among multiple alternatives. An examination of the average length of the sequences of intradimensional processing for the six subjects classified as having intradimensional and variable search patterns given in Table 6.1 supports this view: As the number of alternatives available increases, the average length of an intradimensional processing sequence increases. The fact that the average length of sequence for the four-and eight-alternative choice situations is substantially larger than 1.0 indicates that these subjects were not using the sort of standard revision version of the additive difference model suggested by Russo & Rosen (1975) as a way of dealing with a multialternative choice problem. Instead, the length of the sequences of intradimensional processing suggests that these subjects may have employed the heuristic intradimensional processing rule elimination-by-aspects (Tversky, 1972). It is interesting to note that those subjects who were classified as having interdimensional and variable search patterns have an average processing sequence length shorter than the subjects who were classified as having interdimensional and constant search patterns. The relatively short sequence of interdimensional processing, together with the variable search pattern, is consistent with either a conjunctive type process or the contingent processing model proposed by Payne and Braunstein (1971).

The reasons for these individual differences are not clear. The individuals who processed information in terms of the wins and losses, for example, may have been using the probabilities as weights to be applied to the outcomes of the gambles. This would be consistent with the information integration model. It is also possible that some of the subjects may have possessed statistical knowledge that would have led to an expectation approach to decision making. Some support for such an effect has been found by Schoemaker (1977). He found a positive relationship between the amount of statistical training of undergraduates and the extent to which bids for gambles were consistent with expected values. On the other hand, Lichtenstein, Slovic, and Zink (1969) found that telling people about the expected value concept did not lead to a singificant increase in the use of that concept as a guide to action. Our knowledge of how knowledge already possessed by a decision maker influences his or her decision processes is still limited.

A possible explanation for the processing of the probability to win and the probability to lose together and then the amount to win and the amount to lose together may involve the issue of dimensional commensurability raised by Slovic and MacPhillamy (1974). It may be that comparing the two probability dimensions of a gamble and then comparing the two amount dimensions is easier than attempting to integrate probability information with amount information separately for the win and loss components. In other words, the "chunking" process may be easier for commensurate dimensions. This explanation is only speculative, but it does suggest an important question: What happens as the complexity of a risky alternative is increased through increases in the number of outcomes and probabilities? The problem space formulation is likely to be affected, but how? A variety of mechanisms might be used by a decision maker to simplify such a task. For example, outcomes with very small probabilities might be ignored (Slovic, Fischhoff, Lichtenstein, Corrigan, & Combs, 1977). Another possibility would be for the decision maker to treat all outcomes below a certain level as similar. That is, a decision maker might establish a target level of return (Fishburn, 1977) and combine all the probabilities associated with outcomes below that level into one composite probability of failure to meet the aspiration level. As Kahneman and Tversky (1979) note, the manner in which complex options are reduced to simpler ones is yet to be investigated.

Another important individual difference was whether a subject tended to process information in an interdimensional fashion or in an intradimensional fashion. This sort of difference has appeared in several studies of individual search behavior (e.g., Bettman & Jacoby, 1976; Payne, 1976; Russo & Dosher, 1975). A possible explanation for this difference has been offered in terms of individual differences in how the decision maker represents the knowledge he or she acquires about the alternatives in a decision task (Payne, 1976).

The study just discussed is part of a series of process-tracing studies of decision making (Carroll & Payne, 1977; Payne, 1974 1976; Payne & Braunstein, 1977). Most of those studies also recorded some form of information search data. Results have been pretty consistent in indicating that a given decision maker would use a variety of decision rules contingent upon the demands of the task. This contingent processing notion fits in with the view of decision behavior as a multistage process. The response to task characteristics would seem to call for at least a control or evaluation stage prior to the application of a particular choice rule. The Payne and Braunstein (1971) model is of this type. Several of the chapters in this volume also cite evidence for task-contingent decision processes (Ebbesen & Konecni; MacCrimmon, Stanbury, & Wehrung; Pitz; Wallsten). However, the strongest evidence for multistage processing is provided by studies using another process-tracing method.

Verbal Protocols

The best known process-tracing technique is the collection of verbal protocols. In the method, a subject is simply asked to give continuous verbal reports, "to think aloud," while performing the task. The verbal protocol is then treated as (Newell & Simon, 1972): "a record of the subject's ongoing behavior, and an utterance at time t is taken to indicate knowledge or operation at time t [p. 184]." Note that this method of research is designed to provide information on the sequential (time-ordered) behavior of subjects. To the extent that decision behavior does involve multistage processing, verbal protocols may be a valuable tool for developing and testing models of that behavior.

As a method for obtaining psychological data, the collections of verbal reports is an old idea in experimental psychology. For researchers such as Wundt and

Titchener, introspection, the trained observation of the contents of consciousness under controlled conditions, was *the* method of investigation in psychology. However, the introspective method was virtually abandoned in 20th-century America because of criticisms by Watson and other behaviorialists directed at the objectivity of the method as a basis for a scientific psychology. It is interesting to note that Watson apparently was prepared to accept verbal reports as data ("verbal behavior") when they were verifiable and repeatable. (See Marx & Hillix, 1963, for an extensive historical discussion of the introspective method and the behaviorists criticisms.)

Unfortunately, the apparent parallel between verbal protocol analysis and introspection has undoubtedly discouraged some modern experimental psychologists from adopting the verbal protocol technique of process tracing (Hayes, 1968). It is important, therefore, that the distinctions between verbal protocol analysis, and introspection and other types of verbal data be made clear. First, subjects under the process-tracing strategy are naive about the theoretical constructs of interest to the researcher. In contrast, highly trained subjects (sometimes even the researcher) were used to generate introspective data. A related point is that in collecting verbal proctocol data, the subject is not asked to theorize about his or her behavior. Instead, the subject is asked (Newell & Simon, 1972): "only to report the information and intentions that are within his current of conscious awareness [p. 184]. The researcher, not the subject, is supposed to do the theorizing about the causes and consequences of the subject's knowledge state.

Another distinction between verbal proctocol analysis and other forms of verbal data is the emphasis of the former on the collection of protocols during the actual performance of the task rather than through later questionnaires or interviews. This emphasis relates to the concern with obtaining measures of behavior over time. In contrast, the collection of verbal reports after the response has been the traditional method of obtaining verbal data in psychology.

This last distinction is crucial, for the controversy of what subjects can verbally report has reemerged many times. Nisbett and Wilson (1977) recently argued that people have little or no ability to directly observe and verbally report upon higher order mental operations that result in a response of some kind. Although the research they review is impressive in supporting their argument, the fact that the evidence is derived entirely from verbal reports collected *after* the responses limits its relevance for evaluating the process-tracing technique of verbal protocols. On the other hand, the evidence from years of research on human problem-solving behavior does indicate that protocol data can serve as a valuable basis for model building. Obviously, more research is needed to determine the quality of information about cognitive processes that can be provided by verbal protocols collected in various task environments. In that regard, one hypothesis that can be derived from Nisbett and Wilson (1977) is that protocols collected during the performance of tasks where strong norms of behavior exist may be less informative about individual cognitive processes. For a further discussion of Nisbett and Wilson, see Smith and Miller (1978).

As a final note, although protocols provide a method for collecting a relatively high temporal density of decision data, there is no a priori reason why the verbalizations of a subject should provide a complete record of the subject's state of knowledge at every moment (Newell & Simon, 1972). To illustrate this point, Payne (1974) found that protocols from a risky choice task contained an average of 1.7 words per second. Such a density is similar to the density of words per second found in problem-solving studies. However, it still seems like a rather low density of data given how much we suppose can go on in a few seconds of thinking. Protocols, therefore, like other forms of behavioral data, will only provide partial information about the cognitive processes of an individual.

Examples of the use of verbal protocols in decision research are provided by Bettman (1970), Clarkson (1962), Kleinmuntz (1968). Montgomery (1976), and Svenson (1974), as well as by several studies I have undertaken (Carroll & Payne, 1977; Payne, 1974, 1976; Payne & Braunstein, 1977).

Of special interest are the indications in several of the protocols collected in the studies just cited that subjects use more than one choice rule within the same choice problem. To illustrate, the protocol of one subject that very clearly shows a combination of decision rules is presented in Table 6.2.

The protocol is from a subject faced with a 12 alternative (apartments) choice problem (Payne, 1976). The protocol indicates that the subject first used a strict elimination-by-aspects process to eliminate alternatives. The subject reduced the choice problem from 12 alternatives to eight alternatives, and eventually to just a pair of alternatives. At that point, the protocol shows the decision maker shifting from an elimination-by-aspects procedure to what appears to be an additive-difference strategy. Eventually, after directly comparing the final two alternatives, the subject chose apartment *J*. The protocol of other subjects collected by other researchers also indicate similar combinations of decision process (e.g., Svenson, 1974).

A model based on the protocol in Table 6.2 has been developed. The model consists of three subroutines in a general choice program: (1) an elimination of alternative process; (2) a compensatory comparison process; and (3) a control process that selects decision processes on the basis of an evaluation of the structure of the task.[3] The detailed structure of this particular process model is presented in Fig. 6.1. The model has been coded in BASIC and seems to generate sequential behavior that corresponds fairly closely to the actual sequen-

---

[3]Abelson (1976) references a personal communication from Amos Tversky that also conceives of decision making in terms of a single comprehensive program consisting of many special components. In addition, Newell and Simon (1972) have argued that the representation of human problem solvers in terms of a set of basic functional clusters of methods "to be used separately or in mixtures appears both parsimonious and provocative [p. 846]."

TABLE 6.2
Protocol for a Subject Selecting among 12 Apartments

(A) Protocol	(A) Protocol (continued)
Let's just see what the rents are in all the apartments first. The rent of A is $140. The rent of B is $110. The rent of C is $170. . . . Um, $170 is too much. But, if the other ones aren't good, I'll look at them later. But, right now I'll look at the other ones. . . . I'm going to look at landlord attitude. In H, it's fair. In D, it's poor. B, it's fair, and A, it's good. So, one of them . . . is poor. So that's important to me. . . . So, I'm not going to live any place where where it's poor. . . .	Kitchen facilities in A are poor. In A, poor. In B, poor. In J, fair. In H, they're good. Oh, J and H have better kitchen facilities than A and B. And everything else is about the same. So eliminate those two. And, decide between these two. . . . Let's see furniture quality. In H, it is below average. In J, it's below average, so that's about the same there. . . . Landlord attitude in J is better than in H. . . . In J, the rooms are larger, so, I guess, J will be better.

tial behavior of one subject. The model and the development and testing of computer models of decision behavior based on verbal protocols are discussed further in Payne, Braunstein, and Carroll (1978).

The idea contained in the model, that an early stage in a complex decision process might involve the reduction of alternatives, has been suggested by a number of researchers on both theoretical and empirical grounds (MacCrimmon, 1968; Montogomery & Svenson, 1976; Park, 1978; Wright & Barbour, 1977). The general rationale seems to be that such a procedure provides a way for the decision maker to simplify a complex choice task.

Although limited in generality, the model presented in Fig. 6.1 illustrates the use of a number of concepts from cognitive psychology in explaining decision behavior. There is an explicit recognition of the importance of a task determinant, number of alternatives. Also consistent with research on human problem solving is the presentation of at least two decision rules as complementary. The model also suggests that a decision maker stores information about the decision alternatives in the form of list property structures. This type of knowledge representation is widely used to build theories of human cognitive processes. Finally, the model describes decision making in terms of a dynamic process.

In that regard, the interactive structure of routines *CØ* and *EØ* is particularly interesting. If the elimination process represents a simplification mechanism, then the structure of the model suggests that the problem space may be modified several times during the course of the decision. Newell and Simon (1972) have stated that "the problem space and the specific set of methods used with it need not remain constant through a whole problem solving attempt [p. 860]."

CØ: Evaluation of decision task complexity.
   CI: If number of alternatives greater than two then EØ.
   C2: If number of alternatives exactly two then DØ.
   C3: Goto RØ.
EØ Elimination process.
   EI : Search list-dimensions for first (next) most important dimension (D),
      If end of list then RO.
   E2: Set goal--eliminate by dimension (D).
   E3: Search list-alternatives for first (next) alternative (A), if end of
      list then CØ.
   E4: Search environment for dimension (D, value) for alternative (A).
   E5: Search memory for list-acceptable dimension (D) values.
   E6: If dimension (D, value) on list-acceptable values then E2, else mark
      alternative (A) eliminated and remove from list-alternatives.
   E7: Goto E2.
DØ Direct comparison process.
   DI: Search list-alternatives for first alternative (X) and next alternative (Y).
   D2: Set goal--comparison (X) and (Y).
   D3: Search list-dimensions for last (next) most important dimension (D),
      if end of list then D6.
   D4: Search memory for dimension (D, value) for alternatives (X) and (Y), if not
      avaialble search environment for dimension (D, values) for (X) and (Y).
   D5: Compare dimension (D, value) for alternative (X) and dimension (D, value)
      for alternative (Y) with ordered list-acceptable dimension (D) values. If
      dimension (D) values equal then D3, else if dimension (D value) for
      alternative (X) higher than dimension (D value) for alternative (Y) then re-
      spond--alternative (X) better, and increment overall worth of alternative
      (X) by relative importance value of dimension (D) from list-dimensions, else
      respond--alternative (Y) better, and increment overall worth of alternative (Y
   D6: If overall worth of alternative (X) greater than overall worth of alternative
      (Y), then respond--alternative (X) preferred, else if overall worth of alter-
      native (Y) greater then respond alternative (Y) preferred, else RØ.
RØ: Respond--No choice Possible.

FIG. 6.1.   Detailed structure of the process model.

Montgomery and Svenson (1976) seem to suggest a similar possibility in their structure for decision processes. That structure provides an ordering of decision rules on a continuum of cognitive effort. What is interesting is that the structure also appears to allow for changes in the representation or problem space at different points in time. In particular, the level of metric representation of dimensional values may change. That is, the decision maker's sensitivity to differences in values might change over time. Park (1978) refers to a similar process as "cognitive articulation," or more generally as cognitive categorization. It might be assumed that early in the decision process the sensitivity to dimension values would be more crude. A decision maker might, for example, code all the values possessed by different alternatives on a particular dimension into either a satisfactory or unsatisfactory category (Simon, 1955). Later, perhaps after sone of the alternatives have been eliminated, the decision maker might refine the cognitive categories on the same dimension (Montgomery & Svenson, 1976; Park, 1978). However, Wright (1975) has suggested that decision makers may apply decision rules in such a way as to imply a less sensitive representation of dimensions later in the process.

Finally, the multistage and contingent processing view of decision making being developed may help us to resolve an apparent contradiction in the literature. Linear compensatory models have done a good job of predicting choices among simple gambles. On the other hand, the theory and results of cognitive psychology along with several studies of decision making suggest the widespread use of other processing rules. In particular, Simon (1976) has pointed out that it is hard to reconcile the use of heuristics in problem solving with the use of additive models in decision making. The resolution of this contradiction appears to be in theories of the kind outlined by Kahneman and Tversky (1979). Subjects will first seek to simplify decision problems. This can involve simplifications through the coding of information and the screening and reduction of alternatives, among other mechanisms. Sometimes, such mechanisms will lead directly to a decision. At other times, the subject will be left with a model of the task that allows for compensatory processes. In those cases, subjects will try to maximize the tradeoff among dimensions.

A Comparison of Methods

As might be expected, there are differences of opinion as to whether monitoring information search should be preferred over verbal protocols as a method of collecting process data. Russo and Rosen (1975) argue that eye-movement records are better because "they are unobtrusive, detailed, and difficult to misrepresent [p. 268]." These claims may be true, although it is not clear how unobtrusive eye-movement recording has been given the apparatus used. Nevertheless, Russo (1978) has raised the valid point that verbal protocols require an extra response by the subject—that is, the generation of a verbal description of the thoughts that occur to the subject. Most eye-movement recording techniques do not require such an extra response. More generally, Russo (1978) has posed the question: "Does generating a verbal protocol alter the primary process in important ways [p. 567]?" This question was examined in two studies of decision behavior (Carroll & Payne, 1977; Payne & Braunstein, 1977). The results seem to indicate that the verbal protocol procedure slows down the process slightly but does not change it fundamentally. A similar effect for verbal protocols has been suggested by other researchers (e.g., Dansereau & Gregg, 1966). Other evidence indicating that the collection of verbal protocols does not alter judgment behavior is provided by Johnson (1978) and Montgomery (1976). (See also Simon, 1978.)

Problems with the information search method include the fact that it focuses exclusively on the subject's use of objective, external information. The method does not easily allow for insights into a decision maker's use of information stored in internal memory. Verbal protocols, on the other hand, can provide data on both external and internal search behavior. For example, some data on external search behavior may be acquired through an examination of when and how often different aspects of the decision alternatives are mentioned by a subject. Another problem is that information acquisition methods provide little or no indication of when and if the information being acquired is actually being processed. Information acquisition studies also usually require the decision task to be more structured. This may present a problem as decision researchers attempt to do more "real-world" research. For a further comparison of process tracing methods, see Payne et al. (1978) and Russo (1978).

These process-tracing methods are still being developed. It is clear that each method has a number of problems associated with its use. However, the experience of other areas of cognitive psychology suggests that the process-tracing approach would be a valuable complement to more traditional model-fitting approaches to the study of decision behavior.

A SUGGESTION FOR RESEARCH

This last section of the chapter briefly suggests how a process-tracing approach could be used to study the problem-space construction and editing that may represent the initial stages of an individual's response to a decision situation.

The suggestion is derived from work by Hayes and his associates (Hayes & Simon, 1976; Hayes, Waterman, & Robinson, 1977; Hinsley, Hayes, & Simon, 1977; Simon & Hayes, 1976). The idea is to collect data from the point at which the subject is first exposed to the task instructions up to the time he or she begins to work on the task. Note how this procedure differs from the typical psychological experiment: Usually, the subject is introduced to the task through instructions and is given an opportunity to practice on some examples. Data collection does not start until we are sure the task has been completely understood. Within such a paradigm, there is no opportunity to discover the processes used to generate a problem space (Simon, 1978).

At least two variations of the Hayes and Simon (1976) approach exist. The first is to collect standard verbal protocols from different groups of subjects who have been given different but isomorphic problem instructions. That is, the same problem is disguised in different words. Systematic differences in the responses to isomorphs can provide clues to the manner of problem formulation (Hayes & Simon, 1976). The second procedure is to read the problem instructions to the subjects, one sentence at a time. Subjects are then asked to make relevance judgements about the problem text: what parts are relevant, irrelevant, or uncertain (Hayes et al., 1977).

The work on problem solving demonstrates that the nature of the problem representation depends on the precise wording of the problem text. For example, behavior with respect to a problem depends on the ordering of the sentences in the text (Hayes et al., 1977). In addition, Simon (1978) cites research suggesting that sensitivity to the precise wording of the text depends on the skill or experience level of a subject.

This suggests the value of a program of research in decision behavior that would apply these methods and findings from cognitive psychology. Decision makers could be presented with relatively complex problems in the form of written decision cases of the kind often used by business schools. Using one or both of the protocol methods previously described, it should be possible to track how information is abstracted from the written text, and how that information is turned into a simplified model of the decision task. For example, one might expect that simple variations in the wording of the instructions might cause a decision maker to organize the problem space around attributes or goals on the one hand, or around alternatives on the other.

CONCLUSION

The recognition of the importance of psychological concepts is increasing in both normative and descriptive decision research (Slovic, Fischhoff, & Lichtenstein, 1977). This chapter has tried to further the integration of decision research with the mainstream of psychology through a discussion of how information processing concepts and methods might help us understand decision making. More work in this area seems warranted.

REFERENCES

Abelson, R. Script processing in attitude formation and decision making. In J. S. Carroll & J. W. Payne (Eds.), *Cognition and social behavior*. Hillsdale, N.J.: Lawrence Erlbaum Associates, 1976.

Anderson, N. H. Information integration theory: A brief survey. In D. H. Krantz, R. C. Atkinson, R. D. Luce, & P. Suppes (Eds.), *Contemporary developments in mathematical psychology* (Vol. 2). San Francisco: Freeman, 1974.

Anderson, N. H., & Shanteau, J. C. Information integration in risky decision making. *Journal of Experimental Psychology*, 1970, *84*, 441–451.

Arrow, K. J. Alternative approaches to the theory of choice in risk-taking situations. *Econometrica*, 1951, *19*, 404–437.

Aschenbrenner, K. M. Single-peaked preferences and their dependability on the gambles presentation mode. *Journal of Experimental Psychology: Human Perception and Performance*, 1978, *4*, 513–520.

Bettman, J. R. Information processing models of consumer behavior. *Journal of Marketing Research*, 1970, *7*, 370–376.

Bettman, J. R., & Jacoby, J. Patterns of processing in consumer information acquisition. In B. B. Anderson (Ed.), *Advances in consumer research* (Vol. 3). Chicago Association for Consumer Research 1976.

Carroll, J. S., & Payne, J. W. Judgments about crime and the criminal: A model and a method for investigating parole decisions. In B. D. Sales (Ed.), *Perspectives in law and psychology. (Vol. 1): The criminal justice system*. New York: Plenum, 1977.

Clarkson, G. *Portfolio selection: A simulation of trust investment*. Englewood Cliffs, N.J.: Prentice-Hall, 1962.

Dansereau, D. F., & Gregg, L. W. An information processing analysis of mental multiplication. *Psychonomic Science*, 1966, *6*, 71–72.

Einhorn, H. J. The use of nonlinear, noncompensatory models in decision making. *Psychological Bulletin*, 1970, 73, 211–230.

Fischhoff, B., Slovic, P., & Lichtenstein, S. Fault trees: Sensitivity of estimated failure probabilities to problem representation. *Journal of Experimental Psychology: Human Perception and Performance*, 1978, 4, 330–344.

Fishburn, P. C. Mean–risk analysis with risk associated with below-target returns. *The American Economic Review*, 1977, *67*, 116–126.

Garner, W. R. Interaction of stimulus dimensions in concept and choice processes. *Cognitive Psychology*, 1976, *8*, 98–123.

Gravetter, F., & Lockhead, G. R. Critical range as a frame of reference for stimulus judgment. *Psychological Review*, 1973, *80*, 203–216.

Grether, D. M. & Plott, C. R. Economic theory of choice and the preference reversal phenomenon. *American Economic Review*, 1979, *69*, 623–638.

Hayes, J. R. Strategies in judgmental research. In B. Kleinmuntz (Ed.), *Formal representation of human judgment*. New York: Wiley, 1968.

Hayes, J. R., & Simon, H. A. The understanding process: Problem isomorphs. *Cognitive Psychology*, 1976, *8*, 165–190.

Hayes, J. R., Waterman, D. A., & Robinson, C. A. Identifying relevant aspects of a problem text. *Cognitive Science*, 1977, volume 297–313.

Hinsley, D., Hayes, J. R., & Simon, H. A. "From words to equations." In P. Carpenter & M. Just (Eds.), *Cognitive processes in comprehension*. Hillsdale, N.J.: Lawrence Erlbaum Associates, 1977.

Jacoby, J., Chestnut, R. W., Weigl, K. C., & Fisher, W. Pre-purchase information acquisition: Description of a process methodology, research paradigm, and pilot investigation. In B. B. Anderson (Ed.), *Advances in consumer research* (Vol. 3). Chicago Association for Consumer Research 1976.

Johnson, E. J. *What is remembered about consumer decisions?* Unpublished manuscript, Complex Information Processing No. 372. Carnegie-Mellon University, Pittsburgh, 1978.

Kahneman, D. & Tversky, A. Prospect theory: An analysis of decisions under risk. *Econometrica*, 1979, *47*, 263–291.

Kleinmuntz, B. The processing of clinical information by man and machine. In B. Kleinmuntz (Ed.), *Formal representation of human judgment*. New York: Wiley, 1968.

Kozielecki, J. The internal representation of risky tasks. *Polish Psychological Bulletin*, 1975, *6*, 115–121.

Lichtenstein, S., & Slovic, P. Response-induced reversals of preference in gambling: An extended replication in Las Vegas. *Journal of Experimental Psychology*, 1973, *101*, 16–20.

Lichtenstein, S., Slovic, P., & Zink, D. Effect of instruction in expected value on optimality of gambling decisions. *Journal of Experimental Psychology*, 1969, *79*, 236–240.

MacCrimmon, K. R. *Decision making among multiple-attribute alternatives: A survey and consolidated approach*. Santa Monica, Calif.: Rand Corporation, 1968.

Marx, M. H., & Hillix, W. A. *Systems and theories in psychology*. New York: McGraw-Hill, 1963.

Montgomery, H. A study of intransitive preferences using a think aloud procedure. In H. Jungerman & C. de Zeeuw (Eds.), *Proceedings of the Fifth Research Conference on Subjective Probability, Utility and Decision Making*, 1976.

Montgomery, H., & Svenson, O. On decision rules and information processing strategies for choices among multiattribute alternatives. *Scandinavian Journal of Psychology*, 1976, *17*, 283–291.

Newell, A., & Simon, H. A. *Human problem solving*. Englewood Cliffs, N.J.: Prentice-Hall, 1972.

Nisbett, R. E., & Wilson, T. D. Telling more than we can know: Verbal reports on mental processes. *Psychological Review*, 1977, *84*, 231–259.

Park, C. W. A seven point scale and a decision-maker's simplifying choice strategy: An operationalized satisficing-plus model. *Organizational Behavior and Human Performance*, 1978, *21*, 252–271.

Payne, J. W. *A process tracing study of risky decision making: Examples of protocols and comments*. Complex Information Processing Working Paper No. 274, Carnegie-Mellon University, Pittsburg, 1974.

Payne, J. W. Relation of perceived risk to preferences among gambles. *Journal of Experimental Psychology: Human Perception and Performance*, 1975, *104*, 86–94.

Payne, J. W. Task complexity and contingent processing in decision making: An information search and protocol analysis. *Organizational Behavior and Human Performance*, 1976, *16*, 366–387.

Payne, J. W., & Braunstein, M. L. Preferences among gambles with equal underlying distributions. *Journal of Experimental Psychology*, 1971, *87*, 13–18.

Payne, J. W., & Braunstein, M. L. *Task complexity and contingent processing in decision making: A replication and extension to risky choice*. Unpublished manuscript, University of Chicago, 1977.

Payne, J. W., & Braunstein, M. L. Risky choice: An examination of information acquisition behavior. *Memory & Cognition*, 1978, *6*, 554–561.

Payne, J. W., Braunstein, M. L., & Carroll, J. S. Exploring pre-decisional behavior: An alternative approach to decision research. *Organizational Behavior and Human Performance*, 1978, *22*, 17–44.

Pitz, G. F. Decision making and cogition. In H. Jungerman & G. de Zeeuw (Eds.), *Proceedings of the Fifth Research Conference on Subjective Probability, Utility, and Decision Making*, 1976.

Posner, M. I. *Cognition: An introduction*. Glenview, Ill.: Scott, Foresman, 1973.

Ranyard, R. H. Elimination by aspects as a decision rule for risky choice. *Acta Psychologica*, 1976, *40*, 299–310.

Rosen, L. D., & Rosenkoetter, P. An eye fixation analysis of choice and judgment with multiattribute stimuli. *Memory & Cognition*, 1976, *4*, 747–752.

Russo, J. E. Eye fixations can save the world: A critical evaluation and a comparison between eye fixations and other information processing methodologies. In J. K. Hunt (Ed.), *Advances in Consumer Research* (Vol. 5). (Ann Arbor Association for Consumer Research 1978.

Russo, J. E., & Dosher, B. A. *Dimensional evaluation: A heuristic for binary choice*. Unpublished manuscript, University of California, San Diego, 1975.

Russo, J. E., & Rosen, L. D. An eye fixation analysis of multialternative choice. *Memory & Cognition*, 1975, *3*, 267-276.

Schoemaker, P. J. H. *Experimental studies on individual decision making under risk: An information processing approach.* Unpublished doctoral dissertation, University of Pennsylvania, 1977.

Shanteau, J. An information-integration analysis of risky decision making. In M. F. Kaplan & S. Schwartz (Eds.), *Human Judgment and decision processes.* New York: Academic Press, 1975.

Simon, H. A. A behavioral model of rational choice. *Quarterly Journal of Economics*, 1955, *69*, 99-118.

Simon, H. A. Discussion: Cognition and social behavior. In J. S. Carroll & J. W. Payne (Eds.), *Cognition and social behavior.* Hillsdale, N.J.: Lawrence Erlbaum Associates, 1976.

Simon, H. A. *Models of man.* New York: Wiley, 1957.

Simon, H. A. Information processing theory of human problem solving. In W. K. Estes (Ed.), *Handbook of learning and cognitive process: Vol. 5: Human information processing.* Hillsdale, N.J.: Lawrence Erlbaum Associates, 1978.

Simon, H. A., & Hayes, J. R. The understanding process: Problem isomorphs. *Cognitive Psychology*, 1976, *8*, 165-190.

Slovic, P. *From Shakespeare to Simon: Speculations—and some evidence—about man's ability to process information.* Unpublished manuscript, Oregon Research Institute, 1972.

Slovic, P. The relative influence of probabilities and payoffs upon perceived risk of a gamble. *Psychonomic Science*, 1967, *9*, 223-224.

Slovic, P., Fischhoff, B., & Lichtenstein, S. Behavioral decision theory. *Annual Review of Psychology*, 1977, *28*, 1-39.

Slovic, P., Fischhoff, B., Lichtenstein, S., Corrigan, B., & Combs, B. Preference for insuring against probable small loses: Insurance implications. *Journal of Risk and Insurance*, 1977, *44*, 237-258.

Slovic, P., & Lichtenstein, S. Importance of various preferences in gambling decisions. *Journal of Experimental Psychology*, 1968, *78* 646-654. (a)

Slovic, P., & Lichtenstein, S. Relative importance of probabilities and payoffs in risk taking. *Journal of Experimental Psychology*, 1968, *78*, (3, pt. 2). (b)

Slovic, P., & MacPhillamy, D. Dimensional commensurability and cue utilization in comparative judgment. *Organizational Behavior and Human Performance*, 1974, *11*, 174-194.

Smith, E. R., & Miller, F. D. The limits on perception of cognitive processes: A reply to Nisbett and Wilson. *Psychological Review*, 1978 *85*, 355-362.

Svenson, O. *Coded think-aloud protocols obtained when making a choice to pruchase one of seven hypothetically offered houses: Some examples.* Progress report on project of *Cognitive Processing and Decision Making.* University of Stockholm, 1974.

Tversky, A. Elimination by aspects: A theory of choice. *Psychological Review*, 1972, *79*, 281-299.

Tversky, A. Intransitivity of perferences. *Psychological Review*, 1969 *76*, 31-48.

Van Raaij, F. W. *Direct monitoring of consumer information processing by eye movement recorder.* Unpublished manuscript, Department of Psychology, Tilbury University. The Netherlands, 1976.

Wright, P. Consumer choice strategies: Simplifying vs. optimizing. *Journal of Marketing Research*, 1975, *12*, 60-67.

Wright, P., & Barbour, F. Phased decision strategies: Sequels to an initial screening. In M. K. Starr & M. Zeleny (Eds.), *Multiple criteria decision making: TIMS studies in the management sciences* (Vol. 6) (available as a special issue of *Management Science*). Amsterdam: North-Holland, 1977.

7 Knowing What You Want: Measuring Labile Values

Baruch Fischhoff
Paul Slovic
Sarah Lichtenstein
Decision Research,
A Branch of Perceptronics

An article of faith among students of value, choice, and attitude judgments is that people have reasonably well-defined opinions regarding the desirability of various events. Although these opinions may not be intuitively formulated in numerical (or even verbal) form, careful questioning can elicit judgments representing people's underlying values. From this stance, elicitation procedures are neutral tools, bias-free channels that translate subjective feelings into scientifically usable expressions. They impose no views on respondents beyond focusing attention on those value issues of interest to the investigator.

What happens, however, in cases where people do not know, or have difficulty appraising, what they want? Under such circumstances, elicitation procedures may become major forces in shaping the values expressed, or apparently expressed, in the judgments they require. They can induce random error (by confusing the respondent), systematic error (by hinting at what the "correct" response is), or unduly extreme judgments (by suggesting clarity and coherence of opinion that are not warranted). In such cases, the method becomes the message. If elicited values are used as guides for future behavior, they may lead to decisions not in the decision maker's best interest, to action when caution is desirable (or the opposite), or to the obfuscation of poorly formulated views needing careful development and clarification.

The topic of this chapter is the confrontation between those who hold (possibly inchoate) values and those who elicit values. By "values," we mean evaluative judgments regarding the relative or absolute worth or desirability of possible events. Such events may be general (being honest) or specific (winning a particular lottery). Their consequences (or outcomes) may have one or many salient attributes and may be certainties or possibilities. Such a broad definition captures just about any task ever included under the topics of value, choice, or preference, as well as many that would fit comfortably under attitudes, opinions, and decision making. Our discussion is limited to situations in which people are reporting their values as honestly as possible; the further complication of measuring values in the face of strategic behavior is not considered.

The recurrent theme of this chapter is that subtle aspects of how problems are posed, questions are phrased, and responses are elicited can have substantial impact on judgments that supposedly express people's true values. Furthermore, such lability in expressed preferences is unavoidable: Questions must be posed in some manner and that manner may have a large effect on the responses elicited. Pursuit of the issues raised here can at best alert elicitor and respondent to such impacts, making these effects deliberate rather than covert.

One might hope that such analysis would identify the "right" way to ask about values. To foreshadow our conclusions, we believe that the quest for a right way is, at times, ill-founded. Although there are some obvious pitfalls to avoid, instability is often inherent in our values. Rather than trying to circumvent such lability, we should try to exploit the insight it provides into the nature of values, and their formation, change, and application.

WHEN AND HOW PEOPLE MIGHT NOT KNOW WHAT THEY WANT

People are most likely to have clear preferences regarding issues that are familiar, simple, and directly experienced. Each of these properties is associated with opportunities for trial-and-error learning, particularly such learning as may be summarized in readily applicable rules or homilies.[1] Those rules provide stereotypic, readily justifiable responses to future questions of values. When adopted by individuals, they may be seen as habits; when adopted by groups, they constitute traditions.

The acceptability and perceived validity of such adages as "honesty is the best policy" and "cleanliness is next to godliness" is to some extent appropriate. As guides to living, they have been subjected to some empirical testing (being clean either has or has not brought satisfaction to oneself, one's neighbors, one's ancestors). They are often derived and formulated to be coherent with a wider body of beliefs and values. And, they are readily applicable, both because of their simplicity and because the individual has had practice in working through their implications for various situations. Such facility should help to guarantee that people will give similar answers (regarding, say, the importance of cleanliness), expressing the same underlying views, regardless of how the question is posed.

---

[1]These are, incidently, conditions quite similar to those cited by Nisbett and Bellows (1977) as necessary for valid introspection.

The power of these rules of thumb comes from their development and application to the settings found in a simple and unchanging society with repetitive problems. [2] Their viability becomes quite suspect in a world where the issues are unfamiliar and complex, the old intuitions impotent, the old rules untested and perhaps untestable.

Today we are asked to take responsibility for choosing a mate, a job, a family size, for guiding social policy, and for adopting or rejecting new technologies. Each of these issues confronts us with greater freedom of choice and more lasting consequences than ever before. They take us into situations for which we have never thought through the implications of the values and beliefs acquired in simpler settings. We may be unfamiliar with the terms in which issues are formulated (e.g., social discount rates, miniscule probabilities, or megadeaths). We may have contradictory values (e.g., a desire to avoid catastrophic losses and a realization that we are not more moved by a plane crash with 500 fatalities than by one with 300). We may occupy different roles in life (parents, workers, children) that produce clear-cut, but inconsistent, values. We may vacillate between incompatible, but strongly held, positions (e.g., freedom of speech is inviolate, but should be denied to authoritarian movements). We may not even know how to begin thinking about some issues (e.g., the appropriate tradeoff between the opportunity to dye one's hair and a vague, minute increase in the probability of cancer 20 years from now). Our views may undergo predictable changes over time (say, as the hour of decision approaches) and we may not know which view should form the basis of our decision. We may see things differently in theory than in the flesh. We may lack the mental capacity to think through the issues reliably and therefore come up with different conclusions each time we consider an issue.

One possible partition of the psychological states that might accompany not knowing what we want appears in Table 7.1. Perhaps the most dangerous condition is the first, having no opinion and not realizing it. In that state, we may respond with the first thing that comes to mind once a question is asked. As a defense against uncertainty, we may then commit ourselves to maintaining that first expression and to mustering support for it, suppressing other views and uncertainties. We may then be stuck with stereotypic or associative responses reflecting immediate stimulus configurations rather than serious contemplation.

---

[2]However, one should not tout folk or personal wisdom too highly. Even in those settings, people comfortably hold contradictory adages (''Nothing ventured, nothing gained'' and ''Fools rush in where wise men fear to tred''). The testing procedures for validating such wisdom leaves much to be desired. People may not realize when experience provides a test for their well-worn rules and may not remember their experiences properly when they do consider validity. They may forget a rule's failures and remember its successes, or vice versa. Finally, the translation of subjective feelings to observable judgments has an unavoidable error component due to inattention, distraction, laziness, and mistakes. Such error can introduce enough slippage into the opinion evaluation and formulation process to make clarity somewhat difficult.

TABLE 7.1
Psychological States Associated
With Not Knowing
What You Want

Having no opinion
    Not realizing it
    Realizing it
        Living without one
        Trying to form one
Having an incoherent opinion
    Not realizing it
    Realizing it
        Living with incoherence
        Trying to form a coherent opinion
Having a coherent opinion
    Accessing it properly
    Accessing only a part of it
    Accessing something else

Perhaps the most painful state is to acknowledge having incoherent or conflicted values requiring further analysis.

The states described in Table 7.1 are determined in part by the actual state of our values and in part by how we assess them in a particular situation. The critical elements of that assessment would seem to be: (1) our need for closure, itself a function of the importance of the issue at hand, the need to act, and the audience for our judgments: (2) the depth of the analysis, determined by the thoroughness of the elicitation procedure and our general familiarity with the issue at hand; and (3) our awareness of the problems raised in this chapter—that is, the possibility of not knowing what we want and the power of the elicitor to tell (or hint) to us what our values are.

PSYCHOPHYSICS OF VALUE

Finding that judgments are influenced by unintended aspects of experimental procedure and that those influences are worthy of study is an oft-told tale in the history of psychology. Indeed, McGuire (1969b) describes much of that history as the process by which one scientist's artifact becomes another's main effect. Central to this process is the recognition that the effective stimulus cannot be presumed, but must be discovered (Boring, 1969). A selective survey of this history appears in Table 7.2.[3]

---

[3]No attempt will be made to document this incomplete list drawn from various parts of the lore of psychology. Useful references include Carterette and Friedman (1974), Galanter (1974), Helson (1964), Kling and Riggs (1971), L. E. Marks (1974), Parducci (1974), Posner (1973), Poulton (1968), Rosenthal and Rosnow (1969), Upshaw (1974), and Woodworth and Schlosberg (1954).

Although no attempt has been made at more elaborate categorization of these variables, perhaps the critical factor for experimental design has been whether an effect leads to random or systematic variations in the observed judgments. Recognition of systematic effects is, of course, most productive, leading to the identification of basic psychological principles (e.g., the psychological refractory period uncovered by varying speed of stimulus presentation) or theories (e.g., range–frequency theory derived from effects caused by varying the range and homogeneity of presented stimuli) or design principles (e.g., counterbalancing for situations in which order effects have been observed). The discovery of variables producing random error typically allows little response other than estimation of the size of the effect and the sample size needed to obtain desired statistical power. Although at times noise-reduction techniques may be available

TABLE 7.2
From Artifact to Main Effect

Lability in judgment due to	*Led to*
Organism	
Inattention, laziness, fatigue, habituation, learning, maturation, physiological limitations, natural rhythms, experience with related tasks	Repeated measures Professional subjects Stochastic response models Psychophysiology Proactive and retroactive inhibition research
Stimulus Presentation	
Homogeneity of alternatives, similarity of successive alternatives (especially first and second), speed of presentation, amount of information, range of alternatives, place in range of first alternative, distance from threshold, order of presentation, areal extent, ascending or descending series	Classic psychophysical methods The new psychophysics Attention research Range–frequence theory Order-effects research Regression effects Anticipation
Response Mode	
Stimulus-response compatibility, naturalness of response, set, number of categories, halo effects, anchoring, very small numbers, response category labeling, use of end points	Ergonomics research Set research Attitude measurement Assessment techniques Contrasts of between- and within-subject design Response-bias research Use of blank trials
"Irrelevant" Context Effects	
Perceptual defenses, experimenter cues, social pressures, presuppositions, implicit payoffs, social desirability, confusing instructions, response norms, response priming, stereotypic responses, second-guessing	New look in perception Verbal conditioning Experimenter demand Signal-detection theory Social pressure, comparison, and facilitation research

(e.g., testing in the morning or providing payment for accuracy), they are usually undertaken with some trepidation for fear of turning a large random error into a smaller systematic one and creating a task very unrepresentative of its real-world analog.

We cite these effects for several reasons. One is because many of them seem to be as endemic to judgments of value as they are to the judgmental context in which they were originally observed. Parducci (1974), for example, has found that judged satisfaction with one's state in life may depend highly on the range of states considered. Turner and Krauss (1978) present evidence suggesting that order of question presentation in surveys may have marked effects on people's evaluation of the state of the nation and its institutions. Lichtenstein and Slovic (1973) found that the judged attractiveness of casino gambles is greatly affected by stimulus–response compatibility. The second reason the effects are cited is to set the stage for the following discussion of effects more specific to the judgment of values. Like the phenomena in Table 7.2, these effects may be considered as today's artifacts on the way to becoming tomorrow's independent variables. The third reason is to foreswear any pretense of trying to create a scientific revolution. The pattern we are following is a hoary and respected one in the history of psychology: collecting and sorting a variety of documented and suspected sources of lability in a particular form of judgment. By bringing together such a diverse collection of effects, we hope to: (1) facilitate an appreciation of the extent to which people's apparent values are determined by the elicitor; (2) provide a tentative organization of effects and the contexts in which they may arise; and (3) explicate the implications of these results for various areas in basic and applied psychology.

OVERVIEW

If, as Rokeach (1973) claims, people have relatively few basic values, producing an answer to a specific value question is largely an exercise in inference. We must decide which of our values are relevant to that situation, how they are to be interpreted, and what weight each is to be given. This inferential process is determined in part by how the question is defined and in part by which perspectives we invoke in solving the inferential problem it poses. Once we have reached a summary judgment, we must decide how strongly we believe in it and in the perspectives upon which it is based.

As outlined in Table 7.3, the following three sections describe how an elicitor can affect the expression or formulation of values by controlling the definition of problems, the recruitment and integration of perspectives, and the confidence placed in the result of the inferential process. That control may be overt or covert, deliberate or inadvertent, reversible or irreversible. A fourth section is devoted to the topic of irreversible effects whereby the respondent is actually

TABLE 7.3
Ways that an Elicitor May Affect
A Respondent's Judgments of Value

Defining the issue
    Is there a problem?
    What options and consequences are relevant?
    How should options and consequences be labeled?
    How should values be measured?
    Should the problem be decomposed?
Controlling the respondent's perspectives
    Altering the salience of perspectives
    Altering the importance of perspectives
    Choosing the time of inquiry
Changing confidence in expressed values
    Misattributing the source
    Changing the apparent degree of coherence
Changing the respondent
    Destroying existing perspectives
    Creating perspective
    Deepening perspectives

---

changed by the elicitation process, through having existing perspectives destroyed or new ones created.

The notion of an external elicitor is used mainly as a syntactical device to avoid unclear antecedents. Questions of value must be posed in some way. If an external elicitor does not pose them for us, then we must pose them for ourselves (if only by accepting some "natural" formulation offered by our environment). Indeed, the power of the effects described here may be magnified when we pose problems to ourselves, unless we direct at our own questions the same critical eye that we turn to someone else asking us about our values.

DEFINING THE ISSUE

Is There a Problem?

Before a question of value can be posed, someone must decide that there is something to question. In this fundamental way, the elicitor impinges on the respondent's values. By asking about the desirability of premarital sex, interracial dating, daily prayer, freedom of expression, or the fall of capitalism, the elicitor may legitimize events that were previously viewed as unacceptable or cast doubts on events that were previously unquestioned. Opinion polls help set our national agenda by the questions they do and do not ask. Advertising helps set our personal agendas by the questions it induces us to ask ourselves (two-door or four-door?) and those it takes for granted (more is better).

What Options and Consequences Are Relevant?

Once a question has been broached, its scope must be specified. Bounds must be placed on the options and consequences to be considered. The lore of survey research is replete with evidence regarding the subtle ways in which these bounds can be controlled by the elicitor's demeanor and the implicit assumptions and presumptions in the phrasing of questions (Payne, 1952). There are, it seems, many ways to communicate to a respondent: (1) whether the set of possible options is restricted to the named, the feasible, the popular, or the legal; (2) whether new options may be created; and (3) whether the question may be rejected out of hand. The set of relevant consequences may also be shaped to include or exclude intangible consequences (those without readily available dollar equivalents), ethical (versus efficiency) issues, social (versus personal) impacts, secondary and tertiary consequences, means (versus ends), and the well being of nature (versus that of humans). Control may be inadvertent as well as deliberate. For example, what may seem to the elicitor to be irrelevant and dominated alternatives, sensibly deleted for the sake of simplicity, may provide important contextual information for the respondent.

A tempting solution for the elicitor would be to specify the problem as little as possible, leaving respondents to define the option and consequence sets as they see fit. Unfortunately, this approach increases the probability that the elicitor and respondent will be talking about different things without solving the problem of inadvertent control. Indeed, one might even argue that impassive elicitation is the most manipulative of all. For it means that the entire questioning experience is conducted under the influence of the unanalyzed predispositions and presumptions of the elicitor without even a courtesy warning to the respondent (Rosenthal & Rosnow, 1969): "Here are my prejudices, let's try to be wary of them." There is no reason to believe that people will be spontaneously aware of what has been left out but not brought to their attention (Fischhoff, 1977a; Fischhoff, Slovic, & Lichtenstein, 1978; Lovins, 1977; Nisbett & Wilson, 1977; Tribe, Schelling, & Voss, 1976).

How Should Options and Consequences Be Labeled?

The elicitor's influence on the definition of options and consequences does not end with their enumeration. Once the concepts have been evoked, they must be given labels. As B. A. Marks (1977) suggests, in a world with few hard evaluative standards, such symbolic interpretations may be very important. Although the facts of abortion remain constant, individuals may vacillate in their attitude as they attach and detach the label of "murder." The value of a dollar may change greatly if it is called "discretionary funds," "public funds," or "widows' and orphans' funds."

Political scientists have been accused of ideologically biasing their research by describing acts, options, and outcomes with terms drawn from neoclassical economics with its particular (mostly conservative) political bias (Ashcraft, 1977). More generally, Karl Mannheim (1936) observed that "the political theorist's . . . most general mode of thought including even his categories is bound up with general political and social undercurrents . . . extend[ing] even into the realm of logic itself [p. 117]." Presumably, political scientists' choice of language imposes that perspective on respondents to their surveys and readers of their texts.

Although not new, these issues are still troublesome. Furthermore, they cannot be avoided, for some meaning must be given to events, and the meaning generated by the respondent may be even less appropriate than that imposed by the elicitor (Poulton, 1977). When the respondent sees the validity of contradictory symbolic meanings (e.g., abortion both is and is not murder), conflict in meaning cannot be resolved. In such cases, the only recourse is to step back, somehow, and decide on exogenous grounds just what this elicitation session is all about. If necessary, that longer look should come sooner rather than later. Often, changes in perspective are irreversible (Fischhoff, 1977b). The psychological impact of an offered interpretation may not be rescindable (try to forget that "this is what I, your mother, want you to do, but decide for yourself" or that "this is your childhood sweetheart's favorite restaurant").

How Should Values Be Measured?

After the problem has been structured, the units of measurement must be chosen. It is not difficult to construct options whose relative desirability is changed when the evaluative criterion undergoes any of the following shifts: (1) from profit to regret; (2) from maximizing to satisficing; (3) from the fair price to the price I'd pay; (4) from final asset position to changes in asset position; (5) from the price I'd pay to avoid a malady to the price I'd have to be paid to accept it; (6) from lives saved to lives lost; and (7) from the ratio of benefits to costs to the difference between benefits and costs.[4] As before, choice of units may be specified by the elicitor or left to that nether region created by the "neutral" stance of nonspecification.

Moreover, the size of the unit chosen may affect the responses. Unless some help is provided to the respondent (say, through the use of anchors or logarithmic scales), it may be very difficult to express values that range over several orders of magnitude for a given set of stimuli because people find it hard to use either very small or very large numbers (Poulton, 1968).

---

[4]Kahneman and Tversky (1979) provide the most extensive and insightful discussion of the power of shifts in point of reference, the principle underlying many of these effects.

Should the Problem Be Decomposed?

Many (or most) interesting questions of value are subtle, complex, and multifaceted, with intricate interrelations and consequences. The elicitor must choose between presenting the event to be evaluated as a whole or offering some kind of decomposition. Offering an unanalyzed whole incurs the risk that the respondent will fixate on a single aspect of the problem or treat all aspects superficially, so as to minimize cognitive strain.

Unfortunately, the act of decomposition has consequences besides clarification. One charge leveled against divide-and-conquer strategies is that they destroy the intuitions of the respondent (Dreyfus & Dreyfus, n. d.). Drawing on the work of Gestalt psychologists and Polanyi (e.g., 1962), these critics argue that people think most naturally and adequately by analogy with past experiences and that all such thought (regarding issues of fact or value) is context dependent. Therefore, any attempt to evaluate separately the attributes of a particular event or designate the importance of attributes in the abstract is likely to produce spurious results. In addition to destroying the respondent's natural understanding, decomposition procedures may impose a response mode that does not allow people to articulate their understanding of (holistic) value issues.[5]

Furthermore, decompositions are not unique; different cuts may lead to different judgments of the same issue. Sequential evaluation of alternatives has been found to produce different preferences than simultaneous evaluation (Tversky, 1969). Plott and Levine (1978) have shown that the order in which attributes are considered is a crucial variable in determining preference orderings. Some theories of choice (Aschenbrenner, 1978) predict shifts in the attractiveness of simple gambles as a function of their decomposition. Kahneman and Tversky (1979) demonstrated a variety of reversals in preference depending on whether prospects were considered as a whole or decomposed into two stages. The effective element here was isolating (in the first stage) one suboutcome that was known for certain. Certain losses and gains are weighted more heavily than uncertain outcomes in determining overall attractiveness.

Finally, as Tribe (1972) has argued, decomposition itself typically carries a message. It stresses ends over means. It proclaims the superiority of the elicitor's overall perspective (and the overall social importance of analysis and its purveyors; Gouldner, 1976). It conveys a message of analyzability or solvability where that may be inappropriate.

---

[5]If true, this criticism would attribute the greatest validity to elicitation procedures that leave options in their most natural form. For example, Hammond's social judgment theory approach (Hammond & Adelman, 1976), in which complete options are judged, should be preferred to the Keeney and Raiffa (1976) procedure, in which whole options are evaluated but only two attributes are varied at a time. That procedure, in turn, should be preferred to Edwards' (Gardiner & Edwards, 1975) SMART method that forces total decomposition. Ironically, Dreyfus and Dreyfus (n.d.) chose Hammond and Adelman (1976) as a case in point for the flaws of decomposition.

CONTROLLING THE RESPONDENT'S PERSPECTIVE

Altering the Salience of Perspectives

People solve problems, including the determination of their own values, with what comes to mind. The more detailed, exacting, and creative their inferential process is, the more likely they are to think of all they know about a question. The briefer that process becomes, the more they will be controlled by the relative accessibility of various considerations. Accessibility may be related to importance, but it is also related to degree of associative priming, the order in which questions are posed, imaginability, concreteness, and other factors only loosely related to importance.

One way in which the elicitor may unintentionally prime particular considerations is seen in Turner and Krauss' (1978) observation that people's confidence in national institutions was substantially higher in a National Opinion Research Center poll than in a Harris poll taken at the same time when the latter prefaced the confidence questions with six items relating to "political alienation." Another is Fischhoff, Slovic, Lichtenstein, Read, and Combs' (1978) finding that people judged the risks associated with various technologies to be more acceptable following a judgment task concerning the benefits of those technologies than following a task dwelling on their risks. According to Wildavsky (1966), the very act of asking people for their own personal values may suppress the availability of social values. Indeed, one could speculate that, in general, when conflicting values are relevant to a particular issue, the priming or evocation of one will tend to suppress the accessibility of its counterpart.

Expressed values sometimes reflect the direct application of established rules. Consistency with past preferences is one such rule; cautiousness is another. Whether or not a rule is evoked will depend on situational cues. As an example of a rule that needed to be evoked before it was used, we have found that most people will prefer a gamble with a .25 chance to lose $200 (and a .75 chance to lose nothing) to a *sure loss* of $50. However, when that sure loss is called an *insurance premium,* people will reverse their preferences and forego the $50. For these people, insurance was an acceptable but initially inaccessible rule; without a specific prompt, the sure loss was not seen as a premium.

Altering the Importance of Perspectives

Once an ensemble of relevant values has been elicited, some order must be placed on them. This ordering or weighting may also fall under elicitor control. Such control is, in fact, what experimental demand characteristics are all about: unintentionally telling the subject how to think, what to look at, and what is expected. The unintended impacts of elicitor expectancies show the power of inadvertent influence (Rosenthal, 1969). Although Rosenthal minimizes the importance of operant conditioning in such influence, it is not hard to imagine the impact of an incredulous "hmm" or a querulous "half as important?" on the behavior of a confused or uncertain respondent. Nor is it hard to imagine how the demeanor of the elicitor might encourage or discourage the weight given to intangible or non-western values. Canavan-Gumpert (1977) has shown how reward and criticism can shift people's attention between the costs and benefits involved with a particular event.

One unavoidable decision made by the elicitor that may have great influence on the values that emerge is choice of response mode. Lichtenstein and Slovic (1971, 1973; see also Grether & Plott, 1979, and Lindman, 1971) showed that people use different cognitive processes when evaluating the worth of gambles via a comparative mode ("Which would you rather play?") than they use when judging each gamble separately ("How much is playing each worth to you?"). The different processes triggered by the change in response mode lead people to rather awkward reversals of preference ("I prefer A, but attach a higher value to B."). One possible explanation of such reversals, based on related work by Tversky (1972) and Slovic (1975), is that people make choices by searching for rules or concepts that provide a good justification, that minimize the lingering doubts, and that can be defended no matter what outcome occurs (example: "Quality is more important than quantity."). Different response modes increase the importance of different rules. In the gambles example, A offered a higher probability of winning whereas B promised a greater payoff. Here, the preference mode may have emphasized that "the stakes don't matter if you're not going to win anyway," whereas the bidding mode focused attention on the payoff.

Another effect peculiar to choice behavior was found by Slovic and MacPhillamy (1974), who observed that dimensions common to each alternative had greater influence on choices than did dimensions that were unique to a particular alternative. Interrogation of the respondents after the study indicated that most did not intend to give more weight to the common dimension and were unaware that they had done so.

Choosing the Time of Inquiry

People's values change over time, sometimes systematically, sometimes not. The point in time at which the elicitor chooses to impinge on the respondent will determine in part what the respondent says. Some changes are secular and relatively irreversible. A society and its members may become more or less predisposed to consider environmental values (Harblin, 1977) or equity issues or the rights of women as time goes on. The age distribution in that society as a whole may be shifting, leading to a greater preponderance of young or old people with their characteristic perspectives. By waiting or by hastening, an elicitor has some power to create a different picture of people's expressed values.

Other changes over time, with varying degrees of predictability, are maturation, satiation, cumulative deprivation, increasing risk aversion as one approaches an event, mood changes with time of day, day of the week, or season of the year. Consider people who regularly take stock of the world late at night and whose existential decisions are colored by their depleted body state. Is that value to be trusted or should one rely on the way they value their lives at high noon on a bright spring day? Should an elicitor rely on an auto worker's opinion of the intrinsic satisfaction of assembly-line work on the bus Monday morning or while on holiday and refreshed? In a multiple-play experiment on insurance-buying behavior (Slovic, Fischhoff, Lichtenstein, Corrigan, & Combs, 1977), we found that participants who were generally risk seeking shifted to risk aversion on the final round (just before cashing out). Which attitude should we say characterized them? Or, might not both of these perspectives be part of the individual's value system?

Any gap in time between judgment of an event and its occurrence may introduce an element of random or systematic variation in people's judgment. Hypothetical judgments of what an event would be like may not capture how it will look in the flesh. The contrast between the limited funds budgeted for rescue operations and disaster relief and the almost unlimited resources made available for a particular rescue is one product of this failure of anticipation, as is our greater readiness to pay for the protection of known rather than statistical lives (Fried, 1969). We know relatively little about people's ability to anticipate the impact that specified future contingencies will have on their perceptions and values—nor which perspective, the anticipated or the actual, is a better guide to action (or true preferences). The scanty evidence we have suggests that sometimes, at least, it is better to go with one's anticipations if derived in a relatively thoughtful setting (Fischhoff, Slovic & Lichtenstein, 1979).

CHANGING CONFIDENCE IN EXPRESSED VALUES

The power of values comes from their roles as guides to actions, as embodiments of ourselves, and as expressions of our relation to the world (Rokeach, 1973). It may matter greatly what we think their source to be, how strongly we believe in them, and how coherent they seem. Attitudes towards values may, however, be as labile as the values themselves.

Misattributing the Source

Much of the history of social psychology involves attempts to get people to misattribute the source of their values, by counterattitudinal role playing, by exposure to undirected (overheard) conversations, by conformity pressure, or by inducing social comparison processes. These manipulations lead people to adopt as their own, without critical analysis, attitudes that originated with others (McGuire, 1969a). Cognitive psychology offers some new wrinkles in this misattribution process, showing the ease with which presuppositions are absorbed as facts (Loftus, Miller, & Burns, 1978), inferences are confused with direct observations (Harris & Monaco, 1978), mere repetition improves the believability of statements (Hasher, Goldstein, & Toppino, 1977), and people egocentrically assume that others share their views (Ross, Greene, & House, 1977).

Changing the Apparent Degree of Coherence

People will act and press others to act on values in which they believe most deeply. Depth of belief is a function of source, as mentioned, and of the degree to which such values appear to be in conflict. A superficial analysis may create an illusion of confidence in values simply because conflicting values are not considered. Incoherence in beliefs is typically apparent only when the elicitor adopts or encourages different perspectives. It is easy to avoid taking that extra step, particularly when the respondent is interested in keeping things simple.

Such collusion towards simplicity is encouraged by one implicit message of many elicitation procedures: "This topic is knowable, analyzable; after one session, we will both know your values." It is magnified by the aura of precision and professionalism fostered by elaborate, numerical response modes. That aura manifests the can-do technological-fix, mastery-of-the-world attitude that characterizes our society (Tribe et al., 1976). Ellul (1969) has argued that one way to control people's minds is to lead them to believe that they can have an opinion on anything and everything. Those opinions will necessarily be superficial, guaranteeing that people will have elaborated, thoughtful positions on nothing. When we ask or answer questions of value, a useful antidote to overconfidence might be to recall the effort invested by Rawls (1971) and his colleagues to produce a reasonably coherent position on just one difficult value issue, social justice.

It is, of course, natural to feel that we are the ranking experts, the final arbiters of our own values. Yet, in order to know how good our best assessment of those values is, we must recognize the extent to which they are under the control of factors that we (as scientists as well as individuals) understand rather poorly.

CHANGING THE RESPONDENT

In most of the effects previously cited, the elicitor neither creates nor destroys values, but merely affects the ways in which they are accessed, organized, and evaluated. Some effects, however, suggest ways in which the respondent may be irreversibly changed by the questioning procedure, perhaps for the better, perhaps for the worse. These fall into three generic categories: The elicitor may destroy an existing perspective on a value issue, create a perspective where none existed before, or deepen the respondent's understanding of the issue at hand or of value questions in general.

Destroying Existing Perspectives

As mentioned, one charge leveled against those who break complex questions of value into more manageable component questions is that their divide-and-conquer strategy destroys the intuitions of their respondent. A generalization of this position might be that any elicitation procedure deviating from the normal way in which judgments are made may erode the respondent's "feel" for the issue at hand. The failure of formal decision-making procedures to attract the loyalty of corporate decision makers has repeatedly been attributed to these individuals' refusal to trade the comforts of their intuitions for the promises of the formal methods (Harrison, 1977).

Other aspects of an elicitation mode may destroy parts of our "natural" perspective on issues (Barnes, 1976). For example, the dyadic nature of the elicitation procedure, with an elicitor who is reluctant to influence the response, may deprive the respondent of the opportunity to invoke social comparison processes (Upshaw, 1974). Discussion with others may be a natural part of the way in which many people formulate their judgments. It may also be an effective procedure, perhaps by recruiting additional information and externalizing alternative perspectives that are too difficult to carry in one's head simultaneously. In these examples, the elicitation procedure may be seen as destroying respondents' natural perspective by depriving them of tools upon which they are accustomed to rely (Edwards, 1975).

Creating Perspectives

An insidious possibility when posing unfamiliar questions to individuals with poorly formulated opinions is covertly creating a perspective where none existed. One possible process for accomplishing this feat is for the respondent to satisfy the elicitor's hunger for a recordable response by saying whatever comes to mind. Once emitted, this associative response may assume a life of its own. The respondent may subsequently conclude (Bem, 1972), "If that's what I said, then that must be what I meant." As shown in studies of counterattitudinal role playing (McGuire, 1969a), such positions can show a tenacity that is independent of their source or validity (Ross, 1977). The fact that such spontaneous responses are provided in a formal setting with a relatively esteemed listener may heighten such commitment effects, leading to newly invented but firmly held values. The very fact that one is out of one's depths in such situations makes it quite difficult to get a critical view on this new perspective.

Elicitation may induce people to think about issues they wish to avoid and would have ignored had they not been "bullied" by the elicitor. In some cases, the elicitor cannot be faulted for forcing people to take their heads out of the sand and face the issues implicit in the decisions they must make in any case. The use of decision analysis in medical contexts will create many such situations as physicians and patients are forced to provide explicit values for pain and death (Bunker, Barnes, & Mosteller, 1977). In other cases, the elicitor may be asking respondents to abrogate their own rights by telling, say, how much they would have to be compensated for a particular degradation to their environment without offering the response option (Brookshire, Ives, & Schulze, 1976): "a clean environment is non-negotiable." In the extreme, the elicitor may be guilty of "anaesthetizing moral feeling" by inducing the respondent to think about the unthinkable (Tribe, 1972). The mere act of thinking about some issues in "cold, rational" terms may lead to the legitimation of alternatives that should be dismissed outright.

Deepening Perspectives

Although the preceding discussion has emphasized unsavory aspects of the impact of the elicitor on the respondent, there are obviously situations in which the only valid elicitation procedure is a reactive one. Consider a national poll of values on issues relevant to nuclear waste disposal, the results of which will be used to guide policy makers. An individual who has no elaborated beliefs may not be responding in his or her best interests by giving the value the question seems to hint at. On the other hand, providing no response effectively constitutes disenfranchisement. An elicitor might reasonably be expected to help in translating the respondent's basic predispositions into codable judgments whose implications and assumptions are well understood. Surely, an elicitor does small service to a respondent with incoherent values by asking questions that tap only a part of those values, particularly if that part might be abandoned (or endorsed more heartily) upon further contemplation.

How might the elicitor deepen the respondent's perspective without unduly manipulating it? One reasonably safe way may be to help the respondent work through the logical implications of various points of view. We presented college students and members of the League of Women Voters with the two tasks shown in Fig. 7.1. The first asked them to choose between a high-variance and a low-variance option involving the loss of life. The second asked to choose one of three functions as representing the way in which society should evaluate lives in multifatality situations. Its instructions (omitted in Fig. 7.1) provided elaborate rationales for adopting each of the three function forms. The predominant response pattern, chosen by over half of all subjects, was Option A in the civil defense question and Curve 2 in the second task.[6] The former indicates a risk-

---

[6]These results were not changed appreciably either by changing the degree of elaboration in the rationale given for the three curves, nor by describing civil defense Option B as an action option that

Task 1: Civil Defense

A civil defense committee in a large metropolitan area met recently to discuss contingency plans in the event of various emergencies. One emergency under discussion was the following: "A train carrying a very toxic chemical derails and the storage tanks begin to leak. The threat of explosion and lethal discharge of poisonous gas is imminent."

Two possible actions were considered by the committee. These are described below. Read them and indicate your opinion about the relative merits of each.

OPTION A: carries with it a .5 probability of containing the threat without any loss of life and a .5 probability of losing 100 lives. It is like taking the gamble:

   .5 lose 0 lives
   .5 lose 100 lives

OPTION B: would produce a certain loss of 50 lives.

   lose 50 lives

Which option do you prefer?

_____ Option A
_____ Option B

Task 2: The Impact of Catastrophic Events

(Two pages of instructions explaining the meaning of the curves preceded the following:)

Please rank the three proposals in order of preference.

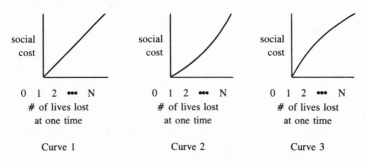

FIG. 7.1.   Two tasks that elicited inconsistency in values towards catastrophic loss of life.

reduced the number of casualties (to a small, but definite, number). The civil defense question was posed in nine ways, varying the variance, expectation, and probability of loss with Option A (with B always a sure loss of A's expectation). Option B was never chosen by more than 10% of subjects except in the one case where A specified a .99 chance of losing no lives and a .01 chance of losing 100 lives, whereas B specified the certainty of losing one life.

seeking attitude towards the loss of life. The latter indicates a risk-averse attitude. Confronting subjects with this inconsistency allowed them the opportunity to reflect on its source and on their true values.

Many social decisions require people to determine desirable rates for growth or for discounting future costs and benefits. Wagenaar and Sagaria (1975) have shown that people have very poor intuitions on the cumulative impact of those rates when they are compounded over a period of years: "Neither special instructions about the nature of exponential growth nor daily experience with growth processes enhanced the extrapolations [p. 416]." When issues with compounded rates arise, the elicitor should work through the details of the extrapolations, leaving nothing to the imagination.

A more difficult intervention is to educate respondents about the assumptions upon which their beliefs are contingent. Tougher still is trying to communicate factual information the respondent may not have known or taken into consideration. Kunreuther, Ginsberg, Miller, Sagi, Slovic, Borkan, and Katz (1978) found that residents of hazard-prone areas typically underestimate the likely property damage from floods and overestimate that to be expected from earthquakes. Although there are obvious problems with presenting damage information without unfairly influencing subsequent judgments, it would seem to be a valid input to helping someone evaluate the national flood insurance program. Likewise, just telling people in vivid detail what they may experience in a new job can increase their probability of success and satisfaction (Mitchell & Beach, 1977).

IMPLICATIONS FOR RESPONDENTS

How do we manage to get by with so much incoherence in our beliefs? Why are we not paralyzed with indecision (to the extent that we are aware of that incoherence) or punished by the consequences of acting on conflicting views?

Paralysis seems averted by the nonintuitive nature of the effects described here and the fact that the world seldom asks us more than one question on a given topic. If we are confronted with inconsistency, it is relatively easy to define our way out of contradictions with specious arguments like "that's different," "things have changed," or "it all depends." There is always some extraneous factor that can be invoked to explain a difference. According to Rokeach (1973), people experience discomfort at inconsistency in their values only when it hints at incompetence or immorality. For better or worse, we are usually spared that experience. Table 7.4 lists some ways one might deal with incoherence.

An intriguing option is just living with incoherence. In the experiment described in Fig. 7.1., half of the subjects had inconsistent preferences. Of those, half decided to deny the incoherence; most of these offered no argument at all, although some tried to demonstrate an underlying coherence by a deeper analysis of their own preferences (typically, by specifying domains in which risk seeking

TABLE 7.4
Ways One May Deal with Incoherence

Nonresolution
Ignore incoherence
Deny incoherence
Live with incoherence
Empirical resolution
Collect evidence (see what you like)
Defer to others
Like whatever you get
Analytical resolution
Create new alternatives
Recognize metaproblem
Analyze values more deeply, creating or uncovering coherence

and risk aversion were appropriate). A more satisfying solution is to think one's way through to coherence. Such analytic resolution might involve devising new, conflict-free options or recognizing that the problem at hand is misstated.

We may escape punishment for acting on incoherent values because: (1) day-to-day life affords us much opportunity for hands-on experience that obviates the need for analytic judgment; (2) we are proficient at convincing ourselves that we like what we get (sour grapes, dissonance reduction); and (3) we cannot easily evaluate the outcomes of our decisions (Einhorn & Hogarth, 1978; Fischhoff, 1980). Unbeknownst to ourselves, we may be stumbling all the time, tripped up by our own inconsistent values. The chaos reigning in our society's attempts to regulate various technological hazards suggests a lot of counterproductive effort (Kates, 1977; Lowrance, 1976).

IMPLICATIONS FOR ELICITORS

The purveyors of formal methods of decision making constitute one group of elicitors. Decision analysts (and economists and operations researchers) not only elicit values, but take the numbers they receive seriously in determining decisions that are (purportedly) in the respondents' best interests. The possibility of instability in values is typically treated by sensitivity analysis. The analyst recalculates the decision model while allowing one value at a time to vary over its range. If the final recommendation is insensitive to changes in each value variable, then the instability is considered to be inconsequential.

Although we have only the rudiments of a theory describing the effect of instability on decisions (Fischer, 1976; Fischhoff, 1980), some preliminary results suggest that the expected value of continuous decisions (e.g., invest X dollars) is relatively insensitive to shifts in individual values. Thus, one dose of one of the psychophysical effects described in Table 7.2 might not have too much impact. Unfortunately, little is known about how multiple errors compound within an analysis, nor what is the effect of correlated errors. The use of one perspective throughout an analysis (the usual practice) may produce many shifts of response in the same direction. For example, one might persistently deflate the apparent importance of environmental values or reduce the discriminability of values of all sorts.

Whatever the promise of sensitivity analysis, in some contexts it completely misses the point. Many of the effects described here reflect the introduction of distorted perspectives or newly created, possibly foreign, values into a decision-making process. Blanket invocation of sensitivity analysis will not excuse the imposition of an elicitor's perspective on the respondent. When shifts in perspective lead to reversals of preference, sensitivity analysis avoids the real issue of which perspective is, in fact, appropriate. Furthermore, the long-range goal of involving people in decision making should be, in part at least, the creation of an informed electorate (or management). That goal will not be served by a procedure that uncritically accepts people's misinformed ideas about their own values.

The resolution of this problem would seem to take one outside the narrow confines of formal decision-making methods. One needs metadecisions on questions such as: Which of several possible inconsistent values is to be accepted? How much education and involvement is needed before people can be treated as though they are expressing their own values?[7] When choosing questions, should axiomatic acceptability be abandoned for the sake of intuitive appeal and ease of response? When parties disagree on an issue, is it fair to adopt a procedure that imposes one perspective so strongly that people are impelled to agree (perhaps with a value that none of them likes)?

A decision analysis that explicitly faced such issues would be much messier than those one usually finds today. However, it would be somewhat better protected from the possibility of the whole enterprise collapsing under the cumulative weight of the issues of value lability that it otherwise ignores or finesses. That "new" decision analysis would probably include an explicit acknowledgment of the artful use of a variety of questions and the gentle development of respondents' opinions, both of which characterize the actual practice of the "old" decision analysis in the hands of its best practitioners.

All elicitors, be they decision analysts or students of judgment, decision making, choice, or attitudes, must decide at some point whether or not they have adequately captured their respondents' values. The usual criteria are reliability and internal consistency (e.g., transitivity). However, where the task is poorly understood because of complexity or unfamiliarity (e.g., preferences for shades of gray), consistency of response within a given experimental mode may tell us

---

[7]Perhaps the only way to ensure meaningful citizen participation in public policy issues is to impanel a representative group of citizens, such as a jury, to follow an issue through the various stages of debate, deliberation, and clarification.

little beyond the power of that mode to impose a particular perspective or generate a consistent, coping heuristic.

Insight into people's values may come rather from posing diverse questions in the hopes of eliciting inconsistent responses. If situation-specific cues play a large role in determining what people express as their values, it is the variance in judgment between situations that reveals what those cues may be. Therefore, one would want to start the study of values with methodological pluralism (Royce, 1974) or even Dadaism (Feyerabend, 1975) designed to elicit the broadest range of variation in expressed values. With a large set of possible determinants of value in hand, one can then try to establish their salience, potency, and prevalence. This approach has the admirable property of (potentially) turning past morasses into silk purses, for any set of inconsistent results becomes a possible source of systematic variance. Inconsistency in values is treated as a success rather than a failure of measurement, for it indicates contexts defined sharply enough to produce a difference. Indeed, this was the approach adopted by Poulton (1968) in producing his six models for the "new psychophysics."

CONCLUSION

Expressed values seem to be highly labile. Subtle changes in elicitation mode can have marked effects on what people express as their preferences. Some of these effects are reversible, others not; some deepen the respondent's perspective, others do not; some are induced deliberately, others are not; some are specific to questions of value, others affect judgments of all kinds; some are well documented, others are mere speculation. Confronting these effects is unavoidable if we are to elicit values at all.

To the extent that these effects are real and powerful, they have different implications for different groups of elicitors.

If one is interested in how people express their values in the real world, one question may be enough. That world often asks only one question (e.g., in a ballot measure). A careful analysis of how an issue is posed may allow one to identify that question and accurately predict responses.

If one is interested in how people create, revise, and express their opinions, the contrast between different procedures may be a source of insight.

If one is interested in what people really feel about a value issue, there may be no substitute for an interactive, dialectical elicitation procedure, one that acknowledges the elicitor's role in helping the respondent to create and enunciate values. That help would include a conceptual analysis of the problem and of the personal, social, and ethical value issues to which the respondent might wish to relate.

The most satisfying way to interact with our respondents and help them make value judgments in their own best interests is to provide them with new analytical tools. Such tools would change respondents by deepening their perspective. In the extreme, they could include relevant instruction in philosophy, economics, sociology, anthropology, and so on, as well as training in decision-making methodology.[8] More modestly, one could convey an understanding of the basic models for values (compensatory, disjunctive, etc.), of useful heuristics (and their limitations), of commonly accepted rules of rationality and their rationales, of common pitfalls, and of new concepts encountered in a particular problem. Perhaps the simplest and most effective message of all might be the theme of this chapter: Consider more than one perspective.

ACKNOWLEDGMENTS

This research was supported by the Advanced Research Projects Agency of the Department of Defense and was monitored by the Office of Naval Research under Contract N00014-79-C-0029 (ARPA Order No. 3668) to Perceptronics, Inc.

REFERENCES

Aschenbrenner, K. M. Singlepeaked risk perferences and their dependability on the gambles' presentation mode. *Journal of Experimental Psychology: Human Perception and Performance,* 1978, *4,* 513–520.

Ashcraft, R. Economic metaphors, behavioralism, and political theory: Some observations on the ideological uses of language. *The Western Political Quarterly,* 1977, *30,* 313–328.

Barnes, S. B. Natural rationality: A neglected concept in the social sciences. *Philosophy of the Social Sciences,* 1976, *6,* 115–126.

Bem, D. J. Self-perception theory. In L. Berkowitz (Ed.), *Advances in experimental social psychology.* New York: Academic Press, 1972.

Boring, E. G. Perspective: Artifact and control. In R. Rosenthal & R. L. Rosnow (Eds.), *Artifact in behavioral research.* New York: Academic Press, 1969.

Brookshire, D. S., Ives, B. C., & Schulze, W. D. The valuation of aesthetic preferences. *Journal of Environmental Economics and Management,* 1976, *3,* 325–346.

Bunker, J. P., Barnes, B. A., & Mosteller, F. *Costs, risks and benefits of surgery,* New York: Oxford University Press, 1977.

Canavan-Gumpert, D. Generating reward and cost orientation through praise and criticism. *Journal of Personality and Social Psychology,* 1977, *35,* 501–513.

Carterette, E. C., & Friedman, M. P. *Handbook of perception* (Vol. 2). New York: Academic Press, 1974.

Dreyfus, H., & Dreyfus, S. *Uses and abuses of multiattribute and multiaspect models of decision making.* Unpublished manuscript, University of California, Berkeley, n.d.

Edwards, W. Comment. *Journal of American Statistical Association,* 1975, *70,* 291–293.

Einhorn, H. & Hogarth, R. Confidence in judgment: Persistence of the illusion of validity. *Psychological Review,* 1978, *85,* 395–416.

Ellul, J. *Propaganda.* New York: Knopf, 1969.

Feyerabend, P. *Against method.* New York: Humanities Press, 1975.

Fischer, G. W. Multidimensional utility models for risky and riskless choice. *Organizational Behavior and Human Performance,* 1976, *17,* 127–146.

---

[8]Rozeboom (1977) has argued that the elicitors themselves should have more of such training.

Fischhoff, B. Cost-benefit analysis and the art of motorcycle maintenance. *Policy Sciences*, 1977, *8*, 177-202. (a)

Fischhoff, B. Perceived informativeness of facts. *Journal of Experimental Psychology: Human Perception and Performance*, 1977, *3*, 349-358. (b)

Fischhoff, B. Clinical decision analysis. *Operations Research*, 1980, *28*, 28-43.

Fischhoff, B., Slovic, P., & Lichtenstein, S. Fault trees: Sensitivity of estimated failure probabilities to problem representation. *Journal of Experimental Psychology: Human Perception and Performance*, 1978, *4*, 342-355.

Fischhoff, B., Slovic, P., & Lichtenstein, S. Subjective sensitivity analysis. *Organizational Behavior and Human Performance*, 1979, *23*, 339-359.

Fischhoff, B., Slovic, P., Lichtenstein, S., Read, S., & Combs, B. How safe is safe enough? A psychometric study of attitudes towards technological risks and benefits. *Policy Sciences*, 1978, *8*, 127-152.

Fried, C. The value of human life. *Harvard Law Review*, 1969, *82*, 1415-1437.

Galanter, E. Psychological decision mechanisms and perception. In E. C. Carterette & M. P. Friedman (Eds.), *Handbook of perception* (Vol. 2). New York: Academic Press, 1974.

Gardiner, P. C., & Edwards, W. Public values: Multiattribute-utility measurement for social decision making. In M. F. Kaplan & S. Schwartz (Eds.), *Human judgment and decision processes*. New York: Academic Press, 1975.

Gouldner, A. *The dialectic of ideology and technology: The origins, grammar and future of ideology*. New York: Seabury Press, 1976.

Grether, D. M., & Plott, C. R. Economic theory of choice and the preference reversal phenomenon. *American Economic Review*, 1979, *69*, 623-638.

Hammond, K. R. & Adelman, L. Science, values and human judgment. *Science*, 1976, *194*, 389-396.

Harblin, T. D. Mine or garden? Values and the environment—probable sources of change. *Zygon*, 1977, *12*, 134-150.

Harris, R. J., & Monaco, R. E. Psychology of pragmatic implications: Information processing between the lines. *Journal of Experimental Psychology: General*, 1978, *107*, 1-22.

Harrison, F. L. Decision making in conditions of extreme uncertainty. *Journal of Management Studies*, 1977, *14*, 169-178.

Hasher, L., Goldstein, D., & Toppino, T. Frequency and the conference of referential validity. *Journal of Verbal Learning and Verbal Behavior*, 1977, *16*, 107-110.

Helson, H. *Adaptation level theory*. New York: Harper & Row, 1964.

Kahneman, D. & Tversky, A. Prospect theory. *American Economic Review*, 1979, *47*, 263-291.

Kates, R. W. *Managing technological hazard*. Boulder: University of Colorado, Institute of Behavioral Science, 1977.

Keeney, R. L., & Raiffa, H. *Decisions with multiple objectives*. New York: Wiley, 1976.

Kling, J., & Riggs, L. *Woodworth and Schlosberg's experimental psychology*. New York: Holt, Rinehart & Winston, 1971.

Kunreuther, H. L., Ginsberg, R., Miller, L., Sagi, P., Slovic, P., Borkan, B., & Katz, N. *Disaster insurance protection: Public policy lessons*. New York: Wiley, 1978.

Lichtenstein, S., & Slovic, P. Reversals of preference between bids and choices in gambling decisions. *Journal of Experimental Psychology*, 1971, *89*, 46-55.

Lichtenstein, S., & Slovic, P. Response-induced reversals of preference in gambling: An extended replication in Las Vegas. *Journal of Experimental Psychology*, 1973, *101*, 16-20.

Lindman, H. R. Inconsistent preferences among gambles. *Journal of Experimental Psychology*, 1971, *89*, 390-397.

Loftus, E., Miller, D. O., & Burns, H. J. Semantic integration of verbal information into visual memory. *Journal of Experimental Psychology: Human Learning and Memory*, 1978, *4*, 19-31.

Lovins, A. B. Cost-risk-benefit assessments in energy policy. *The George Washington Law Review*, 1977, *45*, 911-943.

Lowrance, W. W. *Of acceptable risk*. Los Altos, Calif.: William Kaufman, 1976.

Mannheim, K. *Ideology and utopia*. New York: Harcourt, 1936.

Marks, B. A. Decision under uncertainty: The narrative sense. *Administration and Society*, 1977, *9*, 379–394.

Marks, L. E. *Sensory processes: The new psychophysics*. New York: Academic Press, 1974.

McGuire, W. J. The nature of attitudes and attitude change. In G. Lindzey & E. Aronson (Eds.), *The handbook of social psychology*. Reading, Mass.: Addison-Wesley, 1969. (a)

McGuire, W. J. Suspiciousness of experimenter's intent. In R. Rosenthal & R. L. Rosnow (Eds.), *Artifact in behavioral research*. New York: Academic Press, 1969. (b)

Mitchell, T. R., & Beach, L. R. Expectancy theory, decision theory and occupational preferences and choice. In M. Kaplan & S. Schwartz (Eds.), *Human judgment and decision processes in applied settings*. New York: Academic Press, 1977.

Nisbett, R. E., & Bellows, N. Verbal reports about causal influences on social judgments: Private access vs. public theories. *Journal of Personality and Social Psychology*, 1977, *35*, 613–624.

Nisbett, R. E., & Wilson, T. D. Telling more than we can know. *Psychological Review*, 1977, *84*, 231–259.

Parducci, A. Contextual effects: A range-frequency analysis. In E. C. Carterette & M. P. Friedman (Eds.), *Handbook of perception* (Vol. 2). New York: Academic Press, 1974.

Payne, S. L. *The art of asking questions*. Princeton: Princeton University Press, 1952.

Plott, C. R., & Levine, M. E. A model of agenda influence on committee decisions. *American Economic Review*, 1978, *68*, 146–160.

Polanyi, M. *Personal knowledge*. London: Routledge & Kegan Paul, 1962.

Posner, M. *Cognition: An introduction*. Glenview, Ill.: Scott, Foresman, 1973.

Poulton, E. C. The new psychophysics: Six models for magnitude estimation. *Psychological Bulletin*, 1968, *69*, 1–19.

Poulton, E. C. Quantitative subjective assessments are almost always biased, sometimes completely misleading. *British Journal of Psychology*, 1977, *68*, 409–425.

Rawls, J. *A theory of justice*. Cambridge: Harvard University Press, 1971.

Rokeach, M. *The nature of human values*. New York: Free Press, 1973.

Rosenthal, R. Interpersonal expectations: Effects of the experimenter's hypothesis. In R. Rosenthal & R. L. Rosnow (Eds.), *Artifact in behavioral research*. New York: Academic Press, 1969.

Rosenthal, R., & Rosnow, R. L. *Artifact in behavioral research*. New York: Academic Press, 1969.

Ross, L. The intuitive psychologist and his shortcomings. In L. Berkowitz (Ed.), *Advances in social psychology*. New York: Academic Press, 1977.

Ross, L., Greene, D., & House, P. The "false consensus effect": An egocentric bias in social perception and attribution processes. *Journal of Experimental Social Psychology*, 1977, *13*, 279–301.

Royce, J. R. Cognition and knowledge: Psychological epistemology. In E. C. Carterette & M. P. Friedman (Eds.), *Handbook of perception: Historical and philosophical origins of perception*. New York: Academic Press, 1974.

Rozeboom, W. W. Metathink. *Canadian Psychological Review*, 1977, *18*, 197–203.

Slovic, P. Choice between equally-valued alternatives. *Journal of Experimental Psychology: Human Perception and Performance*, 1975, *1*, 280–287.

Slovic, P., Fischhoff, B., Lichtenstein, S., Corrigan, B., & Combs, B. Preference for insuring against probable small losses: Implications for the theory and practice of insurance. *Journal of Risk and Insurance*, 1977, *44*, 237–258.

Slovic, P., & MacPhillamy, D. J. Dimensional commensurability and cue utilization in comparative judgment. *Organizational Behavior and Human Performance*, 1974, *11*, 172–194.

Tribe, L. H. Policy science: Analysis or ideology? *Philosophy and Public Affairs*, 1972, *2*, 66–110.

Tribe, L. H., Schelling, C. S., & Voss, J. *When values conflict: Essays on environmental analysis, discourse and decisions*. Cambridge, Mass.: Ballinger, 1976.

Turner, C. F., & Krauss, E. Fallible indicators of the subjective state of the nation. *American Psychologist*, 1978, *33*, 456–470.

Tversky, A. Intransitivity of preferences. *Psychological Review,* 1969, *76,* 31–48.

Tversky, A. Elimination by aspects: A theory of choice. *Psychological Review,* 1972, *79,* 281–299.

Upshaw, H. Personality and social effects in judgment. In E. C. Carterette & M. P. Friedman (Eds.), *Handbook of perception* (Vol. 2). New York: Academic Press, 1974.

Wagenaar, W. A., & Sagaria, S. D. Misperception of exponential growth. *Perception and Psychophysics,* 1975, *18,* 416–422.

Wildavsky, A. The political economy of efficiency: Cost–benefit analysis, systems analysis and program budgeting. *Public Administration Review,* 1966, *26,* 292–308.

Woodworth, R. S., & Schlosberg, H. *Experimental psychology.* New York: Henry Holt, 1954.

8 Know, Then Decide

Gregory R. Lockhead
Duke University

Perhaps the most compelling aspect of the deductive systems used in choice and decision theory is that they are well articulated. The normative models are mathematically sound, the data collection methods are tractable, and there are prescribed ways to get about in our uncertain world. Hence, for people who are assigned the task of decision making, normative models are not only compelling, they can also be essential. For the researcher, an important aspect of normative models is that they are easy to disprove if wrong (excepting some linear models whose robustness suggests they account for nearly any findings; see Wainer, 1976) and the variables in the models may be operationally defined.

Normative models proposed as theories of choice have now been studied empirically in some detail. The testable axioms of most of them proposed for use with decision behavior have been treated as hypotheses and evaluated. Unfortunately, the result seems to be that human behavior is not generally consistent with most of the axioms of those models (Lichtenstein & Slovic, 1973; Tversky, 1969; Wallsten, this volume). This produces an enigma. The normative models fully articulate, in a mathematically sound way, what seems to be an appropriate manner for describing decision making, and they function well in predicting the performance of man-made systems. However, the axioms appear to be violated when people are the decision makers. What then are we to do? We cannot scrap the entire enterprise without producing an alternative to replace it. This would be a decision that we cannot improve in decision making and would be inconsistent with most people's introspections (Einhorn & Hogarth, 1978).

CONSIDER THE OBSERVER'S PERCEPTIONS

What seems reasonable, and what is suggested by other chapters in this volume, is to apply normative theory to the task as it is perceived by the observer or decision maker, rather than to the task as it is defined by the experimenter. This observation is one reason dynamic decision models have been proposed (cf. Kleiter, 1970; Rapoport, 1975) and is the basis for these invited comments on the chapters by Fischhoff, Slovic, and Lichtenstein, by Payne, and by Pitz. Decision models must describe the perceptual and cognitive processes involved in making a choice. The concept of information as it is employed in current normative models is not sufficient to account for many of the behaviors those models are designed to predict. What is necessary is to determine what information people actually use in making choices.

This claim shifts the emphasis from motivation to cognition, or perhaps it removes the distinction between these two, as the psychological basis of a theory of choice or decision. A choice entails a response in light of one's understanding of the world and of oneself. Hence, the problem of choice requires study of how people come to know. This is perception–cognition in the full sense of that field. By this view, some prior work in choice and decision making may have confounded problem solving with decision making. These are two different but intertwined processes; the person seeks information to test against hypotheses for solving problems and, when necessary, makes a choice or decision based on the information available. To successfully predict behavior, decision models must incorporate information resulting from problem-solving behavior as well as information based on value assumptions.

Many early decision theories did not include the person's perceptions in their formal models. This is clear in the work of Newell and Simon (1972), which asserts we must account for the facts that people are plastic and that different people have different memories. Each person has different capacities and capabilities; these abilities are sometimes employed by the person in a serial system and are always employed in regard to the person's problem space. By this view, problem solving takes the form of a search through the problem space or internal representation of the situation, where the task and the person's knowledge interact with the "programs" he or she uses in arriving at a decision. To add flesh to this structure, Newell and Simon (1972) skillfully employed the use of protocols collected during the performance of different tasks. Here, we see the use of an introspective method to track analogs to some of the processes involved in problem solving, with the added advantage that any suggested process is open to later test for, at least, consistency of predictions.

The chapter by Payne (this volume) is in this same spirit. Payne is concerned with what information the subject uses and with how that information is used. He guesses that a situation is often processed differently by the observer than is presumed by the experimenter. He conjectures that, by a process-tracing procedure, one might learn what information is being used. The view is that the assumptions of some normative models may not be what are violated. Rather, it may be that the measurements taken by the experimenter are inappropriate. Consistent with this, Pitz (this volume) is seeking to learn how the observer understands an aspect of the situation not usually considered, the variance of stimulus events in addition to some average of those events. This is because we cannot write appropriate normative equations to predict behavior if we do not know the parameters employed by the observer.

There are examples outside of choice theory that also show we need to understand how observers perceive situations. In the field of psychophysics, discriminability and choice between simple events depends on the other events in the stimulus domain. Factors such as context, stimulus range, adaptation, and information feedback are just some of the variables known to affect judgment. For example, two stimuli that are seen as very different from each other when no other stimuli can occur will be confused with each other when more stimuli are added to the set. Moreover, these same two stimuli will be confused increasingly often as the added stimuli are made more and more physically different from the first two (Gravetter & Lockhead, 1973). The categorization of items depends on what other events can occur in the situation. Another difficulty is that an event or stimulus that the experimenter considers as two or more distinct objects can be treated by the observer as a single item, and, conversely, sometimes what the experimenter treats as a single entity is treated by the observer as two or more independent events (Monahan & Lockhead, 1977). Thus, observers may not, as Payne considers, process stimuli in the manner prescribed by the theory being tested. Sometimes, the events considered by the experimenter are not the same events considered by the observer. This allows the suggestion that the observer's behavior might be consistent with the tested theory, but that the parameters entered into the equations by the researcher to test that theory are not those parameters used by the observer.

Because context and stimulus properties greatly determine discriminability and categorization, they also greatly determine choice behavior. We cannot predict decisions without knowing how the stimulus situation is perceived, and we cannot assume a priori what it is of the complex environment that observers select. Indeed, we have been unable to discover even a posteriori what information observers use when the stimuli are as simple as rectangles varying in height and width (Glushko, 1975; Krantz & Tversky, 1975; Monahan & Lockhead, 1977). In light of this, we certainly cannot be sanguine in assuming that we know what people use in complex situations. Perhaps process tracing can help us determine what aspects of the stimulus situation are used. Monitoring eye movements, evaluating protocols, and recording the order in which people request information may help us infer how experimenter-defined stimuli are actually used. This approach has led Payne to a program, to describe the decision process, that has three ordered stages:

1. Because of overwhelming information load, some less important processes are eliminated.
2. The surviving alternatives are then compared by dimensions in terms of importance regarding some goal.
3. The decision is made.

Payne suggests that process tracing might reveal characteristics of how the decision maker stores information and in what order, and that it might reveal dynamic characteristics of the process. Like Newell and Simon (1972), Payne suggests that one should study how the problem space (Simon, 1978) is constructed and how it is edited.

EARLY STIMULUS EVENTS ARE IMPORTANT

One attractive feature of process tracing is the call for data collection beginning from (Payne, this volume) "the point at which the subject is first exposed to the task instructions . . . [p. 26]." The purpose is to discover processes used by the observer in generating the problem space. In an older language, this is an interest in acquisition, in how the observer comes to understand the situation. Hence, the suggestion is to examine our preconceptions as to what information is essential to a theory. Such examination has been useful in other disciplines and it may help us to better understand decision behavior.

As an example from a different field, it was the case only several years ago that psychophysiologists interested in nerve-cell behavior discarded their neural response data until the system had "settled down." It had been common procedure to insert a recording microelectrode into nervous tissue and then to probe with a stimulus—say, with a steady light moved about to different sites on the retina—until a response occurred at the electrode. The initial neural response is often a high rate of activity in these situations. Once this "noisy" transient behavior ceased, the experimenter would turn on a recorder to obtain a record of the activity of the fiber in its steady state. This technique was based on the presumption that initial events somehow disturb the normal state of neural events and thus mask the fiber's normal function of reporting the presence and the magnitude of the stimulus. In many single-cell and gross nerve recordings studies intended to determine the functions of neurons and of their associated neurons and receptors, the transient response of the system was commonly ignored. Such a procedure results in easily described data and is appropriate if the task of individual fibers is to mirror the magnitude of the stimulus over time.

Today, this assumption appears unwarranted. Disregarding the transients often means ignoring the important data. Consider Yarbus' (1967) demonstration that a visual stimulus is not seen if there are no temporal illuminance changes on the retina, such as when the retinal image is stabilized. The stimulus is clearly seen when it is first turned on out of darkness, but it disappears completely in less than 2 seconds. This means that the transient in the stimulus is the important aspect for the perceiver. When a temporal change occurs in the system, as when the stimulus is turned on, there is a perceptual response; when no subsequent change in the system occurs over time, as is the case when the image is optically fixed to one retinal site, there is no response and the stimulus is no longer seen. Our normal visual world does not disappear because of the small tremor movements in our eyes that provide continuously moving contours over the retina and, thus, continual transients to the visual system. Because temporal transients are essential to perception, it follows that transients in the neural response are likely to also be important. Indeed, the existence of on–off type nerve fibers allows the suggestion that transient activity could be the only important aspect for some functions of nervous systems. To not record and study early events, the transient neural activity in this case, may be to not study the information that the system uses.

A similar conclusion may be available from another discipline. In recording operant behavior, B. F. Skinner does not (except early in his career) carefully study what his animals do while being shaped to achieve steady-state performance under some reinforcement schedule. But, here may lie the major story of how an animal decides that pushing the bar is what pays off. There are marked regularities in the behaviors of animals as they learn about a new environment or task, and these changes in behavior during the training procedure might tell us how the animal decides about its world (see Staddon & Simmelhag, 1971; also recall Tolmon's demonstration of hypothesis testing by rats, 1948). A continuous record of the animal behaviors prior to steady-state performance is similar to the verbal protocol as used by Simon. During acquisition, the subject may reveal what hypotheses are being tested and how he or she moves among hypotheses.

Payne records (see Table 6.1, this volume) that different people acquired information in different ways in his study. This is similar to the fact that different animals do somewhat different things when solving a problem (consider superstitious behavior). In both situations, the past history of each subject was slightly different, or a different aspect of the problem space happened to catch attention first, or a different hypothesis was selected among a pool of nearly equal hypotheses. Whichever might be the case, the early behaviors all show regularity and structure. Process tracing is an attractive technique to abstract these regularities. As a bonus, process tracing may also allow discovery of events not previously considered important in the model or by the investigator.

Pitz's apporach (this volume) is similar to Payne's in this regard: "Once we know how a person interprets a problem, what he or she is trying to do, and what mechanisms are available for achieving that purpose [p. 27]," we may find that the decision behavior is not as irrational as it sometimes appears to be. This is why Pitz is interested in learning what the observer knows of the distribution of possible events. If we are to apply normative models based on the use of parameters of distributions, then we must know those parameters that are used by the observers. We need to discover and model what assumptions are made by subjects, and what information they maintain, before we can fully predict choice and decision behavior.

INCONSISTENCIES IN VALUE JUDGMENTS

Fischhoff, Slovic, & Lichtenstein (this volume) demonstrate that people's values can be affected by the interviewer. They also show that it is more difficult to learn individuals' values than many others have thought. I question their guess that today's world presents people with more difficult judgment situations than did the days of yore, particularly in light of problems with sheer survival before antibiotics, fertilizers, looms, electricity, and paternalism. But, this is of no substantive matter to their chapter. They undertook a difficult task and did it well. Their bottom line is a call to determine values by more than one method. This calls for a methodological pluralism that, by convergence, might demonstrate what is salient or otherwise important to the judgment process. This search for invariance across situations is the time-honored method of science.

One might infer from Fischhoff et al.'s data, as I do, that most people implicitly know a lot about the effects on themselves of making value judgments. The very act of making a judgment affects other held values, and the particular judgment made depends on what information the person has. Thus, it is important not to form a value judgment concerning each new piece of information (see Corbin, this volume), even at the expense of potentially forgetting that information. This is particularly so if the judgments based on the new information require modification of already held values. Hence, the discovery that judgments concerning all known facts were not already formed when the pollster came to the door is appropriate; people "know" this is disadvantageous. Indeed, Fischhoff et al.'s evidence that the polled person's values change when a judgment is made argues strongly that opinion surveyors must be cautious and well trained.

Fischhoff et al. also report that people are sometimes inconsistent in their decisions, in terms of the predictions of decision models. As described in the discussion of Fig. 7.1, half of their observers had inconsistent preferences; sometimes the observers were seen to be risk seeking, sometimes risk avoiding. Rokeach (1973) and others have noted that such inconsistencies occur frequently. Yet, one wonders if all such reported difficulties are truly inconsistencies, either in regards to the underlying model or to the observer's actual behaviors. Rather, perhaps the data sometimes reflect different understandings between the experimenter and the observer concerning the task itself.

To get some sense of this possibility, I attempted Fischhoff et al.'s two studies described by Fig. 7.1, and successfully replicated their results. Most people choose Option *A* in the civil defense question (10 out of 10 tested people) and choose Curve 2 in the catastrophe study (7 out of 10 tested people). I then asked the observers (psychology undergraduates, graduate students, and faculty) on what they had based their decisions. In the civil defense case, every observer reported (in different words) invoking a negatively accelerating loss function; the marginal loss of an additional life was reported to become less as the number of people killed increased. This is consistent with the choice of Option A to minimize expected loss.

In the catastrophe situation, several observers reported interpreting the term ''catastrophe,'' and reported the presence of ''N'' on the abscissa of the curves, as meaning the entire population could be eliminated. They reported this to be an added element of cost; losing the entire population (the country, the world) adds a component not involved in the 100 lives maximum loss in the civil defense case. By this, the function relating social cost to lives lost may be concave until some new feature, such as the end of the world, is perceived to be involved, and then become convex. I cannot know that Fischhoff et al.'s observers, or even mine, made these assumptions when choosing alternatives in the study. But, if they did, the choices in the studies are consistent with the normative theory and with the observers' performances. In both cases, the judgments were to minimize expected perceived loss. It is intuitively more pleasing for me to consider that observers have difficulty perceiving the experimenter's meaning of complex situations than that the observers are risk seeking and risk avoiding in inconsistent ways.

Whenever we obtain what appears to be inconsistent behavior in studies, we should consider that how people interpret the situation may have been misunderstood. The identical information presented in different ways ought to result in common judgments; when it does not could be evidence that the data-collection procedures are inappropriate. More importantly, it could provide a method to discover what information people are using. Data-collection methods could serve as independent variables, with the judgments as dependent variables, in experiments designed to determine the bases of choice. This is consistent with Fischhoff et al.'s recurrent theme ''that subtle aspects of how problems are posed, questions are phrased, and responses are elicited can have substantial impact on judgments that supposedly express people's true values [p. 2].'' If we do not know how people interpret our questions, we are not in a position to measure values as abstractions from their answers.

AN HISTORICAL PRECEDENT

A decision or a choice is a categorization. Observers categorize into go or don't go; into mildly pleasant or very pleasant or extremely pleasant; into left or right and so on. A decision is a choice of some alternative, just as is any other categorization or response. Because categorization behavior is a central concern of cognitive psychology, there is considerable precedent for the cognitive emphasis of this book. One important precedent is recalled in this section.

In 1956, Bruner, Goodnow, and Austin emphasized that what was needed in the analysis of categorizing phenomena ''is an adequate analytic description of the actual behavior that goes on when a person learns how to use defining cues as a basis for grouping events of his environment [p. 23]." Their study was to determine the bases on which a person decides to assign some particular label to an event. Their conclusions were very much like those of Newell and Simon (1972) and of some of the chapters in this volume. Bruner et al. discussed concept attainment in much the manner we are now discussing how the observer translates complex information to make a decision. Bruner et al. concluded that decision or classification tasks have at least the following elements:

1. There is an array of instances to be tested that can be characterized in terms of their attributes and attribute values.
2. The person makes a tentative decision concerning the relation between each instance and the criterion task.
3. Information given the observer concerning the relation between that decision and the criterion is used as validation of the decision.
4. The sequence of decisions made is the person's strategy and this embodies certain objectives that can be different depending on aspects of the task.
5. There are consequences, the payoff matrix, associated with each decision.

From this analysis, it follows that the strategies used will be systematically affected by changes in such things as information load and risk (Bruner et al., 1956): "If, for example, cognitive strain is increased, one might expect a change in strategy that reduces informational intake and increases risk of failure . . . [p. 234]." This sounds remarkably like information overload, mostly leading, in their studies, to elimination by aspects. It becomes instructive to read, or to reread, the following several pages in that book. We are told that (Bruner et al., 1956): "Strategies can be located and described . . . and a shift in strategy can also be described and related to changes in the requirement of the task set [p. 236]."

Their method was process tracing. They report that (Bruner et al., 1956): "It is possible . . . to 'get into' the *process* of concept attainment rather than being limited to evaluations simply in terms of whether a subject succeeds . . . [p. 236]." There are "general tendencies in information-getting and information-using behavior that are worth especial note . . . people tend to fall back on cues that in the past have seemed useful." There is the "inability or unwillingness of subjects to use efficiently information which is based on negative instances . . .;" there is "the tendency to prefer common-element or conjunctive concepts and to use (often inappropriately) strategies of cue searching that are relevant to such concepts [p. 237]." "In general, we are struck by the notable flexibility and intelligence of our subjects in adapting their strategies to the information, capacity, and risk requirements. [p. 238]." "Oftentimes subjects were unable to tell us in any coherent way how they had proceeded although the sequence of behavior showed systematic features . . . (cf. Nisbett & Wilson, 1977)."

"As a step towards formalizing the description of the series of decisions that make up a strategy, we have introduced the concept of the *ideal strategy*. An ideal strategy is basically an analytic device used as a yardstick against which to compare the performance of human operators in the situations we set them in . . . the way we would set a computer to do what the subject appears to be doing . . . [p. 241];"

i.e., a normative model.

Bruner et al. go on to make additional points relevant to the issues of this book. They report that people often cannot handle all the information given and are capable of many strategies that represent different sets of seeking behaviors. They note that people decide on ways to reduce the task, overweigh correlated information, and require relatively less evidence before making a judgment if the incoming information is consistent with their previous assumptions than if it is not.

It might seem that these issues that were laid out so clearly in 1956 have been rediscovered. But I think this is not the case. Bruner et al.'s book was widely read when it first appeared and their ideas were well known. My guess is that their observations were not immediately developed for the good reason that we had no well-articulated ideal strategy or normative position against which to compare performance. Without a measurement method, theory can only remain conjecture. Given the efforts in choice theory and in perception and cognition during the intervening 20+ years, perhaps we now have the bases and the incentives to fully develop requisite methods for evaluating Bruner, Goodnow, and Austin's ideas. To do so may allow us to observe discrepancies between the normative and the real. Depending on our motivations, we might then change the models so as to better predict people's choices or so as to educate people so they can make more consistent predictions. What we seem to know is that an ideal strategy might occur all the time, and that we must learn more about the observers' perceptions and strategies. I hope at least, it should be clear by now, that Bruner, Goodnow, and Austin (1956) will be read afresh.

A SUGGESTED FRAMEWORK

There is now a rich normative structure against which to measure concepts in the field of choice and decision theory. Perhaps a framework within which to view the conclusions and results from studies of choice is also now available. One possibility, proposed here, is to invert the title of this book. Perhaps we should study choice and decision behavior in cognitive processing, rather than cognitive processes in choice and decision behavior. The recommendation is to consider perception and cognition as the bases for guiding people to decisions.

Although perhaps still a bit fuzzy, a framework for this approach, which may hold promise, is that one proposed by Neisser in his courageously titled book

Cognition and Reality (1976). Rather than view the person as a simply ordered information processor, with information flowing process by process to the decision, consider the process as a cycle. The suggestion begins for the same reason all other processing models in cognitive psychology do; we are capacity limited. Because we cannot process everything simultaneously, we select. Controlled by motivations, what we select depends on the stimulus (or, more generally, the world) and on our internal representation of that stimulus or of the world. New information from the world modifies our internal representation, or schemata, or problem space, which in turn directs our activity (e.g., eye scanning in terms of Payne's concerns) to further sample information from the environment, which further modifies our cognitive map or internal representation, which directs exploration, and so on. When the representation ceases to be modified, the observer either "knows" or cares too little in comparison to other pressures to continue evaluation, or is forced to respond by some pressure; this is consistent with Simon's (1957) concept of Satisficing. The effects of number of dimensions, of the amount of information searched by the observer, and of how information combines are thus partially determined by relations between the internal representation and the mode of stimulus presentation.

Sometimes, the experimenter or interviewer considers the observer to have made a decision in terms of one hypothesis, whereas the observer has a different schema from that presumed by the data collector. In such cases, the behavior may seem inappropriate to the experimenter and to the normative model, but it might actually be appropriate. According to this framework of interaction between the world and the person, sometimes the information first sampled is consistent with the subject's schema; in this case, he or she may sample no further and decide. If the information is discrepant, the person might ignore the facts, or selectively incorporate only some of the facts, or require much added information before incorporating them. This last is because changing a schema, which is essential if the fact does not fit and yet is to be fully accepted, is difficult. It is especially difficult if a widely encompassing schema is involved, as must be the case for the value systems considered by Fischhoff et al. (this volume), because marked restructuring of the internal representation would be required. Hence, when complex information presented to the person is uncertain or is unclear, one should expect distorted perceptions. This is because those features that fit well into the schema are more readily selected and more likely to be incorporated than are those that do not fit easily.

Irwin Rock (1977) has a compelling demonstration, which may be of interest here, of the interaction between search mechanisms and the incorporation of visual information into memory. Rock constructed a video tape showing one set of silhouette figures moving across the screen from left to right, and another set moving simultaneously from right to left. Each figure was easy to identify: There was a tree, a patriot, an elephant, a chair, and so on. The figures were large, nearly the height of the television screen, and were generated to be semitransparent. When two figures passed through each other on the screen, both could readily be seen and identified at all times. By this stimulus arrangement, it is not possible to view an object moving in one direction without at the same time viewing the object that was moving in the opposite direction. When people are instructed to attend to the left-to-right moving figures in this display, they are able to do so quite easily, as shown by a later recognition test. These people remember essentially all of those figures. The same is true for the figures moving from right to left when people are instructed to attend to that direction of movement. The point of importance is that the left-to-right attenders could report essentially nothing of the figures that moved in the right-to-left direction, and vice versa. This is the case even though all people had "seen" all of those other objects. Only that information that fits is incorporated into the schema; other equally available information is not selected to be encoded in this demonstration of the importance of selective perception. Surely performance by subjects in choice experiments is similarly affected by what is selected to be processed.

Consistent with this demonstration, Pitz (this volume) sees the "process whereby a person translates the stimulus information into some internal structure [p. 5]" as encoding and as essential to understanding the decisions made. Payne (this volume) stresses the importance of paying attention "to the cognitive representation actually used by the individual decision maker [p. 3]." Fischhoff, Slovic, and Lichtenstein accentuate Rokeach's assertion that "The power of values comes from their roles as guides to actions, as embodiments of ourselves, and as expressions of our relation to the world [p. 17]." These encodings, cognitive representations, and values all relate to this concept of the internal representation guiding and directing behavior. This is what I think each of these authors means by "process." The internal state of the person determines what information will be sought next, and determines the importance of information producing a decision or value judgment. Thus, the important question for researchers is to learn where these internal states come from, what their antecedents are, and how these are manipulated.

In light of this argument, it may prove fruitful to turn our normative models around. As well as asking about optimal behavior to achieve some goal, we should attempt to determine how the observer's internal representation predicts his or her behavior. Success here might aid us in determining ways to teach people the essential structure of the environment so they can behave optimally in terms of some external representation.

REFERENCES

Bruner, J. S., Goodnow, J. J., & Austin, G. A. *A study of thinking.* New York: Wiley, 1956.
Einhorn, H. J. & Hogarth, R. M. Confidence in judgment: Persistence of the illusion of validity. *Psychological Review,* 1978, *85,* 395–416.

Glushko, R. J. Pattern goodness and redundancy revisited. Multidimensional scaling and hierarchical clustering analyses. *Perception and Psychophysics*, 1975, *17*, 158–162.

Gravetter, F., & Lockhead, G. R. Criterial range as a frame of reference for stimulus judgment. *Psychological Review*, 1973, *80*, 203–216.

Kleiter, G. D. Trend-control in a dynamic decision making task. *Acta Psychologica*, 1970, *34*, 387–397.

Krantz, D. J., & Tversky, A. Similarity of rectangles: An analysis of subjective dimensions. *Journal of Mathematical Psychology*, 1975, *12*, 4–34.

Lichtenstein, S., & Slovic, P. Response induced reversals of preference in gambling: An extended replication in Las Vegas. *Journal of Experimental Psychology*, 1973, *101*, 16–20.

Monahan, J. S. & Lockhead, G. R. Identification of integral stimuli. *Journal of Experimental Psychology: General*, 1977, *106*, 94–110.

Neisser, U. *Cognition and reality*. San Francisco: W. H. Freeman, 1976.

Newell, A., & Simon, H. A. *Human problem solving*. Englewood Cliffs, N.J.: Prentice-Hall, 1972.

Nisbett, R. E., & Wilson, T. D. Telling more than we can know: Verbal reports on mental processes. *Psychological Review*, 1977, *84*, 231–259.

Rapoport, A. Research paradigms for studying dynamic decision behavior. In D. Wendt & C. Vlek (Eds.), *Utility, probability, and human decision making*. Dordrecht, Holland: Reidel, 1975.

Rock, I. *Form perception as a process of description*. Presented at the 10th Symposium of the Center for Visual Science, University of Rochester, June, 1977.

Rokeach, M. *The nature of human values*. New York: Free Press, 1973.

Simon, H. A. *Models of man*. New York: Wiley, 1957.

Simon, H. A. Information processing theory of human problem solving. In W. K. Estes (Ed.), *Handbook of learning and cognitive processes: Vol. 5: Human information processing*. Hillsdale, N.J.: Lawrence Earlbaum Associates, 1978.

Staddon, J. E. R., & Simmelhag, V. L. The superstition experiment: A reexamination of its implications for the principles of adaptive behavior. *Psychological Review*, 1971, *78*, 3–43.

Tolman, E. C. Cognitive maps in rats and men. *Psychological Review*, 1948, *55*, 189–208.

Tversky, A. Transitivity of preference. *Psychological Review*, 1969, *76*, 31–48.

Wainer, H. Estimating coefficients in linear models: It don't make no nevermind. *Psychological Bulletin*, 1976, *83*, 213–217.

Yarbus, D. L. *Eye Movement and Vision* (B. Haigh, trans.). New York Plenum, 1967.

9 Real Money Lotteries: A Study of Ideal Risk, Context Effects, and Simple Processes

Kenneth R. MacCrimmon
William T. Stanbury
Donald A. Wehrung
University of British Columbia

INTRODUCTION

All decisions involve risk taking. A decision is risky to the extent that it involves uncertain outcomes and possible losses. So, even in minor situations, such as the weekly grocery shopping, one runs risks, such as getting spoiled merchandise, missing bargains at another store, and so forth. In major situations, risk pervades the decision process.

A paradigm for studying risk taking is given in Fig. 9.1. We first characterize the decision situation as part of the general environment faced by the decision maker. The actual situation and the characteristics of the decision maker will determine the situation as it is perceived by him or her, in particular its riskiness. This perception and the characteristics of the decision maker, especially his or her risk-taking disposition, will determine the evaluation process and lead to specific behaviors.

The analyst is interested in characterizing the *riskiness of the behavior,* but in order to do this, it is necessary to characterize the riskiness of the decision situation (e.g., the riskiness of the alternatives). By studying the behavior in various situations, one may be able to infer the *risk-taking disposition* of the decision maker.

A first step, then, would seem to be to develop a way to characterize the *riskiness of situations*. This could be very difficult to do in general decision settings, so attention has often been confined to those decisions in which there is a single numerical outcome (e.g., monetary return on investment) and the probability of the outcomes can be specified. In such situations, when the mean is constant, risk has been equated to variance (Markowitz, 1952). Sometimes, this

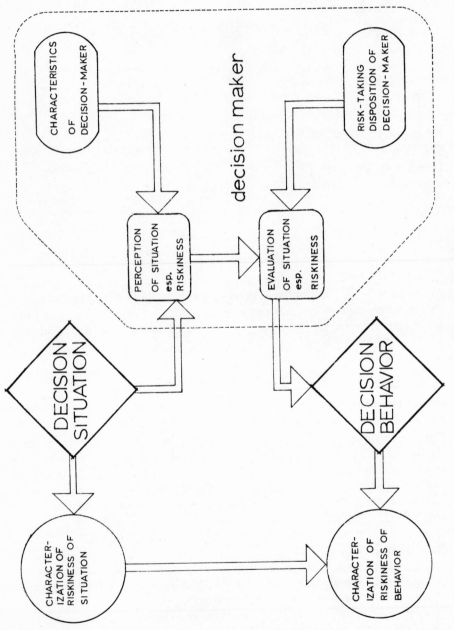

FIG. 9.1. Paradigm for studying risk taking.

has been modified to include just the variance over losses, i.e., the negative semivariance (Mao, 1970). In the more general case of unequal means, a linear function of mean and variance has been developed from more basic axioms (Pollatsek & Tversky, 1970). On the basis of empirical evidence, Payne (1975b) has shown riskiness to be related to probability of loss.

Correspondingly, there have been attempts to specity the risk-taking disposition of the decision maker. In conjunction with the previously mentioned measures, this has at times taken the form of slopes of mean–variance indifference curves (Markowitz, 1959). The most common measure of an individual's risk-taking propensity, though, is based on the individual's having a utility function (satisfying the usual axioms) and then using the Arrow–Pratt measure of the negative of the ratio of the second derivative of the utility function to the first derivative (Arrow, 1971; Pratt, 1964).

We have undertaken a major study of risk taking in decision making based on the paradigm of Fig. 9.1. We have studied naturally occurring decision situations, and we have created some artificial ones that could be suitably manipulated. The latter were based on a variety of risk-taking theories from a range of disciplines, most notably psychology and economics. The participants in our study were top-level business executives—individuals whose profession it is to take, or avoid, major risks.

In this chapter, we discuss one decision situation from stage I of our study. The situation is not a naturally occurring one, but, in creating it, we tried to retain a business context and used *real payoffs*. Our subjects could win our money, or lose some of their own.

An example of the decision situation we used is given in Fig. 9.2. Note that

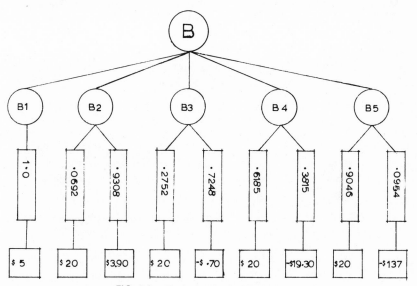

FIG. 9.2.   Example of a decision situation.

there are five alternatives, *B1* to *B5*. Alternative *B1* is a sure alternative—it yields a certain $5. The remaining four alternatives have uncertain outcomes. For instance, *B5* involves a slightly greater than 90% chance of gaining $20, but a complementary (almost 10%) chance of losing $137. All five alternatives have an expected payoff of $5. Suppose you have to rank these five alternatives in order of your preference; how would you rank them?

Because these alternatives represent part of the decision situation, we need to characterize their riskiness. It should be clear that the variance increases monotonically from *B1* to *B5*. Hence, if risk is proportional to variance, then *riskiness* increases monotonically from *B1* to *B5*. Similarly, other possible measures (such as negative semivariance, a linear function of mean and variance, loss amount, expected loss, and payoff range) all increase monotonically from *B1* to *B5*. It would seem reasonable, then, to call *B1* the least risky alternative and *B5* the most risky alternative, with the riskiness of the others increasing monotonically between these extremes.

RESEARCH ISSUES

Riskiness of Preferences: Variance and Ideal Risk

Once we have a characterization of the riskiness of a decision situation, we can turn our attention to the behavior of the decision makers. We can attempt to characterize the riskiness of their preferences and choices and can infer something about their risk-taking dispositions. We look first at the kinds of risk-taking dispositions one might expect to encounter in such situations. Because it is desirable to have the simplest theory consistent with the data, let us consider the possibilities, starting with the most specialized assumptions and moving towards the more general.

A very restrictive assumption, but a strong predictor if it is true, is that individuals are uniformly averse to risk. This can be stated as:

HYPOTHESIS 1:   Preferences monotonically decrease as risk increases.

Many theories in finance and economics begin with "we assume risk-averse individuals . . ." When dealing with continuous utility functions, the associated concavity assumption is a powerful analytic tool. Because we are dealing with the special case of alternatives with equal means but different variances, we can restate the hypothesis for our purposes as:

HYPOTHESIS 1':   Preferences monotonically decrease as variance increases.

As has been shown previously, this is equivalent to assuming a (suitably truncated) two parameter utility function with a general probability distribution (Borch, 1969; Tobin, 1958). A variation on these hypotheses that would be equally parsimonious, but presumably more unlikely, is that people are uniformly attracted to risk.

Realizing that uniform risk aversion is rather specialized, the next step to more generality is to assume that people exhibit risk aversion and risk taking, but do so in a specialized manner. Such a person would increasingly prefer alternatives up to an ideal level of risk, and then his or her preferences would decrease after this point. This may be stated in general as:

HYPOTHESIS 2:   Preferences exhibit an ideal level of risk.

This assumption has been made in some recent theoretical and empirical studies in the psychological literature (Combs & Huang, 1970). This assumption also restricts utility functions (see Fishburn, 1975). In the earlier economics literature, the need for a utility function allowing both insurance and gambling was recognized (Friedman & Savage, 1952). Because our study deals with a special case, we can restate the hypothesis as:

HYPOTHESIS 2':   Preferences are unimodal in variance.

An ideal level of variance with falloff in preference on either side obviously requires a single mode at the most preferred variance level. So, for example, if *B4* is the most preferred alternative, *B3* would have to be preferred to *B2*, which in turn would be preferred to *B1*. Alternative *B5* would be dispreferred to *B4*, but could fit into the rest of the ranking at any point and still be consistent with the unimodality assumption. Note that hypothesis 1' is just a special case of hypothesis 2': a case in which the mode falls at the end of the variance scale.

At this stage, we do not suggest more complex hypotheses because we hope that our results are consistent with one of these special cases. Instead, we turn our attention to some special preference assumptions of a different kind. The ones we have considered so far are simply restrictions on preference representations. If they do not hold, we simply move up to a more general preference form. In contrast, the ones we consider next are building blocks for general preference representations. If they do not hold, then we need to consider revisions of our theories.

Context Effects

Virtually all theories of uncertain decision making incorporate sure alternatives as a special case of uncertain prospects. It is a prospect in which the probability of a particular outcome is identical to 1.00 instead of strictly less than 1. Such sure alternatives are very important to most theories because they help to scale preferences for the uncertain prospects (e.g., by allowing certainty equivalents to be developed). Thus, it is assumed that preferences for constant alternatives fit into the overall preference pattern in a consistent way. This may be stated as:

HYPOTHESIS 3:   Preferences are consistent over the combination of certain and uncertain alternatives.

This hypothesis has been questioned in various ways. For instance, the Allais paradox (see MacCrimmon & Larsson, 1975) of utility theory is based on the presumption that people have a special concern for sure alternatives and this preference cannot be represented in a (von Neumann–Morgenstern) utility function. Here again, we are dealing with a special case in our decision situation. We might be led to question this hypothesis if a unimodal ordering of variances could not be developed when the constant alternative was included, but could be developed when the constant alternative was excluded.

The hypothesis, thus, might be restated as:

HYPOTHESIS 3':   Frequency of preferences that are unimodal in variance are independent of the presence of constant alternatives.

It should be noted that any effect due to constant alternatives is based on the assumption that unimodal preference orderings are an indicator of consistency of preference. In our decision situation, we are saying that if the preference ordering (from best to worst) is $B1$, $B4$, $B3$, $B5$, $B2$, then removing the constant alternative $B1$ will allow a unimodal preference ordering. However, it is not unimodal as it stands and the removal of any other single alternative would not allow a unimodal representation. To the extent that we are willing to accept the ideal level (i.e., unimodality) as a criterion, we are led to question whether our theories that merge constant and uncertain alternatives are appropriate.

Most theories of risky decision provide for calculating the riskiness of an alternative independent of the characteristics of the accompanying alternatives. Thus, we would expect that a person's preference ordering would be independent of any variance in payoff or probability characteristics that were held fixed in particular choices, as long as these factors appeared properly in the risk characterization of an alternative. This hypothesis may be stated as:

HYPOTHESIS 4:   Preferences are independent of the particular characteristics of the available alternatives, beyond what is accounted for in the risk measure.

If theories have to take into account the particular set of alternatives displayed, the theories can become cumbersome. On the other hand, some studies have shown that the payoff–probability characteristics or the variance characteristics that are perceived and evaluated depend on the interrelation among them across alternatives—that is, they have varying salience (Fryback, Goodman, & Edwards, 1973; Slovic & Lichtenstein, 1968a,b). In our specific case, we considered three decision situations. In the one shown in Fig. 9.2, the best outcome is held constant over all the uncertain prospects. In another set, we held the loss amount constant, whereas in a third set, we held the probability constant. We would expect that a person who is risk averse in one set would be risk averse in the other sets (given the same range of variances). More particularly:

HYPOTHESIS 4':   Preference rankings will be unaffected by which particular payoff and probability values are held fixed over all alternatives presented.

An implied assumption is that there are no preferences for particular payoff or probability levels, such as a probability of one-half (Edwards, 1953). If we observe that such independence does not hold, then we may have to revise our ways of characterizing the (perceived) riskiness of alternatives. Not only may the characterization have to take into account the particular probability and payoff levels (see Payne, 1975b; Pruitt, 1962), but it may also have to depend on the characteristics of the other alternatives being evaluated.

OUR STUDY

A number of studies have been conducted in which subjects must express choices over sets of alternatives characterized by particular payoffs and probabilities. The study we describe is somewhat unusual, however, in that it uses *professional decision makers* as subjects, and involves *real gains and losses*.

Most studies of risky decision making are done with college students. Although college students make decisions like anyone else, they are relatively inexperienced in dealing with major risks. If we want to learn about risk taking, we should try to study people who get paid for their risk-taking (or averting) behavior. Perhaps the most prominent large group of such people are top-level business managers. The participants in our study were 40 business executives from the United States (Washington state) and Canada (British Columbia). As a rough characterization, their average annual salary was $35,000, their average wealth was $230,000, their average age was 41 years, and 75% had university degrees. (Dollar amounts are in 1972 dollars). About 40% were chairmen, presidents or vice presidents; the rest were primarily division managers. Both large and small companies were represented.

At least as unusual as using professional decision makers in this study was the use of real payoffs. In the few cases in which business executives have been studied, the payoffs were hypothetical. In the usual studies with college students, the payoffs are either hypothetical or involve only pennies. Slovic (1969) found that college students used different focal strategies depending on whether the choices involved hypothetical amounts or real money (under $2). On the few occasions where more significant money has been involved, the subjects were usually given a prior stake, or had an expectation of not losing money. In our study, on the other hand, we had wagers involving possible losses up to $137 and possible wins up to $140. As it turned out, neither of these extreme amounts was realized. No subjects lost $137, because all subjects avoided choosing that alternative. Of the wagers played out, the largest win was $31.30 (twice) and the largest loss was $5 (13 times). The overall average payoff was $4.13.

The *decision situation* was realized as follows: Each executive was given a booklet containing instructions and three pages of alternatives with five alternatives on each page. For each of these three sets of alternatives, the subjects were asked to rank the five alternatives in order of their personal preference. The characteristics of all three sets are given in Table 9.1; set *B* is the same one shown earlier in Fig. 9.2. As may be seen from Table 9.1, the first alternative in each set is a sure amount—a certain $5. The remaining four lotteries can be characterized by a best outcome, a worst outcome, and a probability of obtaining the best outcome (the probability of the worst outcome is 1 minus the probability of the best outcome). In set *A*, the worst outcome was held constant at a loss of $5; in set *B*, the best outcome was held constant at $20; in set *C*, the probability was held constant at .6185.

When using professionals, it is desirable (for motivational reasons) to use a context related to their special knowledge and interest. Hence, we avoided a probability mechanism that used urns, dice, cards, and so on, and developed a mechanism based on stock prices; this was used to generate the desired probabilities. We presented a list of prices of 100 stocks on the NYSE (on September 8, 1972). The instructions stated that five of these stocks would be chosen at random and the number of "favorable" stocks in this group would determine whether they got the best outcome or the worst outcome. A favorable stock was one whose fractional part was ¼, ½, or ¾ (correspondingly, unfavorable stocks were those that were whole numbers or had fractional parts of ⅛, ⅜, ⅝, or ⅞).

TABLE 9.1
Summary of the Alternatives

	Wager Number	Best Outcome	Worst Outcome	Probability of Best Outcome	Variance
Set A	A1	$ 5.00	$ 5.00	1.00	0
	A2	6.10	−5.00	.9046	11
	A3	11.20	−5.00	.6185	62
	A4	31.30	−5.00	.2752	263
	A5	140.00	−5.00	.0692	1354
Set B	B1	$ 5.00	$ 5.00	1.00	0
	B2	20.00	3.90	.0692	17
	B3	20.00	−.70	.2752	85
	B4	20.00	−19.30	.6185	364
	B5	20.00	−137.00	.9046	2127
Set C	C1	$ 5.00	$ 5.00	1.00	0
	C2	10.00	−3.10	.6185	40
	C3	15.00	−11.20	.6185	162
	C4	20.00	−19.30	.6185	364
	C5	25.00	−27.40	.6185	648

TABLE 9.2
Basic Data

Subject Number	Data	Subject Number	Data
1	12345:12345:12345:ABC	21	24135:35214:41235:CAB
2	13245:12345:21345:CAB	22	45321:31245:31245:CBA
3	13245:12345:12345:ABC	23	54312:23145:21345:BAC
4	32145:31245:12345:BAC	24	45321:32145:21345:BCA
5	32145:23135:21345:ACB	25	45321:32145:21345:ABC
6	32145:31245:21345:BCA	26	45321:32145:21345:ABC
7	34215:31245:12345:ACB	27	54321:32145:21345:ABC
8	32145:41235:31245:BCA	28	42135:43215:42135:ACB
9	43215:41235:21345:ABC	29	32145:43215:51234:ACB
10	43215:32145:31245:ABC	30	54213:43125:42135:ACB
11	54213:32145:21345:BAC	31	54312:51234:51234:BCA
12	54213:32145:21345:ABC	32	52134:54312:21345:CAB
13	54123:32145:21345:ACB	33	45321:41235:31245:ABC
14	32145:14352:51234:CBA	34	53412:31245:51234:BCA
15	12345:35421:12345:BAC	35	54321:45123:51234:BCA
16	12345:15432:12345:ABC	36	45321:43215:51234:ACB
17	21345:25431:12345:BAC	37	32145:34215:54321:ACB
18	15423:15324:12345:CAB	38	54321:31245:54321:ACB
19	35421:21345:21345:BAC	39	45321:32145:54321:ABC
20	54213:34251:12345:ACB	40	54321:43215:54321:ABC

There were 38 favorable stocks and, hence, the probabilities in the wagers were generated by the binomial distribution: $P(r|n = 5, p = .38)$. As an example of how the alternatives were stated, *B4* read:

You will receive *$20* if at least two of the five randomly chosen stocks are favorable.
However, you must pay *$19.30* if none or only one of the five stocks is favorable.

The chances of winning (to two decimal places) were also given.

The participants were asked to provide a preference ranking for the five wagers within each set and finally to rank their top choices across the sets. They were not told which set would be chosen to play out. They had 15 minutes to make their rankings and then the wagers were played out. It was made clear before the session that we would pay if they won, and we expected to be paid if they lost.

The basic data can be easily summarized and are presented in Table 9.2. The sequence of numbers, in each of the three sets of five numbers for a given subject, indicates the place in the preference ranking of the associated alternative. For example, the choices of subject 20 are described by the ranking 54213 for alternatives *A1, A2, A3, A4,* and *A5,* respectively. That is, he puts *A1* in fifth place (i.e., least preferred), *A2* in fourth place, *A3* in second place, *A4* in first place, and *A5* in third place. The ACB at the end of the line indicates he preferred his top choice in set *A* (i.e., *A4*) to his top choice in set *C* (i.e., *C1*) to his top choice in set *B* (i.e., *B5*). From this data, the reader can check any of the following analyses. (The order in which the subjects are listed is based on a subjective assessment of risk aversion, from highly risk averse to risk preferring.)

RESULTS AND DISCUSSION

Riskiness of Preferences: Variance and Ideal Risk

Are Risk Preferences Monotonically Decreasing with Variance? Remember from our earlier discussion that hypothesis 1' asserts that individuals are uniformly risk averse in the sense that an alternative with a lower variance (for a given mean value) will always be preferred to a higher variance. The results need to be examined in two stages: (1) including the constant alternative; and (2) excluding the constant alternative.

In the first case, we can easily see that there are 5! (= 120) possible rankings of all five alternatives. Only one of these, 12345, is monotonically decreasing in variance. Do the observed cases of 12345 rankings constitute significantly more than the expected number, 0.8% (i.e. = 1/120 × 100%), of cases? On this undemanding comparison, the three, three, and nine observed cases for sets *A*, *B*, and *C*, respectively, are all highly significant ($p < .001$). In none of the sets, though, is the monotonically decreasing ranking the most common one. It rates fifth place, fourth place, and second place, respectively. So, we would conclude that although it occurs significantly more than by chance, there are seven times (= 105/15) as many other rankings as there are monotonically decreasing rankings over all three sets.

As we have mentioned, the presence of the constant alternative perhaps does not belong in a theory of risky decision making, so we can eliminate it and repeat our comparisons. With just four alternatives, there are 24 (= 4!) possible rankings, and the one rank consistent with a preference for monotonically decreasing variance occurs four, 15, and 34 times in the three sets. These are also significantly different from a chance occurrence (ranging from .05 in set *A* to .001 in set *B* and in set *C*). Here too, though, there are more cases of nonmonotonically decreasing variance over all sets (67 to 53). The 85% of actual preference orderings that are monotonically decreasing in set *C* is striking.

We conclude that although we do observe some nonrandom preference for decreasing variance, it is a long way from being a universal preference. An assumption of monotonically decreasing variance preference would fail to explain half the cases even when the constant alternative is removed.

Although an assumption of pure risk attraction is uncommon, if it were true, it also would have the analytical tractability of pure risk aversion. By looking at rankings 54321, which indicate a preference for monotonically increasing variance, we can see whether pure risk attraction occurs. With all five alternatives, there were four, zero, and four cases, respectively. This is significantly different from chance in sets A and C. Without the constant alternative, these figures changed to 12, zero, and four; hence, it did not make a difference in sets B and C, but did in set A.

We note that there were 15 monotonically decreasing and eight monotonically increasing rankings with all five alternatives, and 53 and 16 such rankings, respectively, without the constant alternative. Thus, it appears that pure risk attraction is considerably less common than pure risk aversion.

We defer until a later section a discussion of differences among sets A, B, and C, but it is striking that risk attraction occurs primarily in set A and risk aversion is lowest in set A. Set A is the set in which the low amount is held fixed. This point is explored later.

In the closest cases for comparison from previous studies, Coombs and Pruitt (1960) used sets of alternatives with fixed probabilities of the best outcome of .50 and .67 (compared with our .62). The monotonically decreasing cases made up 18% and the monotonically increasing cases constituted 38% of each set. This contrasts with our 85% and 10% (omitting the constant alternative because Combs and Pruitt dealt only with uncertain lotteries). The reason for the higher risk aversion in our case may be due to the real payoffs.

Do Risk Preferences Exhibit an Ideal Variance Level?   According to hypothesis 2′, preferences exhibit an ideal level of variance and decrease monotonically as variance deviates from this ideal on either side. Because the majority of preferences were not monotonic, we ask if they exhibit this unimodal preference property. The analysis is identical to asking which preference orderings can be unfolded with respect to the ordered variance scale (Coombs, 1964).

The data are summarized in Table 9.3. We first list the two ranks that are monotonic because this is the case of having the ideal point at the highest or lowest variance. Next we list the eight cases that have the ideal point next to the end, and then we list the six cases in which the ideal point is in the middle. Note that these 16 cases (out of 120 possible rankings) account for 26, 29, and 40 of the 40 actual ranks found in sets A, B, and C, respectively. Hence, on the average, over the three sets, we observe that although the unfoldable rankings are only 13% of the total possible rankings, they represent 79% of the actual cases. Assuming random order as a benchmark, the unfoldable cases are highly significant ($p < .001$).

If we focus our attention only on the uncertain wagers (i.e., omit the constant alternative), we find a much higher degree of unfolding. With four alternatives, there are 24 possible ranks of which eight are unimodal. These eight cases

TABLE 9.3
Frequency of Ideal Risk Orderings

Ranks Consistent with an Ideal Variance (Unimodal)	Set A	Set B	Set C
Monotonic (ideal at end)			
12345	3	3	9
54321	4		4
	7	3	13
Ideal adjacent to end			
21345	1	1	14
54312	2	1	
31245		7	4
54213	4		
41235		3	1
53214			
51234		1	6
43215	2	4	
	9	17	25
Ideal in middle			
32145	7	8	
54123	1		
42135	1		2
53124			
52134	1		
43125		1	
	10	9	2
	26	29	40

Additional Ranks Consistent with an Ideal Variance when Constant Alternative is Omitted			
Monotonic			
15432		1	
25431		1	
35421	1	1	
45321	7		
	8	3	
Ideal (in middle adjacent to end)			
13245	2		
15423	1		
15324		1	
24135	1		
23145		1	
23135		1	
34215	1	1	
35214		1	
45123		1	
	5	6	
	13	9	

(Continued)

TABLE 9.3
(*Continued*)

Ranks Consistent with an Ideal Variance (Unimodal)	Set A	Set B	Set C
Other Ranks			
14352		1	
34251		1	
53412	1		
	1	2	
TOTAL	40	40	40

account for 39, 38, and 40 cases (out of 40) in sets *A*, *B*, and *C*, respectively. Thus, there is strong evidence for the ideal level of risk (i.e., unimodal) hypothesis when only considering the uncertain prospects.

Although our main attention has been on variance because of the interest in this parameter, we could assume that the preferences are exhibiting unimodality with respect to some other property that is monotonic with variance in each set. So, in set *C*, in which all the actual ranks exhibited an ideal level of variance, we could as well say that they were unfoldable with respect to an ideal gain amount, expected gain, loss amount, expected loss, negative semivariance, payoff range, and so forth. It was not our purpose to discriminate among those cases, but we discuss some of them in a later section in which we look at differences among sets *A*, *B*, and *C*.

Context Effects

Are Constant Alternatives Handled Commensurably with Uncertain Wagers? Because there are only three cases that are not unfoldable by variance (when only the uncertain lotteries are considered), it does not seem worthwhile to consider more general preference assumptions. It seems more useful to ask why removing the constant alternative seems to make such a major difference in the unfoldable ranks. What implications might this have for our theories of decision?

Recall that the number of rankings that could not be unfolded with respect to variance went down from 25 to three when the constant alternative was eliminated. This seems to be a major change and suggests that somehow the constant alternative complicates the original preference ordering. Before we make too much of this difference, though, we must determine that the effect is not due entirely to the set of alternatives being reduced from five to four. Perhaps if some other alternative were removed, the effect would be at least as great. Table 9.4 shows that this is not so. Only the removal of the lowest variance wager has an

TABLE 9.4
Effect on Unimodal Ranks Due to Eliminating One Alternative

	Set A	Set B	Set C
Proportion Unfoldable with All Five Alternatives	$\dfrac{26}{40}$	$\dfrac{29}{40}$	$\dfrac{40}{40}$

Proportion of Those Unfoldable Ranks That Can
be Folded When One Alternative is Removed

	Set A	Set B	Set C
Remove constant alternative	$\dfrac{13}{14}$	$\dfrac{9}{11}$	
Remove alternative at random	$\dfrac{6}{14}$	$\dfrac{3}{11}$	—
Remove lowest variance wager	$\dfrac{12}{14}$	$\dfrac{5}{11}$	—
Remove middle variance wager (i.e., second lowest)	$\dfrac{3}{14}$	$\dfrac{2}{11}$	—
Remove highest variance wager (or second highest)	$\dfrac{0}{14}$	$\dfrac{0}{11}$	—
Remove least preferred alternative	$\dfrac{7}{14}$	$\dfrac{2}{11}$	—
Remove most preferred alternative	$\dfrac{3}{14}$	$\dfrac{4}{11}$	—

effect close to the removal of the constant alternative; note that removing the highest variance alternative (or the second highest) has no effect at all. The effect due to removing the constant alternative is significantly greater than removing an alternative at random ($p < .001$). The removal of the constant alternative allows all the unfolding that all the others do (except for a single case by the low variance alternative). Two rankings (out of the 120) cannot be made unimodal by removing some single alternative.

The results suggest that the constant lottery is perceived differently from the others. We might interpret the results as suggesting that the constant alternative is misplaced in the ranking more than any of the others. Perhaps there is confusion as to where it should be located because it is a sure amount.

We may tentatively conclude that the presence of sure amounts in rankings of uncertain wagers causes irregularities in preference rankings. When we couple these results with those from the Allais paradox (MacCrimmon & Larsson, 1975) and other decision studies (Kahneman & Tversky, 1979), we are led to a concern about a certainty effect that may make usual preference representations, including expected utility theory, inappropriate. Perhaps new theories that obtain separate orderings for sure and uncertain lotteries are needed and then comparisons might be made by discounting uncertain lotteries appropriately. A simple process model in which the uncertain lotteries are ranked separately from sure amounts is presented later in this chapter.

Does Risk Preference Depend on Payoff and Probability Attributes Common to all Alternatives? If a person is disposed to risk aversion, we would not expect him or her to exhibit a risk-averse attitude in one set and a risk-attraction attitude in another set. Because the differences among sets are only based on what attribute is held constant (i.e., loss amount held constant in set *A*, win amount held constant in set *B*, and probability held constant in set *C*), why should there be differences in a subject's ranking from one set to another? Yet an examination of the data shows that only one subject has an identical rank between sets *A* and *B*, only six subjects between sets *A* and *C*, and only five subjects between sets *B* and *C*. Only one subject has an identical ranking across the three sets and that is a monotonic one (indeed, eight of the 12 rankings that are identical across pairs of sets are monotonic).

These results seem to indicate that even though the range of variances are roughly the same across the three sets, some other factors are influencing preferences. As we observed earlier, the regularity in preferences as displayed by the unfolding analysis could be due to attributes other than variance. Perhaps further light can be shed on this by considering the extent to which the constant alternative and the lowest and highest variance lotteries are preferred most or preferred least in each of the sets. This is shown in Table 9.5. From these data we can develop the following conclusions: The constant wager does not seem to be placed differently in the three sets except for it being infrequently in last place in set *B*. The differences are more striking for the lowest variance lottery. It is seldom preferred in set *A* and strongly preferred in set *C*. Dislike of it in these sets is complementary to the liking for it. The highest variance lottery is only much preferred in set *A* and is strongly dispreferred in sets *B* and *C*.

These results need to be interpreted jointly. It seems that individuals do not mind the high variance lottery, and some like it very much, when the possible losses are restricted (to $5 in set *A*). However, when the losses can be larger (up to $27 in set *C* and $137 in set *B*), the high-variance lottery is avoided; in fact,

TABLE 9.5
Frequency of Preference Locations of Focal Alternatives

	Constant Alternative			Lowest Variance Alternative			Highest Variance Alternative		
	Set A	*Set B*	*Set C*	*Set A*	*Set B*	*Set C*	*Set A*	*Set B*	*Set C*
Preferred most	6	6	9	1	12	25	13	3	4
Preferred least	13	2	10	9	6	0	18	30	30

three-quarters of the subjects in each case place it last. The low-variance lottery is very popular when it offers an amount distinctively different from the sure payoff, yet has a low probability of only a modest loss (as it does in set C).

Further information about the effect of the different set formats can be gained by looking at the preferences across sets. Table 9.6 records the top choice of each subject across all three sets. (When alternative 1 was ranked first, the four cases could be interpreted as a choice from any of the three sets, because alternative 1 yielded a sure $5 in each set; therefore, we ignore the set preference for these four individuals.) Looking at the uncertain lotteries, we see the overall popularity of alternatives increases monotonically with variance in set A but decreases monotonically with variance in sets B and C. This suggests that the restricted losses in set A influenced the choice considerably.

In summary, from all three sources—(1) unfolded ranks across sets; (2) most and least preferred lotteries across sets; and (3) rankings of top choices across sets—we see that the loss amount seems to influence the choice. A theory that only incorporates variance (or expected value) without specifically focusing upon the possible losses is likely to be inadequate.

More evidence for hypothesis 4', context influences choice, can be obtained by comparing the ordering of two identical pairs of alternatives in two different sets. Note, in Table 9.1, the $B4$ and $C4$ have identical probabilities and payoffs. Because $B1$ and $C1$ are also identical, we can check if subjects have the same ordering in both sets. That is, according to the principle of "the independence of irrelevant alternatives," if someone preferred $B1$ to $B4$, we would expect that person to prefer $C1$ to $C4$.

Surprisingly, nine (22.5%) of the 40 subjects had a different ordering for this pair in set B from that in set C. Four of these nine subjects ordered the constant alternative ($B1$) over the uncertain wager ($B4$) in set B, but reversed this preference in set C.

One interpretation of this result is that the subjects are quite inconsistent in their preferences. Perhaps they did not think very carefully about their choices. This conclusion, however, seems somewhat at odds with the very regular choice patterns that we observed from the unfolding analysis. A more reasonable con-

TABLE 9.6
Frequency of Top Choice Across the Three Sets

	Set A	Set B	Set C
Alternative 1	3	—	1
Alternative 2	—	6	5
Alternative 3	5	4	—
Alternative 4	6	—	—
Alternative 5	8	2	—

clusion is that the individuals thought carefully about their choices, but that the context influenced their preferences. The large possible losses in set *B* may have made them more attentive to loss in that set and hence have a stronger preference for the sure thing. It appears that the other alternatives (i.e., numbers 2, 3, and 5), which should be irrelevant, are influencing the choice.

Expected utility theory, of course, allows for a consolidated effect of win and loss amounts, probability, and variance. It is quite conceivable, then, that some of the effect of the larger losses in sets *B* and *C* would be reflected in high risk aversion in the utility function below losses of $5. It is unlikely, however, that any reasonable utility function could be constructed for major discrepancies in rankings such as we observed. An attempt to assess the fit of a utility function by setting up the utility inequalities from the data was precluded by the fragmentary nature of the data.

CONCLUSIONS AND A SIMPLE PROCESS MODEL

Conclusions

Our hypotheses have been concerned with the choices of experienced decision makers in risk situations. In general, riskiness may be operationalized in ways that may conflict; in our study, however, riskiness as measured by variance, a linear combination of mean and variance, negative semivariance, range, and so forth, would imply the same preference ordering over the data. The first hypothesis asserted that individuals prefer ordering alternatives from the least risky to the most risky. The analysis of our data from 40 top-level business executives showed that such a monotonic preference for less risk occurred in less than 15% of the cases. Because preferences for less risk do not show up in simple lotteries such as we used, it seems unlikely that such preferences will occur in complex, real situations in which it would be extremely difficult to perceive, or calculate, the riskiness of the alternatives. The mean–variance rule used in financial decisions is a special case of the hypothesis considered here. When we couple the dubious descriptive validity from our study with the concerns about its normative merit (see Borch, 1969, and Fishburn, 1977), little of interest is left in the rule.

If a monotonic ordering over the riskiness of alternatives is invalid, the next step is to ask whether a unimodal preference for riskiness is to be found. This is equivalent to examining for an ideal level of risk with monotonically decreasing preference as one moves away from the ideal. This hypothesis accounted for an aggregate of 79% of the preference orderings in our study and so had considerably more descriptive validity than the simple monotonic preference hypothesis. (It should be remembered, though, that 16 rankings are consistent with the unimodal hypothesis within a set, whereas only one rank is consistent with the monotonic hypothesis.) Other studies have examined more complex alternatives (although a more narrow payoff domain) and also found the unimodal model to fit well (Coombs & Huang, 1970). Our data provides evidence that motivated real decision makers playing for significant amounts of actual money exhibit an ideal level of risk. This supplements earlier findings with bored subjects playing for low, or no, stakes (Slovic, Lichtenstein, & Edwards, 1965). Whether a model of ideal risk would describe preferences over investment alternatives in their real complexity and over major gains and losses remains an open question. The normative aspects of this rule (e.g., the implied utility and probability forms) also need further investigation. At this time, we cannot rule out some other risk dimensions as being more responsible than variance for the observed preference rankings because of the confounding of probability and payoffs with variance (Slovic & Lichtenstein, 1968a).

A next step in studying the risk behavior of decision makers is to recognize that an individual does not necessarily apply the same rule in every situation. Decisions will depend on the context of the choice situation. We incorporated two main tests for context effects. First, we mixed a constant alternative with the uncertain lotteries to see if the constant payoff had an untoward effect on the preference ordering. The results indicated that the constant alternative was treated differently from the other alternatives. When analyses were conducted that examined the effect of removing the constant alternative, the percentage of monotonic risk preferences increased from 15% to over 40% and the percentage of unimodal risk preferences increased from 79% to 98%. This effect was not due solely to decreasing the number of alternatives an individual had to consider when forming his or her preference ordering. Analyses involving the removal of any other alternative had no such major effect. When this result is coupled with the results of other studies in which "sure things" seem to lead to utility paradoxes, we are led to question the automatic merging of sure and uncertain alternatives in theories of preference. If a sure prospect creates a different mental set from uncertain alternatives, we must be cautious about theories that value uncertain prospects according to their certainty equivalent. Although some theories allow a separation (e.g., Luce & Krantz, 1971), most theories of risky decision use sure and uncertain alternatives interchangeably.

The second context effect was the presentation of alternatives in three different sets. In one set, all the uncertain lotteries had the same loss amount; in a second set, they had the same gain amount, and in the third set, they had the same win (and loss) probability. If an individual bases his or her choice solely on a concept of riskiness derived from the characteristics of the alternatives then the ordering of alternatives should be the same from one set to another, because the sets had identical means and comparable risk levels. The results, however, show very different preference patterns from one set to another. Only one person had the same ranking within each set and many people had very different rankings. We concluded that the specific levels of payoffs and probabilities had a major effect beyond that incorporated into the measure of the "riskiness" of an alterna-tive. The characteristics of other alternatives in the set seemed to impinge on the ordering; supposedly "irrelevant" alternatives were not irrelevant. Because this irrelevance notion is a key element in most theories of choice, the results suggest that we should take a closer look at modifying this assumption in descriptive, and perhaps in normative, models.

A Simple Process Model

The study of context effects begins to move the research away from a focus solely on results, and begins to suggest elements of how an individual processes information in making choices. The emphasis shifts from complex calculations and sophisticated decision rules to selective perception and simple decision rules. Although we did not collect data in a form that is conducive to checking on the steps an individual goes through in making choices (see Payne, 1975a), the design does allow us to make some inferences about the process. Very few current decision models incorporate context effects; hence, it seems worthwhile to pre-sent a simple process model that is suggested by our data. This proceeds in the same spriit as the information processing model of risky choice presented by Payne and Braunstein (1971). Our model is not based on detailed protocols and was developed after the analyses of the preceding sections had been performed. It was designed to explain the type of processing observed in individuals rather than to best fit the data we had gathered. Checks on the model, then, can perhaps throw some light on its descriptive validity, although a true, independent test will have to be conducted with other data.

The simple process model that seems to describe subjects making choices, such as the ones in our study, is given in Fig. 9.3. The first step in the process is to put aside the constant alternative(s) so attention may be focused upon the uncertain lotteries as a group. The uncertain lotteries are then examined so that those leading to the chance of an unacceptable loss can be separated out. The remaining alternatives (those not threatening unacceptable losses) are then sepa-rated into two groups: Class I alternatives are those with worthwhile gains; class II alternatives are those with mediocre gains. It is hypothesized that all alterna-tives in class I will be preferred to all alternatives in class II, and, in turn, all those alternatives will be preferred to those initially separated out as having unaccepta-ble losses (class III).

Now that the alternatives have been sorted into general classes and prefer-ences have been established between classes, attention shifts to alternatives within a class. The clearest cut situation involves class III in which the alterna-tives will be ordered on the basis of loss amount, with lower loss amounts obviously being preferable. Within class II, where, by definition, the gain and loss amounts are not salient, the ordering will be by probability of gain (from high to low). Within class I, the internal ordering is not as clear cut and may be

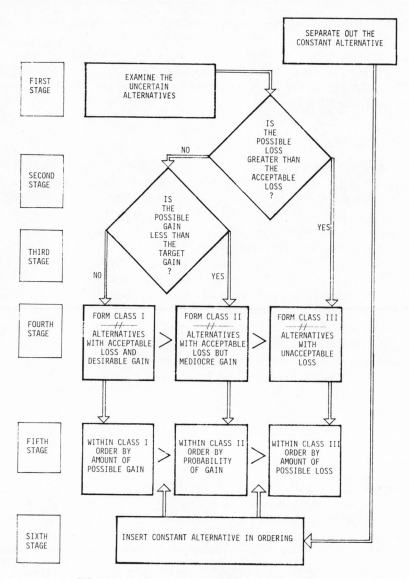

FIG. 9.3. Simple process model of risk-taking behavior.

based on either gain amount or on probability of gain (with the former seeming more likely). The final stage, in this multistage process, is to bring the constant alternative back into the picture, and to place it in relation to the three classes. We would expect that it would not appear between elements of a given class, nor would it be preferred to class I, nor dispreferred to class III. This limits it to appearing between class I and class II or between class II and class III, with the former seeming more likely.

This, then, represents the simple process model we are proposing. It seems to be consistent with other general process models (e.g., Newell & Simon, 1972). Note that it involves only very simple comparisons of characteristics of the presented alternatives and assumes no calculations of risk levels or other complex statistics. To complete the model, though, we do need to incorporate a target gain and an allowable loss so that the comparisons can be made. In general, we would expect that these levels would vary from individual to individual. We did not collect such data, so we shall assume a common level to apply to each subject in order to check the predictions of the model. Because the sure payoff was $5, we assume that the allowable loss was $5 and the target gain was $10. Although these figures are arbitrary, they were not chosen to fit the data and if they provide reasonable results, then, clearly, different levels based on individual preferences should yield considerably better predictions.

When these comparison levels are used in the model presented, we can see that the uncertain lotteries in the sets form into the following classes:

Set *A*:   class I: *A3, A4, A5;* class II: *A2;*   class III:—
Set *B*:   class I: *B2, B3;*   class II:—;   class III: *B4, B5*
Set *C*:   class I: *C2;*   class II:—;   class III: *C3, C4, C5*

Note the differential effect of these predictions over classes. For example, the model predicts that alternative 3 in set *A* will be preferred to alternative 2; that 2 will be preferred to 3 in set *C;* and that the set *B* perference will not be as strong because they are members of the same class.

Although we will not get into a detailed analysis of the results of this model, we note that not only do the predicitions of the preceding paragraph hold, each of the 10 binary predictions between classes is in the correct direction and most of these are highly significant. On the average, 77% of the subjects choose the alternatives predicted. Even when comparisons among blocks of alternatives and not just binary choices are made (e.g., in set *A*, alternatives 3, 4, and 5 must jointly be preferable to alternative 2), the model predicts from 50% to 85% of the choices. Not only is this far better than a random model, it is only a little less than the percentages obtained by piecing together the ex post highest individual preferences (which would yield a preference pattern with no conceptual or logical basis). Our model with a strong conceptual and logical basis, then, seems quite promising. It seems inappropriate here to provide a detailed analysis, but because we provide our basic data, the interested reader may check the model's descriptive validity.

ACKNOWLEDGMENTS

We wish to acknowledge our appreciation for the major financial support of the Technology Branch of the Canadian Department of Industry, Trade and Commerce. We are also grateful for the financial support provided by the Social Sciences and Humanities Research Council, the Associates Workshop of the University of Western Ontario School of Business Administration, and the President's Grants Committee of the University of British Columbia.

REFERENCES

Arrow, K. J. *Essays in the theory of risk bearing*. Chicago: Markham, 1971.

Borch, K. A note on uncertainty and indifference curves. *Review of Economic Studies*, 1969, *36*, 1–4.

Coombs, C. H. *A theory of data*. New York: Wiley, 1964.

Coombs, C. H., & Huang, L. Polynomial psychophysics of risk. *Journal of Mathematical Psychology*, 1970, *7*, 317–338.

Coombs, C. H., & Pruitt, D. G. Components of risk in decision making: Probability and variance preferences. *Journal of Experimental Psychology*, 1960, *60*, 265–277.

Edwards, W. Probability preferences in gambling. *American Journal of Psychology*, 1953, *66*, 349–364.

Fishburn, P. *On the foundations of mean–variance analysis*. Mimeo, Pennsylvania State University, 1975.

Fishburn, P. Mean–risk analysis with risk associated with below-target returns. *American Economic Review*, 1977, *67*, 116–126.

Friedman, M., & Savage, L. J. The expected-utility hypothesis and the measurability of utility. *Journal of Political Economy*, 1952, *60*, 463–475.

Fryback, D. G., Goodman, B. C., & Edwards, W. Choices among bets by Las Vegas gamblers: Absolute and contextural effects. *Journal of Experimental Psychology*, 1973, *98*, 271–278.

Kahneman, D., & Tversky, A. Prospect theory. *Econometrica*, 1979, *47*, 263–291.

Luce, D., & Krantz, D. Conditional expected utility. *Econometrica*, 1971, *39*, 253–271.

MacCrimmon, K., & Larsson, S. Utility theory: Axioms vs. paradoxes. Working paper, 1975, to appear in M. Allais & O. Hagen (Eds.) *Expected utility and the Allais paradox*. Dordrecht, Holland, Reidel, in preparation.

Mao, J. Models of capital budgeting, EV vs. ES. *Journal of Finance and Quantitative Analysis*, 1970, *4*, 657–675.

Markowitz, H. Portfolio selection. *Journal of Finance*, 1952, *7*, 77–91.

Markowitz, H. *Portfolio selection*. New York: Wiley, 1959.

Newell, A., & Simon, H. *Human problem solving*. Englewood Cliffs, N.J.: Prentice-Hall, 1972.

Payne, J. A process tracing study of risky decision making: Examples of verbal protocols and comments (W.P. 274, Department of Psychology). Pittsburgh: Carnegie-Mellon University, 1975. (a)

Payne, J. Relation of perceived risk to preference among gambles. *Journal of Experimental Psychology: Human Perception and Performance*, 1975, *104*, 86–94. (b)

Payne, J., & Braunstein, M. Preference among gambles with equal underlying distributions. *Journal of Experimental Psychology*, 1971, *87*, 13–18.

Pollatsek, A., & Tversky, A. A theory of risk. *Journal of Mathematical Psychology*, 1970, *7*, 540–553.

Pratt, J. W. Risk aversion in the small and in the large. *Econometrica*, 1964, *32*, 122–136.

Pruitt, D. G. Pattern and level of risk in gambling decisions. *Psychological Review*, 1962, *69*, 187–201.

Slovic, P. Differential effects of real versus hypothetical payoffs on choices among gambles. *Journal of Experimental Psychology*, 1969, *80*, 434–437.

Slovic, P., & Lichtenstein, S. Importance of variance preferences in gambling decisions. *Journal of Experimental Psychology*, 1968, *78*, 646-654. (a)

Slovic, P., & Lichtenstein, S. Relative importance of probabilities and payoffs in risk taking. *Journal of Experimental Psychology Monograph*, 1968, *78* (No. 3, Pt. 2). (b)

Slovic, P., Lichtenstein, S., & Edwards, W. Boredom-induced changes in preferences among bets. *American Journal of Psychology*, 1965, *78*, 208-217.

Tobin, J. Liquidity preference as behavior towards risk. *Review of Economic Studies*, 1958, *25*, 65-87.

10 Current Developments in Research on Cascaded Inference Processes

David A. Schum
Rice University

INTRODUCTORY COMMENTS

My interests involve both formal and empirical issues arising in research on the intellectual process we call probabilistic or inductive inference. Thus, I am interested in how individuals should and actually do revise opinion about the relative likeliness of two or more hypotheses or propositions on the basis of inconclusive evidence. One important feature of inference tasks in a variety of natural settings, such as medical diagnosis and jury deliberations, is that the logical connection between observable evidence and one's hypotheses is frequently indirect and involves various catenations of other events interposed between observables and the hypotheses. Such inferential processes are alternatively called cascaded, hierarchical, catenated, or multistage processes. The research I describe in this chapter involves such cascaded inferences, a class of intellectual processes I have found most interesting and challenging to investigate.

Most of the research I discuss is formal in nature; I have more to say about the task of inference than I have to say about the behavior of individuals who perform this task. Probabilistic inference is one of those infrequently occurring but fortunate areas of study within psychology in which there exists a reasonably suitable axiomatic base from which to proceed; such a base allows one to study the formal requisites of a task in terms of its essential ingredients and the manner in which they should be combined. My research on cascaded inference has led me to consider scholarship in a variety of disciplines whose number and diversity I did not anticipate when I began my work in this area nearly 10 years ago. In order first to generate and then to interpret formalizations that I believe capture the essentials of cascaded inference, I have had to draw upon scholarship in such (apparently) diverse areas as evidence law, philosophy, and sensory psychology.

The diversity of disciplines upon which the study of cascaded inference processes rests, as well as the variety of behavioral tasks that involve such processes, allow me to comment on one of the major objectives of interest to the organizers of this book. They hoped each contributor would be able to illustrate how decision research is important in the mainstream of cognitive psychology and is not an isolated endeavor insensitive to the contexts in which such decisions occur. For some time, I have been concerned about whether or not the formalizations I study are rich enough to capture the essential behavioral requisites of inference in various decision contexts (Schum, 1977a). In fact, this very concern led me to consider scholarship in areas outside of psychology in which I was confident that cascaded inference processes occur.

For reasons I discuss, I believe that our formalizations of cascaded inference processes are "behaviorally rich" in the sense that they incorporate many expected behavioral requisites of inference. Furthermore, our formalizations have helped me to fill in the gaps left by the inadequacies of my own intuition about the basic ingredients of complex inference and about how these ingredients should be combined.

MAJOR ROOTS OF PRESENT ENDEAVORS

We tell students of psychology that it is not a trivial task to identify the crucial stimulus or stimuli for some behavioral action. Pressed to tell you what are the essential roots of stimuli for my current research activities, I did experience predictable difficulties. The following three factors I believe to be the most important.

Feelings of Inadequacy

The major stimulus for the work I am now doing had its onset in the middle 1960s, was visceral in nature, and involved the uncomfortable feeling that I knew very little about the task of inductive inference. One reason for discomfort was that I was studying human performance on such tasks; even more discomforting was the fact that I was asked to make specific recommendations, based on this research, about how inference functions ought to be allocated among people and devices in complex systems with diagnostic or inferential missions. I began to compare the complexity of the laboratory and simulation tasks we were studying with the complexity I thought evident in inferences performed in a variety of natural settings; the results of this comparison occasioned my feelings of discomfort.

Our ealry empirical research on probabilistic inference was stimulated by the work of Ward Edwards (1962) and was, as I have indicated, a mixture of basic and applied research. Excellent reviews of this early research are found in papers by Rapoport and Wallsten (1972) and by Slovic and Lichtenstein (1971). It now appears that much of our applied research was premature; we spent a large amount of time evaluating various task-allocation paradigms before we were certain we knew about the formally required ingredients of inference tasks. Our essential problem, as I now see it, was that we thought Bayes' Rule, as it appears in most probability treatises, says nearly all there is to say about probabilistic inference. We did know that sequential application of Bayes' Rule does require attention to possible conditional nonindependence among the evidentiary events of concern; this was not always adequately explained in treatises of that period. However, we were unaware of the cascaded or hierarchical structure of most inference tasks and of the fact that there are several species of evidence that, in combination, require very careful formal treatment.

Interest in Source Credibility and Testimonial Evidence

In applications of conditional probabilities, it is frequently no easy task to specify which event actually conditions opinion; in other words, we usually have to be very careful in deciding just what information we have received. As an example, Let D = event that the streetlight at the scene of the accident was on, and let D^* = the event of my testimony that the streetlight at the scene of the accident was on. As far as you (a juror in a negligence case) are concerned, events D and D^* are not the same events and you can be misled if you treat them as such. For various reasons, you might easily suppose that my testimony D^* is consistent with the truth of *both* D and its complement D^c. In short, you may have reason to question my credibility as a source of information about D, whose occurrence or nonoccurrence you did not actually observe. You may doubt the accuracy of my powers of observation or my veracity in reporting what I saw. Your problem is that, even in light of my unequivocal testimony D^*, you have uncertainty about whether or not D actually occurred.

Studies of the formal requisites of testimonial evidence represented my first attempt to discover more about the task of inference, because I believed (and still do) that source-credibility issues are obvious complicating features of virtually all inference tasks performed in legal, medical, military, and other contexts. I must remark that others have been interested in formalizing probabilistic opinion revision when there is uncertainty about what is the conditioning event. Earlier, John Dodson (1961) attempted a revision of Bayes' Rule that would allow one to incorporate evidence in the form of equivocal responses from a source. As an example of such evidence, suppose I told you I was 70% sure D occurred and 30% sure it did not. A few years later, Gettys and Willke (1969) pointed out certain normalization difficulties in Dodson's original algorithm that resulted in its lack of path independence; they offered a revised version in which such difficulties were removed.

In a series of papers, various colleagues and I began to formalize the process of determining the inferential value of testimonial evidence from sources with less than perfect credibility. In our formalizations of the inferential value of testimonial evidence (as well as other evidence I discuss later), such value is indexed by likelihoods and likelihood ratios, the specific ingredients in Bayes' Rule that incorporate the inferential value of evidence. There was only a very small legacy of research within probability theory on credibility–testimony issues. Todhunter (1865) reviewed some of the earliest studies. Both Laplace (1795) and Keynes (1957) were particularly interested in credibility-related issues. In the work of Laplace and Keynes, credibility-related inference problems were posed in a similar manner; an attempt was made to determine how much weight to assign testimony, *given that the source (or witness) testifies correctly.* A serious difficulty is encountered when the problem is posed in this manner because the exact event witnessed is not incorporated into the formalization. As we see later, we must specify exactly what event the witness reports having occurred.

Our first effort (Schum & DuCharme, 1971) concerns the following rather simple case: Suppose H_1 and H_2 are two disjoint hypotheses or propositions at issue; let $\{D, D^c\}$ be a class of events linked probabilistically to H_1 and H_2 via the conditional probabilities $P(D \mid H_j)$, $P(D^c|H_j)$, $j = 1, 2$; let $\{D_i^*, D^c_i*\}$ be a class of events representing testimony where D_i^* is the testimony or report from source i that event D occurred and D^c_i* is the testimony from source i that D did not occur. This is, in fact, one of the simplest cases of cascaded inference; an event representing testimony is inconclusive evidence of related events in another class, which are, in turn, circumstantially related to one's hypotheses. In determining the inferential value of the testimony from source i, we must specify exactly what the testimony was (either D_i^* or D_i^c*). Consider K_i = the event that source i "testifies correctly," as considered by Laplace and Keynes. This event will not suffice in conditioning opinion about H_1 and H_2 because there are two ways in which the source can testify correctly: D_i^* when D occurred, and D^c_i* when D did not occur. A basic problem is that the source's credibility in reporting D_i^* may be different from his or her credibility in reporting D_i^c*. Using event K_i as a conditioning event on H_1 and H_2, we cannot account for such credibility differences, nor can we incorporate the fact that certain credibility-related probability values may also be conditioned by H_1, H_2, or both.

Suppose source i reports D_i^*; the likelihood ratio for testimonial event D_i^* prescribes the inferential value of D_i^* on H_1 and H_2 and is given in the general case by:

$$\Lambda_{D_i}{}^* = \frac{P(D_i^*|H_1)}{P(D_i^*|H_2)}$$

$$= \frac{P(D|H_1)[P(D_i^*|DH_1) - P(D_i^*|D^cH_1)] + P(D_i^*|D^cH_1)}{P(D|H_2)[P(D_i^*|DH_2) - P(D_i^*|D^cH_2)] + P(D_i^*|D^cH_2)} .$$

$$(10.1)$$

This apparently simple case in fact allowed us to resolve some long-standing problems concerning credibility–testimony issues. Intuition suggests that $\Lambda_{D_i}^*$ should incorporate two kinds of information: information about the inferential value of the *event* being reported and information about the credibility of the source. The former is encoded by the conditional probabilities $P(D|H_j)$, $j = 1$, 2; the latter is encoded by the conditionals $P(D_i^*|DH_j)$, $P(D_i^*|D^cH_j)$, $j = 1$, 2. We chose to term these latter conditionals "hit" and "false-positive" probabilities because of the established convention in signal-detection theory. Intuition is not always complete; there are other important considerations. Notice that Eq. (10.1) requires the likelihoods $P(D|H_j)$, $j = 1$, 2, and *not* the likelihood ratio $L_D = \dfrac{P(D/H_1)}{P(D/H_2)}$. *The ratio L_D suppresses information about the rareness* of event D, whereas the conditionals appearing separately preserve such information. In short, $\Lambda_{D_i}^*$ depends on the rareness of event D under H_1 and H_2. Because this is true, we were able to study the precise nature of the interaction between the credibility of a source and the rareness of the event being reported. Such an interaction was suspected by Keynes, but his formalization did not allow him to study its effects.

Notice in Eq. (10.1) that the credibility-related hit and false-positive values are, possibly, conditional upon H_1, H_2, or both. Suppose, for example, that $P(D_i^*|DH_j) = P(D_i^*|D)$, for every J. In words, D_i^* and H_j are independent conditional upon the truth of D. This implies that $P(H_j|DD_i^*) = P(H_j|D)$, an implication that there is no inferential value in the source's report that is not contained in the event the source reports. If hit and false-positive probabilities for a source *are* conditional upon one or both of the hypotheses, then there may be "extra" inferential value in the source's testimony in probabilistic discriminations between H_1 and H_2. If $P(D_i^*|DH_j) = P(D_i^*|D)$, and $P(D_i^*|D^cH_j) = P(D_i^*|D^c)$ for $j = 1$, 2, then Λ_D^* can be written in simpler form

$$\Lambda_D^* = \frac{P(D|H_1) + \left[\dfrac{h_i}{f_i} - 1\right]^{-1}}{P(D|H_2) + \left[\dfrac{h_i}{f_i} - 1\right]^{-1}} ,$$

$$(10.1a)$$

where hit probability $P(D_i^*|D) = h_i$, false-positive probability $P(D^*|D^c) = f_i$, and where we assume $f_i \neq 0$ and $h_i \neq f_i$.

I have always carefully avoided saying that the "credibility" of a source is *defined* by the conditionals $P(D_i*|DH_j)$ and $P(D_i*|D^cH_j)$, which appear in Eq. (10.1), or by the ratio $\dfrac{h_i}{f_i} = \dfrac{P(D_i*|D)}{P(D_i*|D^c)}$, which appears in Eq. (10.1a). In fact, in our earliest paper on the topic (Schum & DuCharme, 1971), we discussed several problems inherent in attempts to define source credibility or reliability in terms of these ingredients. As the signal detectability theorists have made us well aware, the response D_i* or D_i^c* from source i depends on both the source's sensitivity in discriminating between D and D^c and on the source's response criterion. This response criterion, in turn, depends on the source's expectancies about the prior likeliness of events D and D^c and on costs and payoffs associated with the four possible response–event outcomes. Thus, our assessment of the credibility of source i actually involves a variety of considerations having to do with the source's sensitivity or competence as an observer and with motivational considerations that presumably affect the source's testimonial biases and veracity. The question is: To what extent do the credibility-related ingredients of our Λ expressions allow one to incorporate these sensitivity, expectancy, and motivational considerations in assessments of the inferential value of testimony?

In a recent paper (Schum, 1979), I have attempted to show how $\Lambda_{D_i}*$ as defined in Eq. (10.1) and (10.1a), is sensitive to a remarkable array of subtleties associated with witness observational sensitivity, expectancy, and motivational factors. Incorporating the formal elegance of signal-detection theory in determining hit and false-positive rates, I considered a special case involving a normal-normal, equal-variance observer. The observational sensitivity of such an observer, indexed by d', can be varied independently of the observer's response criterion $L(x_o)$, which, as already mentioned, depends on prior probability (expectancy) of signal occurrence and on costs and payoffs. In a signal-detection task, the observer can be instructed to respond in accordance with any one of a number of decisional strategies, such as maximizing payoff, maximizing hits while holding false positives at some fixed rate, maximizing the probability of a correct response, or minimizing maximum error. For each one of these strategies, there are algorithms for determining formally ideal $L(x_o)$ (see Egan, 1975). For any given setting of d' and $L(x_o)$, corresponding values of h_i and f_i can be determined under the normal distribution assumptions. Thus, one can vary d' and $L(x_o)$ independently for an observer and examine how $\Lambda_{D_i}*$ behaves in response to corresponding changes in the h_i and f_i values associated with different settings of d' and $L(x_o)$.

The results of this study permit three general conclusions. The first conclusion seems obvious from Eq. (10.1a). Under any decisional strategy, when the h_i and f_i values are *not* conditional upon H_1 or H_2, there are simple tradeoffs possible between observer sensitivity and observer response-criterion setting in determinations of the inferential value of the observer's response. As an example, suppose W_i is a high-criterion, low-sensitivity observer; for W_i, $h_i = .05$, $f_i = .01$, and $d_i^* = .68$. Further, suppose W_j is a low-criterion, high-sensitivity observer; for W_j, $h_j = .95$, $f_j = .19$, and $d_j' = 2.52$. For each of the observers, the ratio of hit rate to false-positive rate is the same, and, as Eq. (10.1) shows, for any fixed set of conditionals $P(D|H_k)$ for $k = 1, 2$, Λ_D^* is identical for the testimony from W_i and W_j. The reason why these tradeoffs between observer sensitivity and response criterion are possible is that the values h_i and f_i, not conditional upon H_1 or H_2, are also not, by themselves, inferentially important. Their precise role is to show how much of the inferential value contained in the event being reported is preserved when we consider the credibility of the observer.

The second conclusion of this study was that $\Lambda_{D_i}^*$ is definitely sensitive to the observer's decisional strategy. Plots of $\Lambda_{D_i}^*$ as a function of d' are quite different for various decisional strategies. The third conclusion was that a remarkable array of evidence subtleties can be incorporated in Eq. (10.1) when h_i and f_i are conditional upon H_1 or H_2. Within the signal-detection paradigm, one can make either or both of d' and $L(x_o)$ conditional upon H_1 or H_2. Making $L(x_o)$ conditional upon H_1 or H_2 allows one to represent a wide variety of observer bias effects such as testimony against preference. Suppose a witness is a very close friend of the defendant. This witness testifies to the occurrence of an event that is damaging to the defendant. Intuition suggests and our formalizations verify that this testimony should have more inferential value than testimony to this event from an unbiased or "neutral" observer. Making d' conditional upon H_1 and H_2 allows one to represent situations in which observational sensitivity may be conditioned by knowledge of H_1 or H_2. For example, we might encounter a radiologist whose capacity for detecting some diagnostically important signal on an X-ray is higher for pneumonia than for tuberculosis patients. Finally, making d' and $L(x_o)$ jointly conditional upon H_1 or H_2 allows one to represent a variety of evidential subtleties, some of which are counterintuitive.

After studying elementary forms of Λ_D^*, we performed an empirical study hoping to determine the extent to which subjects change the inferential value of testimony in a manner consistent with the credibility of the source (Schum, DuCharme, & DePitts, 1973). The results, consistent with other studies (see Peterson, 1973), showed that subjects tend to overvalue evidence from unreliable sources. That is, they fail to make the inferential value of D^* smaller than the inferential value of D by an amount Eq. (10.1a) says is appropriate.

Another formal effort (Schum & Kelly, 1973) concerned the multisource case in which n sources, sensors, or witnesses are queried about whether D or D^c occurred. There are several interesting problems in this case. First, the n reports are inferentially redundant in the sense that they all refer to D, which either occurred or did not occur. Second, the n sources can either agree (all report D^* or all report D^{c*}) or they can give contradictory testimony; r sources report D^*, and $(n - r)$ sources report D^{c*}. Thus, there is concern, not only about the inferential strength of the joint testimony, but also about the direction (towards H_1 or towards H_2) of opinion revision. Finally, in addition to concern over whether or not credibility-related values are conditional upon H_1, H_2, or both, there is a new concern about whether or not the sources are behaving independently of one another. Thus, we have two conditional independence issues to worry about; a variety of special cases can emerge depending on the pattern of assumptions that applies in any particular case.

Let R_i be the report from source i about whether or not D occurred; R_i can be either D_i^* or D_i^{c*}. Let $F^* =$ the event of the *joint* testimony from the n sources—that is, $F^* = \bigcap_{i=1}^{n} R_i$. In the special case in which the sources' reports are independent of each other and are not conditional upon either H_1 or H_2,

$$\Lambda_F^* = \frac{P(D|H_1) + V}{P(D|H_2) + V} \tag{10.2}$$

where:

$$V = \left[\frac{\prod\limits_{p \in P} \dfrac{h_p}{f_p}}{\prod\limits_{q \in Q} \dfrac{c_q}{m_q}} - 1 \right]^{-1}.$$

In the credibility-related value V in Eq. (10.2), P is the set of r sources who report D^*, and Q is the set of $(n - r)$ sources who report D^{c*}. The value $c_q =$ "correct rejection" probability for source q where $c_q = 1 - f_q$, and m_q is "miss" probability where $m_q = 1 - h_q$.

In Eq. (10.2), the term V shows the direction as well as the strength of opinion revision. If the aggregate h/f ratio of the P sources reporting D^* exceeds the aggregate c/m ratio for the Q sources reporting D^{c*}, we move opinion towards the hypothesis favored by event D; if the reverse is true, we move opinion towards the hypothesis favored by D^c. We also notice that what matters is the aggregate credibility on either side (P or Q) and *not* the number of sources on either side. We might have one source in P and 20 in Q; if the single source in P is more credible than the aggregate of those in Q, we side with P. Other interesting features of this formalization are discussed in Schum and Kelly (1973) and in Schum (1979). Finally, we extended our multisource formalizations to the more general case involving multinomial event classes (Schum & Pfeiffer, 1973).

At this point, I asked myself two questions that influenced the subsequent direction of my research. I wondered, in connection with Λ_F^* in Eq. (10.2), what evidence law says about the number of witnesses and the impact of testimony, and I wondered whether or not formalizations like Eq. (10.1) and (10.2) would incorporate the various credibility impeachment issues that arise in juridical proceedings. To answer these questions, I started to rummage about in evidence law treatises. I found the answers to my specific questions and I found *much* more. What I found is the next part of my story.

Juridical Evidence Scholarship

Information about cascaded inference has been revealed to me over time and not necessarily when I have needed it most. I wish I had read certain treatises on evidence law before I began my formal work; there is a wealth of information in these treatises for persons interested in the logical requisites of inference. Juridical scholars, at least since the time of Jeremy Bentham, have systematically investigated a variety of evidentiary issues as they arise in litigation. The earliest comprehensive effort appears to be Bentham's treatise *The Rationale of Judicial Inference* (1839). I have wondered why there has been such extensive scholarship on inference in the substantive area of law and not in other substantive areas such as medicine in which inductive inference is equally important; I believe there are three essential reasons: First, litigation is a contentious process in which adversaries present evidence favorable to their own positions. For this reason, a variety of unique credibility-related issues arise in juridical applications. Second, because of the contentious nature of litigation, the court exerts control over which evidence can be given; no such controls exist in other contexts. Finally, in juridical inference, the fact finders are only rarely experts in substantive matters and are almost certainly not knowledgeable about the logical requisites of the tasks they perform. Thus, systematic study of *evidence,* the stock-in-trade of juridical proceedings, has been a necessity.

As you may recall, I said that I began to read in evidence law hoping to discover whether or not legal evidence prescriptions were consistent with prescriptions given by our early Λ formalizations. I discovered consistency with respect to the weight of evidence and the number of witnesses on either side; I also discovered that our Λ formalizations were ''behaviorally rich'' enough to incorporate all the recognized legal grounds for impeachment and support of witness credibility (Schum, 1977a). I also discovered something even more valuable, namely, the scholarship of an eminent jurist named John Henry Wigmore. His most influential works appear to be his treatise *The Science of Judicial Proof* (1937 latest edition, 1901 first edition) and his monumental 10 volume *Treatise On The Anglo-American System Of Evidence In Trials At Common Law* (each volume has a different publication date because the work has been periodically revised; in subsequent references to this work, I cite *Evidence,* followed by the volume number and the most recent date of publication).

Four aspects of Wigmore's work have been of particular interest to me: his classification of evidence, his categorization of the ways in which evidence is used, his study of ''catenated'' inference (Wigmore's term for what we, at least

40 years later, call "cascaded" inference), and his analyses of masses of mixed evidence representing actual cases or portions thereof. Wigmore's diagrammatic analyses of evidence, though systematic in nature, were nonformal in the sense that he offered neither probabilistic characterizations of evidence nor prescriptive rules about how evidence should be combined. He believed that science, though offering canons of reasoning for single inferences, could not provide canons of reasoning for masses of contentious evidence such as that appearing in juridical proceedings (Wigmore, 1937). This sounded like a challenge to me, one that I have accepted, as the next section shows.

CURRENT RESEARCH ON CASCADED INFERENCE

In this section, I tell you about some of our current research objectives and about the progress we have made. I do have other objectives, but they concern relating our research to other areas of psychology generally, and decision theory and analysis specifically. I discuss these latter objectives in the next section.

Formalizing Cantenations of Various Species of Evidence

It may seem presumptuous for anyone to announce interest in formalizing the complex inference tasks individuals perform on the basis of inconclusive, contradictory, and conflicting evidence often obtained from unreliable sources. Anyone who has ever performed such tasks in the role of juror, medical diagnostician, or intelligence analyst knows something about the bewildering array of evidence that must be evaluated and combined. On the surface, it may appear that formalization is nearly impossible in the face of unlimited varieties and large volumes of evidence.

I now believe that, although the substance of evidence may be unlimited, there are, in fact, just a few basic logical *forms* of evidence. These I discuss momentarily. I also have reason to believe that volume of evidence, by itself, should not be frightening; this issue I defer discussing until later. These two revelations have given me hope that we can formalize the process of evaluating and aggregating masses of evidence mixed with respect to logical form.

There is not complete agreement among jurists about how evidence ought to be classified. Wigmore (*Evidence, IV,* 1972 rev.) presents a scheme in which he partitions all evidence into three categories. In more recent work (e.g., Lempert & Saltzburg, 1977), somewhat finer distinctions are made. The classification scheme I will briefly discuss violates neither the older approach of Wigmore nor the modern approach of Lempert and Saltzburg. It is based upon two considerations that are apparent in virtually every classification scheme I have yet seen. In studying the formal requisites of inference, I have the problem of translating descriptions of evidence into the language of events. The reason is that probability is a measure assigned to events and to Boolean functions of events. The classification of evidentiary events I consider must be precise, parsimonious, and yet flexible enough to represent important behavioral distinctions in a variety of inferential or diagnostic contexts.

As far as I can tell, there are two major questions implicit in evidence classification schemes I have seen. The first is: What is the source of the evidence? The second is: What is the nature of the logical relation between the evidence and the propositions, hypotheses, or facts in issue? As I discuss these questions, I introduce notational and diagrammatic conventions I use throughout this chapter. The person "you" referred to in discussion is the person performing the inference task, for example, the fact finder in a court trial or the medical diagnostician.

Source of Evidence: Testimonial versus Real Evidence. A distinction is usually made between instances in which you receive information from your own senses and other instances in which you receive information either from the senses of someone else or from some nonhuman sensing device. Suppose for some inferential purpose we need to know whether or not the index finger on Person A's left hand is missing; let D = event that the index finger on A's left hand is missing and let D^c = event that this finger is not missing. You have never seen A and, therefore, must rely on the report or testimony from a witness W_i who, we assume, nows A and can help us determine whether D or D^c is true. The report by W_i to you is called *testimonial evidence:* Let D_i^* = the event that W_i testifies that D occurred (or is true), and let D_i^{c*} = event that W_i testifies that D did not occur (or is not true). Unless the credibility of W_i is perfect, the testimony D_i^* is consistent with the truth of both D and D^c; the testimony D_i^{c*} would also be similarly consistent with D and D^c. Thus, both reports D_i^* and D_i^{c*} are inconclusive evidence of D or of D^c. Fig. 10.1a shows our diagrammatic convention for illustrating inconclusive evidence; the arrow means "consistent with the truth of" or "has nonzero probability under." In Fig. 10.1a, testimony D_i^* is consistent with the truth of both events in the class $\{D, D^c\}$.

Testimonial evidence of some sort is present in nearly every inference task. However, there are instances, of course, in which you, the fact finder or diagnostician, make direct observations yourself. Person A is brought into the courtroom and holds up his or her left hand. Let D_o = event that you observe the occurrence of event D and D_o^c = event that you observe the nonoccurrence of event D. Objects or other materials available for your own direct observation are frequently called *real* evidence. The question now arises whether or not D_o is conclusive evidence of D. It depends, of course, on whether or not the observational conditions were perfect and on whether or not your senses are completely accurate. If the conditions of observation were poor or your senses less than perfectly accurate, then the formal distinction between D_o and D_i^* vanishes; both could be thought of as testimonial evidence from unreliable sources and, therefore, inconclusive evidence of D.

I shall preserve the distinction between testimonial and real evidence under one special condition. Suppose a situation in which we can accept some event as having, in fact, occurred. In some cases, a fact finder's observational conditions and senses may be virtually perfect. In other cases, we may reasonably assume the occurrence of some event.[1] In such cases, we treat D_O and D as equivalent events. This allows us to use a smaller number of conditioning steps in our formalizations, which, as you will see, rapidly become difficult even in apparently simple cases.

Direct versus Circumstantial Evidence.   Our next concern is with the manner in which our observables (real or testimonial evidence) are related to the basic hypotheses, propositions, or facts in issue. One form of evidence, termed *direct evidence*, would resolve or be conclusive about the matters at issue if the evidence came from a completely credible source. Absent perfect credibility, however, direct evidence is inconclusive. With direct evidence, the only inferential issues concern the credibility of the source and whether or not the evidence is authentic as described in Footnote 1. Another form of evidence is *always* inconclusive about basic matters at issue, whether or not it comes from a perfectly credible source. Such evidence is said to be *circumstantial, indirect,* or *presumptive* (an obsolete term). As Table 10.1 shows, both direct and circumstantial evidence can be either real or testimonial.

Following are several examples that should convey the distinctions made in Table 10.1. Let $\{H_1, H_2\}$ be a class of events representing the hypotheses, propositions or facts in issue of *basic* or *ultimate* interest in an inference task. Although we assume $\{H_1, H_2\}$ to be a disjoint class, it may or may not be exhaustive. First consider *direct-testimonial* evidence. Let H_1 = event that A shot B, and let $H_2 = H_1^c$ = event that A did not shoot B. Witness W_i testifies H_{1i}^*, that A shot B. Here we have a direct-testimonial assertion about our major fact in issue. As Fig. 10.1b shows, H_{1i}^* is consistent with the truth of (or is inconclusive regarding) H_1 and H_2, assuming that W_i is not perfectly credible. Notice that there is no intermediate reasoning step between observable H_{1i}^* and hypotheses $\{H_1, H_2\}$. This is why we label the direct-testimonial cell "never cascaded" in Table 10.1.

Next, consider the *circumstantial testimonial* situation in Table 10.1 with $\{H_1, H_2\}$ defined as in the preceding paragraph. Let D = event that A and B had

---

[1]In jurispi .dence, a special category of evidence called *judicial notice* exists. It refers to clearly indisputable facts whether or not they are commonly known. Such evidence is accepted without proof. I also note that the introduction of real evidence in court trials often requires elaborate procedures for *authenticating* the evidence. Generally, such procedures identify the evidence and show how it is linked with a litigant.

TABLE 10.1

| | | Linkage to Basic Hypotheses | |
		Direct	Circumstantial
SOURCE	Testimonial	1. Never cascaded	2. Always cascaded
	Real	3. Never cascaded	4. Sometimes cascaded

Evidence according to source and linkage with basic hypotheses.

fought on an occasion previous to the one in question; D^c = negation of D. Notice that event D is consistent with the truth of H_1 and H_2; the fact that A and B had a fight in the past may cause us to change our opinion about the relative likeliness of H_1 and H_2, but certainly not conclusively so. Notice that we would say this regardless of the credibility of the source of information about event D. Suppose that our information comes from witness W_j; let D_j^* = event that witness j testifies that A and B had a fight on a previous occasion. Fig. 10.1c shows that the chain of reasoning from testimony D_j^* to $\{H_1, H_2\}$ involves the intermediate step concerning $\{D, D^c\}$. Thus, we have a simple cascaded inference task; D_j^* is inconclusive testimonial evidence regarding events $\{D, D^c\}$ that are circumstantially related to $\{H_1, H_2\}$. Fig. 10.1c happens to depict the simplest possible cascaded inference task. More complex examples appear in a later discussion.

The *direct–real* evidence situation seems rare in most inference tasks. In jurisprudence, a person who had made a direct observation relative to a fact in issue would be employed as a witness and not a fact finder. The fact that I witnessed Jack Ruby shoot Lee Harvey Oswald (as did several million others who saw it happen on television) would probably have precluded my being a juror should this matter have come to trial. One can, of course, imagine showing jurors films or television tapes of some crucial events at the discretion of the court. In medical diagnosis, it would seem a rare occurrence for a doctor to have made an observation that conclusively resolves a diagnostic problem. I do not dwell on this noncascaded inference situation except to point out that the inferential issues seem to involve the accuracy of your own observation and perhaps, authentication issues if the inference is juridical.

The *circumstantial–real* evidence situation is encountered in both cascaded and noncascaded forms. The noncascaded form, in fact, characterizes most of the "bookbag and poker chip" experiments so popular in laboratory inference research in the 1960's. Suppose Bag H_1 contains 90% red (D) and 10% blue (D^c) poker chips; Bag H_2 contains 30% red and 70% blue chips. Under ideal viewing conditions, showing a color-normal subject, a red or a blue chip is real but circumstantial evidence regarding H_1 and H_2. Our diagrammatic convention for real evidence is shown in Fig. 10.1d. A subject's observation D_o (of a red chip)

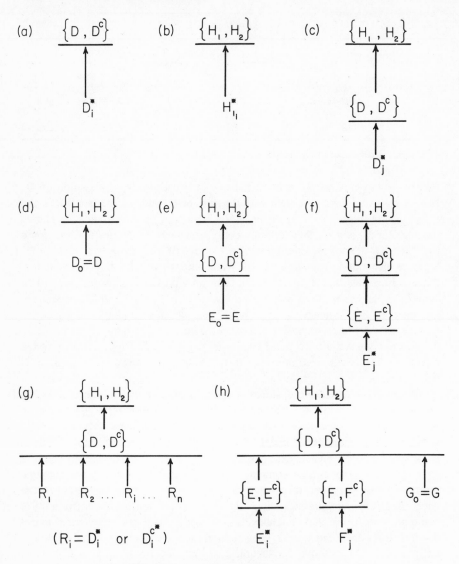

FIG. 10.1. Evidence forms and catenations.

is taken to be equivalent to the occurrence of event D because of the subject's assumed perfect sensitivity and the optimal viewing conditions. In other cases, such as the one in Fig. 10.1e, real evidence may be part of a cascade or catenation. In this case, we accept or assume the occurrence of event E, which is inconclusive evidence regarding $\{D, D^c\}$; events $\{D, D^c\}$, in turn, are circumstantial evidence regarding $\{H_1, H_2\}$. We expect that the situations depicted in Fig. 10.1c and 10.1e are formally similar.

We now consider the process of forming cascades or catenations of circumstantial evidence. Forming appropriate catenations of events that lead inferentially from observables to hypotheses is precisely where the fun starts. In the first place, there is an element of arbitrariness in actual applications. Two individuals might form slightly different catenations of intermediate circumstantial events between the same sets of observables and hypotheses. This is rather akin to the arbitrariness of determining a set of attributes from an objectives hierarchy in a multiattribute utility assessment task (Kenny & Raiffa, 1976). Wigmore (1937) noted the arbitrariness and the essentially deductive nature of the task of forming catenations for some actual set of evidence. However, if we stay in the abstract, we encounter no difficulties because we can form any catenation for illustrative purposes and for detailed study.

The second problem is that there is a virtually unlimited array of possible catenations. My hope is that there is a reasonably sized class of recurring catenations that we can study carefully. Consider Fig. 10.1 again; Fig. 10.1c is the now familiar case in which a single source (witness or sensor j) reports the occurrence of event D, where the class of events $\{D, D^c\}$ is circumstantial evidence regarding $\{H_1, H_2\}$; the formalization of $\Lambda_{D_j}^*$ was given in Eq. (10.1). We shall say that the catenation here is *single-stage* because one event class is interposed between the observable D_j^* and $\{H_1, H_2\}$. In general, the *level* of cascading refers to the number of event classes interposed between an observable and the final hypotheses. Fig. 10.1f shows *two-stage* catenation between E_j^* and $\{H_1, H_2\}$. In the general case, the expression for $\Lambda_{E_j}^*$ in Fig. 10.1f involves 14 conditional probabilities as ingredients. Fig. 10.1g represents the multisource case we discussed in the section interest on Source Credibility and Testimonial *Evidence* (Λ in the special case discussed in this section was prescribed in Eq. (10.2)). The catenation in Fig. 10.1g is also single-stage, because there is one event class interposed between each of the observables (the n reports) and the hypotheses. Finally, Fig. 10.1h illustrates a catenation in which there is real and testimonial evidence.

You may be wondering what order of cascading I am going to assign to the catenation in Fig. 10.1h. With respect to testimonial evidence E_i^* and F_j^*, and have a second-order cascade, and with respect to $G_o = G$, we have a single-order cascade. The difficulty with the catenation in Fig. 10.1h is that we must be careful to acknowledge the inferential redundancy that exists here, as it does in the catenation in Fig. 10.1g (which we discussed in the previously mentioned section). In short, we must either determine Λ for the *joint* occurrence of E_i^*, F_j^*, and G, or determine $\Lambda_{E_i}^*$, $\Lambda_{F_j^* | E_i}^*$, and $\Lambda_{G | E_i^* F_j}^*$. Such formalization acknowledges the redundancy that exists.

The term "cascaded" inference arose because it was apparent that events representing "hypotheses" at one inferential level become, in turn, evidence bearing upon other hypotheses at a higher level. If you look at Fig. 10.1f again, I can make this clearer. Events $\{E, E^c\}$ are possible explanations for our observed testimoney E_j^*. In turn, $\{E, E^c\}$ represent circumstantial evidence for $\{D, D^c\}$ which, in their turn, represent circumstantial evidence for the highest or terminal level events $\{H_1, H_2\}$. The major complication in cascaded inference involves two major conditional independence issues. The first concerns conditional independence of events *within* a catenation. For example, considering Fig. 10.1c together with Eq. (10.1) and (10.1a), we saw how it was necessary to decide whether or not D_j^* is conditioned by $\{H_1, H_2\}$ or both when event D is given. Fig. 10.1h illustrates how complex these conditional independence considerations can be. Take E_i^*, for example; given E, is E_i^* also conditional upon events in $\{D, D^c\}$, upon events in $\{H_1, H_2\}$, or upon events in both classes? As another example, are events E and F conditionally independent of $\{D, D^c\}$ when H_1 is assumed? Quite simply, conditional independence considerations form the basis for articulating the subtle interrelations that frequently exist among evidence items.

A scenario or collection of evidence may consist of many catenations like those in Fig. 10.1. The next question concerns whether or not there are probabilistic linkages existing *among* different catenations. Formal complexity is greatly increased when events in one catenation are conditionally nonindependent of events in another catenation. I provide an example and more discussion of this problem in the later section *Studies of the Dimensions of Inferential Complexity*.

Formalizing the Process of Evaluating and Aggregating a Mass of Mixed Evidence

I believe we have at least the rudiments of a system adequate to uncover the essential formal requisites of the task of evaluating and aggregating a collection of mixed evidence. I have now formally analyzed the evidence from several actual juridical trials, one of which I tell you about in this section. Naturally, I have begun with simple cases and am now extending my work to more formidable ones. The case I discuss here concerns a defendant named Salmon who sold various all-purpose nostrums or remedies on the streets of London at the turn of the century. Briefly, Salmon was accused of causing the death of one MacKensie, who allegedly took some of Salmon's pills. The prosecution offered two witnesses: One was a forensic expert whose postmortem examination of the deceased led him to conclude that Salmon's pills were the cause of death; the other prosecution witness was MacKensie's servant who testified that MacKensie took Salmon's pills and died a short time later. The case for the defense involved what Wigmore (1937) terms "explanation by inconsistent instances [p. 40]." Several witnesses testified that they had also taken Salmon's pills and were not harmed by them.

The essential events in the case are shown diagrammatically in Fig. 10.2. Observe that there are three catenations of events, two representing prosecution

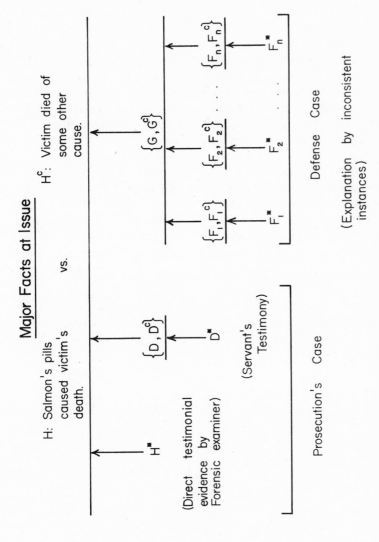

FIG. 10.2. Principal events in Salmon's case as presented by Wigmore.

195

evidence and one representing defense evidence. This case is fairly simple because there appear to be no probabilistic linkages among catenations. Also, of course, the amount of evidence presented was not very large and was all testimonial in nature.

The forensic expert's testimony ($H*$) is a direct testimonial assertion about a major hypothesis or fact at issue; the only inferential issue related to this testimony concerns this witness' credibility. The servant's testimony ($D*$) is the report that the following event occurred: D = event that MacKensie took Salmon's pills and died a short time after. We are first concerned about the servant's credibility because, for example, MacKensie may have taken pills other than Salmon's. In addition, even if MacKensie took Salmon's pills, he might have died of some other cause. This means that D is only circumstantial or indirect evidence regarding the major fact at issue. Thus, the servant's testimony involves a single-stage circumstantial–testimonial catenation.

The defense argument is based upon a more complex circumstantial–testimonial catenation. Let F_i* = the event that witness W_i (alive and in good health) reports having taken Salmon's pills. The credibility of any W_i is an issue because any witness may or may not actually have taken these pills. Let F_i = event that W_i actually took Salmon's pills; let F_i^c = event that W_i did not take Salmon's pills. Thus, F_i* is only inconclusive evidence regarding F_i or F_i^c. Because we must determine the aggregate inferential or probative value of the n witnesses, let $F* = \bigcap_{i=1}^{n} F_i*$. Now, let G = event that Salmon's pills are generally harmful; G^c = event that Salmon's pills are generally harmless. We note that the events F_i, F_i^c are only circumstantial evidence regarding G and G^c. Further, we note that events G and G^c are only circumstantial evidence regarding the major facts at issue (H and H^c); for example, the pills might be harmful, but MacKensie could have died from some other cause.

Now, to formalize the inferential problem facing a juridical fact finder, we begin with Bayes' rule:

$$\frac{P(H|H*D*F*)}{P(H^c|H*D*F*)} = \frac{P(H)}{P(H^c)} \cdot \left[\frac{P(H*|H)}{P(H*|H^c)} \cdot \frac{P(D*|H*H)}{P(D*|H*H^c)} \cdot \frac{P(F*|D*H*H)}{P(F*|D*H*H^c)} \right].$$

$$(10.3)$$

The inferential or probative strength of the evidence is represented by the product of the three likelihood ratios shown inside the brackets in Eq. (10.3). The remaining term $P(H)/P(H^c)$ represents the fact finder's initial or prior opinion about the facts at issue before evidence is presented. We now consider the three likelihood ratios.

1. $\Lambda_H* = \dfrac{P(H*|H)}{P(H*|H_c)}$

As we asserted earlier, the probative value of a direct testimonial assertion about a major fact at issue depends only on the assertor's credibility. Our formalization for the probative strength of $H*$ makes this clear; $P(H*|H)$ is analogous to a hit probability and $P(H*|H^c)$ is analogous to a false-positive probability. Thus, the probative strength of testimony $H*$ depends simply on the fact finder's assessment of the forensic expert's credibility in terms of hit probability relative to false-positive probability.

2. $\Lambda_D* = \dfrac{P(D*|H*H)}{P(D*|H*H^c)}$

In formalizing the probative value determination for the servant's testimony $D*$, we encounter *two* conditional independence issues. We must first ask whether or not the probative value of the servant's testimony depends on what the expert witness testified. Then, we must ask whether or not the witness' testimony depends on H or H^c. Various combinations of these circumstances can occur and the formal process makes clear what is required in each case. As one example, suppose a fact finder decides that testimony $D*$ does not depend on $H*$ *but* could possibly depend on H or H^c—that is, the witness might have some bias (Schum, 1977a). In this case, a formally appropriate expansion results in:

$$\Lambda_D* = \frac{P(D|H)\ [P(D*|DH) - P(D*|D^cH)] + P(D*|D^cH)}{P(D|H^c)\ [P(D*|DH^c) - P(D*|D^cH^c)] + P(D*|D^cH^c)}$$

(10.4)

which is identical to Eq. (10.1) discussed earlier.

3. $\Lambda_F* = \dfrac{P(F*|D*H*H)}{P(F*|D*H*H^c)}$

You should recall that $F* = \overset{n}{\underset{i=1}{\cap}} F_i*$ represents the aggregate testimony of all n witnesses who say they took Salmon's pills. In establishing the probative value of $F*$, there are many subtle linkages possible among the events of concern (see Fig. 10.2). Consider the special case involving the following conditional independence assumptions that seem entirely plausible in Salmon's case.

1. Suppose $F*$ is not conditioned by previous testimony $H*$ or $D*$ when either H or H^c is true. This makes

$$\Lambda_F* = \frac{P(F*|H)}{P(F*|H^c)}$$

2. Suppose the testimonies of the n witnesses are independently given (i.e., there is no collusion) and, for any witness W_i, depend only on events $\{F_i, F_i^c\}$.

3. Suppose, for any W_i, $\{F_i, F_i^c\}$ depends only on $\{G, G^c\}$ and not on $\{H, H^c\}$.

If we let $h_i = P(F_i^*|F_i)$ = hit probability for witness W_i, and $f_i = P(F_i^*|F_i^c)$ = false-positive probability for W_i, then in expanded form:

$$\Lambda_F^* = \frac{P(G|H) + \left\{ \displaystyle\prod_{i=1}^{n} \left[\frac{P(F_i|G) + \left(\dfrac{h_i}{f_i} - 1\right)^{-1}}{P(F_i|G^c) + \left(\dfrac{h_i}{f_i} - 1\right)^{-1}} \right]^{-1} - 1 \right\}^{-1}}{P(G|H^c) + \left\{ \displaystyle\prod_{i=1}^{n} \left[\frac{P(F_i|G) + \left(\dfrac{h_i}{f_i} - 1\right)^{-1}}{P(F_i|G^c) + \left(\dfrac{h_i}{f_i} - 1\right)^{-1}} \right]^{-1} - 1 \right\}^{-1}}.$$

$$(10.5)$$

This expression prescribes how the ingredients necessary in "explanation by inconsistent instances" should be aggregated.

For the person who agrees with the various assumptions we have introduced in this example, Λ_H^*, Λ_D^*, and Λ_F^* show the necessary ingredients and the manner of their combination for each testimonial assertion in Salmon's case as presented by Wigmore. Other assumptions are possible, of course; however, our formal procedure can show what is required under *any* pattern of assumptions about the probabilistic linkages among events in this case. The product of these three likelihood ratios represents the net or aggregate probative value of the evidence in this case.

Studies of the Logical Structure of Various Inferential Arguments

The formal process developed thus far allows one to study the details of various forms of inferential argument. I mentioned that I had hoped there would be recurring catenations whose structure we should study carefully. One such catenation is the defense argument by inconsistent instances in Salmon's case. This form of argument is controversial in legal proceedings and evidence regarding inconsistent instances is not always deemed relevant by the courts (e.g., Cleary, 1972), though the reasons given are often vague. Systematic study of Eq. (10.5) shows why, in this special case, such evidence might not be deemed relevant in the juridical sense.[2]

---

[2]Briefly, juridical evidence is *relevant* if the evidence bears upon an issue in the case and if the evidence has probative or inferential value. Essentially, this means that the likelihood ratio for the evidence has value not equal to one.

Essentially, explanation by inconsistent instances is a statistical argument involving a completely biased sample and is heavily contingent upon the number n of witnesses employed by the side using it. This raises the spectre of a trial by numbers guaranteed to try the court's patience. Fig. 10.3 shows how the inferential value of joint testimony $F*$ varies as a function of n and witness credibility in a special case involving fixed values of the following ingredients of Eq. (10.5):

1. $P(G|H) = .900$, $P(G|H^c) = .001$.
2. For every witness i, $P(F_i|G) = .100$, $P(F_i|G^c)$ h $.700$.

$[\Lambda_F*]^{-1}$ is plotted for four levels of credibility: perfect; $h_i/f_i = 100$, all i; $h_i/f_i = 5$, all i; and $h_i/f_i = 2$, all i.

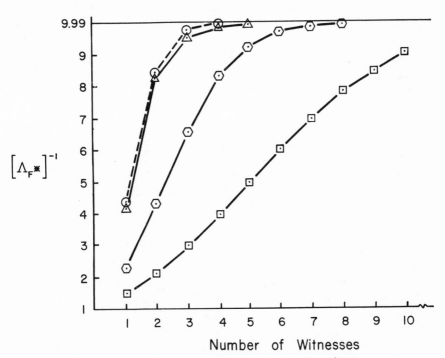

FIG. 10.3. Sensitivity analysis: explanation by inconsistent instances.

There is an upper bound on $[\Lambda_F{}^*]^{-1}$; this bound is given by

$$\left[\frac{P(G^c|H)}{P(G^c|H^c)} \right]^{-1,} = \left[\frac{.100}{.999} \right]^{-1,} = 9.9.$$ Boundedness is a conse-

quence of the assumption that the credibility of each source does not depend on events $\{H, H^c\}$ or on $\{G, G^c\}$. The first thing to notice is that the sensitivity of $\Lambda_F{}^*$ to number of witnesses n depends on witness credibility; $\Lambda_F{}^*$ changes more drastically by adding witnesses of high credibility than it does by adding witnesses of low credibility.

The most important consequence of the analysis, however, concerns the curve for *perfectly* credible witnesses (those for which h_i/f_i approaches infinity). Formally, the full probative value of joint testimony F^* (i.e., the value 9.9) is not justified for any finite number of *perfectly* credible witnesses; $[\Lambda_F{}^*]^{-1}$ does, however, come close to its maximum possible value for only three witnesses. It is very interesting to compare $[\Lambda_F{}^*]^{-1}$ with the corresponding likelihood ratio for joint *contradictory* testiony given in Eq. (10.2). It is easy to show that under the same set of assumptions applicable to credibility, as in our present case, $\Lambda_F{}^*$ in Eq. 10.2) reaches its maximum value for just *one* perfectly credible witness. In short, in evaluating the probative value of contradictory evidence, a single perfectly credible witness on one side can "swamp" any finite number of less-than-perfectly credible witnesses on the other. The basic fact about explanation by inconsistent instances is that it is essentially a statistical argument the strength of which, like other statistical arguments, depends on sample size, regardless of how reliable are the data.

Unlike most conventional statistical arguments, "inconsistent instances" does not involve random sampling. In any case, the user of this argument will only present a "sample" of n witnesses whose testimony is favorable to the case. This is why we said the argument involved completely biased sampling.

Studies of the Dimensions of Inferential Complexity

It has been long been believed that the following factors contribute to the cognitive or intellectual difficulty of inference: amount of evidence, whether or not the evidence was conflicting or contradictory, and whether or not source credibility was an issue. In fact, these are examples of the kinds of variables we studied in early empirical research. I now believe that there are other, perhaps more important, factors:

1. The level or order of cascading between observables and final hypotheses determines inference difficulty. From a purely formal point of view, each level of cascading introduces a new class of events that must be incorporated into the logical structure of the task. The fact that there is often arbitrariness in the determination of these interposed event classes makes the process all the more difficult.

2. A second factor concerns the nature of the probabilistic linkages between events *within* a catenation. I provided examples of such difficulty when I discussed the catenation shown in Fig. 10.1h. This second factor, of course, interacts with the first because the higher the order of cascading, the more conditional independence issues there are to worry about. Another related consideration concerns the particular nature of a catenation. There are very many possible paradigms for a catenation. Appropriate formalization of Λ for a catenation is difficult in many cases, as we have observed.

3. A third factor concerns the extent of probabilistic linkage among events in two or more catenations. I believe this to be the most vexing problem of all. Following is an example of the complexity involved. Consider Fig. 10.4, which shows two catenations of events that form a portion of the evidence in a hypothetical juridical example concocted by Wigmore (1937). Let H = the event that defendant X shot victim Y; D = the event that a rifle with a spent chamber was found in X's apartment; D_i^* = the event that witness i reported event D; G_j^* = the event that witness j reports hearing a loud "crack" coming from the window of X's apartment; G = the event that the loud "crack" came from the window of X's apartment; F = the event that a rifle was fired in X's apartment.

In evaluating testimony G_j^*, I find it impossible to avoid thinking about previous testimony D_i^*. In short, the inferential value of G_j^*, testimony of a loud "crack" coming from the window of the apartment, seems to be enhanced by the previous testimony that someone found a rifle there. We assume, of course, that the times match for events in these two items of testimony. Formally, these two catenations seem somehow linked together; the precise problem is to determine the inferential value of G_j^* given knowledge of previous testimoney D_i^*. Formally, we must determine an appropriate expansion of $\Lambda_{G_j^*|D_i^*} = \dfrac{P(G_j^*|D_i^*H)}{P(G_j^*|D_i^*H^c)}$.

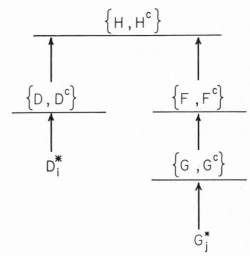

FIG. 10.4. Example   catenation explained in text.

Samuel Johnson once defined a lexicographer, like himself, as a "harmless drudge." I believe that persons who attempt to study catenated inference will also come to think of themselves as drudges because the process of expanding Λ is certainly tedious and frequently vexing. It turns out that, in the general case, there are 32 probabilistic ingredients in $\Lambda_{G_j}{}^*|D_i{}^*$. Under various patterns of conditional independence assumptions, this number of ingredients can be reduced, to a minimum of eight. Looking at the general expansion of $\Lambda_{G_j}{}^*|_{D_i}{}^*$ (which stretches from one side of my desk to the other), I suppose that the major reason why I judged the testimonies to be related concerns the conditional nonindependence of event classes $\{D, D^c\}$ and $\{F, F^c\}$ given H. Quite simply, I would suppose that $P(F|HD) \neq P(F|H)$. There may be other nonindependencies as well, particularly if we knew further that witnesses i and j were friends or relatives.

I return to this example in the next section to illustrate what I believe is an interesting connection between inference and other mental activity.

4. The final dimension of inference difficulty I will mention concerns the particular mixture of evidence in an inference problem. It occurs to me that we may now be in a better position to articulate distinctions between inferences performed in different contexts. For example, much laboratory research on inference usually involved all real–circumstantial evidence without cascading. Psychiatric diagnosis might usually involve a preponderance of testimonial evidence and very high-order cascading from testimonial events to hypotheses that may not be too adequately articulated. Medical diagnosis might involve mixtures of real and testimonial evidence also cascaded towards hypotheses frequently, though not always, well defined. Juridical inference, as Wigmore (1937) tells us, usually consists of a small proportion of real evidence and a large proportion of testimonial–circumstantial catenations, leading, I might add, to hypotheses that are usually well articulated, such as "he did it" or "he didn't do it." I would suppose that military intelligence analysis involves little real evidence, mostly testimonial evidence, and frequently high-order cascading.

The observation that nature is complex is not, by itself, particularly profound. The interesting question is: How can we best cope with this apparent complexity. I tell you about two strategies now and one later on. The first strategy is to filter out events that do not belong on an inference "tree." Consider the transcript of a jury trial; it consists of hundreds, perhaps thousands, of items of evidence. Surely this would be enough to make even the most dedicated drudge lose interest in trying to formalize the process of evaluating and aggregating the evidence. Another of Wigmore's (1937, p. 31) contributions was his discussion of the various inferential uses of evidence in trials at law. He talks about four basic inferential processes, two of which are relevant in connection with our simplification issue. He says that a very large proportion of effort by one side is devoted to explaining away and to denying the existence of evidence presented by the other side. Formally, the act of explaining away your opponent's evidence really amounts to showing that his or her evidence is inconclusive; for example, it points towards H_2 as well as towards H_1. In addition, the act of denying your opponent's evidence is the substance of credibility impeachment. Your opponent offers a witness who testifies D^*, hoping to convince you that D occurred, because D favors H_1 being defended by our opponent. You offer evidence that the witness has diminished powers of observation, making D^c and, hence, H_2 more probable. The point here is that much of the evidence, offered for explanation or denial purposes, may have no inferential significance by itself. Such evidence is presented because it allows a fact finder to evaluate the weight of other evidence that does have inferential significance.

Very simply, it appears that there are two classes of inferential events: those that belong on any inference "tree" (such as Fig. 10.2) and thus represent the basic logical structure of the task, and those that exist for the purpose of allowing the decision maker to make the requisite probabilistic connections among events that do belong on the "tree." As an example, consider the right-hand catenation in Fig. 10.4. We might have, as Wigmore's example illustrates, a substantial amount of testimony regarding the linkages among events in this catenation. A psychoacoustics expert might be brought in; he/she might go into considerable detail in an effort to show how difficult it is to locate sound sources in groups of buildings. This would enforce the idea that G_j^* is consistent with G^c as well as with G. A firearms expert might further testify that the sharp "crack" heard at the window also could be made by a bursting tire as well as by a rifle; this tends to make event G consistent with F^c as well as with F.

Thus, one route to at least some formal simplification consists of filtering out events that do not belong on the tree. The basic logical structure of a task may be simpler than the amount of evidence suggests and may be formally tractable even for large amounts of evidence.

A second route to simplification concerns the problem of deciding which conditional independencies to assume. The complexity of any Λ formulation for some catenation is directly related to the extent of conditional independence among the events in the catenation. The more conditional independence you assume, the fewer the number and the greater the simplicity of the ingredients of Λ in a catenation. As an example, in Eq. (10.1) there are six possible ingredients of $\Lambda_{D_i}^*$ if there is no conditional independence of D_i^* and H_j, $j = 1, 2$, given D or given D^c. If, however, $P(D_i^*|DH_j) = P(D_i^*|D)$ and $P(D_i^*|D^cH_j) = P(D_i^*|D^c)$ for $j = 1, 2$, then Eq. (10.1a) shows that there are just three necessary ingredients. Notice that the h_i and f_i terms appear as a ratio; this means that exact values of h_i and f_i need not be supplied, only their ratio, as we discussed earlier.

Suppose you had difficulty deciding whether or not to assume $P(D_i^*|DH_1) = P(D_i^*|D)$. One thing you could do is to test the implications of this assumption. If you disagree with any of the implications of an assumption you contemplate, you better not make the assumption if you have logical coherency as an objective. One such implication is that $P(H_1|DD_i^*) = P(H_1|D)$; if you knew D occurred, you would not further change your opinion about the likeliness of H_1 if source i told you D occurred. In cases involving many conditioning events, this implication-testing process can become rather tedious. Fortunately, this is one place where a computer can help. My colleague, Carlo Giannoni, of the Rice University Philosophy Department, has developed a computer program written in a language called FORMAC, an extension of PL/I. This program allows one to evaluate implications of a conditional independence assumption, thus relieving an inference analyst of the necessity of performing extensive Boolean manipulation of events.

ON THE RELATION OF CASCADED INFERENCE TO OTHER MENTAL PROCESSES

There is evidence that inferential processes are involved in a wide assortment of mental activity. Inferential processes have been discussed in connection with pattern recognition, concept learning and other learning activity, signal detection and recognition, and attributional mechanisms. I would like to believe that the formalizations we study will someday assist other persons to clarify and extend theory and empirical research in a variety of areas of psychology. I have chosen to relate our work first to an area I believe falls within "cognitive" psychology. The term "cognitive" is very popular now and, as far as I can tell, is rather diffusely applied to virtually every mental process including human reasoning, of which inductive inference is one species.

Cognitive Processes

It should be clear, by now, that I have not taken an approach common in many areas of mathematics. I have not attempted to formalize a "general case" of cascaded inference and then proceed to look at interesting special cases. Such an approach has been attempted (Kelly & Barclay, 1973); in this approach, "general case" formalizations, though not in Λ form, are offered when all conditional independence assumptions are met. I do not find this approach informative as far as the essential ingredients of evidence evaluation are concerned. I have preferred to start at the bottom by looking at simple cases, and then go on to more complex cases. Perhaps equally obvious is that I have not had any descriptive considerations in mind as I have proceeded; I have, however, looked at specific inference *tasks* people have performed. In the process, I have become aware of apparent similarities between inference processes and other mental activity.

Contrast Mechanisms.   Suppose, as is common in most inference tasks, that evidence items arrive sequentially over time. As each one arrives, you revise your opinion about the relative likeliness of hypotheses of interest to you. Let e_{t+1} = some new item of evidence. In evaluating this new item, it may be true that its inferential impact on your hypotheses depends on what other evidence you have; let the class $C = \{e_1, e_2, \ldots, e_t\}$ represent all previous evidence you have that bears upon your hypotheses. In establishing the inferential weight or value of e_{t+1}, there may be events in C that, if taken into account, may alter the weight of e_{t+1}. Formally, what we must determine are appropriate expansions of:

$$\Lambda_{e_{t+1}} = \frac{P(e_{t+1}|H_i \cap C)}{P(e_{t+1}|H_j \cap C)}$$

for every i and j.

I could not help noticing that the process of determining the inferential weight of e_{t+1} appears analogous to certain contrast processes in sensory/perceptual mechanisms. The perceived color and brightness of an object depend, in part, on the background against which the object is presented. Previous evidence, I thought, represents a "background" against which one must evaluate a current item of evidence. Such background, in the form of other evidence, may tend to enhance or diminish the inferential value of your current evidence item. Change the background and you may change the inferential significance of e_{t+1}. For example, the significance of G_j^* in Fig. 10.4 may be altered substantially if we do not take prior testimony D_i^* into account. The sharp "crack" from the window of the defendant's apartment seems to have enhanced impact on H if you also have discovered that someone found a rifle with a spent chamber in this apartment.

Relating probabilistic inference and sensory/perceptual processes is certainly not a novel idea. Hume (1888) said: "All probable reasoning is nothing but a species of sensation . . . When I give preference to one set of arguments above another, I do nothing but decide from my feeling concerning the superiority of their influence." In modern times, the signal-detectability theorists have made us aware of the inferential requisites of detection and recognition tasks (e.g., Egan, 1975; Green & Swets, 1966). In a recent paper (Schum, 1977b), I have turned things around by trying to explain certain inferential mechanisms by using sensory/perceptual analogies when they seem appropriate. I have found such analogies highly useful in interpreting the meaning and significance of various ingredients necessary in determining the weight of evidence in cascaded inference.

Some item of prior evidence may "stand out" in the background if it is an item having inferential significance and if it comes from a credible source. Generally, the "contrast effect" of this prior evidence item upon the current item you are evaluating involves conditional nonindependence of the two items. Each evidence item in the form of real or testimonial evidence may have other circumstantial event classes interposed between these observables and one's final hypotheses. Consequently, the possible conditional nonindependencies that exist between one catenation and another may be very large and the relationships they articulate very subtle. A substantial part of my effort in studying inferential "contrast" has concerned the problem of sorting out the various probabilistic interconnections between two or more catenations and interpreting their meaning. I have found this task to be the most challenging I have yet encountered. In my paper (Schum, 1977b), I elaborate upon six general considerations that appear to influence the "contrast effect" of prior evidence on current evidence. I note that what I have termed "contrast effect" is described by modern jurists as the process of "connecting up" prior and current evidence (Lempert & Saltzburg, 1977).

Decision Theory and Analysis

Cascaded Inference and Multiattribute Utility. Systematic study of the process of assessing multiattribute value and utility ingredients in decision tasks has recently occupied the attentions of many decision theorists. There is no doubt about the intellectual difficulty of generating attributes of consequences, assessing their value or utility, and arriving at a single index of their value or utility. Not to be overlooked in decisions under uncertainty are corresponding difficulties in the task of assessing the probabilities of those states (hypotheses) that act to produce different consequences for different courses of action. If it is true that most, if not all, inference is cascaded in nature, then the inferential side of decision making appears no less difficult than the value/utility side. It appears that there are some common difficulties in multiattribute utility assessment and cascaded inference.

The process of defining attributes of consequence and the process of establishing catenations are somewhat arbitrary, as I have mentioned. Two reasonable, sensitive, and informed persons, each confronted with the "same" choice task, might perceive the attributes of the consequences to be different and also the circumstantial catenations between observables and hypotheses to be different. This serves to remind us that choice prescriptions are, after all, prescriptions for individuals. Decision analysts tell us that the analysis process itself is valuable in locating points of disagreement between individuals. Thus, the process of forming circumstantial event catenations between observables and hypotheses may serve to settle arguments about the weight of evidence in the same way that a systematic attribute generation process can help to settle disagreements about the dimensions and evaluation of consequences.

We have seen how the establishment of appropriate probabilistic linkages among events within and between catenations requires careful attention to conditional independence issues. The general concepts of independence and conditional independence, though conceptually different in inference and in utility assessment, appear to be *the* mechanisms for articulating the subtleties of choice. In utility assessment, we ask whether or not preferences for lotteries involving levels of attributes X and Y are conditional upon knowledge of a level of Z. In inference, we ask whether or not the probability of D^*, given D, also depends on further knowledge of H. In either case, independence and conditional independence judgments are often *exquisitely* subtle. Independence and conditional independence assumptions, when they are appropriate, make for algorithmic simplicity in utility and in inference. Additive independence in multiattribute utility assessment leads to simple additive models for composite utilities. Conditional independence within and between catenations drastically reduces the number and complexity of Λ ingredients. The issue seems to be: How badly off are we if we make these assumptions even when they may not actually be justified? This question has been dealt with in the case of general choice models (e.g., Dawes & Corrigan, 1974); to my knowledge, no one has yet faced it in complex inference.

Divide and Conquer: It Seemed Like Such a Good Idea.   The basic approach in the applied area of decision analysis is to take a complex decision, break it down into its essential ingredients, have the decision maker supply the ingredients, and then recombine the ingredients according to formally coherent algorithms. The basic idea is that it is supposedly easier for individuals to make judgments about the ingredients than to make the global or wholistic judgments individuals already make in the absence of any assistance. Further, individuals are relieved of the task of mental aggregation of the necessary ingredients (or what they think are the necessary ingredients). This "divide-and-conquer" strategy is not new at all and is certainly not an approach initiated by decision analysts. In fact, in the July 9, 1751, issue of the *Rambler*, Samuel Johnson wrote:

> Divide and conquer, is a principle equally just in science as in policy. Complication is a species of confederacy, which, while it continues united, bids defiance to the most active and vigorous intellect; but of which every member is separately weak, and which may therefore be quickly subdued if it can once be broken.

In decision theory, we are now acquiring the formal sophistication necessary to identify the ingredients of choice and the manner in which they should be combined; but now we have other problems. I believe nobody realized how many ingredients there would be and how complex the judgments about these ingredients would be even in apparently simple cases. Just take the inferential side of Salmon's trial. Assume the defense offered just five witnesses and that all conditional independence assumptions hold. The minimum number of probabilistic ingredients is 27, counting a prior odds judgment. In more complex situations, by the time you couple multiattribute utility assessment and cascaded inference, both the decision maker and the decision analyst are bound to lose further interest in their encounter. I note that Johnson also remarked (*Rambler,* August 14, 1750):

> There is, indeed, some danger lest he that too scrupulously balances probabilities, and too perspicaciously foresees obstacles, should remain always in a state of inaction . . .

Carried to an extreme, task decomposition may perish by being too ponderous. Fortunately, it appears that there are alternatives to total task decomposition in cascaded inference.

A LOOK AHEAD

I am sorry to say that my crystal ball is usually occluded. About the only thing I see clearly in it is trouble for the task-decomposition strategy in decision analysis; less clearly defined are possible alternatives. A shroud of mist surrounds what might be novel and useful strategies for descriptive studies of human inference. We are proceeding, nonetheless, with both formal and empirical studies of inference. The research we have planned involves studies of cascaded inference in a juridical context. We have selected a juridical context because there is awakened interest among jurists in the formal details of evidence and in the role of the fact finder as one who revises subjective probabilities on the basis of evidence (e.g., Kaplan, 1968; Lempert, 1977; Lempert & Saltzburg, 1977). Another reason, of course, is that there is existing scholarship on, and abundant examples of, cascaded inference processes in the juridical area. I would expect, however, that our research will be applicable to medical, military, business, and other inferences.

In our formal research, we shall continue to develop and study likelihood ratio expressions for a variety of evidence paradigms; some are suggested by juridical treatises and others by certain logical catenations of circumstantial evidence. Another major formal task will concern the analysis of the evidence in a fairly large collection of actual juridical cases (or portions thereof). Such analysis will be similar to the one illustrated in Salmon's case. The purpose of such formal analysis of cases relates to empirical objectives we have. We wish to be able to present subjects with evidence from cases that have all been analyzed in the manner of Salmon's case. This will allow us to study various ways in which subjects evaluate and combine the evidence under several conditions representing total, partial, and zero task decomposition.

ACKNOWLEDGMENTS

The research described in this chapter is being supported by the National Science Foundation under grant number SOC77-28471 to Rice University.

The author wishes to thank Professor Richard O. Lempert of the University of Michigan Law School for his most helpful comments. Any remaining errors regarding juridical applications are due solely to the author's continuing innocence of the finer points of evidence law.

REFERENCES

Bentham, J. *The rationale of judicial evidence* (Bowring edition). Edinburgh: William Tait, 1839.

Cleary, E. *McCormick on evidence*. St. Paul, Minn.: West, 1972.

Dawes, R., & Corrigan, B. Linear Models in Decision Making. *Psychological Bulletin, 81*, 1974, 95–106.

Dodson, J. Simulation system design for a TEAS simulation research facility (Report #4). Los Angeles, Calif.: Planning Research Corp., November, 1961.

Edwards, W. Dynamic decision theory and probabilistic information processing. *Human Factors*, 1962, *4*, 59–73.

Egan, J. *Signal detection theory and ROC analysis*. New York: Academic Press, 1975.

Gettys, C., & Willke, T. The application of Bayes' Theorem when the true data state is unknown. *Organizational Behavior and Human Performance*, 1969, *4*, 125–141.

Green, D., & Swets, J. *Signal detection theory and psychophysics*. New York: Wiley, 1966.

Hume, D. *A treatise of human nature* (Book 1, Part 3, Section 8). Oxford: Clarendon, 1888.

Kaplan, J. Decision theory and the fact-finding process. *Stanford Law Review*, 1968, *20*, 1065–1092.

Kenney, R., & Raiffa, H. *Decisions with multiple objectives: Preferences and value tradeoffs*. New York, Wiley, 1976.

Kelly, C., & Barclay, S. A general Bayesian model for hierarchical inference. *Organizational Behavior and Human Performance*, 1973, *10*, 388–403.

Keynes, J. M. *A treatise on probability*. London: Macmillan, 1957.

Laplace, P. S. *A philosophical essay on probabilities (1795)* (Rev. ed.). New York: Dover, 1952.

Lempert, R. Modeling relevance. *Michigan Law Review*, 1977, *75*, 1021–1057.

Lempert, R., & Saltzburg, S. *A modern approach to evidence*. St. Paul, Minn.: West, 1977.

Peterson, C. (Ed.) Special issue on cascaded inference. *Organizational Behavior and Human Performance*, 1973, *10*, (3).

Rapoport, A., & Wallsten, T. Individual choice behavior. *Annual Review of Psychology*, 1972, *23*, 131–175.

Schum, D. A. The behavioral richness of cascaded inference models: Examples in jurisprudence. In Castellan, Pisoni, & Potts (Eds.), *Cognitive theory* (Vol. 2). Hillsdale, N.J.: Lawrence Erlbaum Associates, 1977. (a)

Schum, D. Contrast effects in inference: On the conditioning of current evidence by prior evidence. *Organizational Behavior and Human Performance*, 1977, *18* 217–253. (b)

Schum, D. A. Sorting out the effects of witness sensitivity and response-criterion placement upon the inferential value of testimonial evidence (Report #79–01). Rice University Department of Psychology, January 15, 1979.

Schum, D., & DuCharme, W. Comments on the relationship between the impact and the reliability of evidence. *Organizational Behavior and Human Performance*, 1971, *6*, 111–131.

Schum, D., DuCharme, W., & DePitts, K. Research on human multistage probabilistic inference processes. *Organizational Behavior and Human Performance*, 1973, *10*, 318–348.

Schum, D., & Kelly, C. A problem in cascaded inference: Determining the inferential impact of confirming and conflicting reports from several unreliable sources. *Organizational Behavior and Human Performance*, 1973, *10*, 404–423.

Schum, D., & Pfeiffer, P. Observer reliability and human inference. *IEEE Transactions on Reliability*, 1973, *R–22*, 70–176.

Slovic, P., & Lichtenstein, S. Comparison of Bayesian and regression approaches to the study of information processing in judgment. *Organizational Behavior and Human Performance,* 1971, *6,* 649–744.

Todhunter, I. *A history of the mathematical theory of probability.* Cambridge: Macmillan, 1865.

Wigmore, J. H. *The science of judicial proof.* Boston: Little, Brown, 1937.

Wigmore, J. H. *A treatise on the Anglo-American system of evidence in trials at common law* (10 vols.). Boston: Little, Brown.

11 Comments on the Chapters by MacCrimmon, Stanbury, and Wehrung; and Schum

R. Duncan Luce
*Department of Psychology and Social Relations,
Harvard University*

One risk of being a discussant at a conference is that the author takes one's criticisms seriously in making revisions so that little remains to write when preparing written remarks. To a degree that is the situation in which I find myself. My initial major comment about the chapter by Kenneth MacCrimmon, William Stanbury, and Donald Wehrung was that the most striking finding—and it certainly is that—was not sufficiently emphasized. I have in mind the fact that in two of the ranked sets of gambles, there was a pair of gambles in common, and a substantial fraction of subjects ranked them differently depending on the context. In the revised chapter, this result is given prominence, and so I am left with nothing really to say except to note that this result is enough to cast in doubt our whole current enterprise of model building in this area.

Concerning David Schum's highly interesting and informative chapter on cascaded inferences, my original comments entailed a somewhat extended discussion of a particular example, which I found very disturbing. So, I gather, did Schum, for he has examined it and a number of related examples in considerable detail, written a long memorandum about the issues involved, and prepared a paper on it, which will be published elsewhere. He alludes to these considerations in his revised manuscript for the present volume, but I have the impression that these remarks, although clear enough for those who heard my comments at the conference, will seem a bit elliptic to others. It may, therefore, not be amiss for me to repeat the example here.

I was led to consider it because, despite the fact that I had the reprints in which his equations for cascaded inference are derived, I found it difficult to sense exactly what these formidible equations said. In such a situation, it is usually wise to examine a bare-bones case that still retains the basic idea—here, that of cascading information. Being a part-time psychophysicist, I thought immediately of a simple two-stimulus, two-response design, such as yes–no detection, in which there are independent repeated observations—say, by a set of distinct observers—that are to be aggregated into a group decision. In the usual psychophysical notation, $H_1 = s$ stands for the hypothesis that a signal (in noise) was presented and $H_2 = n$ stands for the hypothesis that no signal (noise alone) was presented. Let us identify the event D with the presentation of a signal, so in this special example:

$$P(D|H_1) = 1 \text{ and } P(D|H_2) = 0.$$

The testimony of observer i, D_i^*, is simply the observer's assertion that a signal was presented; in this context, this is called the yes response, Y. And, the testimony D_i^{c*} is the no response, N. To maintain the simplicity of the example, let us assume that all of the observers are independent and statistically identical, and so their performance is completely described by two conditional probabilities, $P(Y|s)$ and $P(Y|n)$.

From these assumptions, it is not difficult to show that Schum's Eq. (1) is (in this special case only) an uninteresting triviality and that Eq. (2) simplifies to:

$$\Lambda_F^* = \frac{1 + V}{V}$$

$$= \frac{\displaystyle\prod_{p \in P} h_p / f_p}{\displaystyle\prod_{q \in Q} c_q / m_q}$$

$$= \left(\frac{P(Y|s)}{P(Y|n)} \right)^y \left(\frac{1 - P(Y|s)}{1 - P(Y|n)} \right)^{n-y}$$

where y is the number of observers saying Y and $n - y$ the number saying N.

What possible merit can there be to this change of notation? None—except for one thing. The psychophysical example reminds one of the very firm and important psychophysical discovery of the third quarter of this century that well-practiced, conscientious observers are not adequately characterized by a single pair of conditional probabilities, as had been implicitly and explicitly assumed during the preceding hundred years, but rather by a continuum of such pairs. The locus of such points is called the ROC curve (engineering lingo standing for receiver operating characteristic) or isosensitivity curve (psychological lingo for the same thing) or power of the test (statistical lingo). If one alters the stimulus conditions, for example, by making the signal stronger or weaker, then the ROC curve alters. But, if one holds the stimulus conditions fixed and only alters cognitive or motivational factors (for example, instructions, payoffs, presentation probabilities), then a single curve is involved and these factors determine the point actually observed. We speak of the mechanism for selecting a point on the curve as the setting of a criterion or a response bias.

I dwell on this point not because psychophysics is so intrinsically interesting, but because there is every reason to believe that this tradeoff phenomenon is very widespread whenever observers are engaged in making difficult observations for which their performance is less than perfect. That is usually the case for eye witnesses. If this is accepted, then I wish to demonstrate that the process of cascading greatly exaggerates the extent of the response bias.

Consider a symmetric, Gaussian ROC curve that has a value of $d' = 1.80$ (this is generated by noise and signal distributions that are Gaussian with unit variance and means that differ by 1.80). One pair of probabilities that lie on this curve is $P(Y|s) = .7$ and $P(Y|n) = .1$. These would arise under instructions that mildly invite the observer to be conservative when saying yes or, equally, under a payoff matrix that made the error of saying yes when there is no signal (false alarm) several times more costly than the error of failing to respond to a signal (miss). A second pair of probabilities that also lie on the same curve is .9 and .3. These would arise by instructions or payoffs favoring, to about the same degree, a more liberal criterion for saying yes. Suppose that there are 20 observers, equally split between saying Y and N. If you are dealing with observers under the first condition, then Schum's Eq. (10.2) yields:

$$\Lambda_F{}^* = \left(\frac{.7}{.1} \right)^{10} \left(\frac{.3}{.9} \right)^{10} = 4784;$$

whereas for observers under the second condition:

$$\Lambda_F{}^* = \left(\frac{.9}{.3} \right)^{10} \left(\frac{.1}{.7} \right)^{10} = 1/4784.$$

The ratio between these two likelihoods is over 22 million, a rather staggering difference when you consider that the only difference between the two cases is a relatively slight tendency to be conservative or to be liberal in saying yes.

In sum, a criterion shift that seems relatively modest to a psychophysicist—and I dare say to any student of human decision making—one that is well within the reach of judicial rhetoric, is reflected in a highly amplified form when judgments are cascaded. I am by no means sure what we should make of this fact. It is inherent in the nature of the situation, but I am sure it is important for us to be aware of it. In particular, the apparent certainty that can arise in cascaded inferences must, I believe, be closely tempered by the realization that it may reflect little more than a consistency of response bias on the part of observers. Care must be taken to try to separate the impact of response bias from that of accumulated information and to heed only the latter. Exactly how this should be done in practice is far from clear.

12 Processes and Models to Describe Choice and Inference Behavior

Thomas S. Wallsten
University of North Carolina at Chapel Hill

Research in behavioral decision making has shifted dramatically in recent years. Whereas earlier work was dominated by linear and normative models (many of the latter of which were themselves linear), present research is guided primarily by theories that specify a wider variety of processes and heuristics, each of which is used in a different context.

My research in the area of probabilistic inference is an attempt to combine the advantages of the two approaches (Wallsten, 1976, 1977). The present chapter describes the resulting theoretical structure and suggests its application to additional decision problems. Accordingly, the chapter is organized as follows: I first review the use of linear and other formal models, reminding us of why they are currently in disrepute, and also indicating why I think they should not be abandoned. Then, I discuss heuristic theories, indicating their weaknesses. Following that, I outline one framework for combining formal models with process theories in a manner that extends over a wide range of decision problems. The usefulness of this approach is illustrated with some recent data collected in the study of probabilistic information processing.

FORMAL MODELS

Formal models of judgment have been investigated primarily within the context of multiple linear regression, functional measurement, normative theory, and conjoint measurement. According to the multiple linear regression model, originally suggested by Brunswik (1940), the decision maker's final (quantitative) judgment concerning a criterion variable is a linear function of the cues or

215

information upon which the judgment is based. The cues themselves either have objective quantitative measures or can be scaled by the decision maker. This model has been applied in dozens of contexts, and extensive reviews of the research have been supplied by Slovic and Lichtenstein (1971) and by Dawes and Corrigan (1974).

By certain criteria, the simple multiple linear regression model has been successful in reproducing the policy of the decision maker. That is, in general, for the tasks studied (Goldberg, 1970): "a simple linear regression equation can be constructed which will predict the responses of a judge at approximately the level of his own reliability [p. 423]." However, we now know that the linear regression model may fit as well as it does, not necessarily because it provides a good description of the decision maker's cognitive processes, but rather because it is very robust both with respect to nonlinearity (Yntema & Torgerson, 1961) and with respect to variations in the beta weights (Dawes & Corrigan, 1974; Wainer, 1976). Thus, criticism has mounted against the descriptive use of the linear regression model because its robustness makes it difficult to falsify.

An alternative approach to assessing the additive and other algebraic models as descriptions of judgment is functional measurement developed by Anderson (1970) in conjunction with his information integration theory (Anderson, 1974). Unlike the multiple linear regression techniques, functional measurement relies on factorial designs and the analysis of variance. As a result, functional measurement is far more sensitive to the presence of interaction than is multiple linear regression. However, when interactions are detected, the question arises as to whether they should be interpreted in terms of an averaging or some other nonlinear model, or whether the data should be rescaled, leaving an additive model with new parameters. Various subtle but important problems arise when deciding whether to rescale data in this manner. These problems and some possible solutions have been discussed in Budescu and Wallsten (1979).

Nevertheless, from the information integration literature a general picture emerges that I interpret as follows: The tasks studied can be classified into two groups. Information is combined for the purpose either of estimating a point on a continuum or of choosing between two or more alternatives. In the former case, the averaging model seems appropriate, and in the latter case, the additive model does. Examples of the former task can be found in studies of impression formation (Anderson, 1965), of the estimation of population parameters from sample statistics (Levin, 1974, 1975), and of the estimation of a numerical criterion on the basis of two cues (Lichtenstein, Earle, & Slovic, 1975). Examples of the latter task include choosing between gambles (Anderson & Shanteau, 1970) or deciding which of two data generators was more likely the parent of a sample of observations (Leon & Anderson, 1974; Shanteau, 1970, 1972).

Despite the greater sensitivity of the functional measurement techniques and the support they have demonstrated for additive and averaging models, the models have been criticized because they emphasize the description of observable input–output relationships of decision behavior rather than the description of processes (Payne, Braunstein, & Carroll, 1978). An extreme statement of this point of view was provided by Simon (1976) who said: "the variance analysis paradigm, designed to test whether particular stimulus variables do or do not have an effect upon response variables, is largely useless for discovering and testing process models to explain what goes on between appearance of stimulus and performance of responses [p. 261]." Even Payne et al. (1978) admit that this is rather overstating the case.

Another context in which linear models have been thoroughly investigated is that of normative decision theory. For example, both the expected utility model and the Bayesian model for independent events (in log odds form) are additive. Although these models are consistent with human choice behavior in many situations, they are not now taken to be generally descriptive. This is because in many other contexts it is possible to demonstrate strong and systematic violations of the normative models' predictions (Becker & McClintock, 1967; Edwards, 1961; Rapoport & Wallsten, 1972; Slovic, Fischhoff, & Lichtenstein, 1977). Two of the demonstrations are mentioned here. First, Lichtenstein and Slovic (1971, 1973) showed that the relative preference values of two gambles depends on the method of evaluation. This preference reversal phenomenon, which is inconsistent with any maximization theory, is quite robust (Grether & Plott, 1979). Secondly, Kahneman and Tversky (1972) demonstrated that subjects are insensitive to sample size and to other statistical properties when performing in a Bayesian inference task, which is quite inconsistent with a Bayesian model of inference. Thus, simple normative models cannot serve as general descriptions of choice and decision processes.

I have reviewed, thus far, three frameworks within which algebraic models have been investigated: multiple linear regression, functional measurement, and normative models. The criticisms in the literature are, respectively, that they are too robust to be falsified, insufficiently concerned with intervening processes, and demonstrably false in various situations. To conclude, however, that such models are wrong in general, or to give them up altogether, would be, in my opinion, a mistake. It should be remembered that quite frequently, algebraic, particularly linear, models do provide very good descriptions of the subject's information processing. Indeed, given what we know about subjects' adaptive strategies (e.g., Newell & Simon, 1972; Slovic, 1972), it is quite likely that when faced with informational cues that are monotonically related to the likelihood of the hypotheses, subjects will process the cues in something like an additive fashion. The preceding review does suggest two conclusions, however. One is that regression techniques alone are not suitable for investigating theories about the nature of the cognitive processes underlying decisions, and the second is that simply asking whether such processes are, for example, additive is asking the wrong question. One might ask what conditions determine whether processing is additive, what formulations describe processing when additivity is either sustained or violated, or what general principles of cognitive processing operate regardless of how cues are combined. Furthermore, a properly formulated theory of judgmental information processing should indicate the conditions under which such processing can be described as additive, or as consistent with some other composition rule, and the reasons why that particular rule is appropriate. Finally, the rule should be tested in such a manner that it has a reasonable chance of being falsified.

My research using conjoint measurement and nonmetric scaling techniques has been an attempt to use additive and additive-difference models in this fashion (Delaney & Wallsten, 1977; Wallsten, 1976, 1977; Wallsten & Sapp, 1977). The studies have all been concerned with how sample information is used to decide which of two alternative hypotheses is more likely correct. Generally, additivity was sustained, although under specifiable conditions, it was clearly violated (Wallsten, 1978). More interesting, however, was the pattern of scale values representing the subjective diagnostic impact of the information, derived with the conjoint measurement techniques. A number of independent variables in the experiments had minimal effects on additivity, but profound effects on the scale values. With such data, it is not enough to argue, as Dawes (1975) has, that subjects processed information in an additive fashion because that was an appropriate strategy in those cases. Rather, one must account for the strong and systematic changes that were observed in the diagnostic impact of the various pieces of information, which nevertheless were generally additively combined. The theory I have been developing is strongly influenced by the current research in judgmental heuristics. Thus, we turn now to review that work briefly, concentrating on what I see as its merits and faults.

PROCESSING THEORIES

Much of the recent research in decision theory has been influenced strongly by cognitive and information processing theories. The general thrust of this work is that (Hogarth, 1975): "man is a selective stepwise information processing system with limited capacity [p. 273]" who employs (Payne, 1974): "a number of different decision procedures... depending on the structural characteristics of the decision task [p. 1]." This research has been reviewed by Hogarth (1975); Slovic, Fischhoff, and Lichtenstein (1977); and Pitz (1977).

The two approaches to cognitive limitations in decision making that have been most influential have stressed the concepts of bounded rationality (Simon, 1957) and judgmental heuristics (Tversky & Kahneman, 1974). According to the former approach (Slovic, 1972), decision makers are characterized by what Simon (1957) has termed bounded rationality, such that they construct a simplified model of the world and then act according to it. The argument continues that decision makers process only a subset of the information available to them, and that the nature of the subset is strongly affected by the structure of the task. Data consistent with this perspective were obtained in the research on choosing or evaluating gambles by Slovic and Lichtenstein (1968), Lichtenstein and Slovic (1971, 1973), and Payne (1973, 1975). In a similar vein, Slovic (1975) demonstrated that when people were required to select one from a pair of two-dimensional stimuli that they had previously equated in value, they consistently chose the stimulus that had the greater value on the more important dimension. Presumably, this result occurred because the decision makers differentially attended to dimensions of the stimulus in a manner dictated by the task at hand.

The work on judgmental heuristics (summarized by Tversky & Kahneman, 1974) is consistent with that utilizing bounded rationality. This latter research has defined and demonstrated three heuristics apparently used by people in making probabilistic judgments: representativeness, availability, and anchoring and adjustment. When using the representativeness heuristic, people make predictions, judgments, or diagnoses according to the degree that the sample evidence is similar to or representative of a particular population. That is to say, a sample is judged according to the degree that it (Kahneman & Tversky, 1972) "reflects the salient features of the process by which it is generated [p. 431]."

Compelling as this explanation of experimental results may be, it suffers from the problem of having very little predictive value. What determines how representative a sample of a different sort is in a new context? To my knowledge, there has been no attempt to independently define and measure the determinants of representativeness. Furthermore, alternative, equally valid explanations have been proposed for the data in question. Nisbett, Borgida, Crandall, and Reed (1976), for example, suggest that Tversky and Kahneman's results are due to people's tendency to use concrete rather than abstract information, and not because subjects are judging how representative the information is. Additionally, Olson (1976) ran experiments very similar to those of Kahneman and Tversky, but obtained very different results. Olson interpreted his (1976) results in terms of the nature of "concrete thinking, the importance of task characteristics, and the difficulty of a priori specification of the salient features with respect to which representativeness is assessed [p. 599]." Additional but similar criticisms were made by Pitz (1977).

When following the availability heuristic (Tversky & Kahneman, 1973), "a person evaluates the frequency of classes or the probability of events by . . . the ease with which relevant instances come to mind [p. 207]." Whether something is easily recalled depends on such factors as search strategies and the item's salient features. The anchoring and adjustment heuristic (Slovic, 1972; Tversky & Kahneman, 1974) states that a judgment is initially made on the basis of a particular most-salient dimension of the stimulus, and is then crudely adjusted as additional dimensions are considered. As with representativeness, both the definitions of the concepts employed in the heuristics and the determinants of the heuristics' use are sufficiently vaguely specified that experimental tests of the heuristics are difficult.

The primary problem with bounded rationality and heuristic theories has been stated succinctly both by Pitz (1977) and by Slovic, Fischhoff, and Lichtenstein (1977). Pitz (1977) has written that:

> ... as yet the assault on normative approaches to decision theory, led by the concepts of bounded rationality and heuristic theory, has not been developed to the point where a systematic model will lead to testable predictions. The experimental support for these alternatives consists mostly of demonstrations that, under appropriate conditions, subjects will behave in an irrational manner [p. 420].

According to Slovic, Fischhoff, and Lichtenstein (1977):

> ... the evidence ... suggests that the heuristic selected, the way it is employed, and the accuracy of the judgment it produces are all highly problem-specific; they may even vary with different representations of the same problem. Indeed heuristics may be faulted as a general theory of judgment because of the difficulty of knowing which will be applied in any particular instance [pp. 5–6].

The problems with these theories as they are now formulated in no way detracts from the important experiments they have inspired. The experiments have demonstrated convincingly that judgment is influenced by the task, that different features of the task are attended to and processed under different circumstances, and that simple algebraic or normative models will not describe judgment in any satisfying and complete fashion. Thus, "bounded rationality" and "heuristic" theories should not be abandoned. Rather, they should be formulated in such a manner that they apply over a range of situations but can be tested rigorously in any particular situation. Frequently, the testing can be accomplished after representing the theory by a well-defined formal model with suitable identification of parameters.

FORMAL MODELS AND A GENERAL THEORY

In order to achieve the present goal of expanding the merger of process theory and formal model to areas other than probabilistic inference, let us consider these areas of decision research within a single conceptual scheme. Decision research has been concerned primarily with choice and inference situations. In the former, decision makers are presented with two or more stimuli, and are required to select one of them for some purpose. In the latter, decision makers are presented with informational or sample stimuli, and either must decide which of two or more alternatives is most likely true or provide an estimate of a value. These choice and inference paradigms can be conceptually related as follows: Refer to Fig. 12.1, in which a choice problem is diagrammed on the left and the two kinds of inference problems are diagrammed on the right. In the choice situation, the person must select one of I alternatives, each of which takes values on J dimensions. In the inference situation, the person is presented with an informational stimulus that varies on J dimensions and then is required either to decide which of I alternative hypotheses is more likely correct, or to generate a single estimate. In the latter two cases, the decision maker must evaluate alternative hypotheses in accordnce with the dimensions of the informational stimulus. Thus, in the inference situations, as in the choice situation, the decision maker is asked to evaluate or compare multidimensional alternatives in order to select one that is best in some sense.

Our general theory assumes that in any choice or inference situation, the dimensions of the stimuli are arrayed from most to least salient and that the person's choice depends on the most salient dimensions. The decision maker's initial or anchor judgment is determined by the values of the stimuli on the most salient dimension. This judgment is adjusted according to the values of the stimuli on the next most salient dimension, and so forth. Adjustments become successively smaller and rougher until either all the dimensions have been processed or a criterion has been reached following which an overt choice or decision is made. The theory at this point is open with respect both to how dimensional salience is determined and how opinion is modified as successive dimensions are considered. It does, however, provide a framework within which specific assumptions can be made, tested, and evaluated.

Let us consider first how dimensions are combined. The possibilities are shown in Table 12.1. Past research suggests that people use either a holistic or a dimensionwise strategy. According to the former, each alternative is evaluated

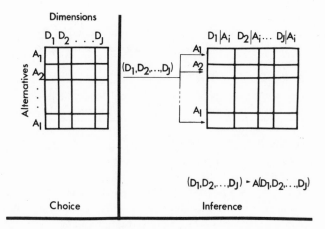

FIG. 12.1.   Schematic representations of choice and inference problems.

TABLE 12.1
One Scheme for Classifying Various Choice and Inference Tasks, with the
Models the Classification Suggests

Evaluate Alternatives	Evaluation Procedure		
	Threshold	Additive	Averaging
Holistic	Conjunctive, disjunctive	Expected utility, multiple linear regression	Functional measurement (selecting alternatives)
Dimensionwise	Elimination by aspects	Additive– difference	Functional measurement (point estimation)

with respect to its most salient dimensions, and the alternative that comes out highest is selected. According to the dimensionwise strategy, the most salient dimension is selected and all the alternatives are evaluated with respect to it. The alternatives are then evaluated on the next most salient dimension, and so on. At some point, either a single alternative has survived, or one alternative has a sufficiently high aggregate score, and it is selected.

Within either the holistic or dimensionwise strategy, subjects may pursue either a threshold, an additive, or an averaging evaluation procedure. This yields a total of six distinct methods by which information can be combined, each of which has been represented formally in at least one fashion. Threshold methods are those in which alternatives are evaluated according to whether or not their dimension values exceed certain fixed or required levels. Examples of holistic threshold strategies are the conjunctive and disjunctive methods, which have been represented as multiplicative models by Einhorn (1971), whereas an example of a dimensionwise threshold strategy is Tversky's (1972) elimination-by-aspects model. Holistic additive strategies are represented by the expected utility and multiple linear regression models discussed earlier, and dimensionwise additive strategies are represented by additive-difference models by Tversky (1969) and Wallsten (1976). Finally, both holistic and dimensionwise averaging models are represented by appropriate functional measurement models.

Thus, within our framework, there are six methods by which stimulus dimensions can be processed prior to a choice. The method that is used depends on individual and task determinants. For example, holistic strategies are preferred to dimensionwise methods if the dimensions of the alternatives are interdependent (Rosen & Rosenkoetter, 1976), and the choice of holistic and dimensional methods depends on the number of alternatives and dimensions (Payne, 1976). I suggested earlier that people may combine dimension additively when choosing among alternatives, but according to an averaging strategy when estimating a point on a continuum. In any event, because each of the models can be formally stated and has testable consequences, it should be possible to determine the conditions under which each holds.

Both dimensions and alternatives may vary in salience as a function of task and individual differences. If the approach I am suggesting is to be at all useful, it must turn out that the determinants of saliency are the same regardless of the method by which dimensional information is combined, so that predictions can be made from one situation and method to another. The literature on concept formation (Trabasso & Bower, 1968) provides a good initial foundation for the discussion and manipulation of dimension salience. Also, Nisbett et al. (1976) may be correct that the salience of dimensions depends on how concrete they are. Other indicators of dimension and alternative salience may be obtained by careful study of the current literature on heuristics.

To summarize the approach I am suggesting, the general theory provides a broad statement of how multidimensional information is evaluated for the purpose of making a decision, and provides a vehicle for extending generalizations over a variety of tasks. Without further development, the theory is no more predictive than any of those previously reviewed here. It does, however, provide a framework within which specific models can be tested, compared, and related to each other, and within which the determinants of salience can be assessed across paradigms. The question, then, is not whether the theory is right or wrong, but is it useful? If the models can be evaluated and related to each other in a specific fashion, and if conclusions about dimension and alternative salience hold over a variety of paradigms, then the general theory will indeed be useful.

INFERENCES BASED ON MULTIDIMENSIONAL INFORMATION

Much of my recent research has dealt with how people process equivocal or probabilistic information for the purpose of deciding between two alternative hypotheses. Several studies have supported the suggestion that informational stimuli are evaluated in a dimensionwise fashion. The alternatives are evaluated with respect to the most salient dimension of the information, and an initial judgment is formed concerning which of the two alternatives is more likely correct. This judgment is modified on the basis of the next most salient dimension, and so forth, until either all the dimensions have been processed or a certainty criterion is reached. Then one of the hypotheses is overtly selected. The contribution of each dimension to the final opinion depends both on its salience and on how strongly it is associated with each of the two alternatives. The two strengths of association, in turn, depend on such factors as how likely the dimension value is given each alternative, how salient or important each alternative is, and so forth. Because the contribution of each dimension to the decision depends on relative strengths of association, it can be represented naturally by a difference function. Similarly, the modification of opinion as dimensions are considered can be represented by an additive function. Thus, the basic model is an additive–difference one, and, as such, falls in cell (2, 2) of Table 12.1 (Wallsten, 1976).

Because the model is quite general, we have applied it in situations where constraints on the model's generality could be formulated and tested, thereby resulting in tractable submodels that could be evaluated and used (Delaney & Wallsten, 1977; Wallsten, 1976; Wallsten & Sapp, 1977). Our research has generally involved three phases. First, nonmetric properties of the data were used to evaluate the adequacy of the models, both in terms of goodness of fit measures obtained in scaling, and in terms of necessary conditions from the theory of conjoint measurement. Next, predictions from one situation or submodel were made to another via the general additive–difference model, and these predictions were tested. Finally, the scale values derived under various conditions were inspected to determine the effects of those conditions on dimension and hypothesis salience. Various manipulations were found to have large effects on the scale values, but no effect at all on the fit of the models. Because the algebraic models described the data well, we took the derived scale values seriously and interpreted them within the framework of our general theory, thereby allowing conclusions to be drawn and extended beyond the particular paradigms under consideration. This work has been recorded in detail (Delaney & Wallsten, 1977; Wallsten, 1976; Wallsten & Sapp, 1977) and also summarized elsewhere (Wallsten, 1977), and therefore, is not treated further here.

Experiment 1: Inferences Based on Three-Dimensional Information.   I now use some very recent work to illustrate the fruitfulness of the approach just advocated. This research has been done in collaboration with a graduate student, Curtis Barton (Wallsten & Barton, 1980).

In the first experiment, subjects had to decide whether alternative A or B was more likely correct on the basis of information consisting of either one or three binary dimensions. At the beginning of a trial, subjects saw on a cathode ray tube (CRT) the portion of the display below the horizontal line in Fig. 12.2. They were instructed to interpret the display in the following fashion: The computer, with equal probabilities, was going to select alternative A or alternative B and then use the probabilities listed under that alternative to sample the horizontally arranged pairs of symbols. The symbols were arranged so as to delimit line intervals, and so that pairs of intervals were identical in their delimiters but different in their length. The pairs of delimited intervals are referred to as bracket, brace, and slash intervals, respectively. If the computer had decided to sample according to alternative A, then it would sample the top bracket interval (to be symbolized subsequently in the text as $[T]$) with probability .8, or the bottom bracket interval ($[B]$) with probability .2, and would also sample one brace ($\{T\}$ or $\{B\}$) and one slash ($|T|$ or $|B|$) interval, each with the probabilities

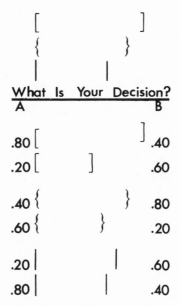

FIG. 12.2.   Facsimile of a single trial.

shown. If the computer had decided to sample according to alternative *B*, then the sampling would occur with the probabilities listed under *B*. When the subject indicated he or she was ready, the computer wrote the results of its sampling above the horizontal line as shown in Fig. 12.2, followed by WHAT IS YOUR DECISION? Note that the sampling results written above the horizontal line consist of information that varies on three binary dimensions: bracket, brace, and slash. The subject was to judge if this information was more likely sampled according to *A* or *B*. Upon deciding, the subject responded *A* or *B* and gave a confidence estimate from 50 to 100 inclusive. Decision times were recorded, and feedback was provided in terms of the correct answer, how much was won or lost for that trial, and the total earnings thus far for the session. Subjects were paid according to a strictly proper scoring rule (Wallsten, 1976), which rewarded them as a function of both their correctness and their confidence rating. We assumed that in the display shown in Fig. 12.2, the bracket intervals would represent the most salient dimension of the informational stimulus, both because people tend to read from top to bottom and because [*T*] and [*B*] were most discriminable, and that on similar grounds, the brace intervals would be the next most salient, and the slash intervals would be the least salient.

The following manipulations were imposed on the task: First, on each trial, subjects received either a three-dimensional informational stimulus as shown in Fig. 12.2, or a one-dimensional stimulus. In the latter case, the computer wrote above the horizontal line only a single one of the three randomly selected intervals, either a bracket, a brace, or a slash. Second, the sampling probabilities under alternatives *A* and *B* for each pair of intervals varied from trial to trial.

This was done in such a fashion that on each trial, each sampled dimension independently took on one of four likelihood ratios, 3/1, 2/1, 1/2, or 1/3, specified for A relative to B. (For example, in Fig. 12.2, the sample likelihood ratios are $P([T]\|A) / P([T]\|B) = 2/1$, $P(\{T\}\|A) / P(\{T\}\|B) = 1/2$, and $P(\|B\|\|A) / P(\|B\|\|B) = 2/1$.) Thus, on each trial, each of the three differentially salient dimensions took on one of four possible likelihood ratios.

The appropriate model for trials with the three-dimensional samples is the additive model:

$$\Psi(S) = \sum_{k=1}^{3} \Psi_k(D_k), \qquad (12.1)$$

where $\Psi_k(D_k)$, $k = 1, 2, 3$, is a real valued function representing the subjective contribution of dimension D_k to the final opinion and $\Psi(S)$ is a real valued function representing the degree to which the total sample subjectively favors A over B. In the full additive–difference model, $\Psi_k(D_k)$ would be elaborated to reflect the difference in D_k's strengths of association between A and B. We need not do so here because features of A and B, such as the sampling probabilities, are never themselves orthogonally varied and, therefore, the difference portion of the full model cannot be assessed. It is, instead, treated as a constant for each of the four likelihood ratios.

Three predictions were made. First, we predicted that ordinal properties of the responses to the three-dimensional informational stimuli would be adequately described by the additive Eq. (12.1). Second, we predicted that to the degree that the equation did not fit the data, violations of additivity would be due primarily to the least salient dimension, which, according to the theory, should have the least consistent effect on opinion. Third, we predicted that when scale values were derived from responses to the three-dimensional informational stimuli, they would be most extreme for the most salient dimension and least extreme for the least salient dimension. However, we expected that when the information consisted of a single dimension, the responses would be the same regardless of which of the three dimensions was presented.

Analyses were done separately for each of the 13 subjects, but I present here only summary data showing either the extreme and the median subjects, or an average over all subjects. The question of whether the three-dimensional information stimuli were processed in an additive fashion was investigated with various analyses, with results summarized in Table 12.2. The three-dimensional informational stimuli fit into a $4 \times 4 \times 4$, $D_1 \times D_2 \times D_3$, design, where D_1 refers to the bracket interval, D_2 to the brace, and D_3 to the slash interval, and where each level of each dimension (line interval) was represented by one of the four likelihood ratios. Eq. (12.1) was fit for each subject separately by means of the computer program ADDALS (de Leeuw, Young, & Takane, 1976), which obtained the best nonmetric additive fit to the data by searching for nine parame-

TABLE 12.2
Summary of Additivity Tests for Experiment 1

| | τ | Interaction[a] | Overall | Percent of Double Cancellation Tests Satisfied | |
				Including Homogeneous Sample	Excluding Homogeneous Sample
Low τ subject	.66	18.5	60	56	65
Median τ subject	.80	3.2	73	73	73
High τ subject	.98	3.2	77	65	92

[a] Cell entries are percents of accountable variance due to interactions.

ters to describe the 64-cell design. Kendall's tau, measuring the rank-order correlation between the best fitting model and the approximately 400 data points, is summarized in the first numerical column of Table 12.2. Shown in the table are data from the subjects with the lowest tau, the highest tau, and the median tau, respectively.

In addition to the scaling analysis, analyses of variance (ANOVA) were run for each subject on both the original responses and on responses monotonically transformed in the manner suggested by Budescu and Wallsten (1979). The two ANOVAs yielded similar results and only the former is summarized here. The three main effects corresponding to D_1, D_2, and D_3 were always highly significant. In addition, some interactions were significant for some subjects, although no pattern over subjects was apparent. The important question, however, concerns the percent of accountable variance due to interaction terms. This percentage varies from a low of .4% for one subject to a high of 18.5% for another, with a median over subjects of 4.4%. The percentages for the three subjects listed in Table 12.2 are shown in the table. Taken together, the scaling and variance analyses suggest that at least to a good first approximation, the separate dimensions do contribute to the final responses in an additive fashion.

Additivity is not perfect, however, and the axioms of conjoint measurement were investigated with the program CONJOINT (Holt & Wallsten, 1975) to determine whether violations of additivity were due primarily to D_3. The axioms of independence, joint independence, and double cancellation (Krantz & Tversky, 1971) were assessed for each subject. There was simply no indication that any one of the dimensions contributed more to additivity violations than did any other dimension. Both independence and joint independence were satisfied to a very high degree and those tests are not reported here. There were, however, consistent violations of double cancellation. It will be recalled that double cancellation is a test of transitivity in any 3 × 3 submatrix drawn from the full design. In the present design, 192 nonindependent tests of double cancellation were possible for each subject, and Table 12.2 provides a summary of the average percentage of tests that were satisfied for the three subjects listed. Over the 13 subjects, the percentages ran from 57 to 84. Thus, the axiom analyses indicate that upon close examination, additivity does not hold precisely, but that the violations do not vary as a function of the three dimensions.

We were able to isolate one interesting cause of nonadditivity. On some trials with three-dimensional information, the three dimensions all had identical likelihood ratios. Additivity tended to break down in these cases, as can be seen by evaluating double cancellation separately for those submatrices including a homogeneous informational sample, and for those not including such a sample. This was done for all subjects and the results for our representative subjects are shown in the last two columns of Table 12.2. Of the 13 subjects, 11 showed greater satisfaction of double cancellation when homogeneous samples were excluded, one showed the reverse pattern by a single percentage point, and one subject, shown in the table, had equal percentages in the two cases. We think that additivity was violated with homogeneous data samples, because subjects tended to ignore redundant data, but we have not verified that yet. If this conjecture is correct, it would be consistent with previous results (Wallsten, 1976).

Because the departures from additivity were generally small, we can look now at the scale values that were derived with the program ADDALS. These values represent the subjective diagnostic contribution favoring A over B of the four likelihood ratios of each dimension. Data from two subjects are shown in the right panels of Fig. 12.3. For each subject, the scale values are plotted separately for each dimension, as a function of the likelihood ratios logarithmically spaced. Because the scale values are unique up to multiplication by a positive constant, it is meaningful to compare slopes of the three functions at corresponding points. If dimension D_1 is most salient and therefore influences opinion to the greatest degree, it will manifest the steepest slope. Similarly, if D_3 is the least salient dimension, it will have the least effect on opinion, and consequently demonstrate the most shallow slope. Contrary to these predictions, the slopes are identical for the three dimensions in the case of both subjects shown in Fig. 12.3. This held true for all other subjects as well.

The second noticeable feature about the right panels of Fig. 12.3 is that the two subjects demonstrate quite different patterns of scale values. The scale values of the subject shown in the upper right-hand panel are monotonic, indeed almost linear, with the log likelihood ratios. Apparently, this subject was attending equally to both hypotheses in making a decision. In contrast, the scale values for the subject shown in the lower right-hand panel are monotonic with the greater of the two sampling probabilities specified by the two alternative hypotheses, and not with the log likelihood ratios. This subject apparently attended only to the hypothesis specifying the greater sampling probability for a dimension, and, therefore, for this subject, the effective association between that dimension value and the other hypothesis was roughly zero.

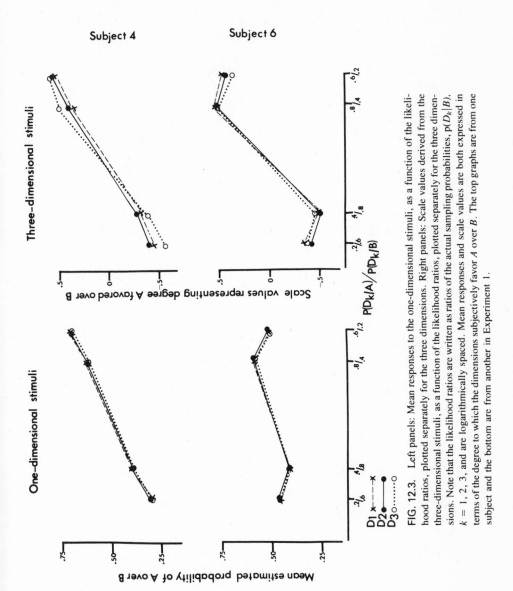

FIG. 12.3. Left panels: Mean responses to the one-dimensional stimuli, as a function of the likelihood ratios, plotted separately for the three dimensions. Right panels: Scale values derived from the three-dimensional stimuli, as a function of the likelihood ratios, plotted separately for the three dimensions. Note that the likelihood ratios are written as ratios of the actual sampling probabilities, $p(D_k|B)$, $k = 1, 2, 3$, and are logarithmically spaced. Mean responses and scale values are both expressed in terms of the degree to which the dimensions subjectively favor A over B. The top graphs are from one subject and the bottom are from another in Experiment 1.

229

The left panels of Fig. 12.3 show mean responses to the one-dimensional information. It can be seen that the two subjects followed their respective strategies as well when the informational stimuli consisted of only a single dimension. I call the strategy illustrated by the upper panels of Fig. 12.3 a *likelihood ratio strategy* and the one shown at the bottom a *probability strategy*.

We inspected the corresponding graphs for each subject in order to classify each in terms of the strategy he or she used in response to one-dimensional and three-dimensional stimuli. The result of this classification is shown in Table 12.3. Of the seven subjects who used a probability strategy in response to the one-dimensional stimuli, six of them retained that strategy for the three-dimensional stimuli. However, of the six subjects who used a likelihood ratio strategy in the one-dimensional situation, three of them used a probability strategy in the three-dimensional situation.

It is useful to obtain independent verification of the existence of the two strategies. This can be done by inspecting the decision latencies for 13 specific pairs of conditions in the design, 12 for three-dimensional stimuli, and one for one-dimensional stimuli. In each case, if we make the assumption that, after equating for the number of dimensions in the sample, latency varies inversely with decision confidence, the probability and likelihood ratio strategies predict opposite orderings of latencies within the pairs. For example, in the one-dimensional case, the probability strategy predicts that the latency in response to the likelihood ratio .8/.4 will be less than the latency in response to .6/.2, whereas the likelihood ratio strategy makes the opposite prediction. Using mean latencies, the number of pair orderings consistent with each strategy was calculated for each subject. The mean result over all subjects is shown in Table 12.4, broken down according to the strategy inferred from the scaling. It can be seen that the majority of latency pairs are consistent with the strategies inferred from the scaling analyses in both the one-dimensional and the three-dimensional situations. In the one-dimensional case, this consistency holds for 11 of the 13 subjects and in the three-dimensional case, it holds for nine of the subjects. Thus, the latency measures do provide some independent verification of the inferred strategies.

In retrospect, it is easy to understand why half the subjects in the one-dimensional situation and about three-fourths of the subjects in the three-dimensional situation treated the two alternative hypotheses as differentially

TABLE 12.3
Number of Subjects Demonstrating Probability and Likelihood Ratio
Strategies in Response to One- and Three-Dimensional Stimuli

One-Dimension Strategy	*Three-Dimension Strategy*	
	Probability	*Likelihood Ratio*
Probability	6	1
Likelihood Ratio	3	3

TABLE 12.4
Mean Number of Latency Pairs Consistent with the Probability and
the Likelihood Ratio Strategies

Strategy Inferred from Scaling	Latency Pair Ordering			
	One Dimension		Three Dimension	
	Prob.	LR	Prob.	LR
Probability (Prob.)	.7	.3	6.8	5.2
Likelihood Ratio (LR)	0	1.0	4.5	7.5

important in arriving at their final decision. The nature of the display made this strategy a good one for simplifying the task and reducing the cognitive strain. In the present case, the two hypotheses (A and B) were arrayed on opposite sides of the screen and expressed in numerical form. It is clearly easier to attend to one side of the screen in forming an opinion, than to glance back and forth and integrate the numerical information from both sides. This is particularly true when the informational stimulus has three dimensions. It is quite likely that other displays could be created, such as those we used in our earlier studies, that would cause attention to be divided more equally between the two hypotheses, or, alternatively, that would cause attention to focus even more strongly on one hypothesis.

Experiment 2: Inference Based on Five-Dimensional Information. Although the additive model provides a reasonable fit to the data and the derived scale values are consistent with, and interpretable in terms of, the general theory, the prediction concerning relative dimension salience was clearly not sustained. This could be either because the general theory is wrong in this regard or because the salience manipulations were not successful. A second experiment, run by Barton and myself (Wallsten & Barton, 1980), suggests that the latter explanation is correct. Because the experiment is rather complex, I describe only a single aspect of it here.

In this study, there are five pairs of line intervals arrayed below the horizontal line on the CRT (cf. Fig. 12.2), and on each trial the informational stimulus contained all five dimensions. The likelihood ratios of the dimensions varied from trial to trial, however. Half the problems were of Type I, in which case the sampling probabilities under A and B for each dimension were such that the likelihood ratio associated with each dimension in the informational stimulus was either 4/1, favoring A, or 1/4, favoring B. The other half of the problems were of Type II, in which case the likelihood ratio of each dimension was either 3/2, favoring A or 2/3, favoring B.

There were two between-subjects manipulations. Half the subjects were required to respond within 20 seconds of the presentation of the information, which provided them with plenty of time. The other half of the subjects, however, were under considerable time pressure, as they were required to respond within 9 seconds. Crossed with this time manipulation was a payoff manipulation. The subjects were paid according to a strictly proper scoring rule, with half of the subjects having parameters resulting in lenient payoffs, and the other half of the subjects having parameters resulting in severe penalties for errors. Thus, this study was concerned with how time and payoff pressure affected the processing of the information dimensions.

The general theory assumes that the dimensions are evaluated in order from most to least salient, and, therefore, from top to bottom in the present situation. Thus, we expected that those subjects who were under time pressure would be less likely to attend to the bottom few dimensions prior to responding. The theory also suggests that subjects will process more available information dimensions when the situation requires a greater degree of certainty. We therefore expected that in the present situation subjects under extreme payoff pressure would attend to more dimensions than would the other subjects.

There were nine subjects in each of the four groups and I present here only the mean result of a single analysis. For each subject, a contrast score was calculated for each of the five dimensions in problem Type I and in problem Type II. This was done for each dimension by subtracting the mean response to all displays when that dimension had one likelihood ratio from the mean response to all displays when that dimension had the other likelihood ratio. The greater role that dimension played in the subject's response the larger its contrast should be. Fig. 12.4 shows the mean contrast of the five dimensions for problem Type I and problem Type II for each of the four groups of subjects. When there was no time pressure, as shown in the bottom two panels, the contrasts were all equal, indicating that subjects attended equally to all five dimensions. However, when subjects were under time pressure and the payoff was not severe, as shown in the upper right-hand panel, decisions were based primarily on the first few dimensions. When there was time pressure and the payoff was severe, as shown in the upper left-hand panel, there was a considerably greater tendency to process all dimensions, but the decisions still turned primarily on the first three dimensions. This is demonstrated by the fact that the graph slopes downward for both problem types after Dimension 3. It should be emphasized that this slight dip is a reliable one because it is reflected in 15 of the 18 individual protocols (nine subjects times two problem types). Thus, these data are consistent with the notion that informational dimensions are processed sequentially, and that in the absence of sufficient time or incentive, the less salient dimensions receive little or no attention.

Summary and Discussion of Experiments. Overall, the data presented are consistent with the dimensionwise processing theory outlined earlier. In particular, the theory was usefully represented as an additive model in the present context, and provided a vehicle for interpreting results in a manner that easily

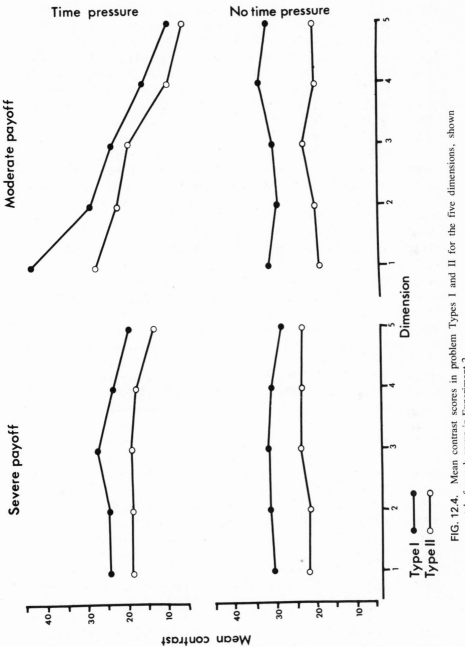

FIG. 12.4. Mean contrast scores in problem Types I and II for the five dimensions, shown separately for each group in Experiment 2.

233

generalizes to other situations. Consistent with the earlier studies in this program of research, it appears that dimensions of the stimuli contribute to final opinion in a sequential, approximately additive fashion. The additivity violations that occurred seem to be due to the presence of homogeneous dimensions, which is precisely the same phenomenon found in our previous research. At least as important as the general applicability of the additive model in this case is the fact that we were able to distinguish, by inspecting the scale values, two distinct strategies that differed from each other in terms of the relative salience of the alternative hypotheses under consideration. Furthermore, independent support for the existence of these strategies was obtained from latency measures. It remains to determine what individual differences caused the adoption of one or the other strategy in this case, but the existence of the two strategies is quite consistent with the general theory and the assumption that subjects will seek to reduce their cognitive load.

In addition, data were obtained demonstrating that the number and order of dimensions processed can be manipulated in a predictable fashion. In the presence of a lenient payoff structure and with little time to work, subjects attended primarily to the more salient dimensions. When the payoffs were more severe, but time was still limited, however, they managed to devote almost as much attention to the last two dimensions as to the first three. Thus, the important findings were not simply that processing was more-or-less additive in this situation, but that processing varied with task characteristics in a manner consistent with the general theory.

It would be important within the context of this approach to determine, for example, whether the same display features affect processing in a choice task as in the inference task. Thus, for example, one might replace the delimited line intervals with amounts of money and have the probabilities under A and B represent the chances of winning those outcomes. Subjects would choose to play the gambles listed under A or under B. It might be assumed that processing in this task would be described by models in cell $(1, 1)$ or $(1, 2)$ of Table 12.1. Analyses similar to those discussed here would be carried out to determine if the salience and order of processing of dimensions depend on the same factors shown to be operative in the inference task.

FINAL COMMENTS

The work I have just reviewed indicates how a general theory can be combined with a formal model to yield both specific predictions and conclusions that generalize in a natural fashion to other situations. This strategy has, of course, been used in other areas of psychology, for example, by Atkinson and Shiffrin (1968) in their work on memory. I believe it can be applied more widely in the area of decision behavior. The research I have described falls in one cell of the matrix shown in Table 12.1. That matrix suggests one framework for organizing most of the research in the area of decision behavior, and suggests how the general theory can be applied to each area in a specific fashion. It is to be hoped that a scheme such as this will provide for a merger of the good features of formal models with those of the general process theory approach, even if not doing away entirely with all of their bad points.

ACKNOWLEDGMENTS

This work has been supported by Grant No. BNS76-20759 from the National Science Foundation. I thank Jerome Busemeyer, John B. Carroll, Michael Kubovy, and Amnon Rapoport for very useful comments on an earlier draft of this chapter.

REFERENCES

Anderson, N. H. Averaging versus adding as a stimulus—combination rule in impression formation. *Journal of Experimental Psychology,* 1965, *70,* 394–400.

Anderson, N. H. Functional measurement and psychophysical judgment. *Psychological Review,* 1970, *77,* 153–170.

Anderson, N. H. Information integration theory: A brief review. In D. H. Krantz, R. C. Atkinson, & P. Suppes (Eds.), *Contemporary developments in mathematical psychology* (Vol. 2). San Francisco: Freeman, 1974.

Anderson, N. H., & Shanteau, J. Information integration in risky decision making. *Journal of Experimental Psychology,* 1970, *84,* 441–451.

Atkinson, R. C., & Shiffrin, R. M. Human memory: A proposed system and its control processes. In W. K. Spence & J. T. Spence (Eds.), *The psychology of learning and motivation* (Vol. 2). New York: Academic Press, 1968.

Becker, G. M., & McClintock, C. G. Value: Behavioral decision theory. *Annual Review of Psychology,* 1967, *18,* 239–286.

Brunswik, E. Thing consistency as measured by correlation coefficients. *Psychological Review,* 1940, *47,* 69–78.

Budescu, D. V., & Wallsten, T. S. A note on functional measurement and analysis of variance. *Bulletin of the Psychonomic Society,* 1979, *14,* 307–310.

Dawes, R. The mind, the model, and the task. In R. Restle, R. M. Shiffrin, N. J. Castellan, H. R. Lindman, & D. B. Pisoni (Eds.), *Cognitive Theory* (Vol. 1). Hillsdale, N.J.: Lawrence Erlbaum Associates, 1975.

Dawes, R., & Corrigan, B. Linear models in decision making. *Psychological Bulletin,* 1974, *81,* 95–106.

Delaney, H. D., & Wallsten, T. S. Probabilistic information processing: Effects of a biased payoff matrix on choices and bids. *Organizational Behavior and Human Performance,* 1977, *20,* 203–237.

de Leeuw, J., Young, F. W., & Takane, Y. Additive structure in qualitative data: An alternating least squares method with optimal scaling features. *Psychometrika,* 1976, *41,* 471–503.

Edwards, W. Behavioral decision theory. *Annual Review of Psychology,* 1961, *12,* 473–498.

Einhorn, H. J. Use of nonlinear, noncompensatory models as a function of task and amount of information. *Organizational Behavior and Human Performance,* 1971, *6,* 1–27.

Goldberg, L. R. Man versus model of man: A rationale, plus some evidence for a method of improving on clinical inferences. *Psychological Bulletin,* 1970, *73,* 422–432.

Grether, D. M., & Plott, C. R. Economic theory of choice and the preference reversal phenomenon. *American Economic Review,* 1979, *69,* 623–638.

Hogarth, R. M. Cognitive processes and the assessment of subjective probability distributions. *Journal of the American Statistical Association,* 1975, *70,* 271–289.

Holt, J. O., III, & Wallsten, T. S. A user's manual for CONJOINT: A computer program for evaluating certain conjoint-measurement axioms. *J.S.A.S. Catalog of Selected Documents in Psychology,* 1975, *5,* 317 (Ms. No. 1079).

Kahneman, D., & Tversky, A. Subjective probability: A judgment of representativeness. *Cognitive Psychology,* 1972, *3,* 430–454.

Krantz, D. H., & Tversky, A. Conjoint-measurement analysis of composition rules in psychology. *Psychological Review,* 1971, *78,* 151–169.

Leon, M., & Anderson, N. H. A ratio rule from integration theory applied to inference judgments. *Journal of Experimental Psychology,* 1974, *102,* 27–36.

Levin, I. P. Averaging processes and intuitive statistical judgments. *Organizational Behavior and Human Performance,* 1974, *12,* 83–91.

Levin, I. P. Information integration in numerical judgments and decision processes. *Journal of Experimental Psychology: General,* 1975, *1,* 39–53.

Lichtenstein, S., Earle, T. C., & Slovic, P. Cue utilization in a numerical prediction task. *Journal of Experimental Psychology: Human Perception and Performance,* 1975, *1,* 77–85.

Lichtenstein, S., & Slovic, P. Reversals of preference between bids and choices in gambling decisions. *Journal of Experimental Psychology,* 1971, *89,* 46–55.

Lichtenstein, S., & Slovic, P. Response induced reversals of preference in gambling: An extended replication in Las Vegas. *Journal of Experimental Psychology,* 1973, *101,* 16–20.

Newell, A., & Simon, H. A. *Human problem solving.* Englewood Cliffs, N.J.: Prentice-Hall, 1972.

Nisbett, R. E., Borgida, E., Crandall, R., & Reed, H. Popular inductions: Information is not necessarily informative. In J. S. Carroll & J. W. Payne (Eds.), *Cognition and social behavior.* Hillsdale, N.J.: Lawrence Erlbaum Associates, 1976.

Olson, C. L. Some apparent violations of the representativeness heuristic in human judgment. *Journal of Experimental Psychology: Human Perception and Performance,* 1976, *2,* 599–608.

Payne, J. W. Alternative approaches to decision making under risk: Moments versus risk dimensions. *Psychological Bulletin,* 1973, *80,* 439–453.

Payne, J. W. *An information search and protocol analysis of decision making as a function of task complexity.* C. I. P. Working Paper No. 287, Carnegie-Mellon University, 1974.

Payne, J. W. Relation of perceived risk to preferences among gambles. *Journal of Experimental Psychology: Human Perception and Performance,* 1975, *1,* 86–94.

Payne, J. W. Task complexity and contingent processing in decision making: An information search and protocol analysis. *Organizational Behavior and Human Performance,* 1976, *16,* 366–387.

Payne, J. W., Braunstein, M. L., & Carroll, J. S. Exploring pre-decisional behavior: An alternative approach to decision behavior. *Organizational Behavior and Human Performance,* 1978, *22,* 17–44.

Pitz, G. Decision making and cognition. In H. Jungermann & G. De Zeeuw (Eds.), *Decision making and change in human affairs.* Dordrecht, Holland: Reidel, 1977.

Rapoport, A., & Wallsten, T. S. Individual decision behavior. *Annual Review of Psychology,* 1972, *23,* 131–176.

Rosen, L. D., & Rosenkoetter, P. An eye fixation analysis of choice and judgment with multiattribute stimuli. *Memory and Cognition,* 1976, *4,* 747–752.

Shanteau, J. C. An additive model for sequential decision making. *Journal of Experimental Psychology,* 1970, *85,* 181–191.

Shanteau, J. C. Descriptive versus normative models of sequential inference judgment. *Journal of Experimental Psychology,* 1972, *93,* 63–68.

Simon, H. A. *Models of man: Social and national.* New York: Wiley, 1957.

Simon, H. A. Discussion: Cognition and social behavior. In J. S. Carroll & J. W. Payne (Eds.), *Cognition and social behavior.* Hillsdale, N.J.: Lawrence Erlbaum Associates, 1976.

Slovic, P. From Shakespeare to Simon: Speculation—and some evidence about man's ability to process information. *Oregon Research Institute Research Monograph,* 1972, *12,* No. 12.

Slovic, P. Choice between equally valued alternatives. *Journal of Experimental Psychology: Human Perception and Performance,* 1975, *1,* 280-287.

Slovic, P., Fischhoff, B., & Lichtenstein, S. Behavioral decision theory. *Annual Review of Psychology,* 1977, *28,* 1-39.

Slovic, P., & Lichtenstein, S. The relative importance of probabilities and payoffs in risk taking. *Journal of Experimental Psychology Monograph Supplement,* 1968, *78,* No. 3, Part 2.

Slovic, P., & Lichtenstein, S. Comparison of Bayesian and regression approaches to the study of information processing in judgment. *Organizational Behavior and Human Performance,* 1971, *6,* 649-744.

Trabasso, T. R., & Bower, G. H. *Attention in learning: Theory and research.* New York: Wiley, 1968.

Tversky, A. Intransitivity of preference. *Psychological Review,* 1969, *76,* 31-48.

Tversky, A. Elimination by aspects: A theory of choice. *Psychological Review,* 1972, *79,* 281-299.

Tversky, A., & Kahneman, D. Availability: A heuristic for judging frequency and probability. *Cognitive Psychology,* 1973, *5,* 207-232.

Tversky, A., & Kahneman, D. Judgment under uncertainty: Heuristics and biases. *Science,* 1974, *185,* 1124-1131.

Wainer, H. Estimating coefficients in linear models: It don't make no nevermind. *Psychological Bulletin,* 1976, *83,* 213-217.

Wallsten, T. S. Using conjoint measurement models to investigate a theory about probabilistic information processing. *Journal of Mathematical Psychology,* 1976, *14,* 144-185.

Wallsten, T. S. Processing information for decisions. In N. J. Castellan, D. B. Pisoni, & G. Potts (Eds.), *Cognitive theory* (Vol. 2). Hillsdale, N.J.: Lawrence Erlbaum Associates, 1977.

Wallsten, T. S. *Bias in evaluating diagnostic information.* L. L. Thurstone Psychometric Laboratory Report #157, Chapel Hill, N.C., 1978.

Wallsten, T. S., & Barton, C. N. *Processing probabilistic multidimensional information for decisions.* Manuscript in preparation, 1980.

Wallsten, T. S., & Sapp, M. M. Strong ordinal properties of an additive model for the sequential processing of probabilistic information. *Acta Psychologica,* 1977, *41,* 225-253.

Yntema, D. B., & Torgerson, W. S. Man-computer cooperation in decisions requiring common sense. *IRE Transactions of the Professional Group on Human Factors in Electronics,* 1961, *HFE-2(1),* 20-26.

13 Process Models of Probabilistic Categorization

Michael Kubovy
Alice F. Healy
Yale University

Probabilistic categorization is that task analyzed from a normative point of view by statistical decision theory. There are two overlapping distributions: An observation is sampled from one of the distributions; a decision is sought regarding which distribution was the source of the observation. The normative aspects of this task are well understood, but how people make such decisions without the benefit of the analytic tools of statistical decision theory is not clear. That is the topic of this chapter.

We chose to study a simple version of probabilistic categorization: The distributions are univariate normal, and the prior probability that an observation will be drawn from either distribution is known to the decision makers, as are the relative costs and benefits for errors and correct responses. The reason for our choice is that this simple version embodies standard assumptions about how people go about detecting faint acoustic or optical signals embedded in noise (Egan, 1975; Green & Swets, 1974). In such a signal detection task, one distribution represents the effect of noise; the other represents the effect of a signal added to the noise.

Although the theory of signal detection is one of the best-developed mathematical theories in psychology, its assumptions regarding the nature of the sensory input to the subject have been tested far more thoroughly than its assumptions regarding the process whereby the subject makes a decision. The standard signal detection model essentially assumes an ideal decision maker. Specifically, it assumes that the subject chooses a cutoff point on a decision axis (an axis monotonically related to the likelihood-ratio axis) and makes one choice for any observation below that cutoff and another for any observation above it. The subject is assumed to hold a static deterministic decision rule: It is deterministic

239

because to every possible observation corresponds only one of the two available responses; it is static because the cutoff is not assumed to shift.

Until quite recently, there has been relatively little concern for the development of process models, or nonnormative models, that describe the decision making in signal detection or, more generally, in probabilistic categorization. In this chapter, we present several information processing models of probabilistic categorization and summarize some of our empirical results in this area.

THE METHOD OF EXTERNALLY DISTRIBUTED OBSERVATIONS

Our main experimental paradigm has been the method of externally distributed observations. We have chosen this method because in standard signal detection tasks we do not know for a given trial how the randomness inherent in the noise affects the observations on which the subjects must base their decisions. In such tasks, the observations are said to be "internally distributed" (or, in Ulehla's, 1966, terminology, the presentation on each trial causes a "covert cue-producing response"). If, on the other hand, the observations are, for example, dots on a card drawn from one of two populations of dots—one population centered to the right of the card's midline, the other centered to the left—the experimenter can tell exactly which observation was presented to the subject on each trial. In such tasks, the observations are said to be "externally distributed."

To externalize observations does not entirely solve the problem. Even though the experimenter may know which observation was presented to the subject on each trial, there is no certainty regarding how the subject perceived the observation. There is, for instance, no assurance that subjects can reliably discriminate among close observations. Such is the case with the first study of externally distributed observations, the dot task previously described, performed by Lee (1963).

It is for this reason that Lee and Janke (1964) introduced the numerical decision paradigm. In this task, the observations are not only made external but also perfectly discriminable. Specifically, the observations are integer numbers drawn from two distributions S_1 and S_2. In our experiments with this paradigm, we instruct subjects that the observations represent the heights of men and women (in tenths of millimeters or in arbitrary units called "glocks") and that they are to decide for each observation which distribution it came from. (For an expanded discussion of this task, see Kubovy & Healy, 1977a, 1977b.[1])

Although our research has concentrated on the numerical decision task, we are aware of the possibility of task-specific decision processes. Indeed, we have

---

[1] Another use of the numerical decision task, which we overlooked in our reviews, is Pitz (1972).

investigated such effects in some detail. Although we have found some evidence for task-specific determinants of cutoff placement (Healy & Kubovy, 1977), the similarities among tasks are more striking than the differences (Healy & Kubovy, 1978).

TAXONOMY

In order to organize our discussion, we turn now to a taxonomy of decision models of probabilistic categorization with feedback. Two major classes are included: active and passive models. Active models are characterized by a monitoring process whereby subjects adjust their behavior so as to satisfy a well-specified decision goal. It is assumed that decision makers modify their behavior so as to reach a prechosen value of some quantity (such as the probability of obtaining an observation from one of the distributions given one of the responses) or so as to maximize the expected value of some index of performance (such as utility or number of correct responses). Passive models, on the other hand, do involve learning, but the learner is not assumed to have a well-specified decision goal. The passive models we consider are descendents of the classical stochastic learning models, such as stimulus-sampling theory and linear-operator models. It is difficult to devise empirical criteria to distinguish between active and passive models. One possible criterion refers to the subject's behavior at asymptote. An active model would predict asymptotic behavior that follows a fixed decision rule, whereas a passive model would predict asymptotic behavior that continues to fluctuate according to the same learning process as at the start of training.

Deterministic and Probabilistic Models

One important distinction holds for both active and passive models—the distinction between deterministic and probabilistic decision rules. This distinction parallels the one made by Luce and Suppes (1965) between algebraic and probabilistic theories of preference.

The deterministic models of interest for probabilistic categorization decisions are those with cutoff rules. Subjects are assumed to choose a cutoff point along the observation continuum. They then respond to any observation greater or equal to the cutoff point with R_2 ("man") and to any observation less than the cutoff point with R_1 ("woman"). Deterministic models do not imply static cutoff points, however. In fact, a number of dynamic deterministic models have been proposed in the literature (reviewed in Kubovy & Healy, 1977a).

In contrast to deterministic models, probabilistic models assign a probability (not equal to 0 or 1) to the binary responses for each possible observation.

Probabilistic models, like deterministic models, need not be static. In fact, probabilistic models have characteristically been formulated as stochastic learning models (also reviewed in Kubovy & Healy, 1977a).

We performed a numerical decision experiment designed to choose between deterministic and probabilistic models (Kubovy & Healy, 1977a). Two conditions were compared: In one condition, subjects were not constrained in their decision rule; in the second condition, the "cutoff report" condition, subjects were constrained to a cutoff rule (which could either be static or dynamic). Thus, if the unconstrained rule is probabilistic, there should be a difference between the two conditions. The statistic we used as a primary basis for comparison was the minimum number of violations of a static cutoff rule over a short block of trials (Kubovy, Rapoport, & Tversky, 1971). The computation of this statistic is illustrated in Fig. 13.1. A subject's behavior during a block of trials can be summarized by a performance curve, the cumulative probability of responding R_2 ("man") for each observation on the height dimension. The cutoff point that minimizes the number of violations of a cutoff rule is the "critical point" for that block, and the number of violations at that point is the statistic of interest.

Although we found a significant difference between the values of this statistic in our two experimental conditions, the mean minimum number of violations at a symptote for the unconstrained condition (about 5% violations) was much closer to that of the cutoff report condition (1.5% violations) than to that of the best available probabilistic model (Schoeffler, 1965) (over 18% violations obtained by simulation of the model at asymptote). In all other respects, there were no significant differences between the unconstrained and the cutoff report conditions, suggesting that the same decision rule was used in both conditions. Therefore, we tentatively concluded in favor of a deterministic model. Because subjects were not constrained to maintain their cutoff fixed across trials, we concluded in favor of a dynamic deterministic model. Our conclusion was tentative because the significant difference between the two experimental conditions could have been caused by (1) a true probabilistic component in the unconstrained condition; or (2) a task-specific reduction in the likelihood of cutoff shifts in the constrained condition (for example, a tendency to perseverate on the same response when it has to be externalized).

Despite any lingering uncertainty we may have on the empirical validity of deterministic models in probabilistic categorization, in the remainder of our chapter we are concerned exclusively with dynamic deterministic models. Our taxonomy of dynamic deterministic models (which is not meant to be exhaustive) is outlined in Fig. 13.2. We wish to stress that this taxonomy is provisional and should be considered only as a means of organizing the work we have done so far. This tree, like botanical trees, is likely to grow new branches, even if in the course of our research we prune some existing ones. During the remainder of this chapter, we examine all of its branches in turn, evaluating which branches should be trimmed off. We progress through the branches from left to right.

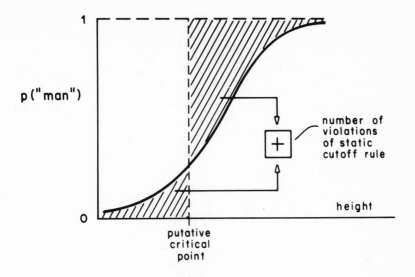

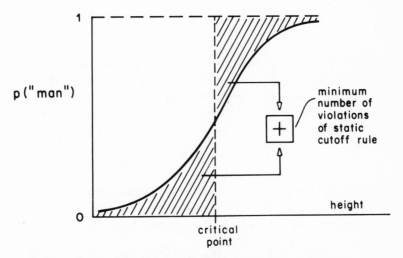

FIG. 13.1.   How to calculate the minimum number of violations of a static cutoff rule.

ACTIVE MODELS

Among the active models are three major subdivisions:

1. In the "quantitatively optimal model," subjects seek to maximize expected value by adjusting their cutoff point on a likelihood-ratio scale. This

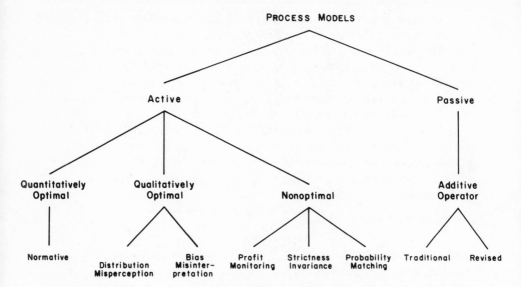

FIG. 13.2.   Taxonomy of decision models of probabilistic categorization with feedback.

model embodies a general Bayesian learner coupled with an ideal decision maker. Fig. 13.3 is a block diagram (adapted from Tanner & Sorkin, 1972) depicting the components of this model. This model is the normative model. As we remark later, subjects do not conform to the normative model when payoffs are not symmetric or prior probabilities are unequal. Hence, we limit our discussion to suboptimal models.

2. In the "qualitatively optimal models" (akin to Tanner & Sorkin's, 1972, "modified ideal observer"), again subjects seek to maximize expected value by adjusting their cutoff point; however, either the learner is not Bayesian or the biaser is not ideal, or both. The diagram in Fig. 13.3 holds for this type of model as it does for the quantitatively optimal model. This class of models has the advantage of being able to account for nonoptimal performance, such as observed under conditions of unequal prior probabilities or asymmetric payoff matrices.

3. In the "nonoptimal models," the subject's behavior does not conform to the diagram in Fig. 13.3 in some respect. For example, the subject's decision goal may not require the calculation of likelihood ratios. In such a case, the likelihood-ratio computer included in the diagram of Fig. 13.3 would be replaced by a computer that calculates another statistic. For example, if the decision goal were to probability match (Parks, 1966), the statistic computer would be the current proportions of R_2 responses and S_2 observations.

Because people do not obey the quantitatively optimal model, it is interesting to inquire into the nature and causes of their suboptimality. Several types of nonoptimality are possible:

1. People may or may not know the optimal rule. For example, a person may not know that in probabilistic categorization a cutoff rule should be used.

2. People may or may not choose the optimal rule, even when they know what that rule is. For instance, psychologists who know signal-detection theory and who are placed in a signal-detection task may choose to apply a simpler strategy, even though they know the optimal one. This type of behavior has been labeled *satisficing* by Simon (1969).

3. People may or may not be able to apply the rule they have chosen. For instance, information-processing limitations may lead an individual to apply an imperfect version of the suboptimal strategy chosen. Table 13.1 outlines the possible combinations of these various alternative causes of suboptimality.

Qualitatively Optimal Models

The Distribution Misconception Conjecture.   It has been observed that subjects choose a cutoff point that is less extreme than one that would maximize expected value (Green & Swets, 1974). We call this pattern of behavior "conservative cutoff placement." Kubovy (1977) has proposed that conservative cutoff placement could be caused by a misconception of the two distributions of observations that leads to overestimating likelihood ratios that are greater than one and underestimating likelihood ratios that are less than one. We refer to this

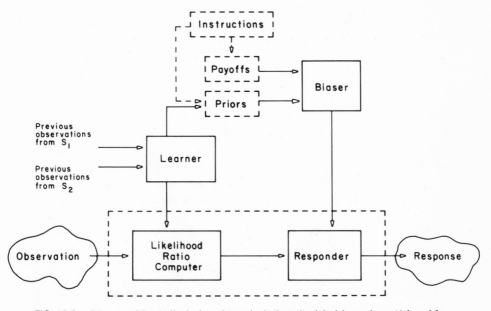

FIG. 13.3.   Diagram of the qualitatively and quantitatively optimal decision makers. (Adapted from Tanner & Sorkin, 1972l.)

TABLE 13.1
Alternative Causes of Suboptimality

Rule Chosen	Knows Optimal Rule		Does Not Know Optimal Rule	
	Perfect Application	Imperfect Application	Perfect Application	Imperfect Application
Optimal	Quantitatively optimal	Qualitatively optimal	—	—
Nonoptimal	Nonoptimal satisficing	Suboptimal application of nonoptimal satisficing	Nonoptimal	Suboptimal application of nonoptimal

pattern as "radical likelihood-ratio estimation." Such a pattern would result from a disregard for rare events in the tails of the distributions.

Indeed, Kubovy (1977) found evidence for such a pattern in a numerical decision task. Specifically, subjects were required to give posterior probability judgments for a set of observations to which they had been exposed previously over a large number (six) of sessions. Because prior probabilities were equal in this experiment, the relationship between posterior probability and likelihood ratio may be expressed as follows: $P(S_2|x) = l(x)/[l(x) + 1]$, where $P(S_2|x)$ is the posterior probability that an observation x was from distribution S_2, and $l(x)$ is the likelihood ratio of observation x. Hence, overestimates of posterior probabilities imply overestimates of likelihood ratios, and underestimates of posterior probabilities imply underestimates of likelihood ratios. Fig. 13.4 shows typical results from three sessions of posterior probability judgments by two subjects in that experiment. These results are clear indications of the pattern of radical posterior probability estimation and, hence, of radical likelihood-ratio estimation.

Testing the Conjecture: Providing Quantitative and Qualitative Information. In order to determine the optimal cutoff point, we can decompose the information needed into thee parts: (1) information from the payoffs; (2) information from prior probabilities; (3) information from the distributions. As previously mentioned, Kubovy (1977) conjectured that information from the distributions was being inadequately processed, leading to conservative cutoff placement.

In an experiment (conducted in collaboration with Martin Guyote), we tested this conjecture in the case of equal prior probabilities, leaving two possible sources of conservative cutoff placement: payoffs and distributions. Our procedure was to isolate each of the two sources of information by providing subjects with one or the other type of information that they would normally have to acquire or derive on their own. Specifically, three tasks were employed: (1) a

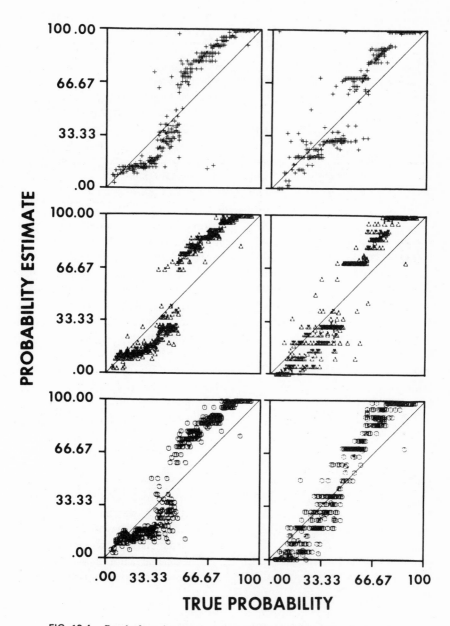

FIG. 13.4.   Results from three sessions (rows) for two typical subjects (columns) reported by Kubovy (1977).

standard binary decision (yes/no) task; (2) a cutoff report task, as we employed
earlier (Kubovy & Healy, 1977a); and (3) a posterior probability judgment task,
as employed by Kubovy (1977).

Fig. 13.5 summarizes the design of this experiment. All subjects began with
the standard binary decision task, after which all were switched to the cutoff
report task. After 100 trials in the latter task, the subjects were assigned to four
groups, differing in the kind of normative information provided to them regarding performance of the task for the subsequent cutoff report trials. The *first
group* ("uninformed") continued performing the cutoff report task without any
additional information. The *second group* ("qualitative information") was given
information that could enable them to become qualitatively optimal. In particular, subjects in this group were told that two kinds of information were necessary
for optimal performance: (1) information about how the structure of the payoff
matrix should influence the choice of cutoff; and (2) information about how the
structure of the distributions should affect the choice of cutoff. The *third group*
("bias information") was provided with the qualitative information given to the
second group followed by quantitative information concerning where to place
their cutoff on the posterior probability continuum in order to maximize expected
value. This information was provided in the form of a posterior probability.
Thus, for the condition where optimal β was 1/4, the optimal cutoff was described as the height at which 20% of the people with that height are men, and

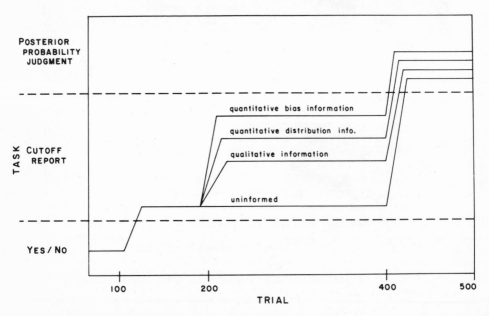

FIG. 13.5.   Design of the experiment providing quantitative and qualitative decision information.

80% of the people with that height are women. The *fourth group* ("distribution information") was also provided with the qualitative information, followed by quantitative information about the distributions. In all subsequent trials, after each observation was presented to the subjects, they were shown the posterior probability that the given observation represented the height of a man. In addition, subjects in this group gave the cutoff report in the form of a two-digit posterior probability rather than a five-digit height. The computer controlling this experiment translated the subjects' reported cutoffs into five-digit heights, which were displayed for the subjects. After 200 additional cutoff report trials, all the subjects performed the posterior probability judgment task.

A preliminary analysis was performed on the posterior probability judgments in order to determine whether the information given to subjects in the distribution information group was understood and retained. The root–mean-square deviation (RMSD) of the obtained posterior probability judgments from the correct posterior probabilities was computed. The RMSD for the distribution information condition was significantly smaller than that for the other three conditions. This analysis confirms that the distribution information condition did lead to superior knowledge about the distributions.

We conducted an analysis to determine whether subjects placed their cutoffs less conservatively in the distribution information group or in the bias information group than in the other groups. Our index of conservative cutoff placement was the directed distance between the median cutoff report for a 50-trial block and the optimal cutoff point for that condition.[2] We found that subjects in the bias information group did not show a significant degree of conservatism in the final block of trials. In contrast, subjects in both the distribution information group and the uninformed group did show a significant amount of conservatism in that block.

These results imply that if subjects are qualitatively optimal, then whatever conservatism they manifest is due to the bias component of the process underlying cutoff placement rather than to the distribution learning component of this process.

Testing the Conjecture: Comparing Ratings and Binary Responses.   Another reason why a qualitatively optimal subject may not be quantitatively optimal has to do with the binary nature of the response. Green and Swets (1974) have pointed out that holding an extreme cutoff necessitates making the same response on almost all trials, behavior that subjects may consider inconsistent with the

---

[2]Unfortunately, the qualitative information group started out less conservative than the other groups, and, moreover, had a significantly greater intersubject variability in conservatism. Thus, although this condition was designed as a control condition, we discuss the results without reference to the data of this group.

demands of a probabilistic categorization task. This explanation of conservatism locates its source in the bias component, rather than the distribution learning component.

In order to test this conjecture, we decided to compare the standard binary-response procedure to a rating procedure, because it is possible to hold an extreme cutoff in a rating task without making the same response on all trials. Hence, to the standard numerical decision paradigm, we added a rating-scale technique. Such a procedure had been used by Lee (1963) and Lee and Zentall (1966) in their tasks with externally distributed observations, but it had not yet been employed in the numerical decision situation. Further, none of the previous studies using a rating-scale technique compared the location of the cutoffs under rating and binary-response procedures. Because we wished to compare the binary and the rating-scale procedures, we introduced explicit payoffs for the various rating categories, as follows:

		Rating					
		1	*2*	...	*j*	...	*m*
Distribution	S_2	V_{21}	V_{22}	...	V_{2j}	...	V_{2m}
	S_1	V_{11}	V_{12}	...	V_{1j}	...	V_{1m}

V_{ij} is the payoff for making the rating response j to an observation from distribution S_i. It should be noted that one can require subjects to order the boundaries between their rating categories in a manner consistent with the rating numbers only if the payoffs satisfy the following inequality:

$$\frac{V_{1j} - V_{1(j + 1)}}{V_{2(j + 1)} - V_{2j}} < \frac{V_{1(j + 1)} - V_{1(j + 2)}}{V_{2(j + 2)} - V_{2(j + 1)}} ,$$

for all $i \leq j \leq m - 2$. By adding the payoff matrix to the rating scale, we were able to specify exactly where the subjects should place their cutoffs. By specifying in this way the same cutoff locations in the rating scale and binary-decision tasks, we were able to compare the two procedures more precisely than had been done previously. The subjects in our experiment were divided into four groups depending on task and response type: binary, binary cutoff report, rating, and rating cutoff report. In each of the two groups giving binary responses, there were five subgroups, corresponding to different payoff matrices, implying optimal β values of 1/4, 1/3, 1, 3, and 4, respectively. Likewise, in each group giving rating responses, there were two subgroups, corresponding to two different four-category rating payoff matrices, one implying optimal β values of 1/4, 1, and 3, and the other implying optimal β values of 1/3, 1, and 4.

The results from this experiment are summarized in Fig. 13.6, which shows the critical points averaged over subjects and blocks as a function of task, response type, and optimal value of β. Subjects in both tasks were less conservative in their cutoff placement when giving ratings than when giving binary responses. These results support Green and Swets's (1974) explanation of conservative cutoff placement, and further support the general notion that conser-

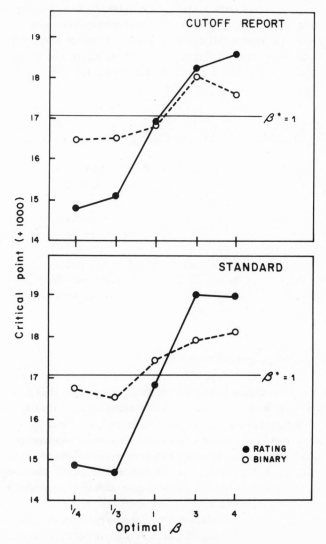

FIG. 13.6.   Critical points averaged over subjects and blocks as a function of task, response type, and optimal β. $\beta^* = 1$ denotes the optimal cutoff location when $\beta = 1$.

vatism is due to the bias component of the decision process, rather than to the distribution learning component.

Understanding the Payoff Matrix: Naive Cost-Benefit Analysis.   In the experiment previously described on the effects on cutoff placement of providing qualitative and quantitative information (conducted with Martin Guyote), we found that when we provided quantitative information on where to place the cutoff, subjects were not conservative in the final block of trials. Although we concluded that subjects have difficulty using the information in the payoff matrix to determine the placement of their cutoff point, we do not have a process model of payoff matrix use. There is, however, on intuitive grounds, reason to believe that subjects may transpose the payoff matrix. The formula for the computation of optimal β is:

$$\beta = \frac{V(S_1, R_1) - V(S_1, R_2)}{V(S_2, R_2) - V(S_2, R_1)} \cdot \frac{P(S_1)}{P(S_2)}$$

where $V(S_i, R_j)$ is the payoff for response R_j given an observation from distribution S_i. It is possible that the subject computes β_r, where the roles of distribution and response are reversed, instead of β:

$$\beta_r = \frac{V(S_1, R_1) - V(S_2, R_1)}{V(S_2, R_2) - V(S_1, R_2)} \cdot \frac{P(S_1)}{P(S_2)}$$

The substitution of β_r for β is similar to the fallacy of *affirming the consequent*. For instance, consider the following fallacious reasoning:

1. If the object is rectangular, then it is blue.
2. The object is blue.
3. Therefore, the object is rectangular.

This rather prevalent fallacy (see Wason & Johnson-Laird, 1972) demonstrates not only that individuals have a problem understanding conditionals, but also, in particular, that they have a tendency to reverse the two terms in a conditional. Subjects might therefore interpret the matrix as if the rows representing distributions and the columns representing responses were transposed. This hypothesis is all the more plausible because (1) the correct identity of the distribution is divulged to the subject only after the response; and (2) the subject has control over the response but not the distribution.

In order to test this hypothesis, we conducted an experiment that varied payoff matrix across subjects. Four payoff matrices were chosen, so that two of them had an optimal β of 1, and two had an optimal β of 5. Furthermore, one matrix in each of these two groups had a β_r of 1, and the other had a β_r of 5. The payoff

TABLE 13.2
Payoff Matrices Used in Experiment on Understanding the Payoff Matrix

	Payoff Matrix						
	$\beta = 1$				$\beta = 5$		
	$\beta_r = 1$		$\beta_r = 5$		$\beta_r = 1$		$\beta_r = 5$	
	R_1	R_2	R_1	R_2	R_1	R_2	R_1	R_2
S_2	0	1	-2	1	0	1	0	1
S_1	1	0	3	0	3	-2	5	0

matrices are shown in Table 13.2. A standard binary-response procedure was employed.

We computed the critical point for each block of 50 trials. The critical point for the blocks with optimal $\beta = 1$ was significantly lower than the critical point for the blocks with optimal $\beta = 5$. Although the effect of β_r was not significant, the interaction of β with β_r was significant. The mean critical points showing this interaction are given in Table 13.3 under Experiment 1.

In order to determine whether this interaction was due to the specific costs and benefits chosen for this experiment, rather than the values of β and β_r, we performed an additional experiment that studied three sets of payoff matrices: One set was identical to that used in the first experiment. The second set of matrices was identical to the first except that each entry of each of the payoff matrices was increased by 3, so that all values were positive. Similarly, the third set of matrices was identical to the first except that each entry of each of the payoff matrices was decreased by 6, so that all values were negative. Again, a binary response procedure was employed, and payoff matrix was a between-subjects factor.

The results are summarized in Table 13.3 under Experiment 2 in terms of mean critical points. For the first set of matrices, which was also used in the first experiment, the interaction of β and β_r was again obtained. In contrast, we did not find such an interaction for the other two sets of matrices, although the effect of β was significant for all three sets of payoff matrices. Hence, we must conclude that subjects are sensitive to the particular entries in the payoff matrix, in a way that is inconsistent both with the normative theory, and with the notion advanced earlier concerning β_r. The data suggest that some additional process is applied to the subjects' interpretation of the payoff matrix when they are in the presence of both positive and negative entries in the matrix. The nature of that additional process is not yet clear, however.[3]

---

[3]On the special nature of negative payoffs, or costs, see Kahneman and Tversky (1979).

TABLE 13.3
Mean Critical Points as a Function of β, β_r, and Type of Payoff Matrices

| | Payoff Matrix | | | |
| | $\beta = 1$ | | $\beta = 5$ | |
Type	$\beta_r = 1$	$\beta_r = 5$	$\beta_r = 1$	$\beta_r = 5$
		Experiment 1		
Original	17378	16629	18180	18985
		Experiment 2		
Original	17201	16118	17671	18265
All positive	17006	16914	18125	17813
All negative	17025	16586	17479	17288

Payoffs Versus Priors. Up to this point in our discussion, we have been concerned only with situations in which priors are equal and payoffs are asymmetric. However, conservative cutoff placement has also been found in situations in which priors are unequal and payoffs are symmetric (for example, Healy & Jones, 1975; Healy & Kubovy, 1977). Determining whether the extent of conservatism is comparable in the two situations (equal priors and asymmetric payoffs versus unequal priors and symmetric payoffs) should help us pinpoint the underlying cause of conservatism. We have not yet completed an experiment with such a comparison for the numerical decision paradigm, but we have compared the two situations in a recognition–memory task (Healy & Kubovy, 1978).

Specifically, a recognition–memory task in which payoffs were fixed at symmetric values and priors varied across blocks of a given subject's session was compared to a task in which priors were equal and payoffs varied across blocks. In each case, the optimal value of β was 1 for half the blocks and 3 for the remaining blocks. The extent of conservative cutoff placement was found to be comparable in the two situations. The observed values of β were larger in the blocks in which optimal β was 3 than when optimal β was 1, but the difference between the observed values of β in the two types of blocks was much smaller than 2 and of comparable magnitude in the two tasks. Unless the correspondence between the magnitudes of conservatism in the two tasks was purely coincidental, the bias misinterpretation hypothesis cannot account for these results.

Before we deal with the next class of models, the nonoptimal models, we pause to summarize our findings to this point. Our evidence appears to favor the bias misinterpretation version of the qualitatively optimal model. We have not, however, been able to develop the bias misinterpretation model so as to account for our experiments on payoff matrix manipulation. Furthermore, the bias misinterpretation approach cannot account for the comparable effects of payoffs and priors on cutoff placement. On the basis of a preliminary examination of data from a numerical decision experiment that we conducted recently, we have reason to suspect, though, that the correspondence between the effects of payoffs and priors we observed earlier in recognition memory may have been a mere coincidence.

Nonoptimal Models

A Nonoptimal Process that Attempts to Maximize Expected Utility.   In collaboration with Jerry Ketron, we have formulated a simple process model that implies conservatism without assuming that subjects are concerned with computing the optimal cutoff on the basis of the payoff matrix or with learning the distributions. Yet, subjects are assumed to formulate a specific decision goal, namely to maximize expected utility (monetary profit). Specifically, we assume that subjects initially place their cutoffs close to the mean of the observations and shift them until they perceive that no additional gain can be expected from further shifting. Because the function relating expected utility to cutoff location (which we shall refer to as the "cutoff–utility function") changes very little in the general region of the optimal cutoff point, we predict that the change in expected utility as a function of cutoff shift will become virtually imperceptible to subjects at a point that is conservative.

In order to test this notion, we conducted with Jerry Ketron an experiment in which we varied, orthogonally and between subjects, optimal d' and optimal β, while keeping prior probabilities equal. We varied d' by translating the distribution of men's heights (S_2) so that d' was .5, 1.0, or 1.5. β was varied by employing three different payoff matrices, implying optimal βs of 1, 2, and 3. For different values of d', the slope of the cutoff–utility function differs for equal values of the likelihood ratio. If the model previously described is correct, we should find differences in cutoff location on the log-likelihood ratio continuum as a function of d' as well as β, in the direction specified by the slope of the cutoff–utility function. Preliminary analyses provided some support for the model, but further work is necessary.

A Nonoptimal Process that Attempts to Keep Strictness Constant.   The decision–theoretic analyses of the quantitatively optimal and the qualitatively optimal varieties assume that whether or not explicit payoffs are provided to subjects, they interpret the instructions as containing implicit payoffs. Hence, in all cases, their decision goal would be to maximize expected utility. However, this need not be so. For example, consider the case in which subjects are not given explicit payoffs but are given instructions to be strict or lax. In such a situation, subjects may choose to regulate hit and false-alarm rates, the probability of obtaining an observation from distribution i given the j-th response,[4] or some comparable index. This is true a fortiriori of subjects who are told explicitly

---

[4]This index, $P(S_i|R_j)$, has sometimes been called the "posterior probability."

to regulate hit and false-alarm rates (Egan, Schulman, & Greenberg, 1959), or to regulate $P(S_i|R_j)$ (Clarke, 1960); they must adopt decision goals incompatible with maximization of expected utility in order to follow instructions. It is not inconceivable, moreover, that subjects adopt such nonoptimal goals even when given an explicit payoff matrix. In other words, subjects may translate the payoff matrix into instructions to attain a given level of strictness, in which case they would choose the same sort of decision goal as they would in the absence of a payoff matrix.

We wish to stress the difference between the notion of strictness and the notion of bias. Whereas bias is ideally independent of sensitivity and is affected by both payoffs and prior probabilities, we think of strictness as being necessarily independent only of prior probabilities. Strictness should be affected by payoffs (and by instructions), but it is not clear whether or not strictness should be affected by sensitivity, and if so, how it should be affected. In any event, because subjects may take sensitivity into account in selecting a given level of strictness, the form of isobias curves (obtained by holding bias constant and varying sensitivity) should not be used as evidence for determining the nature of the strictness index, as Dusoir (1975) mistakenly proposed with respect to the index we describe next.

A plausible interpretation of instructions to be lax or strict, according to Healy and Jones (1973), involves the ratio of hits to false alarms that subjects allow themselves to make. If instructed to be strict, subjects allow themselves very few false alarms, relative to the number of hits they make, whereas instructions to be lax indicate to subjects that they may allow themselves many false alarms relative to the number of hits. It should be noted that as β increases, so does the ratio of hit rate to false-alarm rate. When prior probabilities are constant, the ratio of hit rate to false-alarm rate is directly proportional to the ratio of hits to false alarms. However, when prior probabilities are not constant, the ratio of hit rate to false-alarm rate is not proportional to the ratio of hits to false alarms. Hence, β does not reflect the ratio of hits to false alarms. Indeed, with changes in prior probabilities, β can remain constant although subjects' decisions become either more strict or more lax in terms of the number of false alarms that they allow for each hit. Conversely, β can change with a change in prior probabilities, even if subjects are being neither more strict nor more lax in terms of the ratio of hits to false alarms.

Healy and Jones (1973) have proposed a "strictness index," which—unlike β—is a function of the ratio of hits to false alarms. In a task with n ($n > 1$) confidence ratings ($R_n, R_{n-1}, \ldots, R_1$), this index for the highest (n-th) rating is $P(S_2|R_n)$, the probability of an item being from distribution S_2, given that the highest rating was used. More generally, the index for the j-th rating ($1 < j \leq n$) is $P(S_2|R_n \text{ or } R_{n-1} \text{ or} \ldots \text{ or } R_j)$. This index changes or remains constant just when the ratio of hits to false alarms does. In addition, as Healy and Jones (1975) point out, this index has intuitive appeal. For example, it seems reasonable to demand that subjects hold constant the probability that an item to which they give the highest rating is in fact from S_2. That is, when the prior probability of an item from S_2 changes, subjects may change the number of items they rate R_n, but those items rated R_n should be just as likely to be from S_2 as before the change in prior probability.

Healy and Jones (1973) reviewed some evidence from recall and intelligibility experiments that subjects did maintain a constant strictness index under some circumstances (although not under others). However, in a recognition–memory task, Healy and Jones (1975) found that subjects were not able to maintain a constant strictness index even when specifically instructed to do so and given appropriate feedback. Furthermore, Dusoir (1975) has pointed out that maintaining a constant strictness index may lead to performance below chance level (i.e., hit rate lower than false-alarm rate) under some circumstances and under other circumstances may be impossible (because a hit rate greater than 1 would be required). The implications of Dusoir's findings are interesting not only in terms of the strictness index but also in terms of the probabilities $P(S_i|R_j)$, because holding the strictness index constant is equivalent to holding $P(S_i|R_j)$ constant in a binary response procedure and for the highest rating in a rating procedure. Hence, experimenters like Clarke (1960) who instruct subjects to maintain a given value of $P(S_i|R_j)$ may be imposing unrealistic requirements on their subjects.

However, when the prior probabilities are known in advance, and subjects are permitted to choose any value of strictness or of $P(S_i|R_j)$ they wish, the objection raised by Dusoir does not pose a problem. For a given set of prior probabilities known in advance, subjects may maintain their strictness constant by selecting strictness within the following range: $P(S_2)/P(S_1) \leqslant k \leqslant [P(S_2)/P(S_1)]/FAR$, where FAR is the false-alarm rate and k is the value of the ratio of hits to false alarms. Within this range, hit rate will not be less than false-alarm rate or greater than 1.

To choose k for a set of conditions with changing prior probability levels, subjects should set the prior odds on the left hand of the inequality to the highest ones anticipated, the prior odds on the right hand of the inequality to the lowest ones anticipated, and the false-alarm rate to any value smaller than the ratio of the smallest prior odds to the largest prior odds. The particular value of k selected within this range will presumably be determined by instructions, payoffs, and possibly d'. Once k is chosen, for each level of prior probability, the upper bound for the false-alarm rate is given by the ratio of the prior odds to k. This constraint is probably not so severe as to prohibit subjects from both maintaining constant strictness and adopting a cutoff for typical values of d' and $P(S_2)$. For example, we have been able to calculate cutoff values for a subject who maintains strictness at a constant value ($k = 10$) when d' equals 1.5 and $P(S_2)$ ranges from 1/9 to 9/10.

A Nonoptimal Process that Attempts to Probability Match.   A process that does not have the drawbacks of the strictness index is the probability matching process proposed by Parks (1966) and Thomas and Legge (1970). Unlike the approach considered earlier, Parks and Thomas and Legge assume that subjects necessarily adopt a cutoff rule. They suggest that subjects set their cutoffs so that they will give the response R_2 to a number of items proportional to the number of S_2 stimuli in the task. More formally, the probability-matching rule is $P(R_2) = $ minimum$[kP(S_2),1]$, where k is a function of the payoff matrix, and presumably $k = 1$ when there is no bias favoring either of the two responses. This rule can be thought of as an alternative index of strictness by rewriting it as follows: $P(R_2)/P(S_2) = k$ [except when $P(R_2) = 1$]. Atkinson and Kinchla (1965), Creelman and Donaldson (1968), Dorfman (1969), Parks (1966), Parks and Kellicut (1968), Thomas (1973), and Thomas and Legge (1970) all present data in support of this rule in sensory as well as recogniton–memory tasks. However, as Thomas (1975) pointed out, the probability-matching hypothesis has not always fared well: Subjects are generally more conservative than probability matching predicts. Furthermore, in a numerical decision task, we have presented evidence inconsistent with the probability-matching hypothesis at the individual (but not the group) level (Kubovy & Healy, 1977a).

PASSIVE MODELS

Behavior such as probability matching could be caused by an active strategy on the part of subjects who adopt a well-specified decision goal, or by a passive process such as specified in classic learning models, which are considered in the present section. As mentioned earlier, we consider only cutoff models, because our earlier work ruled out probabilistic models.

One class of model has been proposed to describe the process whereby the cutoff shifts as the decision maker learns to perform the decision task: additive-operator models. The following formulation generalizes all the existing additive-operator dynamic-cutoff models:[5]

Assume that on trial n, the cutoff is c_n and an observation is drawn from distribution S_i and the response outcome O_j is O_E if the response is incorrect and O_C if the response is correct. There is a probability P_{ij} that the cutoff will change to:

$$c_{n+1} = \begin{cases} c_n + d_{1j} & \text{if } i = 1, \\ c_n - d_{2j} & \text{if } i = 2, \end{cases}$$

where $d_{ij} \geq 0$ for all i, j; the probability that the cutoff will remain unchanged is $1 - p_{ij}$:

$$c_{n+1} = c_n.$$

---

[5]A number of additive-operator dynamic-cutoff models have been proposed and studied by Biderman, Dorfman, and Simpson (1975); Dorfman (1973); Dorfman and Biderman (1971); Dorman, Saslow, and Simpson (1975); Kac (1962, 1969); Larkin (1971); Norman (1970, 1972); and Thomas (1973, 1975).

More concretely, suppose that on trial n, the cutoff is c_n and an observation is drawn from distribution S_1, and the subject responded R_2; thus, the response was erroneous and the response outcome is O_E. Then there is a probability p_{1E} that the cutoff on trial $n + 1$ will be $c_{n+1} = c_n + d_{1E}$, and a probability $1 - p_{1E}$ that $c_{n+1} = c_n$—that is, remains unchanged. If the cutoff shifts at all, it will always shift up after an observation was drawn from S_1 (the distribution with the lower mean), and it will always shift down after an observation was drawn from S_2.

In a numerical decision task, we have provided evidence against all existing additive-operator models (Kubovy & Healy, 1977a). In particular, although cutoff shifts after errors were generally in the direction specified by the additive-operator models, there were also shifts in the opposite direction. Furthermore, after correct responses, there were more shifts in the direction opposite to that predicted by the additive-operator dynamic-cutoff models than in the predicted direction.

Although the traditional additive-operator dynamic-cutoff models have been ruled out, the type of model that is suggested by our data (Kubovy & Healy, 1977a) has the following properties:

1. After most errors, subjects shift their cutoff in the direction that will reduce the likelihood of the recurrence of the same type of error.
2. On a small percentage of the trials following errors, subjects shift their cutoff in the direction associated with the gambler's fallacy (according to which the subject believes that the following observation is more likely than is implied by the prior probabilities to be drawn from the distribution not sampled on the present trial).
3. On most trials following correct responses, subjects shift their cutoff randomly in one or the other direction.
4. On the remaining trials following correct responses, subjects shift their cutoff in the direction associated with the gambler's fallacy.

This model could be called a "lose—shift, win—be confused" model, with a sprinkling of gambler's fallacy added on. Although this model has been proposed for the situation with equal priors and symmetric payoffs, it is easily generalizable to other conditions. In particular, what may change is the subjects' tendency to shift in a given direction. The interesting possibility is that no change in the probabilities of shift may occur when only priors are unequal, and that the probabilities would change only if payoffs are made asymmetric.

CONCLUSIONS

We have applied the pruners of Occam and others to our tree of process models for probabilistic-categorization decisions, although we have not reached that ideal (but perhaps not esthetically pleasing state) of a single-branched tree.

Before we began this discussion, we pruned the tree of all branches involving probabilistic models, and at the very beginning of our labors, we cut off the branch of quantitatively optimal models. Subsequently, we cut a twig on the qualitatively optimal branch (namely the one corresponding to the conjecture that conservatism is due to a misperception of the distributions). We also affected two twigs on the nonoptimal branch: (1) We have bruised the strictness–invariance hypothesis; (2) we have weakened the probability-matching hypothesis branch, although it will require some more work before we can get it to fall off the tree. Finally, we have cut off all twigs involving the traditional passive additive-operator dynamic-cutoff models.

Branches still remain both on the active and the passive sides of the tree. On the active side, we still entertain qualitatively optimal and nonoptimal models. Of the qualitatively optimal models, the bias misinterpretation model appears to be the most promising. Of the nonoptimal models, the profit-monitoring and probability-matching approaches appear to have the most merit. Finally, of the passive models, our revised "lose—shift, win—be confused" model is most worthy of further considerations.

ACKNOWLEDGMENTS

The authors contributed equally to this chapter; thus, order of authorship should not be interpreted. Michael Kubovy is now at Rutgers University (Busch Campus), New Brunswick, N.J. The research described here was supported by BNS77-00077 from the National Science Foundation to Yale University. A. F. Healy was supported by a Junior Faculty Fellowship from Yale University during the preparation of this chapter. We are grateful to Tom Wallsten, Martin Guyote, Jerry Ketron, and Loretta Polka for their helpful comments on this chapter.

REFERENCES

Atkinson, R. C., & Kinchla, R. A. A learning model for forced-choice detection experiments. *British Journal of Mathematical and Statistical Psychology*, 1965, *18*, 183–206.

Biderman, M., Dorfman, D. D., & Simpson, J. C. A learning model for signal detection theory— Temporal invariance of learning parameters. *Bulletin of the Psychonomic Society*, 1975, *6*, 329–330.

Clarke, F. R. Confidence ratings, second-choice responses and confusion matrices in intelligibility tests. *Journal of the Acoustical Society of America*, 1960, *32*, 35–46.

Creelman, C. D., & Donaldson, W. ROC curves for discrimination of visual extent. *Journal of Experimental Psychology*, 1968, *77*, 514–516.

Dorfman, D. D. Probability matching in signal detection. *Psychonomic Science*, 1969, *17*, 103.

Dorfman, D. D. The likelihood function of additive learning models: Sufficient conditions for strict log-concavity and uniqueness of maximum. *Journal of Mathematical Psychology*, 1973, *10*, 73–85.

Dorfman, D. D., & Biderman, M. A learning model for a continuum of sensory states. *Journal of Mathematical Psychology*, 1971, *8*, 264-284.

Dorfman, D. D., Saslow, C. F., & Simpson, J. C. Learning models for a continuum of sensory states reexamined. *Journal of Mathematical Psychology*, 1975, *12*, 178-211.

Dusoir, A. E. Treatments of bias in detection and recognition models: A review. *Perception & Psychophysics*, 1975, *17*, 167-178.

Egan, J. P. *Signal detection theory and ROC analysis*. New York: Academic Press, 1975.

Egan, J. P., Schulman, A. I., & Greenberg, G. Z. Operating characteristics determined by binary decisions and by ratings. *Journal of the Acoustical Society of America*, 1959, *31*, 768-773.

Green, D. M., & Swets, J. A. *Signal detection theory and psychophysics*. Huntington, N.Y.: Krieger, 1974 (originally published, 1966).

Healy, A. F., & Jones, C. Criterion shifts in recall. *Psychological Bulletin*, 1973, *79*, 335-340.

Healy, A. F., & Jones, C. Can subjects maintain a constant criterion in a memory task? *Memory & Cognition*, 1975, *3*, 233-238.

Healy, A. F., & Kubovy, M. A comparison of recognition memory to numerical decision: How prior probabilities affect cutoff location. *Memory & Cognition*, 1977, *5*, 3-9.

Healy, A. F., & Kubovy, M. The effect of payoffs and prior probabilities on indices of performance and cutoff location in recognition memory. *Memory & Cognition*, 1978, *6*, 544-553.

Kac, M. A note on learning signal detection. *IRE Transactions on Information Theory*, 1962, *IT-8*, 126-128.

Kac, M. Some mathematical models in science. *Science*, 1969, *166*, 695-699.

Kahneman, D., & Tversky, A. Prospect theory: An analysis of decision and risk. *Econometrica*, 1979, *47*, 263-291.

Kubovy, M. A possible basis for conservatism in signal detection and probabilistic categorization tasks. *Perception & Psychophysics*, 1977, *22*, 277-281.

Kubovy, M., & Healy, A. F. The decision rule in probabilistic categorization: What it is and how it is learned. *Journal of Experimental Psychology: General*, 1977, *106*, 427-446. (a)

Kubovy, M., & Healy, A. F. Numerical decision and the ideal learner: A reply to Dorfman. *Journal of Experimental Psychology: General*, 1977, *106*, 450-452. (b)

Kubovy, M., Rapoport, A., & Tversky, A. Deterministic vs. probabilistic strategies in detection. *Perception & Psychophysics*, 1971, *9*, 427-429.

Larkin, W. Response mechanisms in detection experiments. *Journal of Experimental Psychology*, 1971, *91*, 140-153.

Lee, W. Choosing among confusably distributed stimuli with specific likelihood ratios. *Perceptual and Motor Skills*, 1963, *16*, 445-467.

Lee, W., & Janke, M. Categorizing externally distributed stimulus samples for three continua. *Journal of Experimental Psychology*, 1964, *68*, 376-382.

Lee, W., & Zentall, T. R. Factorial effects in the categorization of externally distributed stimulus samples. *Perception & Psychophysics*, 1966, *1*, 120-124.

Luce, R. D., & Suppes, P. Preference, utility, and subjective probability. In R. D. Luce, R. R. Bush, & E. Galanter (Eds.). *The handbook of mathematical psychology* (Vol. 3). New York: Wiley, 1965.

Norman, M. F. Limit theorems for additive learning models. *Journal of Mathematical Psychology*, 1970, *7*, 1-11.

Norman, M. F. *Markov processes and learning models*. New York: Academic Press, 1972.

Parks, T. E. Signal-detectability theory of recognition-memory performance. *Psychological Review*, 1966, *73*, 44-58.

Parks, T. E., & Kellicut, M. H. The probability-matching rule in the visual discrimination of order. *Perception & Psychophysics*, 1968, *3*, 356-360.

Pitz, G. F. Simultaneous information integration in decisions concerning normal populations. *Organizational Behavior and Human Performance*, 1972, *8*, 325-339.

Schoeffler, M. S. Theory for psychophysical learning. *Journal of the Acoustical Society of America,* 1965, *37,* 1124–1133.

Simon, H. A. *The sciences of the artificial.* Cambridge, Mass.: M.I.T. Press, 1969.

Tanner, W. P., Jr., & Sorkin, R. D. The theory of signal detectability. In J. V. Tobias (Ed.). *Foundations of modern auditory theory* (Vol. 2). New York: Academic Press, 1972.

Thomas, E. A. C. On a class of additive learning models: Error correcting and probability matching. *Journal of Mathematical Psychology,* 1973, *10,* 241–264.

Thomas, E. A. C. Criterion adjustment and probability matching. *Perception & Psychophysics,* 1975, *18,* 158–162.

Thomas, E. A. C., & Legge, D. Probability matching as a basis for detection and recognition decisions. *Psychological Review,* 1970, *77,* 65–72.

Ulehla, Z. J. Optimality of perceptual decision criteria. *Journal of Experimental Psychology,* 1966, *71,* 564–569.

Wason, P. C., & Johnson-Laird, P. N. *Psychology of reasoning: Structure and content.* Cambridge, Mass.: Harvard University Press, 1972.

14 Comments on Directions and Limitations of Current Efforts Toward Theories of Decision Making

William K. Estes
Rockefeller University[1]

Other chapters in this volume have presented a rather wide sampling of current theoretical orientations relative to decision making and the kinds of research on which they are based. The following remarks are intended to relate this contemporary cross section of the field to some long-term trends and to indicate a few points where reorientations or changes of emphasis might prove fruitful.

Research and theory on decision making fall at the crossroads of a number of disciplines. The origins of decision theory are evidently to be found in the thinking of the founders of probability theory, especially relative to gambling, and major advances were associated with economics and the theory of games (von Neumann & Morgenstern, 1944), and with the evolution of statistical theory from Fisher (1935) to Savage (1954) and Wald (1947). More recently, purely mathematical theory has been increasingly complemented by psychological investigations, yielding the vigorous hybrid "behavioral decision theory" (Slovic, Fischhoff, & Lichtenstein, 1977).

Though the making of decisions by people is certainly a psychological process, research on the problem within psychology has come relatively late as compared, for example, to research on problem solving and learning. One reason may lie in the common belief that failures of people to learn or to solve problems result mainly from limitations of capacity, whereas inferior decisions arise mainly from inadequate knowledge of optimal decision strategies. Further, although the criteria of learning and the correct solutions to problems in educational situations are generally well known to the teacher or experimenter, optimal decision strategies often are open research problems. Thus, the study of decision

---

[1]Now at Harvard University.

making has been guided to a major extent by the formulation of normative theories, that is, the development of formal models prescribing decision strategies that are optimal given a characterization of the state of the world and of the individual's value system.

During several decades in which normative theories were the center of attention, it was commonly assumed, especially by economists and game theorists, that the psychological problem of understanding decision and choice could be wholly accomplished by normative theories. This assumption derived from the premise that people are inherently rational and will conform to normative theories once they are informed about them. During the same period, however, psychologists began to develop experimental situations for the study of decision behavior (Coombs & Komorita, 1958; Edwards, 1954; Estes, 1957; Siegel, 1961). Findings emerging from experiments began to throw doubt on the adequacy of the premise and to suggest the need for supplementation of normative theories by descriptive theories founded on facts arising from empirical research and capable of elucidating the reasons why people often are not disposed to or are incapable of conforming to normative theories.

Further, concern with the problem only of characterizing the end result of decision making—that is, choices made and their outcomes—gave way to concern also with the dynamics of the decision process itself: explaining not only what choices are made, but how decisions are generated (Bower, 1959; Estes, 1960). Finally, during the past few years, the focus of research attention has begun to shift somewhat from the way psychology, along with other disciplines, may contribute to understanding decision making in economic and similar situations to the way theories of decision making may contribute to other lines of research and theory in psychology.

COMMON ASPECTS OF DECISION MODELS

Although the researches and models discussed in this volume are extremely diverse, substantial commonality can be detected with regard to basic concepts and the mathematical methods used to work with them. In general, it has been quite uniformly found that decisions prove to be more simply related to appropriately chosen theoretical variables than to observables. In empirical studies, we observe individuals making choices of objects or decisions between possible environmental situations, which in either case can be described and measured quite objectively. However, as principles or laws of decision making begin to take on some simplicity and generality, we find that they do not refer directly to the observable properties of objects or environmental situations, but rather to representations of these in what might be termed the individual's internal cognitive space. It has commonly been believed that once ways are found to measure the attributes of representations in the cognitive space, laws of decision and choice will take on their simplest forms. Hence, a pervasive aspect of research on decision making has been associated with the development of scales of psychological measurement, in particular scales for utility and subjective probability, but also for more general concepts of "strength," as in Luce's choice model (Luce, 1959; Luce & Suppes, 1965).

The idea that tendencies to make choices are simple mathematical functions of utilities and subjective probabilities provided what was, in effect, the standard framework for models of decision making during some two decades following the publication of von Neumann and Morgenstern's (1944) influential volume. In any uncertain situation involving choices with differing probabilities of payoffs, the individual making the decision was conceived to consult his or her subjective probabilities of the various possible outcomes and the values of these on his or her personal utility scales and to choose the alternative with the highest expected utility; hence, the designation MEU (maximization of expected utility) or SEU (subjective expected utility) models (Coombs, Dawes, & Tversky, 1970). The MEU framework was influential both in shaping the structure of some of the more general psychological theories of the period (for example, Greeno, 1968) and for generating the first experimental tests of decision models, one of the earliest being that of Mosteller and Nogee (1951). As a self-sufficient model, MEU has been found inadequate, as cogently indicated by Kahneman and Tversky (1979), but the concepts of utility and subjective probability have remained all but universal components of decision theories.

One reason for the strenuous efforts to formulate psychological scales of measurement for utility and subjective probability over a period of years (reviewed by Luce & Suppes, 1965) was the assumption that once the theoretical variables were adequately measured, the task of theory construction would be virtually completed, because the decision maker in the classical SEU models was assumed to arrive at a decision by way of mental calculations on these theoretical quantities. An alternative possibility, scarcely recognized in the earlier literature, is that utility and probability enter importantly into the decision process, but only indirectly, by determining the magnitudes of other theoretical entities of quite different character. This possibility has indeed been realized in the decision models stemming from signal detectability theory (Kubovy & Healy, this volume; Tanner & Swets, 1954).

The general schema of the decision situation in this latter branch of theory is that the decision maker is presented with a sample observation and the task of deciding which of a number (usually two) of alternative distributions the sample was drawn from. In the original development of the theory with respect to engineering of auditory communication equipment, the sample was an auditory signal and the possible distributions were the collection of samples that might arise from a noisy background (the noise distribution) and the samples that might arise from the noisy background plus the signal (the signal plus noise distribution). The model has been extended to other kinds of psychological situations than auditory perception, but with the terms signal and noise being retained and extended by analogy.

In any version of signal detectability models, the possible samples can be ordered on some dimension. The decision maker is conceived to set some value, the criterion, on this dimension and to follow the rule that when a sample observation falls on one side of the criterion, it is assigned to one population (e.g., signal plus noise), and when it falls on the other side of the criterion, it is assigned to the other distribution (e.g., noise alone). Probabilities and utilities enter into the model only indirectly by determining the value of the criterion. Like the original SEU models, these models deriving from signal detectability theory were originally static, the value of the criterion being some function of objective payoff values and event probabilities. However, in some newer theoretical efforts, the possibility has been recognized that an individual's criterion may be modified in a systematic way by learning that occurs over a series of experiences in a given type of decision situation (Kubovy & Healy, this volume).

The traditional focus of decision theorists on measurement and psychological scales has been advantageous in some respects, but perhaps disadvantageous in others with regard to the relationship of decision theory to other branches of research and theory in psychology. The advantage has been a close connection with developments in some of the areas of psychology, notably psychophysics, where the most precise research and rigorous theorizing have been the tradition. A disadvantage is that the conception of choice behavior as being directly determined by scale values has not encouraged interaction with the emerging body of research and theory in cognitive psychology. Thus, behavioral decision theory has been almost exclusively limited in application to situations in which all admissible alternatives for choice in a situation are presented to the experimental subject by the experimenter, and the task is simply to select from among these alternatives. In a few instances, information regarding alternatives must be gained by some exploratory activity on the part of the subject (Corbin, this volume), but still the framework is a set of alternatives prescribed by the experimenter.

Experiments done in this traditional mold fail to represent common situations leading to decision making outside the laboratory in which an individual starts an episode of decision making with only the motive of achieving some goal in a situation and must proceed to generate a set of relevant alternatives—that is, a set that includes or is likely to include the optimal one. A physician confronted with a sick patient must start by bringing to mind the set of diseases that should be considered; if this phase of the process is inadequate, then a diagnosis based on an incomplete set of alternatives may omit from consideration the actual cause of the illness. In developing a theory to deal with this type of situation, it may be necessary to be concerned less with the values of alternatives on a utility scale than with the way representations of alternatives are stored and organized in memory and retrieved at the point of decision. There are indications in several chapters in this volume (notably those by Corbin and Wallsten) that the need for this more cognitively and less measurement oriented kind of theory is beginning to be felt even by investigators working with classical decision paradigms.

When we go beyond the problem of the representational aspects of the alternatives that enter into decisions and consider how decisions and choices are made, we find two main branches of theory that parallel the distinction just noted between the classical SEU framework and that of signal detectability theory—that is, the two principal classes of deterministic and probabilistic models. In the deterministic models, it is generally assumed that once appropriate measurements have been made of the psychological magnitudes entering into a given type of decision, one can expect to describe or predict the outcomes of decisions by finding what function of these magnitudes the individual making the decision is attempting to maximize or minimize. Models for the process of maximization or minimization have taken a number of forms including the expected value models discussed previously, linear programming (Davidson, Suppes, & Siegel, 1957), elimination by aspects (Tversky, 1972), and Bayesian models (Edwards & Phillips, 1964). In the probabilistic models, the individual is conceived rather to continually sample, or to be presented with samples, from distributions of random variables, to make comparisons on the momentary samples, and, as a result of these comparisons, to move toward or be driven toward a decision. The oldest and most familiar type of model in this category is, of course, the gambler's ruin, predecessor of the random walk models developed for choice behavior by Estes (1960) and Kintsch (1963), among others, for psychophysical judgments by Link and Heath (1975), and for choices or decisions made in the course of memory retrieval by Ratcliff (1978).

So far as I can see, it is difficult to say at this point whether the deterministic and probabilistic models should be viewed as competitive or complementary. In favor of the latter view, one might note that deterministic models, augmented by the increasingly elaborate methods of multidimensional scaling, have been more effectively applied to characterizing end results of decision making in relatively complex situations involving either multidimensional information available to the decision maker or multidimensional outcomes. Probabilistic models, on the other hand, have been developed much further with respect to accounting for the dynamics of decision making and the relations between probabilities of choices and the time taken to make them. At the same time, these achievements of the probabilistic models have been largely limited to binary choice situations and some of the problems involved in extending them to multidimensional situations remain to be solved.

Both types of models have been developed for the most part without a great deal of input from research and theory in other branches of psychology. However, this situation may change as information-processing models in psychology become increasingly sophisticated and provide conceptual machinery for dealing with mental representations and operations on them, for example, "mental rotation'' (Shepard & Podgorny, 1978) or various types of memory search, which enter into decision making. One would hope that in time the models will progress beyond description and begin to provide insight into the sources of capacity limitations that often keep human decision makers from performing close to the optimum levels that might be expected on the basis of purely normative theories.

TASK ORIENTATION VERSUS PROCESS ORIENTATION

It is rather striking that in collected volumes including subsections on decision making—for example, *Handbook of Mathematical Psychology* (Luce, Bush, & Galanter, 1965), or *Cognitive Theory* (Castellan, Pisoni, & Potts, 1977)—one observes high frequencies of cross citations among chapters within the section on decision making, but few citations across sections. Over a period of years, there seems to have been some increase in ''outward'' citations from decision making to other areas, but little sign of increase in ''inward'' citations.

One interpretation of this relative insularity of the literature on decision making may have to do with the distinction between task and process orientation. In the latter, the primary strategy is to focus on a hypothetical process or mechanism, or on some empirical effect presumably indexing such a process, then to attempt to abstract the hypothesized process from a variety of tasks and to look for common determiners across tasks. In this approach, there usually is relatively little interest in the specific tasks themsevles, and new tasks are constructed freely to help bring out the hypothesized process. The next step beyond the abstraction of a process is to seek its rules of combination with others and ways of discriminating its effects from those of other frequently confounded processes. A consequence of the strategy is that, with progress on a given problem, cross-citations to other segments of the literature increase, and major theoretical contributions often manifest this tendency conspicuously (as, for example, Anderson & Bower, 1973; Norman & Rumelhart, 1971; Shiffrin & Schneider, 1977).

In the task-oriented approach, the character of the task itself defines the research area and the focus is much more strongly on determinants of performance in the task than on ways the task might be used to reveal processes cutting across areas. From the beginnings of what could be termed research in cognitive psychology, perhaps the epitome of the task-oriented approach has been problem solving. Whereas nearly all other long-recognized research clusters and traditions in the area are identified with relatively abstract capacities or processes (intelligence, memory, perception), problem solving has been all but synomomous in the minds of psychologists with water-jug puzzles, missionaries and cannibals, and the Tower of Hanoi. Similarly, and almost as pervasively, decision making is identified by psychologists with choices among gambles or guesses at the composition of urns of marbles (Coombs, Dawes, & Tversky, 1970; Wallsten, this volume).

A common correlate of the task orientation is a predilection for proceeding toward theory construction by systematic classification of tasks; this tendency is seen clearly within the decision-making area in the chapter by Wallsten in this volume and, with regard to the problem-solving area, just as conspicuously in a review by Greeno (1978). Undeniably taxonomic efforts can prove valuable, and those just mentioned seem both timely and constructive. Still, it must be observed that theoretically significant classifications more often follow than precede the development of process-oriented models, because a principal function of taxonomy is to specify the combinations of processes or mechanisms implicated in situations defined by empirical boundary conditions. Further, one should not sell short the possibility that current demands for increasing practical relevance of research may be better met in the long run by intensifying efforts toward the construction of functional process models and refinement of methods for their evaluation than by hastening to redirect research from tasks that appear simple (though still incompletely understood) to tasks that appear to mirror the complexity of decision making in business and government.

Within the task-oriented approach, a conspicuous difference between the research traditions on problem solving and decision making is the shift toward a strong emphasis on the detailed course of individual performance and computer simulation models for individual performance in the case of problem solving, but continued reliance on the prediction of statistics of choice data in the case of decision making. Perhaps associated with this difference, one finds, in the decision making area, that there has been a conspicuous lack of attention to the characteristics of the individuals or groups studied in researches designed to test theories. Thus, one commonly finds a model rejected on the basis of an experiment dealing only with a sample of psychology undergraduates at a particular university.

Because a major role of heuristics and strategies in decision making is coming to be widely recognized, and because these must be assumed to depend on individual learning histories, commensurate attention to the educational and experiential backgrounds of subjects utilized in tests of models would appear essential. Further, it must be noted that, to date, investigations of decision making have yielded numerous demonstrations that subjects employ heuristics or strategies, but as yet have not gone on to attempt detailed accounts of the conditions under which heuristics do or do not come into play when appropriate or the sequences of cognitive operations that translate knowledge about heuristics or rules into actions. Here, it would be interesting to see whether our understanding of decision making would be deepened by the employment of computer simulation models of individual performance, analogous to those that have proved fertile with respect to problem solving (Newell & Simon, 1972).

DECISION AND COGNITION

What relations should one expect, or hope, to develop between decision theory and the rest of cognitive psychology? Perhaps it can be agreed that cognitive structures and processes—perceptual and memorial capacities, processes of storage, transformation, organization, and retrieval of information—can be studied only by observing behavior in tasks calling for cognitive functioning. Whatever the task and whatever the investigator's purpose, the experimental subject must continually be making choices and decisions between alternative actions. The investigator can infer properties of internal structure and function only subject to assumptions about the way in which responses are generated given the internal states. This problem has been recognized from the beginnings of experimental psychology and has generated many continuing strands of theoretical development and sometimes controversy.

In theories of learning and behavior, this issue has given rise to the distinction between learning and performance, first implemented in a systematic and formal way in the systems of Tolman (1932) and Hull (1943), and central to current descendants of those systems (for example, Estes, 1959; Logan, 1979). In sensory psychology, it was recognized from the earliest beginnings of research on psychophysics that information entering the organism's sensory system is not translatable in a continuous one-to-one fashion into observed responses. At the very least, one must take account of sensory thresholds—that is, minimum levels of intensity below which stimuli do not influence behavior at all, and minimum differences between stimuli, "difference thresholds," that must be exceeded in order for physically different stimuli to lead to differences in observed behavior. However, continuing research ultimately showed that even the idea that stimuli exceeding intensity thresholds or difference thresholds can be mapped directly onto observed choices is much too simple. Rather, it became clear that all of the observable actions of either animals or people are influenced by experiences with costs and benefits of the actions and current motivations as well as immediate sensory inputs. This insight found a suitable formalism in the importation of signal-detectability theory into psychology beginning with the seminal paper of Tanner and Swets (1954).

From the early 1960's down to the present, major theoretically oriented research efforts in many aspects of perception have centered around efforts to distinguish the contributions of decision factors versus stimulus properties in the determination of the observed responses that are used as a basis to infer internal structures and processes. To mention just one example with which I happen to be personally familiar, a substantial body of research on the recognition and identification of letters in reading and in simpler experimental tasks related to reading has been directed toward the experimental separation and theoretical representation of the factors that limit an individual's capacity for abstracting information from a text or any other type of character display. Some models (for example,

Gardner, 1973; Shiffrin & Geisler, 1973) have explored the viability of the extreme position that capacity limitations are entirely attributable to decision factors. Others (for example, Estes, 1975) recognize the importance of decision factors but assume that these combine with capacity limitations at the level of sensory processing to set the bounds of efficiency on overall performance. Similar problems and similar approaches are to be found in the field of audition and auditory communication.

In all of the various approaches to understanding the role of information processing and decision factors in perceptual situations, investigators currently assume the importance of the concept of the criterion and the other basic concepts and methods of signal-detectability theory; these methods are basic to most attempts to untangle the relative contributions of motivational and informational factors. Further, the idea has gained currency that very similar approaches should be applicable in the study of memory, where problems facing the investigator differ in the important respect that what corresponds to the experimentally controllable "signal" in studies of sensory and perceptual processing is the inferred memory trace (Healy & Jones, 1973; Murdock, 1974). Thus, the central problem in studies of recognition memory is to distinguish the contributions of the state of a memory trace and those of motivational and contextual factors to observable behavior in tests of recognition. It has seemed natural to investigators to carry over the basic machinery of the theory of signal detectability, letting the inferred strength of memory traces correspond to signal strength. But, exchanging an observable for an unobservable independent variable raises major new problems, in that trials on which responses are based on relevant traces and trials on which responses arise from guessing are not experimentally identifiable. One approach to dealing with these problems has been to design experiments in which the tasks closely correspond to those used in investigations of recognition memory, but in which the variable corresponding to strength of the memory trace is externalized in some fashion so that the decision factors and decision processes can be isolated and examined more directly. An important current line of investigation following out this motif is that of Kubovy and Healy as exemplified in a number of earlier contributions (Healy & Kubovy, 1977; Kubovy & Healy, 1977) and in their chapter in the present volume.

The approach of Kubovy and Healy seems to fall on the border line between task-oriented and process-oriented approaches. Most of their data arise from a task of the kind traditionally used in much research on behavioral decision making. However, their interest is not so much in analyzing determinants of performance in the task per se as in abstracting the processes responsible for stability or shifts in the decision criterion. Here, one may note the similarity of some properties of Kubovy and Healy's cutoff model to those of concept identification models in that, for example, in both cases, learning is assumed to occur on errors with random variation or no variation in response tendencies following successes (cf. Atkinson, Bower, & Crothers, 1965, Chapter 2; Millward &

Wickens, 1974). Thus, possibilities emerge, not yet fully realized, for relating Kubovy and Healy's approach to other lines of research on learning outside the decision-making tradition.

Another potential bridge between cognitive psychology and decision research may be found in the distinction between structural and control processes (Atkinson & Shiffrin, 1968). In this very influential categorization, Atkinson and Shiffrin have used the term *structural* to refer to processes or mechanisms constrained by relatively invariant capacities of the individual, *control* to refer to strategies, heuristics, and similar cognitive processes that are under voluntary control and dependent on an individual's learning history. Presumably, control processes are strongly influenced by motivation, incentives, and rewards even though these are rarely identified and explicitly manipulated by researchers in cognitive psychology. However, it seems reasonable to suppose that an individual's decision to engage one or another control process in a cognitive task might be controlled in much the same way and by much the same variables as decisions in what are explicitly labeled decision-making tasks. Consequently, there would seem to be the prospect that the experimental results and theory growing out of studies of explicit decision making might have much to offer cognitive psychologists in their increasing preoccupation with control processes.

REFERENCES

Anderson, J. R., & Bower, G. H. *Human associative memory*. Washington, D.C.: V. H. Winston, 1973.

Atkinson, R. C., Bower, G. H., & Crothers, E. J. *An introduction to mathematical learning theory*. New York: Wiley, 1965.

Atkinson, R. C., & Shiffrin, R. M. Human memory: A proposed system and its control processes. In W. K. Spence & J. T. Spence (Eds.), *The psychology of learning and motivation* (Vol. 2). New York: Academic Press, 1968.

Bower, G. H. Choice-point behavior. In R. R. Bush & W. K. Estes (Eds.), *Studies in mathematical learning theory*. Stanford, Ca.: Stanford University Press, 1959.

Castellan, N. J., Jr., Pisoni, D. B., & Potts, G. R. *Cognitive theory* (Vol. 2). Hillsdale, N.J.: Lawrence Erlbaum Associates, 1977.

Coombs, C. H., Dawes, R. M., & Tversky, A. *Mathematical psychology*. Englewood Cliffs, N.J.: Prentice-Hall, 1970.

Coombs, C. H., & Komorita, S. S. Measuring utility of money through decision. *American Journal of Psychology, 1958, 71,* 383–389.

Davidson, D., Suppes, P., & Siegel, S. *Decision-making: An experimental approach*. Stanford, Ca.: Stanford University Press, 1957.

Edwards, W. The theory of decision making. *Psychological Bulletin, 1954, 51,* 380–417.

Edwards, W., & Phillips, L. D. Man as a transducer for probabilities in Bayesian command and control systems. In M. W. Shelly, II, & G. L. Bryan (Eds.), *Human judgments and optimality*. New York: Wiley, 1964.

Estes, W. K. Of models and men. *The American Psychologist, 1957, 12*(10), 609–617.

Estes, W. K. Component and pattern models with Markovian interpretations. In R. R. Bush & W. K. Estes (Eds.), *Studies in mathematical learning theory*. Stanford, Ca.: Stanford University Press, 1959.

Estes, W. K. A random-walk model for choice behavior. In K. J. Arrow, S. Karlin, & P. Suppes (Eds.), *Mathematical methods in the social sciences 1959*. Stanford, Ca.: Stanford University Press, 1960.

Estes, W. K. Memory, perception, and decision in letter identification. In R. L. Solso (Ed.), *Information processing and cognition: The Loyola Symposium*. Hillsdale, N.J.: Lawrence Erlbaum Associates, 1975.

Fisher, R. A. The fiducial argument in statistical inference. *Annals of Eugenics*, 1935, *6*, 391–398.

Gardner, G. T. Evidence for independent parallel channels in tachistoscopic perception. *Cognitive Psychology*, 1973, *4*, 130–155.

Greeno, J. G. *Elementary theoretical psychology*. New York: Addison-Wesley, 1968.

Greeno, J. G. Natures of problem-solving abilities. In W. K. Estes (Ed.), *Handbook of learning and cognitive processes* (Vol. 5). Hillsdale, N.J.: Lawrence Erlbaum Associates, 1978.

Healy, A. F., & Jones, C. Criterion shifts in recall. *Psychological Bulletin*, 1973, *79*, 335–340.

Healy, A. F., & Kubovy, M. A comparison of recognition memory to numerical decision: How prior probabilities affect cutoff location. *Memory & Cognition*, 1977, *5*, 3–9.

Hull, C. L. *Principles of behavior*. New York: Appleton-Century-Crofts, 1943.

Kahneman, D., & Tversky, A. Prospect theory: An analysis of decision and risk. *Econometrica*, 1979, *47*, 263–291.

Kintsch, W. A response time model for choice behavior. *Psychometrika*, 1963, *28*, 27–32.

Kubovy, M., & Healy, A. F. The decision rule in probabilistic categorization: What it is and how it is learned. *Journal of Experimental Psychology: General*, 1977, *106*, 427–446.

Link, S. W., & Heath, R. A. A sequential theory of psychological discrimination. *Psychometrika*, 1975, *1*, 77–105.

Logan, F. A. Hybrid theory of operant conditioning. *Psychological Review*, 1979, *86*, 507–541.

Luce, R. D. *Individual choice behavior. A theoretical analysis*. New York: Wiley, 1959.

Luce, R. D., Bush, R. R., & Galanter, E. *Handbook of mathematical psychology* (Vol. 3). New York: Wiley, 1965.

Luce, R. D., & Suppes, P. Preference, utility, and risk. In R. D. Luce, R. R. Bush, & R. E. Galanter (Eds.), *Handbook of mathematical psychology*. New York: Wiley, 1965.

Millward, R. B., & Wickens, T. D. Concept-identification models. In D. H. Krantz, R. D. Luce, R. C. Atkinson, & P. Suppes (Eds.), *Contemporary developments in mathematical psychology* (Vol. 1). San Francisco: Freeman, 1974.

Mosteller, F., & Nogee, P. An experimental measurement of utility. *Journal of Political Economy*, 1951, *59*, 371–404.

Murdock, B. B., Jr. *Human memory: Theory and data*. Potomac, Md.: Lawrence Erlbaum Associates, 1974.

Newell, A., & Simon, H. A. *Human problem solving*. Englewood Cliffs, N.J.: Prentice-Hall, 1972.

Norman, D. A., & Rumelhart, D. E. A system for perception and memory. In D. A. Norman (Ed.), *Models of human memory*. New York: Academic Press, 1971.

Ratcliff, R. A theory of memory retrieval. *Psychological Review*, 1978, *85*, 59–108.

Savage, L. J. *The foundations of statistics*. New York: Wiley, 1954.

Shepard, R. N., & Podgorny, P. Cognitive processes that resemble perceptual processes. In W. K. Estes (Ed.), *Handbook of learning and cognitive processes* (Vol. 5). Hillsdale, N.J.: Lawrence Erlbaum Associates, 1978.

Shiffrin, R. M., & Geisler, W. A. Visual recognition in a theory of information processing. In R. L. Solso (Ed.), *Contemporary issues in cognitive psychology: The Loyola Symposium*. Washington, D.C.: Winston, 1973.

Shiffrin, R. M., & Schneider, W. Controlled and automatic human information processing: II. Perceptual learning, automatic attending, and a general theory. *Psychological Review*, 1977, *84*, 127–190.

Siegel, S. Decision making and learning under varying conditions of reinforcement. *Annals of the New York Academy of Science*, 1961, *89*, 766–783.

Slovic, P., Fischhoff, B., & Lichtenstein, S. Behavioral decision theory. *Annual Review of Psychology*, 1977, *28*, 1–39.

Tanner, W. P., Jr., & Swets, J. A. A decision-making theory of visual detection. *Psychological Review*, 1954, *61*, 401–409.

Tolman, E. C. *Purposive behavior in animals and men*. New York: Appleton-Century-Crofts, 1932.

Tversky, A. Elimination by aspects: A theory of choice. *Psychological Review*, 1972, *79*, 281–299.

von Neumann, J., & Morgenstern, O. *Theory of games and economic behavior*. Princeton: Princeton University Press, 1944.

Wald, A. *Sequential analysis*. New York: Wiley, 1947.

Author Index

Subject Index